The Civil War in the
Jackson Purchase,
1861–1862

ALSO BY DAN LEE
AND FROM MCFARLAND

*Thomas J. Wood: A Biography of the Union
General in the Civil War* (2012)

*The L&N Railroad in the Civil War: A Vital North-South
Link and the Struggle to Control It* (2011)

*Kentuckian in Blue: A Biography of Major General
Lovell Harrison Rousseau* (2010)

The Civil War in the Jackson Purchase, 1861–1862

The Pro-Confederate Struggle and Defeat in Southwest Kentucky

DAN LEE

McFarland & Company, Inc., Publishers
Jefferson, North Carolina

LIBRARY OF CONGRESS CATALOGUING-IN-PUBLICATION DATA

Lee, Dan, 1954–
　　The Civil War in the Jackson Purchase, 1861–1862 : the pro-Confederate struggle and defeat in southwest Kentucky / Dan Lee.
　　　p.　　cm.
　　Includes bibliographical references and index.

　　ISBN 978-0-7864-7782-1 (softcover : acid free paper) ∞
　　ISBN 978-1-4766-1271-3 (ebook)

　　1. Jackson Purchase (Ky.)—History, Military—19th century.　2. Kentucky—History—Civil War, 1861–1865—Campaigns.　3. United States—History—Civil War, 1861–1865—Campaigns.　I. Title.
　　F457.J23L44 2014
　　976.9'03—dc23　　　　　　　　　　　　　　2013047144

BRITISH LIBRARY CATALOGUING DATA ARE AVAILABLE

© 2014 Dan Lee. All rights reserved

No part of this book may be reproduced or transmitted in any form or by any means, electronic or mechanical, including photocopying or recording, or by any information storage and retrieval system, without permission in writing from the publisher.

On the cover: Fort Anderson, Paducah, Kentucky, and the camp of the 6th Illinois Cavalry, April 1862 (Library of Congress); background © 2014 Shutterstock

Manufactured in the United States of America

McFarland & Company, Inc., Publishers
　Box 611, Jefferson, North Carolina 28640
　　www.mcfarlandpub.com

To the memory of my parents

The time has come.... We are determined to rush to the rescue of our country.... We want to kill a Yankee—must kill a Yankee—never can sleep sound again until we do kill a Yankee, get his overcoat and scalp. Indian-like, we want a scalp and must have it.
—*Daily Confederate News*, Columbus, Kentucky,
January 3, 1862

Table of Contents

Acknowledgments   ix

Preface   1

Introduction: The Antebellum Jackson Purchase (1820–1860)   3

1. The Secession Crisis (November 1860–August 1861)   13
2. The Federals and the Confederates Make Their Opening Moves (April–August 1861)   20
3. Stalemate (August–September 1861)   30
4. Invasions (September 1861)   40
5. Columbus (September–October 1861)   47
6. The Battle of Columbus-Belmont (November 1861)   57
7. With General C.F. Smith in Paducah (November–December 1861)   73
8. Grant and Polk After the Battle of Columbus-Belmont (November–December 1861)   80
9. The Federal Expedition (January 1862)   96
10. The Attack on Fort Henry and Fort Heiman (February 1862)   106
11. Between Two Battles (February 1862)   119
12. The Battle of Fort Donelson (February 1862)   131
13. The Surrender of Fort Donelson (February 1862)   146
14. Reconnoiters and Evacuations (February–March 1862)   154
15. Island Number Ten (March–April 1862)   161
16. Rebel Incursions and Yankee Injustices (1862–1865)   188

Afterword	210
Chapter Notes	213
Bibliography	227
Index	237

Acknowledgments

The author thanks the friendly staff at Columbus-Belmont State Park, Fort Donelson National Battlefield, and the Lloyd Tilghman House and Civil War Museum in Paducah. At each location, those on duty were abundantly willing to answer questions and to discuss at length the events of 1861–1862. Likewise, the staff at the Forrest C. Pogue Special Collections Library, Murray State University, was most generous with their time and materials.

The author would also like to thank two fine Jackson Purchase historians, Berry Craig and the late Lon Carter Barton, for their groundbreaking contributions to the understanding of antebellum and Civil War life in Kentucky's westernmost province. Patricia Ann Hoskins also deserves high praise for her "'The Old First Is with the South': The Civil War, Reconstruction, and Memory in the Jackson Purchase Region of Kentucky." It is a splendid piece of research and writing.

As always, the author especially thanks his wife, Linda Akins Lee. A careful proofreader, a cheerful traveling companion, and a computer expert, she interrupted her own work at times to render valuable aid on the Jackson Purchase project. To whatever extent this book is a success, the credit is largely hers.

Preface

It is an axiom in sports and in the military that the best defense is a good offense. That was exactly the attitude of both the Northern and the Southern armies in 1861 and 1862 toward the Jackson Purchase region of Kentucky.

The Jackson Purchase was the westernmost area of Kentucky. It was shaped like a clenched fist and in its grip it held the ends of three bright ribbons: the Ohio, the Cumberland, and the Tennessee rivers. In addition, the Purchase was bounded on the west by the Mississippi River, and though it did not control either the source or the mouth of the Big River, it did dominate the transition point where the Northern-controlled portion of the Mississippi ended and the Southern stretch of the river began. This was at the towering bluffs of Columbus, Kentucky.

A glance at the map will show that it was these rivers that gave the Jackson Purchase its greatest military importance. The northeast-to-southwest flowing Ohio River was a valuable supply artery, but more important, a natural boundary between two nations, if it came to that. The Cumberland River, with its mouth at Smithland, Kentucky, dipped deep into Tennessee and flowed by the capital city of Nashville. The Tennessee River, with its mouth at Paducah, plowed even deeper south, into Mississippi and Alabama. The Tennessee was a natural invasion route that had to be protected. The Mississippi River was the greatest prize of all, and Columbus was the key to it. Columbus, the "Gibraltar of the West," was easy to defend and difficult to attack. Whoever held it controlled river traffic all the way to Memphis and Vicksburg. Thus, the Jackson Purchase was the riverine gateway to the Deep South. Every strategist north and south recognized this. One side saw that it must defend the Purchase in order to protect Dixie, and the other realized that it must defend the region against those whose presence would block the invading forces facing south. Both sides began to mass their forces on the edges of the Purchase, waiting for that moment when Kentucky neutrality would end. To move before that would be to risk offending the sovereign sensibilities of this vital region.

The Confederates seemed to hold the early edge, for the Jackson Purchase was really a part of Dixie. In all of Kentucky there was no region more militant in its feelings against the United States. So fervent was the love for the Confederacy that the region was called the "South Carolina of Kentucky." The mood in the Purchase was for secession, and when it appeared—correctly, as it turned out—that Kentucky was going to remain in the Union, the leaders of the Purchase tried to secede from Kentucky and annex the Purchase to Tennessee. Some Jackson Purchase citizens actively sought a Confederate occupation. The Confederates were, in fact, the first to make a defensive-offensive move into the Purchase. Convinced that the Federals were about to pounce, General Leonidas Polk moved into Columbus on September 4, 1861. Two days later, General U.S. Grant occupied Paducah.

Thus sanctity of the Purchase was doubly violated and the issue of which side would prevail was far from settled. It took a year of fighting before the combined talents of Generals U.S. Grant and John Pope and Flag Officer Andrew H. Foote, with the nearly unstoppable power of the United States behind them, were able to leverage, gouge, and maneuver the ever-weakening Confederate forces out of the Jackson Purchase. Four main battles were fought in defense of the Purchase: the Battle of Columbus-Belmont, which straddled the Mississippi River and was fought in both Kentucky and Missouri; the Battle of Fort Henry, which straddled the Tennessee River and was fought in both Kentucky and Tennessee; the Battle of Fort Donelson, which was the climactic contest of the period; and the Battle of Island Number Ten, which was in the midst of a bizarre tangle of Mississippi River turns and state boundaries, and was really fought in all the three states of Kentucky, Tennessee, and Missouri. There were innumerable smaller actions during the period 1861 to 1862. Even afterward, when Federal control over the Purchase was consolidated and irreversible, the fighting continued. Nathan Bedford Forrest and his cavalry continued raiding into the Purchase until October of 1864. The "Wizard of the Saddle" even made so bold as to attack Paducah, the region's largest city. Also, as was true in the rest of Kentucky, the partisan rangers of both sides became a dangerous presence in the late years of the war. The Purchase had its full portion of bloodletting.

The Jackson Purchase was the land where the rivers came together, the heart of the Civil War in the West, and both sides mounted repeated offensives to try to defend it. A cast of characters both great and craven fretted and strutted in this oddly under-studied theater. This is the story of the bloody years 1861–1862 in the Jackson Purchase and the ultimate Union victory.

Introduction
The Antebellum Jackson Purchase (1820–1860)

The Jackson Purchase was settled forty years later than the rest of Kentucky. It was the recognized territory of the Chickasaws and their dominion was respected. Surveyors were prevented by state law from even entering the tribal lands. Then, in the fall of 1818, Isaac Shelby of Kentucky and Andrew Jackson of Tennessee traveled on behalf of the U.S. government to Chickasaw Oldtown (near the site of present-day Muscle Shoals, Alabama) to try to buy the land. By a combination of bribes and threats, the two white officials accomplished their mission. The U.S. Senate ratified the treaty on January 7, 1819, and President James Monroe signed it the same day.

A year later the Kentucky general assembly passed a law to incorporate the Purchase and have it surveyed into townships according to the provisions of the Land Ordinance of 1785. Two hundred military land warrants were issued to veterans of the Revolution and the War of 1812. The old soldiers got the first pick. Some time passed before the eager civilian settlers were allowed to move in, and when they came, they came in a wave. Avoiding the bottoms and sloughs, they began buying up land in quarter-section tracts from the land office in Wadesboro. Patricia Ann Hoskins writes, "Eight thousand [nonmilitary] land warrants were issued to potential settlers attracted by cheap land."[1]

With the influx of settlers, counties began to be formed. Four large counties were created in the first four years of settlement: Hickman (1821), Calloway (1822), Graves (1823), McCracken (1824). Three other counties would be struck from these before mid-century. Combined with the land between the Cumberland and Tennessee rivers and some area east of the Cumberland, this region became the 1st Congressional District of Kentucky. What was undoubtedly of more immediate concern to the settlers was the all-important task of selecting the location of their farms.

The dark soil of the Purchase proved excellent for corn, wheat, and oats, and for both Irish and sweet potatoes. This was not too different from the rest of the state, but the Purchase was unique in two of its crops: cotton and dark-leaf tobacco. The Jackson Purchase was the only area of Kentucky where cotton could be commercially grown, and the tobacco grown there was different from the burley grown in most of the rest of the state. Burley was air-cured: after being cut in the field, the long, leaf-bearing stalks were hung in the rafters of the barns to cure in the still autumn air. Jackson Purchase tobacco was dark-leaf, used for snuff and plugs, and it was smoke-cured. Hung up the same way as burley, dark-leaf tobacco was cured in the aromatic smoke of a small, carefully watched hickory fire smoldering on the dirt floor of the barn. The sight of smoke curling out between the slats of the barn wall during the cool autumn days became one of the most beloved native images of farm life in the Purchase, though it alarmed uninformed travelers who believed the farmer's barn was on fire.

Tobacco was king in the Purchase, superseding in importance even food crops and garden truck. A *New York Herald* reporter in the early 1860s took note of the diet of Jackson Purchase farm families. He said that they subsisted on "salt meat and hominy, hoe cake and molasses, and rye coffee. Butter, sugar, and wheat bread were rare and vegetables were kept for special occasions and weekends." The reporter attributed the poor diet to the fact that the people grew so much tobacco. In addition to its crops, the Purchase was noted for its swine and mules.[2]

The land between the Cumberland and Tennessee rivers (which is now considered part of the Jackson Purchase and will be included as such in this book), was more rugged and "generally retained the unkempt look of the wilderness with heavy timber, deep gullies, and a sparse population." It was isolated, hard to reach because of a lack of bridges. In its gloomy loneliness, it was a perfect refuge for moonshiners, but there was an even more important industry there. The land between the rivers was stippled with iron ore, so even though it did not produce the crop yields of the rest of the Purchase, it did become the home of Western Kentucky iron manufacturing. The fuel for the blast furnaces gave the farmers farther west an additional source of income. As Calloway County historians Dorothy and Kerby Jennings observed, "Thousands of acres of woodlands were harvested of their native timber which in turn were fired and extinguished in home-made brick and mortar kilns after the burning timber began to coalesce into smoldering coals to make the essential charcoal fuel to fire iron furnaces."[3]

The Jackson Purchase furnaces produced over 42,000 tons of pig iron per year valued in excess of $1,200,000. Early on, the most impressive of them may have been Daniel Hillman's Empire Furnace, which had a stack thirty-five feet high and a 9½–foot bosh. By itself, the Empire Furnace turned out over 1,800 tons of iron in a single year, and it was only one of three owned by Hillman. One of his later furnaces, the Center Furnace, could produce up to

2,100 tons a year. In addition to the furnaces themselves and the surrounding workers villages, Hillman owned 72,000 acres where mining and timber operations kept a large workforce busy.

Acquiring an adequate workforce was a constant struggle for Hillman and the other iron magnates. Some whites were employed, but with so much cheap, fertile land available, most white men preferred to become freeholders and work for themselves. Some Kentucky furnace operators hired Indians and it is claimed that even a few Chinese were brought in to work the iron. But, inevitably, they turned mostly to black slaves as a labor force.

The Jackson Purchase was unusual in the variety of work assigned to slaves. Most were farm laborers, of course, and performed the same jobs they did elsewhere in the South: felling and sawing timber, butchering hogs, shucking corn, picking cotton, and working from spring until fall in the labor intensive tobacco fields. While some local tobacco stayed in the Jackson Purchase—there was a state-licensed tobacco warehouse in the Graves County seat of Mayfield—much of the tobacco was shipped on flatboats down the Mississippi River to the New Orleans markets. A typical pattern of tobacco sales may be revealed in the accounts of planter Isaiah Carter of Graves County. Among his tallies for the late 1850s, Carter wrote, "On Feb. 2, 1858—shipped 6 hhds [hogsheads] tobacco to New Orleans, made $915.... On Apr. 29, 1859—shipped 2 hhds tobacco to New Orleans, made $188 in gold."[4]

In 1860, there were 2,845 slaves in the Purchase, about 16 percent of the population, belonging to 514 masters. There were no great planters on the scale of Alabama or Mississippi, however. Lon Carter Barton observes, "The great majority of slave owners—367—possessed five or fewer Negroes." The largest slave owner in the Purchase in 1860 was a widow named Harriet Owen, who owned fifty-two slaves. The second largest owned forty-seven slaves. Hoskins writes that only "three percent held twenty slaves or more." This is not to suggest that slavery was of marginal importance to the antebellum Jackson Purchase. To the contrary, it was considered vital to the increasing prosperity of the Purchase. So demanding was the work of clearing and planting the new land, which was forty years nearer the frontier period than the rest of Kentucky, and so lucrative was the dark-leaf tobacco crop that the Purchase was the only part of the state where the number of slaves was on the increase in the decade preceding the Civil War.[5]

Slavery on the Jackson Purchase farms seems to have been neither more nor less severe than other places in the Upper South. Blacks were bought and sold. There were auction blocks in the county seats (the county clerks' fee for recording the sale of slave property: $2.62½), and slaves were required to carry passes when traveling from the master's property. Barton writes, "Troops of mounted 'paterrollers' kept vigilant watch.... [V]agrant or unruly slaves were often whipped by these men or by the harsher masters." On the other hand, "an indictment delivered by the Graves County Circuit Grand Jury in its 1859 session charged at least one master with cruel and inhuman treatment of slaves." One wonders what was considered cruel and inhuman, for a slave might be whipped pretty badly for even the smallest offense. As an example, if a white person obstructed the toll road between the towns of Columbus and Feliciana he was charged $10 to $20; if it was a Negro, the penalty was thirty-nine lashes.[6]

Christmas seems to have been the only occasion for celebration, and if the memories of the farmers are to be believed, it was a season of great good will between blacks and whites. Pearl Handley, in her scrapbook of Handley family papers, recorded, "On Christmas Eve night, the negroes assembled in front of the big house with fiddle, tambourine, bones, and mouth organs played and danced. When the boss man came out the negroes crossed hands together and made a seat. They lowered their hands so he could sit down and then marched around the big house ... making the wildest music and dancing together. They would barbeque—hog and a lot of chickens and have what they called a 'festibule' and songs, dancing, and feasting were the order of the day until New Year's Night."[7]

Aside from work at the iron furnaces and as field hands, many Jackson Purchase blacks were leased out to work on the paddle wheelers plying the Cumberland, Tennessee, Ohio, and Mississippi rivers. And, after 1853, some were hired out by masters to help build the railroads, fifty-one dollars a month seems to have been the going rate, a sum of money that may or may not have been divided between the owner and the slave.

Though blessed with a web of navigable rivers, Jackson Purchase citizens decided to enter the age of the Iron Road in 1853 with the construction of the Kentucky portion of the Mobile & Ohio Railroad. This railroad, when finished, would stretch some 469 miles between Mobile, Alabama, and Columbus, Kentucky. It was worked on throughout the 1850s and the final spike was driven in late April 1861. It was dedicated to the "support of Southern commerce and the maintenance of Southern institutions."[8] A second railroad was the Nashville & Northwest Railroad. This infrequently mentioned line had its northern terminus at Hickman, on the Mississippi River, and extended into Central Tennessee. According to Charles H. Bogart, the Nashville & Northwest "played a minor, but important part in the war. The N&N, like the M&O, moved considerable northern goods inland, into Tennessee, from the steamboat landing at Hickman during the months before the Confederates seized Columbus.... The N&N fell into Union hands and helped supply troops in Western Tennessee when the Tennessee and Cumberland Rivers were not navigable due to low water."[9]

A third railroad was the New Orleans & Ohio Railroad. This line was not purely Southern in character. It was to become part of the Illinois Central system and connect to the Chicago & Cairo Railroad north of the Ohio River. Since there was no railroad bridge, the locomotives and rolling stock had to cross on ferry boats. Looking south, the railroad would run from Paducah and connect to the Mobile & Ohio near Troy, Tennessee, about ten miles below the Kentucky line. Paducah's citizens were generous in their support of the railroad. The *New York Times* reported that they voted to subscribe $200,000 to the project and that McCracken County subscribed an additional $100,000. Such support paid off. The first rail was spiked down in 1853, and the iron road inched southward. Hoskins writes, "By July of 1854, seven miles of track had been laid and a barbeque was held in Paducah to celebrate. According to *The Paducah Herald*, 'people drove in carriages and ox-teams and came on foot and horse and on mule back from miles around to witness for the first time in their lives the thrilling spectacle of a roaring "iron horse" consuming wood and water and belching forth smoke, fire and steam as it pulled a train of cars at the amazing speed of 15 miles per hour.'"[10]

In a "Letter from Western Kentucky," which was published in the *New York Times* on August 25, 1855, a writer calling himself "Hico" crowed that, when complete, the NO&O extension of the Mobile & Ohio would make the system "one of the longest railroads in the Union, if not in the world." It was likely to grow longer still; a charter had been granted to push the railroad on north until it reached the Great Lakes. He mentioned that large sums of money from Pittsburgh, Pennsylvania, were being poured into the railroad and that a rolling mill for iron was being built, as well as a nail factory, and that "a foundry and machine shop ... are in contemplation" in Paducah. Paducah, said Hico, was "quite a flourishing place" of five thousand residents. He added that "there is not a better location for steamboat building to be found anywhere in the West."[11]

Not every citizen was so enthusiastic about the importance of building a railroad to bisect the Purchase from north to south. Independent-minded Graves Countians refused to approve a bond issue to finance their portion of the NO&O. The line came to an abrupt halt in the country between Paducah and Mayfield from 1854 to 1858. By July 1858, the people, some of them anyway, had changed their minds about the railroad, and they greeted with speeches and a fine barbecue the first locomotive that pulled into Mayfield, July 3, 1858. Regular passenger service was begun shortly afterward, with a train leaving Mayfield for Paducah every morning at 6:30, except Sundays.

The NO&O Railroad brought Irish and German workers to the Jackson Purchase, and also construction engineer Lloyd Tilghman of Maryland. Tilghman was an 1836 graduate of the United States Military Academy and a Mexican War veteran. But more important to the directors of the NO&O was his long years of experience working on various Eastern railroads, including the

Baltimore & Ohio. The NO&O officials courted Tilghman and he responded. In 1852, he moved his family into a new two-story brick house on Paducah's Kentucky Avenue.

Tilghman had chosen well in making Paducah his Kentucky home, for as Hico said, it was quite a flourishing place. The Purchase's infatuation with railroads, however, did not supplant its long-time love affair with its rivers, and it still looked to the river towns as the cultural and political leaders of the region. None was more important than Paducah. The site of Paducah was awarded to frontier hero George Rogers Clark for his Revolutionary War services. The location was familiar to him; he and his men had camped directly across the Ohio River at old Fort Massac before striking out overland toward Kaskaskia in July 1779. Clark never developed his land grant in any way before his death in 1818. The tract passed into the hands of his celebrated brother, William Clark, of the Corps of Discovery. The first cabin on it was built by James and William Pore in 1821, and others soon followed. They called their small community Pekin, a name that did not long endure. After William Clark surveyed the site into town lots in May 1827, he renamed it Paducah. There are many legends about the origin of the unusual name, but nothing is certain, except that it stuck. Clark began selling lots in 1830.

By now, paddle wheelers were a common sight on the interior rivers, and Paducah was well situated to take advantage of the vigorous river trade between Louisville and New Orleans. Also, since it was at the mouth of the Tennessee River, the town was the gateway to the Deep South. Boats could go up the Tennessee as far as Muscle Shoals, Alabama. By 1848, Paducah had grown to two thousand citizens. Four years later that number had doubled.

The wharf at Paducah welcomed all manner of travelers. It was also the port of entry for household and luxury items from Pittsburgh and New Orleans, and the point of departure for tobacco, whiskey, iron, cross-ties, barrel staves, and other manufactured goods of McCracken County and the surrounding area. Hoskins writes, "The waterways quickly established the area as a bustling trade and manufacturing center that included lumberyards and stores, sawmills, brickyards, and distilleries." Paducah also became a market for the home crafts produced in the Purchase: "Items that were made in the home, such as butter, cheese, wine, and molasses, could be purchased or traded at one of the three bakers, seven clothing stores, twenty-three grocery stores, or six wholesale grocery stores that existed in Paducah by 1860."[12]

Yet, as important as commerce was in the young city, the gem of Paducah was not a place of commerce but a place of healing. In 1845, the U.S. government resolved to build a series of inland "Marine Hospitals." Two of them would be in Kentucky, one in Louisville and the other in Paducah. The Treasury Department was given the assignment, and Stephen Harriman Long of the Corps of Topographical Engineers was ordered to manage the job. Work on the Louisville facility began right away, but the Mexican War intervened and ground was not broken for the Paducah hospital until the spring of 1849. One million bricks were ordered and hopes must have been high that construction would speed along, after a four year wait. However, as one historian has observed, "Affairs did not go well at Paducah. Unseasonable rains hampered the work during the autumn of 1849.... The contractor could only lay about one-third his normal rate of bricks. March, April, and May of 1850 proved equally unfavorable. Even the fence surrounding the hospital was washed away." Delayed by the rain, engineer Long nevertheless found ways to improve upon the time. He "managed to excavate the cellar.... He had a well dug, procured dressed stone and lumber, and had the walls and roof framed. Only by September of 1850 was he ready to begin laying bricks, but he hoped to have the walls up and the roof on before winter."[13]

That schedule was overly optimistic. Construction was not complete until late 1851, when Long was at last able to report the Paducah hospital "nearly ready for patients." The main task that remained was the requisition and delivery of medical supplies and furniture. On April 26, 1852, the United States Marine Hospital in Paducah opened its doors. It was a three-story building, shaped like an "H." The design provided for maximum ventilation and light, and the building was topped by a tall cupola and illuminated by high, rectangular windows. The Paducah U.S. Marine Hospital was a handsome addition to a proud city, and if the design was progressive, the mechanical systems were even more so. Visitors were amazed to find water closets and running water fed by cisterns. The hospital had a copper roof.[14]

It may be that the metal roof helped spare the new building from a devastating fire in Paducah the very month the hospital commenced operations. An entire city block burned, and a bit more around the edges, besides. The *New York Times* reported "the fire originated in the livery stable of J.G. Cole, and soon communicated to Heywood's House on the north, and several frame buildings on the south." The offices of two newspapers, the *Democrat* and the *Journal* were damaged, and the bank was burned. Luckily the money was in the vault. The damage to the city might have been far worse if the wind had not died down, for Paducah had no municipal fire engine. Even so, the damage from the fire was bad. The *Times* reported "it entailed a loss of $100,000 over and above the insurances," and added, "the town is a mess of ruins." The fire was a serious, but not fatal, setback. Paducah was soon back on its feet.[15]

Paducah looked forward rather than backward. As its excitement over the railroad showed, the city embraced the latest technology and strived continuously to be better than the year before. In 1853, a telegraphic cable was laid under the Ohio River to connect Paducah to the north bank. The *New*

York Times called it the "longest Submarine Telegraph cable in the United States" at 4200 feet, and praised its sturdy construction, comparing it favorably to a more famous European telegraph wire, saying, "The wire across the Channel from England to France is not so large, nor probably as strong. That has eight wires. This has eighteen. The electric wire in that has but one coating of gutta-percha; this has three. This is lashed spirally; the British wire is not." Through the rest of the decade, Paducah pressed on. On January 30, 1860, civic leader Judge Quintus Quincy Quigley wrote proudly in his journal that, two days earlier, "our town was lighted with gas, which is still another step in improvement."[16]

With all of its hustle, it was inevitable that Paducah would be the most cosmopolitan of the Jackson Purchase communities. In its mix of nationalities, Paducah was more like Louisville or St. Louis. Added to the English and Scots-Irish stock, there were a great many Germans who landed in Paducah to stay, and to the usual congregations of Baptists, Methodists, and Cumberland Presbyterians were added a sizeable number of Catholics and Jews. The presence of all of these many strains made Paducah a political anomaly. In a congressional district noted for its intransigent conservatism, Paducah sometimes strayed from the flock to vote Whig. Outside of Paducah, the citizens were strictly of the Democratic Party. The Purchase was nearer to Nashville than to Frankfort and often identified itself more with the Volunteer State than with the state to which it belonged. It was the one region of Kentucky that idolized Andrew Jackson, its namesake, over Kentucky's own, more liberal Henry Clay. Considering this conservative attitude, it is not surprising that the Purchase's leading spokesmen were loud advocates of slavery and in 1860 inflamed the region's passions with vigorous support of secession. The U.S. representative of Kentucky's 1st Congressional District, Henry C. Burnett, has been described as "the stereotype of a fire-eating secessionist," and his ally John Noble, editor of the *Paducah Tri-Weekly Herald*, has been called "a vociferous mouthpiece of the Democratic Party [and] rabidly pro-secessionist...."[17]

The questions of slavery and its corollary, secession, were discussed everywhere people gathered, in the country stores and across the boundary fences between farms. The churches, too, struggled with the question. Both the Baptists and the Methodists split over the question. Alan Bearman writes, "Although it is probable that the first church in the Jackson Purchase was a Baptist Church, the most powerful denomination in the region on the eve of the Civil War was the Methodist Church." After the schism, the Southern Methodists "argued that slavery was an issue outside of the church's realm of power, that church members could own slaves ... that slavery was biblical and because it was legal in the South it was acceptable for a Methodist to own slaves." Naturally, Southern Baptists felt the same.[18]

It seems that in all of the Purchase, it was only in Paducah that voices in noticeable numbers were heard in opposition to the idea of breaking apart the Union. Newspaper editor John Noble's secessionist braying became such an annoyance to the Unionists of Paducah that on Christmas Day 1860 there was a demonstration directed at him personally. Judge Quigley wrote of that morning in his journal: "The first thing that arrested my attention in coming to my office was an effigy hung by the neck to the telegraph wire at the corner of Broadway and Locust Street with a large card inscribed 'The fate of a disunionist.' The figure also had a copy of the Paducah *Herald* in its hand and the effigy was said to represent J.C. Noble, its Editor. After a short time the mayor had it taken down and then the boys put it on a dray and hauled it up and down the streets and finally in front of Noble's office on Main and then burned it.... The public mind is in an excited and inflammable state."[19]

However boisterous the Paducah Unionists were, they were too few to stem the tide of popular opinion or turn aside the winds of secession blowing from the South. The Jackson Purchase aligned itself with Southern interests as regional conflict grew sharper with the presidential election of 1860.

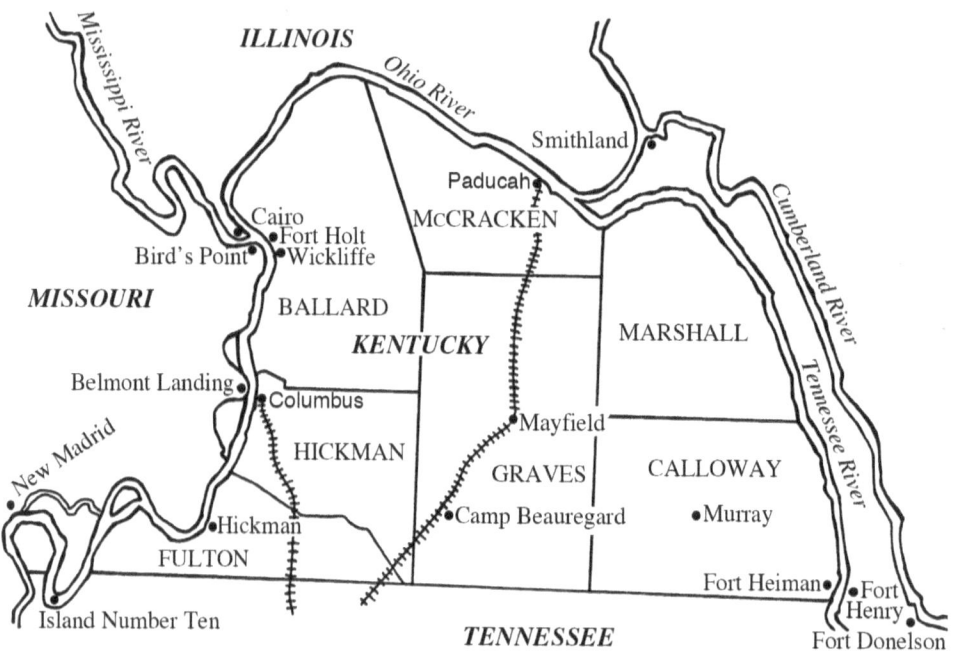

The Jackson Purchase, 1861–1865 (by the author). South of Paducah: The New Orleans & Ohio Railroad. South of Columbus: The Mobile & Ohio Railroad.

1

The Secession Crisis
(November 1860–August 1861)

In the presidential election of 1860, the Jackson Purchase rejected Abraham Lincoln, Stephen A. Douglas, and John Bell in favor of pro-slavery Southern Democrat John C. Breckinridge. The rest of the state supported Bell, the Constitutional Union candidate. Bell's entire platform was made up of one very wide plank: preserve the Union under the Constitution.

In supporting Breckinridge, the Purchase believed that it was voting its economic self-interest. Patricia Ann Hoskins observes that in the last years before the war tobacco production in the Purchase quadrupled, as did the cash value of its farms. So lucrative was the tobacco market that land which was previously considered inferior was now coming under the plow. The demand for field hands was great and growing, and it was answered in the accepted way of the South: slavery. Hoskins observes, "From 1850 to 1860, the number of slaveholders increased 32 percent while the number of slaves increased by 41 percent." As a consequence, she says, "A vote for Lincoln was thought to be a vote for abolition and the Purchase needed its slaves to keep the economic momentum rolling."[1]

Yet, Lincoln won the national election, and before his inauguration day, seven states of the Deep South seceded to form the Confederate States of America. Many in the Purchase were leaning in that same direction. Congressman Henry C. Burnett wrote in the *Paducah Tri-Weekly Herald*: "There is not the slightest hope of any settlement of adjustment of existing troubles." Moderate Kentuckians were alarmed. If a shooting war began, Kentucky would be between the belligerents and her rivers would be dyed red with blood. In the Jackson Purchase there were few moderates. Even a meeting convened in Paducah by Judge Quigley and others to express support for the Union was invaded by vocal pro–Southern men who disrupted the proceedings. More typical than the unproductive Paducah meeting was the one called the next month, January 1861, in Ballard County to advocate disunion.[2]

The supreme irony was that, in their excited state, the secessionists failed to recognize that supporting dissolution of the Union was actually detrimental to their financial interests. R.E. Banta writes, "Kentucky's commerce, aside from the raising of tobacco, hemp, corn, and hogs and the processing of these commodities, consisted of the wholesaling and distribution of northern products to the South and Southern products to the North; friendship with both localities was vital."[3] It was a dilemma to be solved by discussions between calm men, yet the fanatics persisted, both at home and in the national capital. The preeminent Purchase voice in Washington, D.C., 1st District representative Henry C. Burnett, was one of those fanatics. Burnett was doing what he could to defend the Southern cause by obstructing every piece of "military legislation, which included bills to raise money for the Federal treasury and to strengthen the army and navy."[4] He was not averse to feeding the paranoiac sense of oppression felt by Southerners in order to get his way. As just one example, historian Berry Craig writes, "Burnett, in denouncing the navy bill, charged the army and navy were about to be used to coerce the cotton states that had seceded." Burnett's constant stonewalling won him the ire of the Northern press. The *Cincinnati Commercial* said on February 8, 1861, that Representative Burnett was "a big, burly, loud-mouthed fellow who is forever raising points of order and objections to embarrass the Republicans in the House" and who "pops up and objects" whenever a pro–Union member rose to speak.[5]

A less blustery secessionist was Kentucky governor Beriah Magoffin. Magoffin was a forty-six-year-old native of Harrodsburg. He was a broad-shouldered, strapping man, and he had the florid complexion of his Irish immigrant father. He looked more like the village blacksmith than a governor, but his rough-hewn appearance was misleading. Magoffin held degrees from two of Kentucky's finest universities, Centre (Class of 1835) and Transylvania (1838). He was educated well, and he married well, too, when at age twenty-five he wed Anna Nelson Shelby, the granddaughter of Isaac Shelby. Magoffin was elected to the state senate in 1850, and in 1859 he made a run for the governor's chair. He campaigned on a whole raft of pro–Southern issues, including strict enforcement of the Fugitive Slave Act and repeal of the Missouri Compromise. He won—and soon must have wished that he had not, for the situation became turbulent after Lincoln's election.

On January 17, 1861, a special legislative session met in response to a summons from Governor Magoffin. He had been receiving emissaries from Alabama and Mississippi urging secession upon Kentucky. As a result, the governor "had concluded that Kentucky could not—should not—remain in the Union without the guarantees of protection against anti-slavery forces. He recommended [to the legislature] the selection of delegates to a state sovereignty convention that would determine Kentucky's future." He hoped that an ordinance of secession would be the convention's result.[6]

Magoffin had the full support of Henry C. Burnett, who said, "I hope one of the first things our legislature will do, will be to pass a joint resolution strongly denouncing force against the Southern states, either by the present [Buchanan] or incoming [Lincoln] administration.... Our legislature ought to provide at once for the calling of a state convention, so that the sovereign voice of Kentucky can be heard in this most momentous crisis." The Jackson Purchase newspapers also favored a convention to provide for Kentucky's secession. The same day that the special legislative session convened, Len G. Faxson, the editor of the *Columbus Crescent* wrote, "Kentucky may as well prepare immediately to go with the Southern States into a separate Confederacy—the sooner she does so, the better it will be for her." However, Magoffin, Burnett, Faxson, and all of those who were clamoring for secession had underestimated the equally strong determination of the many Unionists in Kentucky's general assembly. Loyal members of the legislature blocked the proposed convention and adjourned until March 20 to give peace efforts a chance to succeed.[7]

Nothing much happened to change anyone's mind before the legislators came back together on March 20. On April 2, John C. Breckinridge, a former vice-president and unsuccessful presidential candidate, spoke to the legislature and issued a personal call for a border state convention to draft a plan of conciliation. If it failed, Kentucky would still have time to decide which course was best to pursue. Breckinridge did not realize how little time there was. On April 12, 1861, Confederate shore batteries opened fire on Fort Sumter in the Charleston, South Carolina, harbor. President Lincoln called for 75,000 volunteers to put down the rebellion. Kentucky's quota was four regiments. All thoughts of conciliation evaporated. The time had come to choose sides. In response to Lincoln's call for volunteers, Magoffin said, "I say, emphatically, Kentucky will furnish no troops for the wicked purpose of subduing her sister Southern states." The governor also summoned the general assembly to reconvene on May 6. Maybe now, shocked by Lincoln's call for troops, the legislators would vote for a secession convention.[8]

Once again, Governor Magoffin's hopes were dashed. On May 16, the Kentucky House of Representatives passed by a vote of sixty-nine to twenty-six a resolution which stated, "The State and citizens thereof shall take no part in the civil war now being waged, except as mediators and friends to the belligerent parties." Kentucky had adopted a purely defensive attitude; she would stand in a state of armed neutrality. On May 24, with the time for the special session about to expire, the state senate followed the example of the house and passed by a vote of thirteen to nine its own resolution of neutrality. The Union-leaning legislators took two additional measures to protect their gains. They created a Home Guard as a counterbalance to the largely pro–Southern State Guard, and further weakened Magoffin's power by creating a five-man military board to conduct the state's military affairs.[9]

The legislature had spoken and the governor was powerless. Neutrality was an unusual position to take, and ultimately an untenable one, but it bought the Unionist forces in Kentucky time to solidify their support. In the meantime, as historian Lowell H. Harrison states, "A bewildered observer from abroad might well have concluded that the United States had become three countries: the Union, the Confederacy, and Kentucky."[10]

In times of trouble, the people need their entertainments. In 1861, there was no better entertainment in America than Dan Rice's Circus. When Rice's Circus set up its tents in Paducah during the second week in April, it must have seemed to the citizenry to be the perfect antidote to their worries. Rice's Circus was like no other. It combined clowns, acrobats, and exotic animals into a dazzling show—"The Greatest Show on Earth"—and it was the creation of clever Dan Rice. Not bad for a man who had begun his life in show business as the human partner of Sybil, the pig who could tell time. On the night of April 13, 1861, an "immense crowd" was watching the twirling trapeze artists and the pratfalls of the clowns when Dan Rice himself came out and stopped the show. He announced that "a telegram had been received that Sumpter [sic] had surrendered. And then there went up a loud and deafening shout." This was how Judge Quigley recalled it.[11] The next morning, Quigley said, "The town is alive ... with inquiry upon every face and dejection upon that of many both Union and Southern men that in all probability much blood and treasure will be expended before the difficulties are settled."[12]

Then, on the 15th, when Lincoln called upon the states for volunteers, Quigley described the reaction by use of a metaphor than recalled the most destructive event in Paducah's history, the great fire of 1852. Quigley said of Lincoln's call to arms, "The news spread like leaping flames over our city, and the same day saw us no longer divided but all united in rejecting him [Lincoln] and his government for the support of the South." Businesses closed their doors, courts adjourned, and cheering men filled the streets. Even Paducah, progressive Paducah, had turned south, and the Jackson Purchase was a monolithic bloc of secessionism. So rabid were feelings there that people began referring to the region as "The South Carolina of Kentucky."[13]

The citizens of the Purchase watched the events in Frankfort in an emotional boom and bust cycle. Hopes that Governor Magoffin would be able to lead the state into secession were repeatedly crushed by the dastardly Unionists in the legislature, and the Purchase howled in outraged frustration. A mere week after Lincoln called for volunteers, some Purchase secessionists decided to take action. A.J. Barry, George B. Moss and other civic leaders in Columbus wrote to President Jefferson Davis. Their letter is remarkable for its militancy. They said, in part:

We approach you, sir, as Kentuckians, and in the spirit of friendship; and here permit us to say that Kentucky is still true to the holy cause of Southern rights, and we trust our confederated brethren will not place an uncharitable construction upon her long silence and seeming indifference. She would long since have spoken, proclaiming the fact and announcing her determination to link her destiny with her sisters of the Confederate States, but her voice has been stifled by politicians, who ... have basely used it to serve their own selfish ends.

The day is not far distant when the traitors who have tarnished Kentucky's fair escutcheon will be dealt with according to their merits. The secession of Kentucky is now a fixed fact.... The war has commenced, and we desire to play our part in it. We long to take our stand in arms by the side of our friends and brothers, to show the world what Kentuckians can dare in defense of Southern rights and Southern honor. Our former allegiance is broken. We acknowledge no Union but that of the Confederate States. We recognize no President but your Excellency.

Barry and his friends went on to suggest that Confederate forces immediately seize Cairo, Illinois, the muddy town at the conjunction of the Ohio and Mississippi rivers, and assured Davis that Cairo's citizens were agreeable. They recommended as well that the Confederates occupy Columbus:

The Mississippi here is very narrow, only half a mile wide, and to the north of the town are the iron banks—immense bluffs, which rise 200 feet above the river. An efficient battery there would effectually command the channel. Nothing could pass without our permission. It is the first high bank below the mouth, which, added to the narrowness of the river here, makes it capable of being rendered an almost impregnable point.

The letter writers referred President Davis to the Honorable H.C. Burnett as witness to their "character and standing." The letter concluded: "Should the suggestions we have thrown out ... meet with your approval, we pledge ourselves to render you every assistance in our power to forward the project mentioned, or any other that may redound to the course of Southern rights and the prosperity of the Confederate States."[14]

Pro-South leaders in the Purchase went a step further than letter writing in May 1861 when they met in Mayfield for a regional secession convention. Mayfield was the appropriate venue. Its supposed founders, John Anderson and his wife, came from South Carolina, and the pretty little town that grew up around their lonely cabin was the most radical in the Purchase. The first of the two meetings, which convened on May 10, amounted to little. The second, which was gaveled to order on May 29, was a more serious attempt to effect a separation. Between 155 and 160 delegates attended the three-day event. Some of them may have come expecting the Jackson Purchase to secede immediately. It was no secret, for it had been reported in the *Louisville Daily Journal*, that on May 21 "six cannon and 1000 small arms belonging to the state ... were transported from Paducah to Mayfield." With such firepower to be had practically for the taking, who could predict what might happen? A consensus was all that was required.[15]

The men who assembled in Mayfield were united in their opposition to the Union, but they came prepared with a variety of ideas for the proper course. One proposal was for the Purchase areas of Kentucky and Tennessee to secede from their respective states, combine into one, and then approach the Confederate government for admission as a brand new state of the CSA. The idea was ambitious, almost visionary, and might have failed among these conservatives even if it had not been opposed by several competing factions, which it was.

Others felt that the Purchase should secede from Kentucky and ask to join Tennessee. Still others held that any scenario involving separation from Kentucky was unnecessary. Over the coming months, they argued, unfolding events—perhaps even a Federal invasion of the state—would outrage a growing number of right-thinking Kentuckians. A great reservoir of latent states rights sentiment would be released, at which point the legislature would certainly drop the notion of armed neutrality and lead the entire state out of the Union.

This last expectation seems to have been held by delegate Lloyd Tilghman, construction engineer for the NO&O Railroad and a major in the pro-South State Guard. When he rose to address the convention, Tilghman began by attending to a matter of personal honor. He said that a person who said he was a Northern sympathizer was a "damn liar." That settled, he pledged to defend Kentucky sovereignty "if he had but 500 men to do it," and suggested to young men who were champing at the bit to go over to the South to just be patient. There would soon be work for them in Kentucky. He could say no more at present than to assure them "that there was a movement on foot which it was not proper for him to divulge at this time." Tilghman's implication was clear.[16]

By the third and final day of the convention, upwards of 3500 citizens had gathered to watch and listen to the discussions. The chairman had to move the meetings out to the shady courthouse lawn to accommodate the interested crowd. It was not, however, only the locals who were interested in the Mayfield proceedings. From his headquarters in Cincinnati, General George B. McClellan, commanding the Department of the Ohio, wrote to President Lincoln on May 30: "A very delicate question is arising as to western Kentucky, that portion west of the Tenna. River.... A convention is now being held in Mayfield which may declare the 'Jackson Purchase' separate from Kentucky, its annexation to Tennessee, and that this will be followed by an advance of Tenna. Troops upon Columbus and Paducah." McClellan's intelligence of the convention's intention was correct, as far as it went, though the threat of secession in Mayfield never developed beyond a lot of spirited talk. No faction of delegates was able get enough votes together to put any one of the three proposals over the top.[17]

Before they adjourned on May 31, the delegates approved four resolutions which were predictable in tone. They denounced the president, they encouraged Governor Magoffin to resist any Federal invasion, they commended Magoffin for refusing to send Lincoln any troops to subdue the South, and they spoke out strongly against the delivery of thousands of "Lincoln guns," which had been sent into the state for use by the Unionist Home Guards. The Mayfield delegates also took action in response to Lincoln's call for an extraordinary election to be held in Kentucky on June 20. Its purpose would be to select senators and congressmen to fill the seats of the many legislators who had resigned or been expelled since the crisis began. They must be elected before Congress convened in a special session, scheduled to begin on July 4 in Washington. The Mayfield delegates had no trouble at all in selecting their candidate. Who could it be other than their long-time champion, Henry C. Burnett? The convention unanimously chose Burnett as their candidate for the 1st District. Then the delegates returned to their homes.

The electoral postscript to the June canvass was discouraging to the secessionist clique. Nine of Kentucky's House seats were filled by Unionists. Only the 1st District elected a States Rights man, Burnett, who defeated his opponent by almost three thousand votes. The Southerners suffered another setback on August 5, when the election of state lawmakers had a similar result to that in June. The Unionists won seventy-six seats in the Kentucky house to the secessionists' twenty-four, and loyal senate candidates won twenty-seven seats to only eleven for the followers of Jefferson Davis.

Kentucky had made its decision. Those who had played for time by imposing neutrality on Kentucky had been proven to have the winning strategy. Their power had increased as weeks grew into months. They had kept Kentucky in the Union and they had won undisputed control of the general assembly, leaving the Jackson Purchase politically isolated.

2

The Federals and the Confederates Make Their Opening Moves
(April–August 1861)

The cannon and small arms that had been delivered via the NO&O Railroad from Paducah to Mayfield in May was just one of many ominous moves made by the militarists of both sides during the spring and summer of 1861. Until August, neutrality was officially the word of the day, but the truth was that Unionists and States Rights men alike were scrambling to gain an advantage during the lull.

In the spring of 1861, Federal forces began to mass on the west bank of the Mississippi at Bird's Point, Missouri, and north of the Ohio River at Cairo, Illinois. Bird's Point belonged to Colonel John Bird, a secessionist. He paid dearly for his sentiments. The colonel's plantation was occupied and fortified and he was arrested as a security measure and confined at Cairo.

Cairo, though in Illinois, was a hotbed of secessionism. With a population of 2220, it was the largest town in that downstate region called "Egypt," an area that had actually considered seceding from Illinois. The alarmed governor, Richard Yates, sent four hundred militiamen and four pieces of field artillery on the railroad from Chicago to Cairo to prevent his fellow citizens from doing anything rash. Within two weeks, there were three thousand troops at Cairo. Their commander was Colonel Benjamin Prentiss of the 10th Illinois Infantry. He oversaw the erection of elaborate works, a short distance below the town, which were described by the English traveler William Howard Russell:

> After breakfast I went down about the works which fortify the bank of mud, in the shape of a V, formed by the two rivers—a fleche with a ditch, scarp, and counter-scarp.... The thermometer was at 100° soon after breakfast, and it was not wonderful to find that the men in Camp Defiance, which is the name of the cantonment on the mud between the levees ... were suffering from diarrhoea.... Cairo, indeed, in not comfortable; the worst barrack that ever asphyxiated the British soldier

would be better than the best shed here, and the flies and mosquitoes are beyond all conception virulent and pestiferous."[1]

With the rebellion in Southern Illinois tamped down and fortifications erected to defend against attack, there was little for the soldiers to do, aside from the hated drill. Jay Carlton Mullens writes, "The volunteers at Cairo spent most of the early summer of 1861 fighting rats, mosquitoes, dysentery, malaria and boredom" in muddy old Cairo. With so few amusements, the mud itself became an item of interest. One soldier was "amazed when he saw a man stuck in the mud and unable to extricate himself not two rods from headquarters."[2] By the second week in May, the number of troops at Cairo had grown to 5250 and there were thirty artillery pieces. It was reported that the men had "been regularly mustered into the United States service, and the encampment is regularly one of the United States Government."[3]

At Bird's Point, too, things were progressing rapidly. Private Charles W. Wills (8th Illinois Infantry), who came across from Cairo to visit, wrote that the soldiers posted there had "thrown up breastworks and dug a deep ditch outside of them, making a pretty strong camp." He was fascinated by the Bird plantation "Big House" and repelled at the conditions he found in the nearby slave village. He wrote, "I went to old Bird's house this morning. It is just like the pictures we have seen in *Harper's* of southern planters homes. A wide, railed porch extends around two sides of the house from the floor of each story.... Back of the house were the quarters filled with the ugliest, dirtiest niggers I ever saw, dressed in dirty white cotton. Awfully nasty!"[4]

There were also Federal troops posted on the Ohio River upstream from Cairo at Mound City, Illinois. There was not much to do there, either, but Corporal D. Leib Ambrose of Co. H, 7th Illinois Volunteers, remembered that patrols were sometimes quietly ordered to cross the river into Kentucky to investigate suspicious activity.

John M. Adair of the 55th Illinois remembered, "At Cairo we imagined we were in the heart of the enemy's country, and the most rigorous discipline was adhered to, as a poor calf which undertook to pass the guard line without giving the countersign found out to its sorrow. One of the boys of Co. 'E' shot it dead for this breach of discipline." The men were touchy and nervous about Rebel incursions. Yet, the days passed, and all the men seemed to do was drill, build fieldworks, and swat mosquitoes.[5]

The officers at Cairo intended to change that. In the last week in May, General Prentiss and some of his fellow officers, including Colonels Eleazer A. Paine and Richard J. Oglesby, signed their name to an ambitious letter to President Lincoln. Neither Kentucky nor Tennessee had seceded, and these men wanted to secure the Purchase areas of both states before they could align themselves with the South. Their proposal was to move south from Camp Defiance with ten thousand men to Columbus, Kentucky, and perhaps as far south as Memphis. They could be ready to mount their expedition in three days. "Should the Government deem it wise and proper to make such a demonstration from this point, upon the seceding States by occupying the states south still in the Union, no just offense can arise in those States, at such a defensive movement.... [W]e are anxious that you should seriously consider the importance of this maneuver." No such advance was authorized. On June 8, 1861, Tennessee seceded, so that opportunity was lost.[6]

It was not only in Southern Illinois that the Unionists were busy that spring. All along the north bank of the Ohio River recruitment and training camps were being established. J.V. Guthrie and W.E. Woodruff were raising what would become two regiments of soldiers at Camp Clay, across the Ohio from Newport, Kentucky. And Colonel Lovell Harrison Rousseau was busy raising two infantry regiments and a cavalry regiment at Camp Joe Holt, Indiana, opposite Louisville.

In neutral Kentucky itself, there was much activity. In May, at President Lincoln's request, Lieutenant William "Bull" Nelson of the U.S. Navy came down to Frankfort to discuss with the head men there the distribution of several thousand rifles with which to arm the loyal Home Guard (the "Lincoln Guns" to which the Mayfield Convention objected). Regarding the guns, General McClellan wrote President Lincoln that "some of the leading Union men in Kentucky ... uniformly represent that the effect has been extremely beneficial, not only in giving strength to the Union party and discouraging the secessionists, but that it has proved to the minds of all reasonable men that the Genl. Govt. has confidence in their loyalty and entertain no intention of subjugating them."[7]

It was this same William Nelson, soon to be a general in the service of the United States, who established Camp Dick Robinson. On August 6, the day after the legislative elections had confirmed Kentucky's Union sympathies, Nelson began his Garrard County camp and by September 1 he had four Kentucky regiments, plus 2000 loyal Tennessee mountaineers who were exiled from their own state. Union camps were also established near Greensburg and Hopkinsville. Magoffin protested to Lincoln that this certainly looked like a violation of the principle of neutrality. However, the August elections had proven the overruling loyalty of most Kentuckians and Lincoln just ignored him.

Kentuckians flocked to Camp Nelson and the other Federal camps, but they did not flock to Cairo or to Bird's Point. The lack of Union volunteers from the Purchase only confirmed that region's devotion to the Confederacy. About 100,000 Kentuckians fought for the Union, including 23,000 black soldiers; fewer than forty thousand fought for the Confederacy. Only in the Purchase did the general attitude swim against the current of Unionist sentiment in Kentucky. Only about six hundred Jackson Purchase men volunteered for Federal service while more than five thousand pledged their fates to the South. There were more CSA soldiers from the Purchase than any other of Kentucky's six regions.

The Purchase's undisguised Rebel sympathies worried the Federals. Through the late spring and summer, General McClellan and President Lincoln received a stream of communiqués about conditions in Kentucky Rebeldom, which leading Unionist Leslie Combs called "our mad dog district." Some of these letter writers made free with strategic advice, as well.[8] Garrett Davis wrote to McClellan in June, "The sympathy for the south and the inclination to secession ... is stronger in the southwestern corner of the state than it is in any other part." As to what to do about it, Davis advised, "You will have to move on Paducah and Columbus, in the State, and Memphis, in Tennessee."[9] In July there came to General McClellan's desk a note from his spy E.J. Allan (who was in reality the legendary operative Allen Pinkerton): "The rebels have taken possession of the Mobile & Ohio Railroad for their exclusive use.... I know the camp at Cairo and Bird's Point is full of spies, good fellows, and gay ladies.... The rebels are in possession of accurate drawings of the whole defense at these points, corrected daily when necessary."[10]

Each week brought new alarms and to many it looked as if delay was inviting defeat.

Ironically, the Confederates and their civilian friends were equally alarmed and for the same reason: what the enemy defined as defense looked awfully threatening. When the Federals occupied Cairo, the *Paducah Tri-Weekly Herald* shrieked, "To Arms!! To Arms!! It is disgraceful to Kentucky and to the South to suffer these vandals to quietly plunder our commerce."[11]

Lloyd Tilghman, ranking officer of the State Guard in the Purchase, placed two cannon at Columbus in response to Prentiss' advance, and traveled to St. Louis to try to obtain more weaponry. Major Josiah Gorgas, commanding the CSA Engineer Bureau, wanted to go even further. He wrote to L.P. Walker, the Confederate secretary of war: "To avoid [an advance down the Mississippi to New Orleans] it would be necessary to fortify some point as Columbus or Richmond [he meant Hickman], lining the banks of the river with cannon and covering them with land works—an intrenched camp, capable of holding 30,000 men. With this the purpose of the river could not be effected, and there would be no use in turning such a work, since nothing could be effected below it without a flotilla." A.J. Barry and the other city fathers of Columbus were perfectly willing for their town to become an armed camp, as shown by their April letter to President Jefferson Davis.[12]

Where were the necessary guns to be found? While Tilghman hoped that St. Louis could supply what was needed, others looked to Montgomery, Alabama; Jackson, Mississippi; or closer, to Nashville or Memphis. Tennessee governor Isham Harris protested that his state was powerless to help. He wrote to secretary of war Walker: "There is very little doubt in my mind that the settled purpose of the troops at Cairo is at a very early date to take possession of and fortify Columbus, Ky., and make that the base of their operations south. This the people of that part of Kentucky are determined to resist, but unfortunately they have no arms, and we are unable to aid them in this respect."[13]

In addition to his travels in an attempt to obtain arms, Colonel Tilghman also undertook a peace mission to Cairo. He visited Colonel Prentiss in his headquarters to assure the Federal commander that recent reports in the *Louisville Daily Journal* that his State Guard were hostile and might aid troops from Tennessee in an aggressive move north were false. The Kentuckians harbored no hostile intents toward the troops at Cairo, Tilghman said, and in addition, he had just come from Tennessee and Governor Harris had no plans for an aggressive move. In the transcript of the interview, Prentiss is represented as saying Tilghman's "friendly feelings are cordially reciprocated," but that he had been informed "that bodies are arming and drilling with a proposed destination ... North; and I will say to you frankly, that we are prepared for the attack and await it."[14]

Tilghman again blamed the newspapers, and said, "The press ought to be restrained in its ready circulation of errors. There is not a word of truth in the statement of there being 12,000 men at Paducah for invasion, or, as to the concentration of troops in any part of Kentucky under my control. As to the recent arrival of arms at Columbus, they were the property of the State. This, as her right, Illinois cannot raise any objection to. Kentucky has her own rights to defend, and no State can do it more powerfully. She is a warm and generous friend, but a hearty enemy."[15]

Tilghman had an objection of his own: Kentucky's commerce was being interfered with. Not even a barrel of flour could be shipped without being the subject of "espionage." He was referring to Yankee inspections and seizures of property. Prentiss said that his instructions were to "seize no property unless I have information that such property consists of munitions of war, destined to the enemies of the United States Government."[16] (The evidence is that Prentiss' directive regarding Kentucky trade—and its distinction between contraband and legal property—was not so carefully followed as he pretended. Commerce suffered south of the Ohio. The camp newspaper at Cairo observed that "businesses of all kinds is [*sic*] perfectly stagnant in Paducah and many houses are said to be closed."[17] Even Judge Quigley gave up on Paducah and relocated his family and himself to Paris, Tennessee, in June.) The two officers went back and forth for a bit on the subject of what constituted contraband and what arms, exactly, were illegal, before Tilghman returned to the main point, that Prentiss' fear of invasion through Kentucky was "groundless," adding, "There are not organized fifty men in Western Kentucky, outside of my command." He said that he was glad Prentiss was in command across the Ohio, for "the position of Illinois and Kentucky relatively is very delicate.... Affairs must be managed on both sides with calmness."[18]

Maybe Colonel Tilghman really did think that he could reassure Prentiss and prevent a possible invasion of Kentucky. Or maybe he was just sowing doubt in the Federal commander's mind, causing him to hesitate, and in that way buy precious time for Kentucky to prepare. Whether Tilghman's personal meeting with Prentiss was sincere or cynical, it seemed clear to many that sooner or later a fight was inevitable. The need for weapons was plain to all and it continued to be an obsession among Kentucky's leading secessionists, including Governor Magoffin.

The governor was doing what he could to get arms to Kentucky's Confederates, just as President Lincoln, using William Nelson as his liaison, was delivering guns to the state's Unionists. In May the governor appointed a known states rights man, Dr. Luke P. Blackburn, to purchase arms for the state. Blackburn visited Mississippi, Arkansas, and Louisiana in his search for weapons. He returned in June. While in New Orleans, Blackburn had delivered a speech saying, "Kentucky was ready to go into the Southern Confederacy and would go immediately if the South would but let her have arms." The South did let her have arms—antiquated weapons at inflated prices—which were stored in local armories before they found their way into the hands of Kentucky secessionists.[19]

Some of these newly arrived Kentucky weapons went right back south again, carried into Tennessee by departing Kentuckians. The *Frankfort Daily Commonwealth* reported on May 24, 1861: "It is reported that some 300 volunteers, with one thousand muskets and six field pieces, left Paducah yesterday for Camp Cheatham near the Kentucky and Tennessee Line. Their ultimate destination is Jackson, Tennessee, where southern troops are concentrating in large numbers. We reckon these cannon had not seen the [neutrality] proclamation."[20]

Tennessee, while respecting Kentucky neutrality insofar as recruiting on her soil was concerned, was busy building up strength immediately outside her borders. There were Confederates stationed within fifty yards of Cumberland Gap in the east, and in the west, just below the state line, were the aforementioned Camp Cheatham and Camp Boone. In addition Governor Isham Harris ordered work to be commenced on two forts, one on the Tennessee River, the other on the Cumberland. Benjamin F. Cooling writes, "Work began that summer on Fort Henry (the Tennessee [River] post named for Gustavus A. Henry, the senior confederate senator and native of nearby Montgomery County), as well as Fort Donelson (located twelve miles away on the Cumberland and named for the state's attorney general, Daniel S. Donelson, who participated in the [site] survey). At the very least, Harris planned to use these positions for traffic check points on the rivers."[21]

Fort Donelson on the Cumberland was well located "upon a steep hillside about one mile from Dover.... The hill—so often styled a bluff—rose 75 to 100 feet above the river and its irregular shape encompassed 100 acres. It was surrounded by deep gullies offering barriers to land assault." The site for Fort Henry on the Tennessee was a low-lying spot called Kirkman's Old Landing. There was a better, higher site across the river, but that bank was in Kentucky and could not be used for reasons of political delicacy.[22]

There were those Confederates who did not share Governor Harris' sensitivity to Kentucky neutrality. General Gideon Pillow wrote to President Jefferson Davis from Memphis on May 16, 1861: "The country near the north boundary line of Tennessee is an open and level one, and is wholly indefensible except by a large force. I can occupy and fortify Columbus, Ky. with half the force required to defend the interior line.... I am now making all my dispositions with that view. I have sent a special messenger to Governor Magoffin, asking his permission to occupy it. My expectation is that he will withhold his consent. I know no alternative but to take responsibility of acting upon my own judgment." In the end, it was Pillow's own superiors, not Magoffin, who refused him permission to "act on his own judgment." But his day would come.[23]

Although Confederate military forces might have to content themselves with waiting at the border of the Jackson Purchase, the homegrown secessionists were under no obligation to hesitate before taking action. Everyone was tense. John M. Johnson, who was sent by Governor Magoffin to study the situation in the Purchase, reported that "there was a 'great uneasiness' felt throughout the border counties, many people having removed their families from the area. The fear of impending crisis ... had resulted in the practice of wearing arms, and it was feared that the whole situation would 'lead to violence toward those of opposite opinions.'" Johnson was a good observer, as events proved.[24]

It was a dangerous time and place for anyone with a Northern point of view. In Mayfield, a states rights man named Henry Clay King threatened to hang Judge R.K. Williams, who was helping to enlist men for what eventually became the 20th Kentucky Volunteer Infantry. For others, it was worse than mere threats. In every county of the Purchase, committees had formed for the purpose of gathering volunteers for Confederate service, and they did not take kindly to the few Unionists who still lived among them, especially those who refused to be recruited. Historian Steven Wright recounts one example, that of a man named Jones, who lived near the village of Boydsville in Calloway County. Mr. Jones was visited by the county vigilance committee one night, abducted, and taken south to the military commander at Union City, Tennessee. Quoting the *Louisville Daily Journal*, Wright says, "The commanding officer there would have nothing to do with [Jones], but, on his return home ... he was shot in three places and left to die in the road. He dragged himself to a small brook ... where he got water and was found by a neighbor; he lingered two days and died, leaving a widow and two small children."[25]

Many who saw such outrages decided that the time had come to refugee north. The Busbey, Boswell, and Harp families of Hickman County constituted themselves into a small wagon train and came straggling into Louisville in August. A *New York Times* correspondent in Louisville reported their arrival. "Their condition is really deplorable," the writer said. "They were forced to leave their farms at a few hours' notice, leaving their crops and household goods at the mercy of the heartless rebels. They traveled with the aged and infirm, and youthful and tender members of their families ... and encountered many hardships. They inform us that fully fifty families in Hickman and Ballard Counties have been forced to leave their houses, and to abandon their crops and nearly all they possessed in the world, their offence being that they entertained Union sentiments."[26]

Through June and July, the men in these states rights bands who were terrorizing their Unionist neighbors would make their way south to join the regular Confederate service. Men went from the Purchase into Tennessee as part of their county's militia company, in small bands, or individually. In July alone, the number of men who went south totaled over two thousand. It was not just farmers going, either. Men with good town jobs gave them up to enter the Confederate service. The case of J.F. Melton, the town marshal of Murray, is an example. Melton turned in his badge and recruited a company of Confederates. Things had not really broken loose in the west, so Melton led his men to Virginia, where they fought in the Battle of First Bull Run. It is remembered that "after that battle, Melton resigned his command and returned to Calloway County, where he recruited a second company with which company he made his way to Fort Henry." Melton would see a lot more of war before his career as a Confederate was done.[27]

The strangest group that passed through the Purchase to Tennessee, however, was not from Kentucky at all, but rather from Illinois. Confederate sympathizer Thorndike Brooks had tried to lead a secession movement in southern Illinois and failed, had tried to organize an attack on some Federals guarding a local bridge and failed, and finally settled for raising a company of men whom he would lead south. He recruited about forty-five men in Williamson and Jackson counties, and on the night of May 25 they rendezvoused near Marion and began walking toward the Ohio River. Two days later, a steamboat called the *Lynn Boyd* ferried them across to Paducah, where they were hailed as heroes. Mr. Augustine Shields, the proprietor of the St. Francis Hotel, gave them rooms and hot meals. Mrs. Shields presented the company with a new Rebel flag when, on May 29, they marched down to the NO&O Railroad depot for the short train ride to Mayfield. In an article with a Mayfield dateline, the *Louisville Daily Journal* reported: "Our town was surprised yesterday evening by the arrival of a company of strangers who came marching up with a secessions flag flying. They were a company from Southern Illinois on its way to the Confederacy. They were received and greatly applauded by the secessionists of this place. The Captain of the State Guard at this place (O.R. Boon) was passing round the evening before they left raising a contribution to pay their expenses while here...." The Illinoisans spent the night at the Cargill Hotel. The day of May 30 was spent recruiting in Mayfield. They left with nine new volunteers that evening and arrived early the next morning at Camp Boone, where no one knew quite what to do with them. They finally were mustered in as Co. G, 15th Tennessee Infantry.[28]

The Illinois company returned to Mayfield in late July, as part of an expeditionary force. A Louisville correspondent had noticed that signs were growing more ominous. From Mayfield he wrote, "Matters are daily growing worse here, and some desperate moves will soon be made." That dreaded desperate move occurred on July 20 when a band of about one hundred Rebels from Union City, led by Captain Henry Clay King (the same man who had threatened to hang Judge R.K. Williams), stole Mayfield's supply of weaponry. King's men had been in Paducah on July 18 and, with the help of a sympathetic sentry, got some guns from that city's arsenal, but that did not compare to the Mayfield haul, where they stole nine hundred muskets and six pieces of field artillery. The Unionists in Mayfield had been alert to the threat and had removed the guns from their arsenal to secret locations. The Rebels found them nevertheless and took them back to Tennessee, except for about four hundred small arms that were handed over to the Confederates in the state-line town of Fulton. The whole caper was thought to have been planned by Colonel Lloyd Tilghman.[29]

Brigadier General Benjamin F. Cheatham, commanding at Memphis, was delighted with the success of King's expedition. Cheatham wrote to the commander at Camp Boone on July 21: "I have this moment learned from a messenger who has just arrived from my camp at Union City that a party of Kentuckians yesterday brought to my camp from Mayfield a large lot of muskets and a field battery of artillery. I presume they are a portion of the State arms that were at Mayfield, Ky. I write this to let you know that they are subject to your order as Kentuckians. I expect that in retaining them you of course get the consent of Governor Magoffin of Kentucky."[30]

In that, General Cheatham was overly optimistic. Governor Magoffin did not give his consent. Or, at least, the Kentucky Military Board that now dominated Magoffin did not. At the board's direction, Magoffin issued a proclamation saying in part, "I do now issue this my proclamation commanding every citizen, or other person, within the jurisdiction of this State, having in his possession any arm or munitions thus unlawfully seized, to deliver up the same to the judge of the County Court of the county in which he resides." In addition, Magoffin authorized board member George T. Wood of Munfordville to travel to Hickman and to Union City to try to recover the stolen weapons. Of course, Wood could not.[31]

So this is where things stood by the end of August. In special elections, Kentuckians had installed Unionist majorities in the U.S. Congress and in the state legislature. However, Kentucky was still considered up for grabs. Soldiers of both sides armed to the teeth were massing on the borders. There had been small military excursions into Kentucky, from Mound City on the north and from Union City on the south, but they had not amounted to much, had not led to a general advance. The season for fighting was passing and would soon be gone. Leading officers on both sides were eager to open the ball. General Prentiss at Cairo wanted to invade Kentucky. General Pillow at Memphis wanted to invade Kentucky. Kentuckians held their breath and wondered who would move first.

3

Stalemate
(August–September 1861)

Forbidden by political considerations from entering the Jackson Purchase, the commanders and men of both sides could only nibble at the edges. The Federals continued to gather in Cairo.

Private Charles W. Wills rather enjoyed life there. Will's mind was often on satisfying his stomach, and since he was free with his money, he was not disappointed at Cairo. "We have a barrel of ice water every day. Milk, cake, and pies are peddled around camp, and I indulge in milk considerably at five cents a pint. Everything is much higher here," he said at one point, and at another, "We have lots of beer sent us from Peoria, and drink a half barrel a day while it lasts."[1] There were also less expensive amusements. Wills said, "The Ohio is warm enough and I swim every night now." He and the men also liked to fish, and even if they did not hook a fat catfish, rations were still pretty good. "Fresh beef every day, potatoes, rice, and beans," he reported.[2]

Wills was one of those buoyant souls who made the best of the situation. He was even upbeat in his acknowledgment of the plague of bugs that called Cairo home. "We do have the richest assortment of bugs here imaginable," he said, "from the size of a pin head up to big black fellows as large as bats." And when he found a "wiggler" in his milk one morning, he said, "Don't you think they out to mix clean water with the cow juice?"[3] In his cheerfulness, Wills was distinctly in the minority. Almost no one else had anything good to say about Cairo. The British war correspondent and gadabout William Howard Russell said about Cairo that it was impossible to believe that some men, even speculators, "could have fixed upon such a spot as the possible site of a great city.... A more desolate woe-begone looking place, now that all trade and commerce had ceased cannot be conceived."[4]

Russell also commented upon the clouds of mosquitoes that became a familiar torment to every visitor. The mosquitoes, the rats, the dampness, and the careless and seemingly eternal nastiness of young men away from home for the first time made Cairo a purgatory of poor health. Between late April and early June, there were 993 cases treated in the military hospital: 614 cases of diarrhea and dysentery; 113 cases of fever; twenty-five cases of pneumonia, including twelve that were complicated by pleurisy; fourteen cases of rheumatism; nine cases of scrofula, three cases of sunstroke; and 114 cases classified as miscellaneous. What was mysteriously called miscellaneous cases may have been gonorrhea and syphilis, for Cairo was developing a thriving red light district. Clearly, the surgeons at Cairo had more than they could handle.

Conditions had improved only slightly when Dr. John H. Brinton of Philadelphia arrived in September. He pointed out in his memoirs that Cairo was "unhealthy to the last degree," but it was not entirely attributable to the vermin, the dampness, and the bad hygiene of the young soldiers. It was partly due to their backgrounds. Brinton wrote, "The men from the country had often not passed through the ordinary diseases of child life, and no sooner were they brought together in camps, than measles and other children's diseases showed themselves and spread rapidly."[5] Still, there was no getting away from the role an unhealthful setting played in the continually high number of hospital cases. Brinton said, "As a pestilential hole fraught with all malarial poisonous influences, the town [Cairo] unquestionably is pre-eminent." And it was only going to get worse as more men crowded into the triangle where the rivers came together.[6]

The men in blue who were gathering at Cairo were a terrific worry to Major General Gideon J. Pillow. That peripatetic Englishman William Howard Russell visited Pillow on his way up the Mississippi toward Cairo, and he said, "General Pillow is a small, compact, clear-complexioned man with short whiskers, cut in the English fashion, a quick eye, and a pompous manner of speech." Russell mentioned that Pillow limped from a wound he had received in the Mexican War battle of Chapultepec, of which he was fond of talking. One would think that Pillow would have avoided the subject of the late war, for he had come away despised by his fellow officers. They despised him, first, for his incompetence. This was the story that Russell heard told: "[Pillow] had made himself ludicrously celebrated in Mexico for having undertaken to throw up a battery which, when completed, was found to face the wrong way, so that the guns were exposed to the enemy."[7]

The second reason that Pillow was held in such disdain was because of his constant plotting behind the back of the popular General Winfield Scott. Pillow was quarrelsome, insubordinate, and ambitious. He faced three courts of inquiry during what was a rather short war. He was acquitted by each court, if not by his fellow officers. Future Union General John Sedgwick expressed the feelings of many in the officers' corps when he said, "The sentiment of the army will never acquit him."[8] Back home after the war, Pillow became a successful speculator in Tennessee and Arkansas land. In 1861, he was probably the richest man in Tennessee, but he apparently still burned to achieve military glory. At the start of the war, Governor Isham Harris appointed Pillow brigadier general of the Provisional Army of Tennessee. He was promoted to major general on May 6, 1861. His martial skills had not sharpened in the years since the Mexican War. A soldier said that General Pillow "does more foolish things than any one I ever saw," and another said that he had a "fool's courage and confidence."[9]

As of July 13, 1861, Pillow found himself a subordinate of General Leonidas Polk, commanding the Confederate Department No. 2. Being reduced to a secondary role did nothing to dampen Pillow's ambitions. From his headquarters in Memphis, he loved to plan and propose grand campaigns and to filibuster his visitors with complaints. Russell said, "General Pillow is particularly indignant with the cowardice of the well-known secessionists of Kentucky, but I think he is rather more annoyed by the Federal troops at Cairo." He wanted to get at them, and by July 1861, he thought that he had found a way.[10]

On July 28, 1861, Pillow crossed the Mississippi River to occupy New Madrid, Missouri. He wrote to Polk that his "Army of Liberation" had moved on eight steamers to New Madrid, where the people greeted him with "a thousand cheers." His men were in good spirits and eager for the "Dutch Hunt." The occupation of New Madrid was only the first step of a plan in which Pillow and his men would march north to St. Louis, joined en route by three thousand men from Pocahontas, Arkansas. This would give him a force of eleven thousand. Generals Sterling Price and Ben McCulloch would demonstrate and distract the Mis-

General John C. Frémont (collection of the author).

souri Federals while Pillow conquered St. Louis. Then he would cross the Mississippi and drive the Federals from Cairo. Voilà! The Yankees would be pushed back from the boundaries of the Jackson Purchase and the virginal neutrality of Kentucky would be preserved.[11]

Pillow's intended sequel to the occupation of New Madrid never came to pass. He finally realized that he did not have sufficient manpower, supplies, or transportation for such a campaign. He was intimidated by the Federal troops blocking his way at Cape Girardeau and Bird's Point, and knew he would have to fight his way through them "before his triumphal march could fairly begin." So, he stopped his army of liberators at New Madrid to await further developments. While they waited, Pillow's Confederates were supplied with large quantities of "tea, liquor, and other things ... by way of Paducah and Columbus, Kentucky."[12]

In July, the same month that Pillow crossed the Mississippi River into Missouri, Major General John C. Frémont assumed command of the sprawling Western Department (formerly the Department of the West), which was defined as "the State of Illinois and the States and Territories west of the Mississippi River and on this side of the Rocky Mountains, including New Mexico." On August 15, the Jackson Purchase of Kentucky was added to Frémont's command, while the rest of the commonwealth was included with Tennessee in the Union Department of the Cumberland, commanded by General Robert Anderson.[13]

Frémont was one of the great heroes of the age. He was The Pathfinder, who had surveyed the Oregon Trail and crossed the Sierra Nevadas into California in mid-winter. His books about his Western exploits were best sellers and made his name familiar to an even wider audience. He had helped wrest California away from Mexico in the previous war, had served in the Senate from California, and had been the first Republican Presidential candidate in 1856. However, he tended to be insubordinate and imperious. He angered the Lincoln administration immediately after his appointment to command by traveling not to his headquarters in St. Louis but to New York, where he spent three weeks buying guns and equipment for his department. It was not until late July that he arrived in St. Louis. He rented from his wife's cousin a mansion on Choteau Street for $500 per month (to be paid by the War Department). Ensconced there, Frémont "surrounded himself with layers of befeathered and gold-braided assistants and guards." It became nearly impossible for anyone to get in to see Frémont. A great many of his inner circle were foreigners. The man who had once sat in council with men like Kit Carson and Thomas "Broken Hand" Fitzpatrick now gathered about him a group of Hungarian and German dandies.[14]

A good many people who had once admired Frémont the Pathfinder came away disappointed after they observed his behavior as departmental commander. Dr. John H. Brinton, that keen observer, had been in St. Louis before he went to Cairo, and he was expected to report to departmental headquarters. He could not get an audience with Frémont. Brinton wrote, "The impression I received from the first, of this somewhat noted person, was not a very favorable one.... He was surrounded by a queer crowd of foreigners ... much over-uniformed, and rejoicing in bold belts and breast sashes unknown to our service. There was much jabbering and gesticulation, and the scene was most un-American.... At the time I was in St. Louis, he was busy creating strange offices, and filling them with strange appointees ... certainly Frémont was little of a real soldier."[15]

Likewise, those who had known him since the Mexican War were not impressed by his conduct as commander in the West. Thomas Ewing, lawyer, former cabinet member and senator (and incidentally, both the foster father and father-in-law of General William Tecumseh Sherman), wrote frankly to President Lincoln about Frémont, saying, "Your appointment of Frémont was unfortunate, and will give you much trouble and produce much mischief.... I knew him in the Senate—He sat beside me, and voted with me generally for three months—I was favorably impressed with him as a sound conservative man, but one of comparatively weak intellect.... Those who knew him in California represented him to me as having there assumed state and pomp and ceremony under circumstances and in a style calculated to provoke ridicule—and that he was withal arrogant and jealous of power, quite disposed to combine the Russian autocrat with the Turkish sultan—The sooner you call him to Washington for the purpose of consultation and dispose of him in a quiet way, the better."[16]

Frémont might have been surprised at how widespread the poor evaluations of his performance as department commander really were. Certainly, he made some serious blunders of both style and substance. However, he did make two strokes in 1861 that were calculated to break the stalemate in the West. The first was his enthusiastic support for a program of construction of a fleet of ironclad gunboats and his personal initiative in ordering thirty-eight mortar boats and the tugboats to pull them. The idea of an inland fleet, or brown-water navy, occurred simultaneously to several practical minded Union men, and it is hard to know who might have heard what from another, who might have influenced whom, who might have planted a seed in another man's imagination. The swirl and eddy of ideas may be impossible to trace, but the several key players are well known.

Two men who conceived of the idea of an inland fleet immediately after Fort Sumter fell were friends from St. Louis. One was attorney general Edward

Bates and the other was the river man James B. Eads. As Eads recalled it, "I received a letter from Attorney General Bates, dated Washington, April 17th, in which he said: 'Be not surprised if you are called here suddenly by telegram. If called, come instantly. In a certain contingency it will be necessary to have the aid of the most thorough knowledge of our Western rivers and the use of steam on them, and in that event I have advised that you should be the one consulted.'"[17]

Eads was the man with the required knowledge. Born in 1820 in Lawrenceburg, Indiana, and raised along the Ohio River in Cincinnati and Louisville, Eads had traded a great river for a greater one at age thirteen when he moved to St. Louis. It was a curious wrinkle in this future river man's life that the steamboat that carried him to St. Louis was on fire as it docked. Eads was caught in the rush of passengers fleeing to shore. Once safe on dry land, he stopped and turned to watch the boat burn in the morning light.

Eads' first job was as a street peddler, but in 1839 he landed a job as a mud clerk on a river packet. Now he began to learn the Mississippi and read its surface signs and submerged secrets. Accounts of wrecks came to fascinate him, and he began to develop a method of recovering cargoes from the river bottom—a diving bell and a twin-hulled, steam-powered salvage boat equipped with a derrick and suction pumps. In the late 1840s, he perfected both his craft and his methods on the Mississippi's tributaries. Eads and his crew became the leading experts in a unique trade, and he prospered. By the mid–1850s, he owned his own salvage fleet and had augmented it with a stump puller.

Bates' expected summons to Washington arrived on April 24, 1861. Eads hurriedly consulted with General Frémont before he headed East. He spent several days in the Capital City, meeting with secretary of the navy Gideon Welles, assistant secretary Gustavus A. Fox, and, on April 29, President Lincoln and his cabinet. Eads urged the creation of an inland fleet able to carry the fight to the enemy. Then, having done all he could, he returned to St. Louis. His presentation had been informative. The question was, had it been persuasive?

On May 3, General Winfield Scott wrote to General McClellan to explain his Anaconda Plan. Part of it, the strangulation of the South, would have to be accomplished by an inland fleet; he believed "from twelve to twenty-seven gunboats" would be required. The army high command appeared now to be on board, but still no word came to Eads. Overflowing with anxious energy, Eads returned to Washington in early May, but the government moved with its accustomed lack of speed which a St. Louis salvage captain could not change. He returned to St. Louis, still not knowing what the outcome of his recommendations would be.[18]

On May 14, his proposals went to the War Department. The logjam was beginning to break. In July, quartermaster general Montgomery C. Meigs was at last ready to let bids for the construction of an inland fleet. The bid notices appeared in the river town newspapers on July 27. Eight men submitted sealed bids. When they were opened on August 5, it was Eads' that was the lowest. He promised to build seven ironclads at $89,000 each and deliver them to Cairo in sixty-five days, "or forfeit $200 per boat per day."[19]

The design was by naval architect John Lenthall and improved by Samuel Pook. The specs for the gunboats called for vessels of "six hundred tons, to draw six feet, to carry thirteen heavy guns [three bow guns, four guns on each side, and two guns in the stern], to be plated with iron two and a half inches thick, and to steam nine miles per hour." Each one was to be "one hundred and seventy-five feet long, and fifty-one and a half wide; the hulls of wood" and with casemates that sloped back at an angle of about thirty-five degrees to deflect shot and shell.[20]

The ironclads were built for war, and not for the comfort of the crew. They were so hot that the gunboat crews would come to call the new-style vessels "Federal bake ovens." In addition, they were so cramped that living aboard one was a form of torture. Below decks were the engine room, fire room, magazines, shell room, shot lockers, coal bunkers, mess hall, quarters for 251 crewmen, and aft, the captain's quarters. As naval historian Jack Coombe observes, "It was a lot ... to cram into a hull 175- by 50-feet."[21]

It was also a lot of work to cram into sixty-five days the building of not one but seven such innovative vessels. The clock was ticking, and Eads hurried back to St. Louis to get started.

All the while, work had been progressing on the construction of three timberclad gunboats under the watchful eye of Commodore John Rodgers in Cincinnati. Rogers had bought three Ohio River side-wheelers for $62,000 and was having them refurbished for wartime purposes at a local drydock. They looked like typical side-wheelers, except that they were completely clad in boards of five-inch thickness (even the paddle wheel), and each carried four 32-pounders and four 8-inch Dahlgren guns. They headed downstream in the first week in August, before the river could reach its summer pool low. Even so, they faced difficulty getting over the limestone ledges at the Falls of the Ohio. One of them had to be dragged "by the united power of the three over a bar having a foot less water than the draft of the deepest of them," reported Rodgers. The Louisville pilots, knowing that they had a certain leverage, also proved difficult. They balked at guiding the boats through until Rodgers promised them what amounted to a fat bonus above their usual pay.[22]

The timberclads landed at Cairo on the afternoon of August 12, 1861, and they were a welcome sight. Until then, the only river-craft to oppose the

Rebels and patrol the rivers around Cairo was one lonely tugboat, the *Swallow*. These three timberclads, the *Tyler*, the *Lexington*, and the *Conestoga*, would win a great name for themselves and saw action weeks before the first of the ironclads came down the ways. On August 15, only three days after reporting at Cairo, Lieutenant Commander S. Ledyard Phelps went on the offensive. He reported that as "the commanding officer at Cairo was very anxious that the gunboats should make a demonstration," he went on a scouting mission down the Mississippi toward New Madrid. He encountered two Rebel steamers below Hickman and chased them, but they got away. No damage had been done in this first timberclad expedition, not a gun had been fired, but the Rebels knew that they faced a new offensive threat.[23]

Soon after arriving back in St. Louis, Eads found that he had nine ironclads to build, not seven. Frémont had decided on his own initiative to buy and convert two boats—a ferry called the *New Era* and Ead's own snag-puller, the *Submarine*—into gunboats. They were renamed the *Essex* and the *Benton*. Of the latter, Eads said that she became "the most powerful iron-clad of the fleet." She was covered with thirteen and a half inch plate iron and mounted sixteen guns.[24]

On Eads' schedule, before the conversion of the *New Era* and the *Submarine*, came the laying of seven new keels, the start of work on the contract vessels. In order to meet his deadline, Eads established two shipyards, one about ten miles south of St. Louis at Carondelet, where he employed five hundred hands, and the other at Mound City, Illinois, where three hundred men worked. Many different trades were represented. The workmen's wages were $2 an hour and twenty-five cents per hour of overtime. Congress appropriated $1 million for the boat-building effort, but the War Department was slow in forwarding the money to Eads—yet another worry for an overworked man whose bills were quickly mounting. By the end of August, he owed more than $700,000. Luckily, the money arrived in late September, and it was needed, for this was not a strictly local enterprise. Eads was ordering gun carriages from Cincinnati, engines from Pittsburgh, iron armor from Newport, Kentucky, and Portsmouth, Ohio, and white oak lumber from all over the upper Midwest and Kentucky.

While the gunboats were being built, Frémont conceived of the idea of using artillery craft on the rivers. Cooling says that Frémont became "fascinated with mounting 17,500-pound seacoast mortars on rafts for use against Confederate shore batteries."[25] Frémont ordered thirty-eight of these mortar barges and the tugboats to pull them, and he awarded Theodore Adams of St. Louis the contract to build them. The mortar barges became one of several points of contention between Frémont and Commander Rodgers. Rodgers had opposed them, as he had the general's purchase of the *New Era* and the *Submarine*. In fact, Rodgers had "vetoed purchase of Eads' snagboat," but "Frémont reversed the decision." Frémont was also suspicious of Rodgers' close connection with quartermaster general Montgomery C. Meigs, whose accountants were nosing around, looking for malfeasance in the St. Louis headquarters of the Western Department.[26]

All of these disagreements considered, Frémont had Rodgers recalled and Captain Andrew H. Foote sent west from the Brooklyn Navy Yard to replace him. Foote arrived at St. Louis on September 5, 1861, and wired secretary of the navy Gideon Welles: "I have reported to Major-General John C. Frémont." It seems an odd statement that navy Captain Foote would report to army General Frémont until one realizes that the inland fleet project was under the auspices of the army. Foote nevertheless took pains to include Secretary Welles among those whom he kept informed. The day after he reported to Frémont, Foote traveled down to Carondelet to assume command.[27] Coombe writes, "Captain Foote would have been impressed by the sprawling shipyard, at the foot of Marceau Street, that contained six long sheds, a dozen ways, a forest of cranes and hoists and a marine railway ... consisting of a series of rails that extended from a boat shed and upon which was a car or cradle that could either run boats out of the water to the shed, or launch a vessel from the shed into the water."[28]

Flag Officer Andrew H. Foote (National Archives).

Seeing Foote, Rodgers was flabbergasted. He had not known that he was being relieved until the moment Foote arrived and presented his orders. The role of Frémont in his recall was not mentioned; the Navy Department's official explanation "was that the riverine force had grown to the point that an officer more senior than a commander should be in charge."[29] Rodgers was gracious to Foote, though he did decline to remain at Carondelet in a subordinate position. However, Rodgers complained to Secretary Welles, in a long letter dated September 7, that years of service in a variety of commands had accustomed him to solving his own problems without bothering his superiors:

> You have naturally supposed that I did nothing because I labored silently. In regard to the new gunboats little on my part remains. I have taken steps to procure the gun carriages, the anchors, rowboats, chains, cooking apparatus; I have appointed the necessary superintendents; I have used means to insure that iron plating shall be properly made; I have ordered additions to the gunboats themselves, rendering them in my opinion more than a match for the smooth water for any frigate in the service...I am not conscious of having been without zeal. I have the consolation of knowing that those are more familiar with my part here give me credit for great efficiency. They think I have proved that I did actually deserve the honor you conferred upon me in the command which I excercised.[30]

Fair or not, the commander was out and the captain was in. There was still a lot of work to be done at the boatyards and not much time. If Foote's temper sometimes spilled over, well, that was what it took to get things moving, and men remembered it. Eads said of the man who became his friend that he was "full of anecdotes, and having a peaceful, easy flow of language. He was likewise, ordinarily one of the most amiable-looking of men; but when angered, as I once saw him, his face impressed me as being most savage and demoniacal."[31] Foote had reason to be temperamental. He complained that he was stuck in "this wilderness of naval wants" and said his work was of "almost insuperable difficulty." His biographer, Spencer Tucker, agreed, saying, "The task before him was daunting. Foote would be a naval officer essentially without resources and subject to army control; and he was well aware that his government's priorities lay with coastal operations. Then there was the lesson of his predecessor. Foote would need all his professional assets as well as his formidable resources of resolution and faithfulness to duty to do this job, as well as the ability to get along with army officers."[32]

To add to his difficulties, Foote was out of his element. He was a blue water man who loved the sea, and operating on interior rivers with untrained crews and an army of landlubbers was foreign to both his soul and his training. Still he persisted, and at last the first Union ironclad on the western waters, the *St. Louis*, came sliding down the ways into the Mississippi River. The date was October 12, 1861. In a short time, the *Carondelet*, the *Cincinnati*, the *Louisville*, the *Mound City*, the *Cairo*, and the *Pittsburg* joined their sister on the brown water, and then came the *Essex* and the *Benton*. It was a formidable fleet, a real threat to the Confederacy, and they were needed now more than ever before. A month earlier, on September 3, the Confederates, feeling pushed and threatened, had broken the stalemate in the West.

4

Invasions
(September 1861)

During the summer and fall of 1861, while the Federals in Missouri and Southern Illinois worked on their ironclads, tensions in the Jackson Purchase increased. The region was filled with homegrown secessionists and they were intent on mischief. Their small acts of malice in turn only drew the ire of the Federals.

There had been two incidents back in June that threw the people of Columbus on the Mississippi into a civic rage. The first involved a militia company from Columbus, the Rangers, who went out on maneuvers. It was little more than a camping trip, but when they began moving north on the east bank of the Mississippi, alarmed Unionists imagined that an invasion had commenced. They alerted Colonel Richard J. Oglesby, now commanding at Cairo, and he "decided he would either capture them or kill them." He dispatched two hundred men who "landed at night and marched toward the encampment." At houses along the line of their stealthy march, the Union patrol aroused sleeping citizens and arrested some of them. They did not arrest any of the Rangers, though. They had ended their maneuvers and gone home. One of Columbus' leading citizens, George Taylor, later protested: "It has never been the pleasure of any person connected with this flagrant infraction of Kentucky neutrality to allege any fault committed by a single individual of that party of Rangers. It was a wanton, unprovoked invasion of Kentucky soil to hunt down and murder Kentucky citizens."[1]

The second incident that enraged the citizens of Columbus occurred when two companies of the 8th Illinois Infantry, accompanied by Colonel Oglesby himself, were reconnoitering downstream aboard a transport called the *City of Alton*. Passing Columbus, they noticed a Rebel flag flying in the town. It was still flying when they came back upstream, and a crowd had begun to gather, seething with defiance. The *Alton* slowed down and pulled near the shore. Colonel Oglesby shouted for the people to haul the flag down. They refused, and Oglesby said he would do it himself. They are reported to have answered, "We'd like to see you try it." The soldiers were lined up in ranks two deep on the deck, their weapons ready, when a captain and a sergeant jumped over the rail, waded ashore, pulled down the Confederate banner, and brought it back as a trophy. The soldiers expected a fight. None developed, but the people of Columbus had another Rebel flag flying within the hour and sent a dare to the men who essentially had held them at gunpoint while their property was violated. If the Yankees wanted this new flag, they could "come and take it." The town did not forget the confiscated flag, though. The editor of the *Columbus Crescent* said of the captured flag, "Would that its folds had contained 1000 asps to sting 1000 Dutchmen to eternity unshriven."[2]

Responding to the Yankee trespass, General Simon Bolivar Buckner of the State Guard sent Colonel Lloyd Tilghman and six companies to Columbus. Buckner tried to obtain tents and other supplies for them, only to find that the government agents in Louisville refused to honor the requisition. Shortly afterward, in the first week in July, having had his fill of neutrality, Colonel Tilghman laid down his neglected draftsman's pen for good and led his five hundred men to Camp Boone, Tennessee, where they became part of the Confederate 3rd Kentucky Infantry. Before he left Paducah, conscious that he might never return, Tilghman wrote his last will and testament. He left all of his personal property, his Paducah town lots, some property in Arkansas, and five slaves to his pretty wife, Augusta.

There were several alarming incidents in August. In the second week of the month, the *W.B. Terry*, a riverboat owned by a Paducah consortium, captured the Louisville packet *Pocahontas* at Pine Bluff, a Calloway County town on the Tennessee River. More or less at gunpoint, the *Pocahontas* and her cargo of tobacco were delivered upstream to Confederate Tennessee. The *Terry* returned to Paducah alone. Ten days later, the U.S. gunboat *Lexington* appeared at Paducah. The *Terry* was positively identified and, Commander R.N. Stembel said, "I ran alongside of her, cut her out, made her fast to the *Lexington*, and immediately returned" to Cairo. As the seizure was taking place, the captain and crew of the *Terry* abandoned the vessel and were not captured. Colonel Oglesby at Cairo, said, "I had indisputable proof ... that she was running in the employment of the Confederate States. *Without hesitating on the neutrality of Kentucky*, I ordered her capture. She turns out to be of no great value, say, vessel and furniture, $3,000. To the Confederates three times that sum will not compensate the loss" (emphasis added).[3]

A few hours later, the crew of the *Terry*, along with forty or fifty armed Paducah citizens, took control of a mail packet called the *Samuel Orr* and stole away with her up the Tennessee, minus the captain and crew, who escaped in skiffs. In reporting the incident, Oglesby said that the capture was "a retaliation more vindictive than sensible, as they thus destroy the last means of illicit trade

Mississippi Gunboats under construction at Carondelet (*Harper's Weekly*, October 5, 1861).

with the border states north of the Ohio. Nevertheless, they have the boat and cargo, worth say, $25,000."[4] (General Frémont took a more sinister view of the event. He wrote to adjutant general Lorenzo Thomas: "Events have thus transpired clearly indicating the complicity of citizens of Kentucky with the rebel forces, and showing the impracticability of carrying on operations in that direction without involving the Kentucky shore.")[5]

At a mass meeting called on the afternoon of the *Terry*'s capture, the people of Paducah angrily met, "condemning the action of the Federals" and calling on Governor Magoffin "for military assistance." If he would not defend them, they warned, they would appeal to their Confederate brethren in Tennessee. Despite all of their foot-stamping, the help did not come and the *Terry* was not returned to its owners.[6]

On the last day of the month, the *New York Times* announced that mail delivery in the Purchase was going to be curtailed: "The Post-office Department having authentic information that the mails here have been repeatedly violated and cannot be carried safely in that part of Kentucky named herein, it is ordered that the Post-offices at Hickman, Columbus, and Paducah, Kentucky, and all other Post-offices in Kentucky west of the Tennessee River, be discontinued." Only the small routes between Russellville to Milburn and Eddyville to Olive were spared. Postmasters in the Purchase were ordered to be watchful for Southern agents and to intercept Southern mail.[7]

Small events led inevitably to larger ones. The Federals were expecting rebellion to break out in the Purchase at any time and patrolled constantly to prevent it. Not only did they prowl the rivers, more than once they also set foot on the soil of neutral Kentucky. The people were feeling crowded. Yankee power (the *misuse* of power, in the view of most natives) was being felt more and more and had to be resisted. The Purchase was caught up in an unhealthy escalation that could lead but to one result. Events were about to take a very serious turn, indeed.

Major General John C. Frémont made two moves in 1861 that continued to benefit the Union cause long after he had left the scene. As discussed earlier, he advocated and materially supported the construction of an inland fleet. Second, he appointed Brigadier General Ulysses S. Grant to command the District of Southeast Missouri, headquarters at Cairo.

Grant had experienced a hard time getting a command. He had left the army in 1854 under a drunkard's cloud and immediately before war commenced in 1861 had been a clerk at his father's retail leather store in Galena, Illinois. When the secession crisis came, Grant was eager to return to military service, but with conditions. He refused a commission as captain of the local militia unit "on the grounds that having been a captain in the regular army, he ought to have something better." The governor of Illinois turned down his application for a commission. The men in power in Missouri and Ohio were likewise uninterested in taking a chance on Grant. A letter to the adjutant general of the U.S. Army went unanswered. One of Grant's traits was a talent for friendship, and as it happened, he had a friend in the congressional delegation from Illinois, the Honorable Elihu B. Washburne. Through Washburne's influence, promotions began to come Grant's way. He was appointed colonel of the 21st Illinois Volunteers in June 1861, and in August, when Lincoln needed to keep the Illinois Republicans happy by appointing some brigadier generals from their state, Grant received one of the commissions. He was subsequently posted in Missouri.[8]

In August, Grant met with Major General John C. Frémont in St. Louis. The former Pathfinder liked what he saw in this scruffy brigadier. On August 28, 1861, he appointed Grant to command the District of Southeast Missouri. In his orders to Grant, Frémont revealed his aggressive plans. Grant "was fully instructed," remembered Frémont, "concerning the actual and intended movements on the Mississippi and the *more immediate movements upon the Kentucky shore*, together with the intention to hold the mouth of the Tennessee and Cumberland rivers. In his written instructions General Grant was directed to ... take possession of points threatened by the Confederates on the Missouri *and Kentucky shores*" (emphasis added).[9]

Grant moved his offices to the St. Charles Hotel on Ohio Street in Cairo, and on September 2, he made his first offensive move. He sent a force to occupy the obscure river landing of Belmont, Missouri, opposite Columbus. To the frightened citizens there, the Federal noose appeared to be tightening. It appeared that way to General Leonidas Polk, too. Like Frémont, he had been thinking about a move into Kentucky. He understood that timing was important. On September 1, Polk had written Governor Magoffin: "I think it of the greatest importance that I should be well informed of the future plans and policy of the Southern party in Kentucky, so as to shape my own plans accordingly.... I think it of the greatest importance to the Southern cause in Kentucky or elsewhere *that I should be ahead of the enemy in occupying Columbus and Paducah*" (emphasis added).[10]

Now Frémont had forced his hand. Believing that the next Federal advance would be into Columbus, Polk ordered General Gideon Pillow to move from his New Madrid base into Kentucky. The object was Columbus, but because of the Yankee artillery at Belmont, Pillow's transport boats had to land in Hickman. He occupied the little town on September 3, 1861. He moved overland into Columbus the next day.

The news that the Confederates had invaded Kentucky and occupied Hickman and Columbus arrived at Cairo from several forces at once. The Federal timberclads *Tyler* and *Lexington* were steaming past Hickman when they saw a Confederate camp a half-mile long on the Kentucky bank. They skirmished there with the oddly named Rebel gunboat *Yankee* and fired twenty shots in her direction. During the fight, the Union boats received fire from two Confederate shore batteries. They escaped serious damage and continued their cruise. As they steamed back toward Cairo later that same day, they were fired upon again, this time by a Rebel artillery crew at Columbus.

It appears that by the time the boats docked at Cairo, Grant had already heard about the invasion from Charles de Arnaud, one of Frémont's foreigners, this one a Russian. Arnaud had been spying down the Kentucky side of the river and had seen the Confederates at Hickman and Columbus. He reported that four thousand Rebels were on their way to Paducah—another day and the city would be lost. Grant hastily wired Frémont in St. Louis and told him that he was going to advance unless orders arrived forbidding it. When no orders came, Grant began to prepare for his move. He took a moment to telegraph the speaker of the Kentucky House of Representatives that the Rebels had invaded the Purchase. Civil War historian James Ramage wrote, "This perceptive, delicate action shielded Grant from any accusation that he was guilty of violating Kentucky neutrality—the Confederates had already violated it, and his message showed that he knew this."[11]

Still no countermanding orders came from St. Louis, so Grant set out for Paducah with three steamboats, plus the timberclads *Tyler* and *Conestoga*, the 9th and 12th Illinois Volunteers, and Battery A, Chicago Light Artillery. They left Cairo at 11:30 P.M. on September 5, 1861. Grant timed his departure so as to reach Paducah about dawn. He hoped to catch the people unawares, and if his *Personal Memoirs* are to be believed, he did. Grant wrote, "When the National troops entered the town the citizens were taken by surprise. I never saw such consternation on the faces of the people. Men, women and children came out of their doors looking pale and frightened."[12]

That was the way Grant remembered it in 1885, but the people of Paducah, while certainly upset, may not have been so surprised as he said. In his report of the expedition, written at the time, he said that he saw the Rebel flags flying when the Yankees approached Paducah, and he saw them begin to come down. One of the flags belonged to Mrs. Emily Gant Jarrett. She ordered a nine-year-old black boy to haul it down, just as Grant happened to notice it. He ordered his men to capture it. As a local writer recounted it more than sixty years later, "A squad of soldiers learning Mrs. Jarrett's name and address, was detailed to bring it to headquarters. She refused their request, whereupon they searched [her] little cottage. After much questioning and intimidation the soldiers reported a fruitless assignment. It is thought she was wearing it as a petticoat."[13]

Grant's Illinois troops quickly "took possession of the telegraph office, railroad depot [where he found and confiscated a supply of rations and two tons of leather], and Marine Hospital," as well as "George Oehlschlaeger's bake shop and Fred Hummel's gun shop." The officers began to choose homes for their headquarters, and

General U.S. Grant (Library of Congress).

churches, schools, and warehouses began to be fitted out to serve as hospitals. The artillery battery moved toward the edge of town and set up camp "on the main street looking west from the city."[14]

Grant had come prepared with a proclamation, which he read to the people and which said in part, "I have come among you not as an enemy, but as your friend and fellow citizen, not to injure or annoy you, but to respect the rights and to defend and enforce the rights of all loyal citizens.... The strong arm of the Government is here to protect its friends and to punish its enemies. Whenever it is manifest that you are able to defend ourselves, to maintain the authority of your Government, and protect the rights of all its loyal citizens, I shall withdraw the forces under my command from your city." Then, to make sure that his words reached the people who were not near when he read them, Grant gave the text to Mayor John S. Sauner so that the proclamation could be published as a broadside.[15]

As the Federals settled in, those citizens of Paducah who could do so were clearing out. Sergeant John McLean, Co. A, 40th Illinois Infantry, remembered that the people "were seized with an immediate desire to leave town, employing any and all kinds of conveyance for the purpose, including drays, wagons, express carts, push carts, wheelbarrows, baby cabs or anything that would hold a trunk.... By noon the town was practically deserted." The citizens were not simply fleeing out of hatred for the Federals; in fact, some of them were crossing the river into Illinois. What they were trying to do was get out from between two armies, for they expected Pillow to arrive at any hour. When he did, the shelling would commence, and families wanted to be as far away as possible by then. Whatever the individual reasons for the exodus, there was an unmistakable atmosphere of urgency in Paducah on that September day. McLean found the sight of people turning themselves into refugees humorous.[16]

Grant did not remain long in Paducah. By 4:00 P.M. he was ready to return to Cairo. He left behind the two timberclads and one of the transports, and left General Eleazer A. Paine in temporary command, instructing him to secure the town and "to take special care and precaution that no harm is done to inoffensive citizens; that the soldiers shall not enter any private dwelling nor make any searches unless by your orders.... Exercise the strictest discipline against any soldier who shall insult citizens or engage in plundering private property."[17]

Grant had no sooner steamed out of sight than Paine began to ignore his instructions. He ordered a gunboat to fire a cannon round, which hit a house, and "when he later ordered a local blacksmith to shoe his horse and the man refused, Paine arrested him and gave him two choices: shoe the horse in five minutes or be shot." In addition, Paine allowed the men of the 9th Illinois to engage in "stealing, plundering, and rampant vandalism." It must have been a welcome relief to the people when General C.F. Smith, a career Regular, arrived to take permanent command of Paducah on September 14.[18]

Back at Cairo that night, Grant found orders awaiting him from Frémont. They were written in Hungarian. Once they were translated, Grant saw that he was instructed to "prosecute with the utmost speed all the preparation of the place selected for the Fort and Entrenched Camp on the Kentucky Shore forming a triangle with Cairo and Bird's Point, which fortification we will call Fort Holt."[19] Also, if he felt "strong enough," Grant was authorized to occupy Paducah.[20]

5

Columbus
(September–October 1861)

The people of Paducah experienced an unpleasant shock in being occupied by the army, but the people of Columbus were overjoyed at the arrival of Pillow's troops. George Taylor was the spokesman for a group of citizens who addressed an adoring letter to General Polk, still at Union City. The letter began, "Honored Sir: Will you permit a few of the citizens of this city and its vicinity, so recently oppressed and suffering from the tyrannical rules of the Northern Government, to express to you our profound gratification at the advent of the army under your command...." It ended several pages later assuring the general of the "pleasure we derive from the sense of restored confidence and the enjoyment of a consciousness that now our families and our property are safe. If it from hearts filled with such emotions at these that this entire community extends to you and to your gallant army a cordial welcome."[1]

On or about September 8, the people of Columbus were able to cheer their hero in person, when General Polk arrived from Union City. The road that led Polk to the camp at Columbus was an unlikely one. Born in North Carolina in 1806, Polk had attended university at Chapel Hill before being accepted at the U.S. Military Academy. One of Polk's roommates there was Albert Sidney Johnston and one of his closest friends came to be a cadet in the class behind him, Jefferson Davis. While still at the academy, he felt the sinner's guilt and had a conversion experience. He soon felt the call to the ministry and almost as soon as he graduated in 1827, he resigned his commission to begin his religious studies at the Virginia Theological Seminary in Alexandria. He graduated in 1830 and moved with his new wife to Middle Tennessee, where he preached—mostly to slaves—and became "quite an industrious farmer." In 1838 Polk was named Missionary Bishop of the Southwest, and in 1841 he became the Bishop of Louisiana. At his plantation there, named Leighton, he owned four hundred slaves. He lost the plantation in 1854—too much of the bishop, too little of the planter.[2]

The secession crisis of 1860 put him in a uniquely delicate position. As a Southern citizen, he believed in the right of secession, but as the bishop in charge of a vast diocese he had to think about its effect on his church and his parishioners. Louisiana's secession "had severed all connection of the Diocese of Louisiana with the Protestant Episcopal Church of the United States." Polk emphasized to his brethren in the North that the separation was not over Christian doctrine and said, "Our relations to each other hereafter will be the relations we both now hold to the men of our Mother Church of England."[3]

In June 1861, Polk traveled to Virginia to visit with all the Louisiana troops who had already begun to gather in the Eastern Theater and also to visit with his old West Point friend, President Jefferson Davis. Within a week, Davis offered Polk a brigadier general's commission. Polk hesitated for a polite three days before accepting. The wait proved beneficial to the bishop, for when the commission came, it was not that of a brigadier, but of a major general. He was assigned to command Department No. 2, with his headquarters in Memphis. Portions of Alabama, Tennessee, Arkansas, Mississippi, and Louisiana were included in his department. On September 2, 1861, his command was expanded to include all of Arkansas and Missouri.

Polk must have been a man of considerable charm. He became an Episcopal bishop with very little pulpit experience and became a major general overseeing an important area of command with no more to recommend him than four years as a West Point cadet and an interview with his friend Jefferson Davis. Part of his appeal may have been his impressive physical presence. Polk was "of good stature and an erect military carriage, broad shouldered and deep in the chest, with a well-poised shapely head, strong but finely cut features, one white lock overhanging his wide forehead, clear complexion, and keen but frank and kindly blue eyes, the first glace recognized him as a man to be obeyed."[4] Almost forty years later, one of Polk's soldiers remembered him as "a great and good man ... an elegant and noble gentleman. He was a strict disciplinarian, and required full service from his officers and strict observance of etiquette in his military family; but he was kind and just. I have many reasons for loving the memory of this good man."[5]

Polk's occupation of Columbus brought on a political crisis. On September 4, the Confederate secretary of war, L.P. Walker, sent Polk a terse note. It was a little behind the curve of events, but its intent was unmistakable: "News has reached here that General Pillow has landed his troops at Hickman, Ky. Order their prompt removal from Kentucky."[6] Governor Harris of Tennessee piled on the same day. He called the invasion "unfortunate," and said, "The President and myself are pledged to respect the neutrality of Kentucky. I hope they [Pillow's troops] will be withdrawn instantly."[7]

Beriah Magoffin, governor of the violated state, tried to admonish both sides equally and demanded that Polk's and Grant's forces be removed from Kentucky. He was frustrated when, once again, the Unionists in the legislature asserted their power and passed a strongly worded resolution calling on the CSA troops—only the CSA troops—to withdraw. The governor vetoed their resolution and the two houses of the legislature easily overrode his veto by a vote of about three-to-one in each house. From this moment on, Magoffin was a governor in name only; the Unionist general assembly ran Kentucky now. Magoffin bowed to their will and issued a proclamation that read, "In obedience to the subjoined resolution, adopted by the general assembly of the Commonwealth of Kentucky, the Government of the Confederate States, the State of Tennessee, and all others concerned, are hereby informed that Kentucky expects the Confederate or Tennessee troops to be withdrawn from her soil unconditionally."[8]

Over a period of days, Polk tried to restore the calm of the politicians whose anxieties he had so obviously aroused. Bypassing the upset L.P. Walker, Polk wrote a respectful letter directly to President Davis in which he said he hoped "that the measure I have taken may meet the approbation of my Government." Three days later he wrote another letter in which he defended himself as the possible savior of the cause in Kentucky, and also protested that he had actually been made to wait too long. He said in part, "I believe, if we could have found a respectable pretext, it would have been better to have seized this place some months ago, as I am convinced we had more friends then in Kentucky than we have had since.... If we make the stand now, and do it vigorously, we shall find we have more allies in the State than we shall ever have at a future day, and if our arms should be successful in a few battles the State will soon abandon the position which fear of the power of the Federal Government alone constrains her now to maintain."[9] Polk wrote to Governor Harris that the advance was "entirely acceptable to the people of Kentucky," and was "essential to the security of Western Tennessee." He offered the excuse for the invasion that he "had never received official information that the President and yourself had determined upon any particular course in reference to the State of Kentucky."[10]

And on September 8, probably the very day that he personally moved into Columbus, Polk wrote to Magoffin: "A military necessity having required me to occupy this town [Columbus], I have taken possession of it by the forces under my command. The circumstances leading to this act were promptly reported to the President of the Confederate States. His reply was, 'the necessity justified the action.'"[11] In a second, longer message dated the same day, Polk offered to leave Kentucky soil if he could obtain a promise that the Federals would do the same simultaneously and also promise not to come back. In a letter to Kentucky state senator John M. Johnson, Polk was particularly forceful. The general said that his occupation of Columbus "finds abundant justification in the history of the concessions granted to the Federal Government by Kentucky ever since the war began, notwithstanding the position of neutrality which she has assumed." Then he detailed Kentucky's duplicity:

> [S]he has allowed the seizure in her ports (Paducah) of property of citizens of the Confederate States. She has by her members in the Congress of the United States, voted supplies of men and money to carry on the war against the Confederate States. She has allowed the Federal Government to cut timber from her forests for the purpose of building armed boats for the invasion of the Southern States. She is permitting to be enlisted in her territory troops, not only of her own citizens, but of citizens of other States, for the purpose of being armed and used in offensive warfare against the Confederate States. At Camp Robinson, in the county of Garrard, there are now 10,000 troops, if the newspapers can be relied upon, in which men from Tennessee, Ohio, Indiana, and Illinois are mustered with Kentuckians into the service fo the United States and armed by that Government, for the avowed purpose of giving aid to the disaffected in the Confederate States and of carrying out designs of that Government for their subjugation...We are here, therefore, not by choice, but by necessity.[12]

General Leonidas Polk in his bishop's robes (Library of Congress).

One thing was clear. Polk was satisfied with both the causes and the results of his occupation of Columbus and no matter how much the politicians might yelp, he was going to stay.

The Confederate soldiers were happy to stay. They loved Columbus. The views of the Mississippi River from the ridge top of the Iron Bluffs were magnificent. The weather was cool and pleasant. The people came with their wagons loaded with chicken, pork, potatoes, fruit, and whiskey. Trooper John Milton Hubbard of Co. E, 7th Tennessee Cavalry, reminisced: "We were now in a 'hog and hominy' country, and the soldiering was of the holiday kind. We made long marches through the Purchase and saw many evidences of Southern sympathy. Indeed, the whole population seemed to be friendly to us, as even those with Northern sympathies prudently kept quiet."[13]

Young men of the Purchase flocked to join Polk until there were enough to fill a new infantry regiment, the 7th Kentucky, CSA. Polk had 17,000 soldiers by the end of October. There was plenty of work to do, of course, and there were also many amusements. The young soldiers courted the local girls. They staged minstrel shows and found fun in "rolling a cannon ball at nine holes in the ground; foot racing, wrestling," and even tree-climbing. They really were just boys, after all.[14]

Their camps were behind the brow of the high ridge. At first, they lived in tents, but the weather was growing cooler. Lunsford P. Yandell, assistant surgeon of the 4th Tennessee Infantry, wrote to his parents: "Every evening and morning we have fires built in front of our tents, but they are but poor substitutes for fireplaces or stoves." Winter was coming, and to fend off its effects the men built their shebangs. Yandell wrote that he and his messmates had built a plank shack ten feet by twelve. It was well furnished, he said, and they frequently entertained.[15]

The best Civil War scholar of the ordinary soldiers' life, Bell Irvin Wiley, writes, "Probably the most industrious of the tent dwellers [at Columbus] were a group of Louisianans.... These soldiers dug cellars under their tents and covered them over with boards. The canvas-enclosed upper story was used as a sleeping room, while cooking and eating were done 'deep in the earth beneath.'" This may have been some men of the 13th Louisiana, a regiment of primarily French-speaking troopers who dazzled the people with a regimental parade through Columbus in December 1861.[16]

The most vocal (and eloquent) malcontent at Columbus may have been Henry Morton Stanley of Co. E, 6th Arkansas Infantry. This young soldier, whose later fame would grow from his search in the African interior for Dr. David Livingstone, wrote of his experience at Columbus that the food was terrible, the shelter was insufficient, and the officers both ignorant and cruel: "The fault of the American generalship was that it devoted itself solely to strategy and fighting.... The officers knew how to keep their horses in good condition, but I do not remember ever to have seen an officer who examined the state of our messes ... it never seems to have struck any officer, from General Lee down to the Third-Lieutenant of an infantry company, that it might be possible to reduce the number of invalids by paying attention to the soldiers' joys and comforts."[17]

As to their cruelty, Stanley said, "I had seen unfortunate culprits horsed on triangular fence-rails, and jerked up by vicious bearers, to increase their pains; others straddled ignomiously on poles, or fettered up with ball and chain; or subjected to head shaving, or tied up with the painful buck and gag; or hoisted up by the thumbs.... Our brigade-commander, and regimental officers were eaten up with a mighty zeal."[18] Stanley also complained about the work of building the defenses at Columbus and soldiering in general: "We had condemned ourselves to a servitude more slavish than that of the black plantation hands.... We could not be sold, but our liberties and lives were at the disposal of a Congress about which I, as least, knew nothing."[19]

The work was very hard. The works were built on the Iron Bluffs, 150 feet above and a bit north of Columbus. There were no entrenchments directly behind the town. Four roads were carved down the face of the bluff to connect the army population and the civilians below. Columbus was a village of about one thousand people, proud of its brick houses of business, its newspaper (the *Columbus Crescent*), its wharf, and its recently acquired status as the northern terminus of the Mobile & Ohio Railroad. Mark Twain called it "a pretty town." He was in a good position to judge; he knew scores of them from his days as a riverboat pilot.[20]

When they were done, the Confederates had erected two miles of rifle pits and trenches among the beech and locust trees. They were connected by a simple and ingenious intercom system—iron pipes were made to serve as speaking tubes. These pipes were undoubtedly left over from the plumbing system that connected the camp to the river. A steam-powered pump drew the water up the steep bluff, saving the boys the constant and heavy job of filling water barrels and loading them on wagons for the winding trip to the camps.

There were five major earthen forts and 140 cannon arrayed in three tiers from the water's edge to the ridge top. The artillery pieces were given affectionate pet names such as "Soul-Searcher," "Snorter," "Rib Smasher," and, in honor of the general's wife, "Lady Polk." That last-named piece was the biggest gun in the Confederacy, a rifled Dahlgren gun able to throw a 128-pound shell three miles. The long, black projectiles from the Lady Polk were called "lampposts." The collective name for this web of trenches and gun emplacements was officially Fort De Russey. It was perhaps better known as "The Gibraltar of the West." Colonel (soon to be General) John P. McCown commanded the guns and also the left wing; the right wing was commanded by General Benjamin F. Cheatham.

In addition to the earthworks, Polk's engineers would eventually line the river and the land approaches with mines, and in the spring Polk would follow General Pillow's advice to stretch a chain across the Mississippi to impede southbound Yankee traffic. Each link of this mighty chain was eleven inches long, six inches across, and weighed twenty pounds. It was secured on the Missouri bank by two large sycamore trees and on the Kentucky side by a great anchor. This monstrous piece of iron weighed six tons and measured nine feet from fluke to fluke. The chain that stretched between the sycamores and the anchor floated on the river on log pontoons placed at regular intervals. The soldiers called the whole thing "Pillow's Folly," and as they expected, it ultimately failed. The chain broke of its own weight, but while it lasted, it was a sight to see.

Polk established another camp across the river at Belmont landing where the Yankees had recently been. It was named Camp Johnston. Posted there were a battery of artillery, a regiment of infantry, and a cavalry squadron. Private William G. Stevenson (Co. B, 2nd Tennessee Infantry) remembered his time at Columbus-Belmont as "hard work and harder drill ... at one time we worked twelve hours out of every thirty-six or so. Every other work turn came at night. Generals Polk, Pillow, Cheathum [sic], and McCown were present day and night encouraging the men with words of cheer. General Pillow at one time dismounted and worked in the trenches himself to quiet some dissatisfaction which had risen." General Polk's work, too, was hard. His challenges consisted of more than merely inspecting and encouraging the work details; he had his hands full with his superiors in the field and with the War Department in Richmond.[21]

On September 15, 1861, Albert Sidney Johnston superseded Polk as commander of Department No. 2. Polk was reassigned to command the 1st (Western) Division of the department. This reduced the area of Polk's command (to all of Western Kentucky west of the Cumberland River and Western Tennessee) and sharpened the focus of his duties to more of military and less of political responsibilities. It also brought into his realm of control Forts Henry and Donelson. Work had languished on the forts through the summer. Polk intended to remedy that at once by appointing a new general to be in charge. On October 31, 1861, he wrote to Johnston in Bowling Green: "I beg leave to call the attention of the general commanding to the importance of having some commander of large experience and military efficiency put in charge of the defenses of the Tennessee and Cumberland Rivers." He had someone in mind. He proposed to appoint Colonel Lloyd Tilghman to the position, and further recommended Tilghman's promotion to brigadier general. Johnston approved both. He wrote Tilghman about his new responsibilities on November 17: "The utmost vigilance is enjoined. The general regrets to hear that there has been heretofore gross negligence in this respect—the commander at Fort Donelson away from his post nightly and the officer in charge of the field batteries frequently absent. This cannot be tolerated." There were six companies at Fort Donelson and Johnston was going to ask Governor Harris for four more Tennessee companies to make a full regiment. With these, plus impressed labor, Tilghman could finish the forts.[22]

Polk was also ordered to begin a new camp, sort of a way station between Fort Henry and Columbus. Camp Beauregard, as it was christened, was in Graves County, the most rebellious of any in the Purchase. Abraham Lincoln had not received a single Graves County vote in the election of 1860, and before war's end, the county would provide almost ten times more soldiers to the Confederacy than to the Union. The nearest village to Camp Beauregard was Feliciana, a thriving little hamlet on the NO&O Railroad. The Confederates placed their camp about two miles east of the village on a high hill, which provided a panoramic view of the valley below. By late September there were roughly 2800 officers and men at Camp Beauregard and reinforcements continued to come in. They were styled finally as the 4th Division (two brigades), commanded by Colonel John Bowen. Bowen's camp resembled one from the Revolutionary War, so predominant were the numbers of flintlocks and shotguns. Modern weapons were practically unseen. At its height, Camp Beauregard may have been home to more than six thousand soldiers, primarily boys from Arkansas and Mississippi. One notable exception was the 1st Missouri Infantry under Lieutenant Colonel Lucius Rich, who was nicknamed "Double Quick Rich" for his love of having his regiment perform the drill at that speed. It paid off. Captain Joseph Boyce recalled that "the regiment became so proficient that it was christened 'The Regulars.'"[23]

When they were not drilling, the Camp Beauregard garrison spent their time on camp duties, but there was the occasional alarm. In late October, the 2nd Brigade raced by train to Mayfield in response to reports of a Union attack. The Yankees were said to have captured an NO&O locomotive, and burned part of the town, as well. When the Confederates arrived, they found that report had been a wild exaggeration. No locomotive had been captured and there had been no arson in Mayfield, but the Federals had come into town and gotten drunk and were rude to the people. The Confederates settled down for the night, some in a defensive perimeter around the town and the rest in downtown buildings, and the next day they returned to their picturesque camp. Mayfield was the object in what came to be an ongoing game. Private Isaac E. Hirsh of Co. G, 22nd Mississippi Infantry, later recalled, "Both sides captured and evacuated Mayfield regularly once a week, the garrison in possession invariably retreating before the enemy appeared."[24]

For the men at Columbus and Belmont, and the men at Forts Henry and Donelson, and for the small groups of defenders at scattered outposts in between, Polk was determined to do his best in acquiring weapons and ammunition. However, the whole Confederacy was strained for resources and Polk had to wait his turn and do what he could with his too-meager share, even as the Yankees increased their power and pressed in around him.

Polk wrote frequent appeals to General Johnston, to the new secretary of war, Judah P. Benjamin, and to Major Josiah Gorgas, the CSA chief of ordnance. On October 14, he wrote to Gorgas: "We still want 12, 18, and 24 pounders as siege pieces"; on October 17, to Benjamin: "We are greatly pressed by want of powder"; on November 14, to Benjamin again: "Just heard of an arrival of arms and ammunition at Savannah, Ga. Can you not send me 4,000 or 5,000 stand of arms and 20,000 pounds of powder?" He bullyragged secretary of the navy Stephen Mallory, as well. On October 15, he wrote Secretary Mallory: "I am very much in need of additional boats to operate upon the Mississippi, Tennessee, and Cumberland Rivers.... Will you please order their purchase and armament immediately?"[25]

In the matter of the boats, Polk got partial satisfaction. He did not get ironclad gunboats; he did get six converted river steamers: the *McRae* (eight guns), the *General Polk* (five guns), the *Ivy* (two guns), the *Livingston* (six guns), the *Jackson* (two guns), and a floating battery called the *New Orleans* (six 8-inch Columbiads). This was uncommonly generous. Usually he had to do with much less than he needed, and adding to his troubles was the fact that he was expected to fill in the gaps in his defenses and even to weaken his own district by sending men to other areas where they were needed. As has been seen, in September Polk had to establish a new camp between Columbus and Fort Henry, and in early November he was ordered to send five thousand men and two artillery batteries to help defend Clarksville, Tennessee. This would leave him with only ten to eleven thousand effectives. He protested to General Johnston at Bowling Green: "I am deeply impressed with the serious consequences that may follow from weakening the force at this place.... [F]or me to protect my flank with the remainder would be impossible."[26]

Frustrations piled on top of frustrations in this most deadly of games, in which Polk was naturally expected to emerge victorious. It seemed impossible. It was like being made to begin a chess game with a third of the pieces missing. It cannot be a coincidence that the hard-pressed Polk asked on November 6 to be relieved. He said that he had consented to accept a commission with "reluctance," and that he wanted to return to his "former pursuits."[27] Before President Davis replied a week later, the situation had changed. By then, Polk had done what few others would ever be able to claim. He had won a significant victory over General Grant.

6

The Battle of Columbus-Belmont
(November 1861)

Major General John C. Frémont was a poor department head and a worse subordinate. He quarreled with President Lincoln, with quartermaster general Montgomery Meigs, and with the Unionist governor of Missouri, Hamilton R. Gamble. He argued with the Blair brothers, postmaster general Montgomery Blair and Francis Blair, Jr. He not only fussed with Frank Blair, he also arrested and jailed him for no worse crime than defending Lincoln's point of view.

What was Lincoln's point of view? Among other things, Lincoln believed that the proper timing of things was paramount. It shows in his actions throughout the war that, whenever it was in his power to do so, the president consciously chose an exact moment to announce this initiative or that. He also believed in the president's prerogative to set policy. In the late summer of 1861, Lincoln believed that General Frémont had violated both of these principles and in doing so had risked losing both Missouri and Kentucky. On August 30, Frémont had issued a unilateral and premature proclamation that announced no quarter for guerrillas and the immediate emancipation of the slaves belonging to Southern-leaning Missourians. Frémont's proclamation of emancipation applied only to Missouri, but like the New Madrid earthquake of 1811, its shock waves rocked Kentucky. Loyal Kentuckians, who believed in union but also believed in their right to own chattel property, saw ominous signs in Frémont's freeing of the slaves. If Missouri's slaves were freed today, why not Kentucky's tomorrow? And if the present war was to be a war of emancipation, Kentucky might well reconsider its adherence to the Union.

General Robert Anderson, commander of the Department of the Cumberland, sat down in his Louisville office and wrote to the president: "I feel it my duty to say that Major General Frémont's Proclamation is producing most disastrous results in this State.... A company which was ready to be sworn into service was disbanded [that very morning]. Kentucky feels a direct interest in this matter, as a portion of General Frémont's force is now upon her soil [the men in and near Paducah]."[1] Before Anderson's message reached him, Lincoln had already moved to reverse Frémont's ill-considered and poorly timed announcement regarding executions and emancipation. On September 2, the president wrote to Frémont, explaining that, in short, the general's course would cost the Union valuable friends in the border states. Missouri and Kentucky might be driven into the Confederacy. He asked Frémont to rescind the orders. Frémont replied, "I acted with full deliberation and upon certain conviction that it was a measure right and necessary, and I think so still." He told Lincoln to rescind the orders himself, if he wanted to. Lincoln did, and the orders were cancelled.[2]

Three weeks later, Frank Blair was released from arrest. Frémont had made another error in picking on the Blairs, who were Lincoln's friends and who had a reputation for delighting in the destruction of their enemies. When the Blairs went into a fight, they never quit until their enemy's name was ruined, his career reduced to rubble. The Pathfinder was now their enemy. Frank Blair pressed multiple charges against Frémont, including everything from waste and corruption to neglect of duty. Lincoln sent two emissaries, adjutant general Lorenzo Thomas and secretary of war Simon Cameron, to investigate matters in Missouri. Cameron was armed with the authority to relieve Frémont of command if he thought it best. When they reached St. Louis, they found that Frémont was gone. Uncharacteristically, the general had left the comforts of the city to lead a campaign in the field.

Confederate General Sterling Price had won the Battle of Wilson's Creek on August 10 and had subsequently pushed north all the way to the Missouri River. On September 20, Price won a second victory. He defeated Colonel James Mulligan in the Battle of Lexington, and thereby drove a wedge between Kansas City and St. Louis. He spent nine days in Lexington, unthreatened and unworried, before he pulled his army together and moved south. Observers argued that Frémont should have quickly and vigorously honored Mulligan's call for reinforcements. Having failed in that, the least he could now do was catch Price while the man they called "Old Pap" was still in Missouri. For once, Frémont agreed, and he took to the field to lead that campaign personally shortly before adjutant general Thomas and secretary Cameron arrived in St. Louis.

While Frémont was pursuing Price, Thomas and Cameron were pursuing Frémont. On October 13, they found him at Tipton, Missouri, and explained the reason for their coming. They spent a day in Tipton, gathering facts. By the end of their brief visit, the prospects for the Pathfinder to continue in command were not good, but Frémont persuaded Cameron to exercise the latitude given him by the president and give him one final chance. Considering that Frémont was actively campaigning, Cameron agreed to do so.

6. The Battle of Columbus-Belmont

That campaign, however, progressed too slowly. It was not until late October that Frémont's cavalry finally caught up with Price's Rebels near Springfield and skirmished with them. Frémont moved into the city and made his battle plans. To prevent Price from receiving reinforcements from the east, General Grant was ordered on November 1 to "make a demonstration on both sides of the Mississippi with the view of detaining the rebels at Columbus within their lines." There was to be no fighting, though; Frémont cautioned Grant not to bring on a battle.[3]

Before Frémont could execute his plan (who is to say that the slow-moving general would *ever* have executed his plan) the order arrived which relieved him of command of the Western Department and assigned General David Hunter in his place. The order was a week old, but it had taken until November 2 for it to reach him. His contrariness, his insubordination, his extravagance, and his failure to win a battle or even fight one during Price's long-lasting invasion of Missouri had brought Frémont down. He took his bodyguard and left Springfield for St. Louis. General Hunter turned the army about face and followed.

Colonel Benjamin Grierson of the 6th Illinois Cavalry saw Frémont at Jefferson City as he returned to St. Louis. Grierson remembered, "He looked careworn and appeared to be considerably depressed in spirits at being deprived of his command and the opportunity, as he thought, to move onward and force the enemy into action and gain a victory."[4] The Confederates were almost as upset as Frémont at his recall. Secretary of war Judah P. Benjamin said that Frémont was known as a general "whose incompetency ... was a guarantee against immediate peril."[5]

Frémont was gone, but the events he had set in motion would take a while to wind down. One of them was Grant's demonstration against Columbus, and it did mean "immediate peril." Grant might have been glad to get out of his Cairo headquarters for a short autumn campaign. In his office, he had to endure various aggravations. One was the quacking flock of newspaper correspondents, forever asking their pesky questions while serious men tried to deal with their many duties and the attendant frustrations. Another was the necessity of overseeing all the military needs for 4800 men at Cairo, 3500 men at and near Bird's Point, 3600 men at Fort Holt, 7000 men at Paducah, and nine hundred men at Mound City. He had only a handful of good subordinates to help ease the burden.

General C.F. Smith at Paducah was one of the best. Even so, because of its importance, Paducah claimed a great deal of Grant's attention. He had to shuffle arms, equipment, and reinforcements to Paducah. He had to arrange for communication between Cairo and Paducah and to that end had ordered a telegraph line to be strung between the two points. He had to keep up to date on the construction of Fort Anderson, the great earthworks around the Marine Hospital, and the ring of smaller forts that studded Paducah's outskirts. He had to deal with the continuing exasperation of a pontoon bridge that stretched between Paducah and the Illinois shore. The bridge caught driftwood and all manner of debris that washed downstream and kept breaking "with every rise and fall of the river." In addition, when it was in good repair, the bridge obstructed river traffic. After only a couple of months of occupation, the Federals decided the bother was not worth the benefit and dismantled the bridge for good.[6]

Grant had to prepare for the defense of Paducah. There were frequent alarms. On October 6, 1861, General Smith informed Grant, "The latest news from Columbus comes thro' the Roman Catholic priest here, tho' he does not want it whispered. Columbus is in his division of duties. He was told that the attack on this place might be looked for on or by next Thursday, the 10th.... I give the information for what it is worth."[7] It was natural that Grant often had to travel up to Paducah to keep an eye on things. He liked General Smith and he also liked the town, though he regretted the changes that war had brought. As he wrote his wife on October 1, "Yesterday I went up to Paducah. It is a beautiful town, but now nearly deserted. This end of Ky. will soon be in the same fix as Mo. is in, a waste. The amount of suffering the coming winter must be horrible."[8]

Not long after he returned to Cairo, Grant had to turn his attention to a new problem in Paducah. There was an outbreak of illness. The medical personnel on hand were not sufficient to handle the many new patients, and reports of suffering men reached Governor Oliver P. Morton of Indiana, who took action. On October 21, he appealed to the Sisters of the Holy Cross at Notre Dame for help. In response, a group of seven nuns traveled to Cairo, went to Grant's headquarters for instructions, and were sent immediately to Paducah for hospital service. So superior were they as nurses that sisters from this same order were requested to come serve in the hospitals at Cairo and Mound City. This they did.

Grant also had to be concerned about defending Smithland, at the mouth of the Cumberland River. He sent six companies of infantry, one of cavalry, and an artillery battery to be permanently posted there. They were under the command of Colonel Augustus L. Chetlain. The men were soon bored. John McLean wrote, "We had little to do there aside from guard duty and building earthworks. It was too cold to do much drilling."[9]

With so many never-ending headaches at headquarters, Frémont's order to make a demonstration must have come as a welcome excuse to get away.

Before his troops could take to the field, Grant received two disturbing reports. The first was that M. Jeff Thompson and a Rebel force of three thou-

6. The Battle of Columbus-Belmont

sand were operating about fifty miles southwest from Cairo, and the second that a detachment was about to leave Columbus to reinforce Price. Grant sent Colonel Richard J. Oglesby with a force from Bird's Point to handle Thompson. To threaten General Polk and force him to keep his men inside the Columbus works, Grant ordered General C.F. Smith to take as many men as possible from Paducah to demonstrate east of Columbus. Smith sent two infantry brigades, with cavalry and artillery accompanying, but they were not expected to actually make an attack.

Grant's expeditionary force left Cairo on the evening of November 6 aboard a small fleet of six paddle wheelers. The timberclads *Lexington* and *Tyler* steamed ahead of them for safety. The *Lexington* was under Commander R.N. Stembel, and the *Tyler* was under Commander Henry Walke, who also had overall command of the escort.

The boats stopped at Bird's Point to take aboard two infantry regiments, one of cavalry, and an artillery battery. Grant now had about three thousand men, divided into two brigades. Brigadier General John A. McClernand commanded one and Colonel Henry Dougherty the other. Their soldiers traveled ready for action, carrying two days' rations and forty cartridges each. An hour before midnight, the little armada stopped about eleven miles north of Columbus and tied up to the Kentucky shore. Several curious farmers came around to see what all the noise was about. That they were not arrested or even detained is a curious thing since they could be expected to hurry to Columbus with the news that a Federal fleet carrying scads of bluecoats was only a few miles away. It seems obvious that Grant was not worried about Polk knowing of his approach; indeed, he was enticing Polk into giving him a battle.

About 2:00 A.M., Grant later said, he received a report from Colonel W.H.L. Wallace that troops from Columbus were crossing to Belmont. Grant decided to attack. He had been ordered by Frémont not to attack, and Grant admitted as much in his *Memoirs*, but he had an explanation. He said that since the beginning of the downriver trip "the officers and men were elated at the prospect of at last having the opportunity of doing what they had volunteered to do—fight the enemies of their country. I did not see how I could maintain discipline, or retain the confidence of my command, if we should return to Cairo without an effort to do something."[10]

So strong was Grant's determination to "do something" that he may have made up the whole incident of the 2:00 A.M. report. There is no evidence—even from Colonel Wallace, the supposed informant—that such a dispatch was ever sent. Grant biographer William S. McFeely believes that Grant knew he was going to make an attack before he left Cairo, and McFeely *does* present evidence. He says, "Clearly he had already made the decision to attack when he left Cairo. Why else would he have taken three thousand men out in those boats? The gunboats alone could have made a 'demonstration' by shelling Columbus; Grant gave his intent away in an order, sent on November 6, to Col. R.J. Oglesby, commanding an Illinois regiment nearby in Missouri. Oglesby was told to 'communicate with me at Belmont.' Grant had set out to fight and to take the fort—not to demonstrate." Whatever his intentions were at Cairo, Grant was committed now to battle. The fleet steamed up and got underway under a blood-red sunrise, a warning, as all sailors new.[11]

At 8:00 A.M., the transports stopped to tie up on the Missouri shore, a few miles north of Camp Johnston, the Rebel camp at Belmont. Their presence was immediately known. A few rifle shots from the nearby trees greeted the soldiers as they disembarked and a cannon spoke from Columbus across the river. Dr. Brinton remembered that he "saw a puff of smoke afar off, and in a few seconds a huge projectile flew past us, and far above our heads. It was not exactly in line, and rather high, and so passed harmlessly by, falling far to our right. But the man who fired this shot soon improved his aim.... [The shot] seemed to me to be making a bee-line for my eye, but fortunately changed its mind, and passing above our heads, and apparently between our smoke-pipes, buried itself in the dirt of the Mississippi bank of the river." Brinton paid two black youths, whom he referred to as "darkies," fifty cents each to go dig out the shell, which he wanted as a souvenir. The Federals, on the morning of their first battle, had not yet learned enough to take the business seriously.[12]

As always seemed to happen, the lined-up men had a long wait before anything happened. It was not until 10:00 A.M. that the skirmishers advanced. The main line followed, with the cavalry screening the right and the artillery behind. Their work was about to begin. There was work for the surgeon, too. Brinton selected "a little one-story house on the edge of the woods" for the field hospital. It belonged to a family named Bratcher. Dr. Amos Witter "of an Iowa regiment" was left behind as the new, temporary head of the house while Brinton followed the troops to serve as a mobile dressing station. He left his sword behind at the Bratcher house and never saw it again.[13]

While the infantry inched forward against light but persistent opposition through the woods, the *Lexington* and the *Tyler* were already in serious action. The soldiers might be green; the sailors were not. This was nothing new to them, in fact. They had been trading shots with the Rebels all through the late summer and early fall. They had patrolled all three of the Rebel rivers (not including the Ohio, where there was little danger), and had fought small actions along the Mississippi—such as those at Beckwith's Farm near Norfolk, Missouri, and at Lucas' Bend, Missouri, in September—until Polk had to complain to the secretary of the navy: "The gunboats the enemy have now in the Mississippi River are giving us most serious annoyance."[14] The timberclads' expeditions on the Cumberland and Tennessee, too, had sometimes led to

6. The Battle of Columbus-Belmont

shooting trouble, and now they were back in the Mississippi, steaming into their biggest battle yet. The sailing men were more experienced than their fellows on shore, and they were ready for the work. They were commanded by career navy man and Mexican War veteran Commander Henry Walke. In his article for *Battles and Leaders*, Walke said that he had received instructions on November 6 from General Grant to prepare to move down the Mississippi to reconnoiter and to escort a convoy of escorts, "but I did not know the character of the service expected of me until I anchored for the night." It was only then that he learned that an attack was pending in a few hours.[15]

As the troops assembled on the Missouri shore at Belmont, Walke "attacked the Confederate batteries, at the request of General Grant, as a diversion, which was done with some effect." The gunboats circled in a tight pattern to maintain their position in the heavy current and to avoid the enemy's shells. They fired at the Rebel artillery as they turned, but their shells only chewed into the bluff below and did no damage to the guns or their crews. The only casualties occurred when a Confederate artillery piece burst in Captain Richard Stewart's battery and killed two men. The other batteries kept firing. The roar was incredible; soldiers at Mound City, Illinois, over twenty miles away, could hear the artillery. After about thirty minutes the gunboats retired upstream, for as Walke said, "The number, as well as the quality of the enemy's guns, proved so formidable that it would have been madness to remain long under their fire and accordingly, having accomplished the object of diverting the fire from our troops, the gunboats withdrew from the contest." The navy's part in the battle was not entirely over, but for the time being, it was.[16]

Camp Johnston was commanded by Colonel J. C. Tappan. Normally, he had his own 13th Arkansas there, along with an artillery battery commanded by Lieutenant Colonel Daniel Beltzhoover and some Mississippi cavalry. However, in the face of the Federal threat that morning, Polk had hurried four regiments of Pillow's infantry and Pillow himself to the Missouri side. Polk might have sent more men over to Belmont if General C.F. Smith's troops had not been marching down toward Columbus on the Kentucky side. The Confederate general had to keep enough strength on hand to defend his works in case the real attack was coming by land. The infantrymen on the Kentucky side of the river were ordered to the east side works to oppose Smith, when he showed up.

Even considering those many men he kept with him, it appeared on paper that Polk had sent an adequate number of reinforcements over to Belmont. There were now upwards of 3000 Confederates there, approximately the same number of troops that Grant had. This fight would be made at even odds, as far as numbers were concerned, but the men who came over to reinforce Tappan were poorly armed and had little ammunition with them, besides. Private Don Singletary (Co. E, 12th Tennessee Infantry) said, "We had muzzle loading guns and had been on picket duty so often that we were all nearly out of ammunition and in our rush and haste no ammunition was given us.... I had only seven cartridges."¹⁷

Colonel Tappan had sent his cavalry out to keep watch on the enemy while he and Lieutenant Colonel Beltzhoover adjusted the artillery. A little after 9:00 A.M., General Pillow came on the scene to take charge of operations. He sent three companies of infantry forward into the woods to oppose the enemy advance and had the rest form in line of battle in an open field, facing northwest, with their backs to the river. William M. Polk, General Polk's son, was bitterly critical of Pillow's ill-conceived deployment. He wrote, "Most of the line of battle, especially the center, was placed in an exposed position, in an open field, with a heavy wood only about eighty yards distant in its front. Under the cover of this wood the Federal force moved forward in its line of battle, and halting at the timber's edge, raked the field with its fire." There were several better positions which Pillow might have chosen for his deployment, and he soon knew it. "He found that he was unable to dislodge the concealed foe by a series of gallant charges. These proved of no avail, and ... he had to give way." The last was a bayonet charge. When it failed, the battle line collapsed and the Rebels retired in confused disorder toward their camp. By 11:00 A.M., the Confederates had been pushed back more than two miles. Beltzhoover's battery could not do much good defensive work; at this point it was running out of ammunition and would soon fall silent.¹⁸

When the Rebels failed in their final charge and began to fall back, the Yankees were still in the trees. The artillerists across the river at Columbus observed the distance between their own men and the Federals and felt that it was upon their shoulders to save the day. If they fired into the still-concealed Yankees before they could form up for a final push, they might be able to prevent the annihilation of Pillow's command. They opened up with everything they had. It was a terrible storm of Confederate iron, but it flew too high. It rattled through the treetops and McClernand's brigade on the right flank and Dougherty's on the left were inconvenienced very little if at all while they dressed their lines for the final push into the Rebel camp.

At their camp, a few Rebels were trying to re-form their lines behind an abatis when General Napoleon Buford's 27th Illinois of McClernand's brigade surprised them with an attack on their left flank. The Rebels had not seen them approaching and when this sudden attack from an unexpected direction broke upon them, it was more than they could take. They joined their comrades below the riverbank and the Yankees charged into their camp.

While the battle was going on near Camp Jackson, Commander Walke ordered the timberclads to steam forward and engage the batteries at Columbus once more. He reported that the enemy's "shell [were] flying around us, but doing no harm, while our shell seemed to go where they could be effective." Even so, the gunboats retired upstream after only about twenty minutes.[19]

More important than the inconclusive action of the big gunboats was that of the little Confederate river packets that steamed back and forth all morning, carrying ammunition and reinforcements to Belmont and carrying the wounded back to Columbus. In mid-morning, early in the battle, General Pillow had sent a call for reinforcements, more ammunition, and a section of artillery. Polk had responded with alacrity, but as the commanding general said, it soon became "obvious that further reinforcements had become necessary." The 15th Tennessee and the 11th Louisiana had been held as a reserve on the Kentucky riverbank and now they were ordered into action. They boarded the steamer *Charm*. Its captain, W.L. Trask, reported that he cast off about 11:30 and "crossed the river under a heavy fire from the enemy's cannon, they having at this time driven in our forces, planted their batteries on the riverbank, and directed them particularly at our boat."[20] If crossing the Mississippi was a harrowing experience, the landing was perhaps worse. Captain Trask continued,

> Upon landing at 12 m. [meridian] on the Belmont side, and at a point about 400 yards above the position occupied by the enemy's battery—at that time playing on our boat—we found the landing obstructed by our disorganized forces, who endeavored to board and take possession of our boat, and at the same time crying: "Don't land!" "Don't land!" "We are whipped!" "Go back!" etc. We, however, succeeded in landing six companies of Colonel [S.F.] Mark's regiment, when the disorganized troops previously spoken of made a rush on our boat and forced me to give the order to back the boat from the landing, leaving my stage planks on the river bank and still having on board the remaining four of Colonel Marks' regiment; also Colonel [T.H.] Logwood's company of cavalry. At this juncture I moved up the river bank some 200 yards, intending to effect a landing of the remaining companies of the boat when she touched the bank. This I accomplished successfully, but found myself unable to land the cavalry company for want of stage planks and the repeated efforts of our disordered troops to board the steamer.[21]

Captain Trask had to return to the Kentucky shore with the cavalry still on board. The *Charm* was struck several times, and the splinters flew, but the boat's name held true; she was charmed and only one man was wounded.

Watching from shore, it became clear to General Polk that Pillow needed still more reinforcements. He ordered General Benjamin F. Cheatham to select one brigade out of his division and send it over. Cheatham chose the 1st Brigade, under Colonel Preston Smith. Cheatham crossed aboard the *Prince* ahead of Preston's brigade, covered from behind by the fire of an artillery battery from his own division. Once on the Missouri shore, he took charge of Pillow's troops and began forming them for a counterattack.

In the abandoned Camp Johnston, the Federals were celebrating. The Confederate flag was pulled down and a U.S. flag was raised, and regimental bands began to play patriotic tunes while officers on top of cannons led the men in singing. McClernand called for three cheers and gave a little speech, as did some other politician-officers. Some in the ranks may have listened while they sat down to eat the Rebels' untouched breakfasts. Others rambled among the tents searching for souvenirs. A few kept to their work. Colonel John A. Logan claimed that of all the Union regiments in Camp Johnston, only his own 31st Illinois "retained their formation in ranks." The best historian of the battle, Nathaniel C. Hughes, writes that "while individual soldiers pillaged Camp Johnston, others worked to salvage valuable military property ... horses, cannon, etc." He specifically mentions Surgeon John H. Brinton, who "did fine work under hard circumstances and managed to see that nearly all the wounded were returned to the field hospital at the Bratcher cabin.... Brinton dumped out the contents of the few ammunition wagons and packed them with the many injured enlisted men. From the field hospital nearly all of these wounded went back on wagons to the transports."[22]

Brinton had an eye-opening morning. The first wounded man he saw as he followed the lines was only slightly wounded, but the next one was unforgettable: "A shell had exploded behind, but close to, the back of a soldier.... I have never seen a worse wound, before or since. The whole of the skin and muscles of the back from the nape of the neck to the thighs and on both sides of the spine had been torn away, as if the tissues had been scooped out by a clean-cutting curved instrument. The surfaces were raw and bleeding, and the sight was a horrible one, and one which I have never forgotten. In a moment or two he expired, and I remounted and rode on."[23]

Back at the field hospital, assistant surgeon H.P. Stearns found himself suddenly swamped with wounded men in numbers for which the medical staff was only partially prepared. He wrote, "There were no hospital stores or ambulances. There was a sufficient supply of morphine, chloroform, instruments, and dressings.... There was an abundance of water; no soup and no food except such as the men had in their knapsacks." The war was young and battlefield medicine would improve, but that did not help the men who suffered now at the Bratcher cabin.[24]

The celebration at the captured camp offended General Grant as both dangerous and unprofessional. Hughes says, "To regain control Grant ordered Camp Johnston to be burned immediately. Field grade officers carried torches and set the fires themselves."[25] While Camp Johnston burned, Dr. Brinton was dressing the wounds of some officers. He looked up and happened to observe "the pipes of two steamers going up the river. I thought to myself, 'These cannot be our gunboats,' and so rode up to General Grant and pointed them out to him. He would not at first credit these as the enemy's transports until I drew his attention to their course.... He then expressed surprise but immediately ordered our men into line."[26]

Grant, who liked to claim credit for things, did not mention Brinton in his *Memoirs*. He simply said, "I saw ... two steamers crossing from Columbus towards the west shore, above us, black—or gray—with soldiers from boiler-deck to roof." He still had not gained complete control of his men, for he said, "Some of my men were engaged in firing from captured guns at empty steamers down the river, out of range, cheering at every shot. I tried to get them to turn their guns upon the loaded steamers above and not so far away. My efforts were in vain."[27]

The burning of the camp, plus the growing understanding that they were about to be cut off from their transports, and the firing of the Columbus guns—especially the Lady Polk, which was beginning to drop some of her enormous "lamp-post" shells among the looting Yankees—focused the attention of the men better than Grant himself could do. The men lined up, McClernand's first followed by Dougherty's, assembled their prisoners, and hurriedly left the open ground of the camp for the shelter of the woods. As fast as he could, Brinton began loading casualties into wagons and on artillery caissons, but, he had to admit, "We had a number of wounded men whom we did not bring off."[28] In the woods, the men formed in column and headed back toward their transports at the landing. Tired and rattled, they were in no shape to meet the Confederate attack that suddenly crashed into them from the direction of the riverbank.

When he arrived on the Missouri bank, General Cheatham began to organize the regiments that Pillow had led into such confusion. Pillow was still there, and he helped Cheatham. They soon had three regiments ready for action. A pilot on the *Hill* later told Mark Twain, "General Cheatham had his men strip their coats off and throw them in a pile, and said, 'Now follow me to hell or victory!' I heard him say that from the pilot house; and then he galloped in, at the head of his troops."[29] Cheatham led his men "directly back from the river in the direction of the enemy's transports and gunboats, intending, if possible, to take them in flank." They went about a half mile and crouched down beside the roadside in the woods, "fifty to one hundred yards to one side." The Yankees appeared, a mixed force of infantry and cavalry. Confederate veteran Don Singletary remembered that, at first, no order came to fire; "then the crash came, and the real battle was on. It was a running fight."[30] General Cheatham remembered it the same way. He said that "under the continuous fire from our columns in pursuit, [the Yankees] were slaughtered from that point to within a few hundred yards of their gunboats lying more than 2 miles from the position in which we engaged them."[31]

During the fight, Colonel Preston Smith and his brigade came across the river and were ordered to hurry forward. Cheatham's men had just overrun the Federal hospital when Smith's column caught up. Major General Polk was at the head. Polk had become convinced that General C.F. Smith's expected attack from the east was not coming and that he was needed now on the other side. Rushing forward to join Cheatham and Pillow, Polk noticed that "the route over which we passed was strewn with the dead and wounded ... and with arms, knapsacks, overcoats, etc."[32] The sight of such destruction and of such waste was fascinating. It was the hospital grounds that especially interested Pillow, who said, "Here we found a yard full of knapsacks, arms, ammunition, blankets, overcoats, mess chest[s], horses, wagons, and dead and wounded men, with surgeons engaged in the appropriate duties of their profession."[33]

The arrival of Preston Smith's men raised the number of Confederates to about four thousand men. The Yankees were outnumbered and they were on the run. Now was the time to finish it. Polk ordered the gray column forward. Polk said, "On arriving at the point where his transports lay, I ordered the column ... under the cover of a field thickly set with corn, to be deployed along the river bank within easy range of the boats.... A heavy fire was opened upon them simultaneously, riddling them with balls, and as we have reason to believe with heavy loss to the enemy. Under this galling fire he cut his lines and retreated from the shore."[34] The retreat was covered by the Federal gunboats, but the transports had to run a mile-long gauntlet of sharpshooters. The Federals slowly disappeared to the north in the gathering gloom and, as Polk said, "It being now sunset, and being left in the possession of the field, I ordered the troops to retire."[35]

When the retreat from the Camp Johnston parade ground began, the seriousness of their situation hit the Federal officers with panic-inducing force. The Kentucky guns across the river were pounding them, and they could see the men in butternut and gray emerging from their hiding places beneath the riverbank and sliding north to block them from their transports. Grant remembered, "At first, some of the officers seemed to think that to be surrounded was to be placed in a hopeless position, where there was nothing to do but surrender. But when I announced that we had cut our way in and could cut our way out just as well, it seemed a new revelation to officers and soldiers. They formed line rapidly and we started back to our boats."[36]

The composure of their leader restored a measure of calm to the officers and through them to the men—until Cheatham's attack on the right flank began slaughtering them. The 7th Iowa and the 22nd Illinois turned to reply. Hughes says, "The Union troops exchanged volleys with the enemy, but the rebels pressed their attack [and] Dougherty's men began to fall at an alarming rate." It looked as if there was no escape from this killing field. The 15th Tennessee was blocking the way to the landing. The 15th Tennessee included that company of Illinois secessionists who had come south through the Purchase in the spring.[37]

John Logan's 31st Illinois, the men who never broke ranks at Camp Johnston, fixed bayonets and charged forward. General McClernand, who had found a rare spot of high ground on this wide river bench, ordered Captain Ezra Taylor's Chicago Battery to unlimber and pump loads of double canister into the Confederates. The combination of cold steel and hot iron was too much. The Rebels gave way. When the 31st charged through the resulting gap, the 30th Illinois followed, and men who were shaken loose from other regiments saw their chance and joined them. Now the rout began. The infantry and the cavalry alike headed north for the landing as fast as they could go. There was still hope. The artillerists were ordered to turn about and open fire. Then, when no infantry could be made to stand and support the pieces, the big guns had no choice other than to abandon the defensive effort and join the race. Those who stayed behind with Colonel Dougherty were overrun. Unit cohesion was lost. Dangerous gaps widened between the regiments. There was indescribable danger in the woods, but safety waited at the transports, and regiments, companies, mixed groups of men, and individuals made their way as best they could toward the landing. Many did not make it.

One who did not was Dr. John H. Brinton. He was with the column when it left Camp Johnston and entered the woods with them. In the trees, he was called to by a wounded man in a gray uniform. He was a major from Louisiana and he asked Brinton to stop and help him. This Brinton did. A quick examination showed him that the man was dying. They chatted while the battle raged and the man asked Brinton how long he could live. Brinton told him honestly that he could live "but a very short time." Brinton continued the story: "He begged me to remain with him, and when I told him that our troops were on their way to their boats, he offered to protect me while he lived, if I would only stay. I assured him that his own people would find him and that I must go. So I mounted and reluctantly left him on the ground." Brinton had waited too long to leave. The way before him was crowded with Confederates. "No sooner had I reached the verge of the woods than I found myself confronted with quite a number of our gray-clad enemies," Brinton said. "I came upon them suddenly, and they instantly covered me with their rifles. Fortunately for myself, I wore a civilian's overcoat of black cloth and my uniform was, therefore, not very conspicuous. I immediately raised my hand in a deprecatory, and at the same time in an authoritative sort of a way, and they lowered their guns." This was his chance. He spurred his horse away and escaped into a thicket, where he lost his way.[38]

The action of the Federal gunboats in the afternoon is hard to determine with absolute confidence, partly because of Commander Walke's own confused narrative. He wrote an after-action report, an article for *Battles and Leaders*, and a memoir, and they each vary somewhat in both detail and sequence. It seems that the gunboats did not go into action for several hours after the second action of the morning ended. They did not confront the Confederate transports head-on, although they did fire at them long-range across Belmont Point. They steamed back into action during the Confederate counterattack in mid-afternoon. The Rebel artillery crews were firing high, and Walke ordered the timberclads to run in close. As they crowded closer "to the frowning battlements," closer than in any other fight of the day, the Confederate gunners on the Kentucky bluffs found their range. Speaking of himself in the third person, Walke wrote that "their shot and shell began to have a telling effect. A cannonball came down obliquely through the side deck and scantling [of the *Tyler*], taking off the head of Michael Adams and wounding several others. The effect of this shot, not one of the largest in use by the enemy, convinced Commander Walke of the necessity of removing his vessels (which had all this time been kept moving in a circle to avoid the range of the enemy's guns) to a greater distance." The *Tyler* and the *Lexington* fired a few defiant broadsides as they pulled back to Belmont Landing.[39]

There was a crisis at the landing. The Rebels were pressing the dispirited Federals hard. No one much was opposing them. The badly overmatched artillery and the cavalry were trying to hold the Confederates at a distance. Walke's gunboats began firing into the graybacks. The effect was gratifying. "The enemy's artillery was seen tumbling over, and his ranks were soon broken," said Walke. "They dispersed in the utmost confusion, or fell on the ground to escape our shot and shell."[40] In his book, Walke quotes a *Missouri Democrat* correspondent who wrote that the gunboats "took up a position between us and the enemy, and opened their guns upon them, letting slip a whole broadside at once." The reporter said that the *Lexington* and the *Tyler* saved Grant's routed army "from a terrible and otherwise certain doom."[41]

Amid the crackle of the Secesh small arms fire and the roar of the responding gunboats, Grant's men boarded the transports. At the railings, those who had not thrown down their weapons began shooting at the Rebels onshore. The mooring ropes were cut and the men still on the bank hurried to try to get onboard. It was a close thing for all of them, particularly the commanding general, if his account is to be believed. In his *Memoirs*, Grant wrote,

> Our men, with the exception of details that had gone to the front after the wounded, were either now aboard the transports or very near them. Those who were not aboard soon got there, and the boats pushed off. I was the only man of the National army between the rebels and our transports. The captain of a boat

that had just pushed out but had not started, recognized me and ordered the engineer not to start the engine; he then had a plank run out for me. My horse seemed to take in the situation. There was no path down the bank and everyone acquainted with the Mississippi River knows that its banks, in a natural state, do not vary at any great angle from the perpendicular. My horse put its fore feet over the bank without hesitation or urging, and with his hind feet well under him, slid down the bank and trotted aboard the boat, twelve or fifteen feet away, over a single gang plank. I dismounted and went at once to the upper deck.[42]

It is an heroic image—the man on horseback, alone between his army and the enemy, staring defiantly at the men who are shooting at him, or perhaps glancing back with fatherly concern to make sure none of the children are being left behind, before performing a calm and agile act of horsemanship—and it may never have happened at all. The Confederates insisted that the soon-to-be-famous account of Grant's composure was a fiction. As an example, in a letter that was reprinted in the May 1910 issue of *Confederate Veteran*, James D. Porter (who was Cheatham's chief-of-staff), wrote, "Cheatham was so close on his heels that Grant just before he went on board the boat—and he was the last man to go aboard—abandoned his horse, which was appropriated by one of Cheatham's staff officers, who was afoot, and who used him until he was shot in the battle of Shiloh."[43]

There was a lot of confusion on the bank and Porter could not have seen everything. Perhaps it did happen as Grant wrote it, but there is another problem with his account. It is the clear implication that Grant left no one behind. "Those who were not aboard soon got there," he said. This is a plump falsehood. Almost every man who wrote about the battle mentioned the scores of wounded who were abandoned to die or to become prisoners of war. In addition, there were the survivors of Colonel Dougherty's brigade, men who Hughes says were "begging to be taken aboard."[44]

Then there was Dr. Brinton. To escape being captured in the woods, Brinton had spurred his horse into a thicket and lost his way. After a while, he encountered "two old darkies," who told him that he was not headed toward the transports, that he was downriver from Belmont. He had been heading south. One of the black men drew him a map in the dirt and Brinton set out in the right direction, a fact that was proven to him when shells began to rattle through the treetops above him. He rode on, not knowing which army he might meet, until he reached an unfinished railroad and encountered Captain James Dollins' Federal cavalry patrol, who were themselves "bewildered." As a major, Brinton was the ranking officer on the scene and they asked him what to do. He simply threw out scouts and moved forward, to who knew where? They crossed a swamp and struck a road which led them to a backwoods cabin filled with sullen people who refused to help them. They were about to resort to persuasion of the forty-four caliber kind until a woman recognized Brinton. She was Mrs. Bratcher, whose cabin Brinton had picked earlier in the day as his field hospital. She was grateful to him for his order that her personal belongings be respected and she offered her son as a guide. The party set out. Along the way, Dollins' cavalry decided to go their own way. Brinton continued with the Bratcher boy, who led him to the riverbank where Brinton soon spotted one of the Union gunboats trolling for stragglers. The doctor boarded the boat just at dark, the end of a very long day, but not quite the end as now he had to help tend the many wounded onboard.[45]

Worse than all of these was the fact that an entire regiment had gone missing and was left behind. Colonel Napoleon Bonaparte Buford was a native of Woodford County, Kentucky, a West Point graduate, and the half-brother of General John Buford, the cavalryman who would later save the Army of the Potomac on the first day at Gettysburg. The Bufords were free-thinking men and it served them well in their military careers. At Belmont, Colonel Buford commanded the 27th Illinois Infantry in McClernand's brigade. During the fight in the woods, the 27th was on McClernand's extreme right, adjoining Dougherty's brigade. In the heat of the fight, taking heavy fire and suffering many casualties, Buford had led his men toward the west, away from the river. He was looking to escape the hellish fire from Cheatham's men and also to find a way around the Confederate 15th Tennessee, which blocked the way to the landing. At some distance out, Buford turned north. He found that he could not hold a true course. There was swampy ground to circumvent and he was still hoping to find a way around the enemy's right flank. Buford veered this way and that; he was simply following his nose, trying to reconnect with his brigade at the landing. If that proved impossible, he was prepared to march all the way to Bird's Point.

While Buford's men followed their circuitous route vaguely north, the transports steamed away from the landing and brigade commander General McClernand grew increasingly upset about his lost regiment. Well north of Belmont, he persuaded the pilot of the *Chancellor* to pull ashore so that he could make a quick reconnaissance. He had barely come down the gangplank when out of the woods stepped Lieutenant H.A. Rust, adjutant of the 27th Illinois. It was an incredible coincidence. The lost regiment was found, and in a short time, so was Captain Dollins' cavalry. Everyone boarded for the trip to Cairo.

The Battle of Columbus-Belmont was over. Hughes says that the flotilla had a "solemn trip" north, but the return was "triumphant," with artillery salutes fired from Fort Holt, Bird's Point, and elsewhere. A crowd waited to greet them at Cairo.[46]

7

With General C.F. Smith in Paducah
(November–December 1861)

No crowd waited to greet General C.F. Smith's troops when they returned from their demonstration east of Columbus. Then again, Smith had obeyed General Frémont's orders not to bring on an attack. General Smith was a man to obey orders. Chetlain says, "He was one of the oldest and most accomplished officers of the regular army. He was a splendid-looking soldier, tall, slender, and straight, with close-cut grey hair and a heavy white mustache. He was the embodiment of the ideal soldier."[1] Brigadier General Lew Wallace wrote a similar physical portrait of Smith and added, "The description is elaborate, I know; and if one asks wherefore, the answer is ready—the man before me was by odds the handsomest, stateliest, most commanding I had ever seen, the one who has since remained in memory my ideal of a general officer." Wallace compared Smith's aura of dignity to that of George Washington.[2]

Charles Ferguson Smith was a Philadelphian by birth and an 1825 graduate of West Point. There was a period later in his career when he returned to serve as the superintendent of the military academy. During that time, two of the cadets were U.S. Grant and William T. Sherman. During the Mexican War, Smith served first in Zachary Taylor's army, and then with that of Winfield Scott. Before the war was over, he received three brevets for meritorious conduct in battle. Various duties in the West followed. He was promoted to brigadier general of volunteers at the start of the Civil War and found himself under the command of his former pupil Grant, a situation that discomfited Grant far more than it did Smith. Assigned to command the post at Paducah, he proclaimed that he intended to pursue a policy designed to show the citizens that the government did not intend to interfere "with their comfort and well being in any respect." He promised that "the person and property of everyone" would be protected and "quiet and good order preserved."[3]

By mid–October 1861, bad behavior on the part of some Paducah citizens convinced Smith "that the conciliatory policy ceases to be a virtue" and he must therefore "take such measures as the circumstances call for and justify." This included requiring passes for persons and "stores of any description" to leave the city. At the same time, he kept his vow to protect private property, including that of Southern sympathizers. Among those who would prefer to make the occupation more terrible, there were mutters that General Smith, himself, was disloyal.[4]

On November 1, General Frémont ordered Smith to cooperate in conjunction with Grant in a demonstration against Columbus. The purpose was to keep any of General Polk's forces from going west to reinforce Sterling Price. Consequently, on November 6, Smith issued identical orders to his 1st Brigade commander, Brigadier General E.A. Paine, and his 2nd Brigade commander, Colonel W.L. Sanderson. They were to leave enough men to guard their camps and to assemble the rest at his headquarters "in full marching order" on that same afternoon, every man carrying three days' cooked rations in their haversacks. The only difference in Paine's and Sanderson's orders had to do with the route each column would take. Paine was ordered to march to Melvin, twenty miles out, and then over to the Lovelaceville and Blandville Road for the return to Paducah on the third day. Sanderson was to march by a more eastern circuit toward Plumley's Station, thence to Viola, thence back to Paducah on the third day. Each would be in supporting distance of the other, and each brigade commander was reminded, as Frémont and Grant had both mandated, that this was merely intended to be a demonstration; there would be no attack. Paine left Paducah with two thousand men at 2:00 P.M. on November 6. Sanderson left an hour later.[5]

The next day, both columns could hear the reverberations of artillery fire from the direction of Columbus. Sanderson kept to his programme, but Paine disobeyed orders. He marched eleven miles beyond Melvin to Milburn. That night he sent scouts to the Mississippi River to make contact with Grant. The Federals had already left for Cairo. A disappointed Paine reported, "If the attack had been renewed to-day [November 8] I should have marched on Columbus. As it is, I am just starting on my return." If that were not damning enough, he added, "My soldiers are almost out of provisions. I wish one day's full rations sent to me to-night."[6] Paine had started out with three days' rations, a sufficient supply if he had not exceeded his orders, but he *had* exceeded his orders. He had marched too far and now his soldiers were likely to go hungry. Hungry soldiers tended to find their own solution. It was not in keeping with the principle of good order, Smith's obsession. General Smith was outraged with Paine's disobedience. He said that Paine's action indicated "a fixed purpose from the start to gain notoriety without reference to the public service or his plain duty as a soldier."[7]

7. With General C.F. Smith in Paducah

On the march back toward Paducah, the discipline in Paine's column broke down. The men of the 40th and 41st Illinois began casting off overcoats, blankets, and cooking gear. Mules were abandoned, an army wagon was wrecked, and a farmer's turkey flock was reduced by saber-wielding troopers. Other thefts were not specified. General Smith said only that "the property of citizens was wantonly destroyed, and in some instances robbery by violence committed."[8]

Historian Steven E. Woodworth says of the return march to Paducah, "the regiments virtually disintegrated." This was not only injurious to good order, it was dangerous. Paine did not know how close to disaster he came, for Confederate Colonel D.W.C. Bonham was on his way from Camp Beauregard to intercept the Federal column. Bonham had two full regiments, parts of two others, a field battery, and a company of horse soldiers behind him and he was coming to do battle, but he started too late and failed to make contact before Paine's men straggled into Paducah. It was a bit of good luck, for the Confederates might well have destroyed Paine's column in detail. The Rebel soldiers hated that they had missed the chance to destroy the Yankees as they crossed Graves County. In a letter home a few days later, a disappointed Lieutenant A.C. Riley of the 1st Missouri lamented that had they started the pursuit sooner "we certainly would have had a fight."[9]

Smith was disgusted by the small groups and the disheveled individuals he saw slouching into Paducah, some of them a day late. He reprimanded Paine for his poor handling of the expedition and had a message of condemnation "read at the head of every company in camp." Further, he announced to all that he intended "to ask for a legal investigation into the conduct of all concerned."[10] The exceptions to the disarray in Paine's column were the 9th and 12th Illinois. Chaplain Marion Morrison of the 9th Illinois said that his regiment returned to Paducah on schedule and "in splendid order," even though this was the regiment's first march. He said, "To prevent [straggling] in the 9th a rear guard was appointed, which compelled all to keep their places. This, some of the boys who were very tired, no doubt, thought to be cruel." They felt better, though, when "General Smith issued an order highly commending the 9th for their orderly conduct."[11]

Paducah, like most army camps, was a fertile ground for rumors. Gossip seemed always to be flying. Augustus L. Chetlain remembered, "Not long after the battle of Belmont.... I had a visit from General Smith. I remarked that there was a rumor afloat that Paducah was threatened by a force under General Albert Sidney Johnson [sic]. The general smiled and replied that Johnson and he were old army friends and knew each other well. 'Johnson knows what forces I have and I know what he has. I don't think he will attack me,' and he didn't."[12] Smith was right in thinking that he had nothing to fear from the

Rebels outside Paducah, but he underestimated the danger within his own camp. The insubordinate and vengeful E.A. Paine did not take his reprimand with good grace. He smoldered, and waited for his chance to take a measure of revenge. He found it later that same month. On November 19, General Smith granted permission for some Rebel officers to enter Paducah to negotiate an exchange of prisoners. The Confederates met at the former Tilghman home. That day, General Lew Wallace decided to drill a company of his Zouaves, the 11th Indiana Infantry, on the street outside. As the brightly dressed soldiers went through their evolutions, Robert Owen Woolfolk raised a window, hung a Rebel flag, and shouted the familiar cry, "Hurrah for Jeff Davis!"[13]

Wallace sent an aide up to the door to demand the flag's removal. Woolfolk refused and the aide called some soldiers over who removed the flag, "tore it to shreds and threw it in the midst of the Confederate officers." When the aide tried to raise a U.S. flag in its place, Woolfolk knocked him down. The squad of Zouaves and the Confederate officers had a brawl inside the house, and the noise was heard outside. Wallace was suddenly in over his head. It appears that it was the brigadier general himself who went to summon General Smith. The old Regular came quickly; the disturbance at Woolfolk's was contrary to the principle of good order.[14]

When General Smith walked through the door, the scuffle ended. He apologized to Woolfolk for the trespass and the destruction of his property. Turning his attention to the soldiers, he placed them under arrest and sent them back to their quarters. Wallace handled those who were milling around outside. Private John B. Day of Battery A, Chicago Light Artillery, remembered years later, "I can plainly see Gen. Wallace as he came walking from Gen. Smith's headquarters and mounting the fence beside the house and hear his tone of utter contempt as he said, 'You have had your will, get back to your camps.' The mob quickly and quietly disappeared." The next day General Smith issued an order condemning the riotous behavior of Wallace's Hoosiers.[15]

The event exploded and the story was told and retold. The 11th Indiana was angry, but the anger was not confined to that regiment. The men of a Missouri regiment were said to have commandeered a municipal fire engine and were on their way to flood General Smith's headquarters with a high-pressure blast, until Colonel Wallace stopped them. Rumors began to swell beyond the limits of the town. This was Paine's revenge. He was undoubtedly the source of the possibly career-ending gossip, though Wallace was accused of being both the author of the original event and the source of the later slander against Smith. Paine may well have been behind this, as well. Wallace smarted under the false accusation and was still upset over the insult to his reputation years later when he wrote, "This affair, apparently so trifling, worked me an injury of long standing. Unfortunately, it furnished the newspapers a welcome theme. Accrediting me with the outbreak, they complimented my patriotism and denounced General Smith." Even the *New York Times* began to report on Smith's disloyalty, and the story continued to spread. Wallace continued: "From Paducah the story passed to headquarters at Cairo, thence to headquarters at St. Louis, in both of which the military offense was seen and discussed as of my incitement."[16]

He went to General Smith to complain about the false reports of his role in the incident. As he recalled, Smith said, "Why, don't you see? If I can stand to be accused of disloyalty, what have you to grumble at?" Wallace wanted to "card the papers" on both his behalf and Smith's, but the old general would not allow it. Smith was calm, he trusted army channels to do him justice.[17] In the end, General Henry W. Halleck, Frémont's successor, had to step in to save Smith's career; the affair had gone that far. Bruce Catton writes that Halleck "telegraphed McClellan (who now commanded all of the Federal armies) insisting that Smith was loyal and that he was needed where he was." Halleck's word had weight and because of his defense of the general in Paducah, "the effort to get Smith out failed."[18]

Smith seems to have known all along who was behind the smear campaign, and he denounced Paine's plot as a "base conspiracy." Finally the true perpetrator of the ruinous gossip was known to all, and the treacherous officer was "banished to Bird's Point on the Mississippi." Unfortunately, Paducah had not seen the last of him.[19]

General Henry W. Halleck (National Archives).

The press had to retract their original presentation of events. The *New York Times*, for one, said, "The late trouble reported between Gens. Smith and Wallace ... proves to have been greatly exaggerated and in reality not worth mentioning. Paducah is now probably the strongest point of defense in the whole Western Department."[20]

After passions cooled, some of the soldiers regretted

the ugly incident of the Rebel flag. Forty-five years after the event, John B. Day was still thinking about it. He wrote that the soldier's life in Paducah was such a pleasant one that "many a time in after days we wished ourselves back again. Paducah has a warm spot in the heart of each of the few of us who are left." However, he said, "There was only one event that occurred to mar our otherwise ideal life in Paducah, and of that we were so thoroughly ashamed that we tried to forget it by never mentioning it. I refer to the raising of the flag on Col. Woolfolk's house. Our battery took no active part in the proceedings but by being there and countenancing it, we were as guilty as those who did take an active part."[21]

Once that incident and the resulting scandal were behind them, the soldiers settled down and could enjoy life again. Day said, "I had never before and have never since seen as many handsome women as I saw in Paducah," many of whom never tired of the campaign to win them over. Charles B. Kimbell, who served in the same artillery battery as Day, wrote that the Union boys sent out "serenading parties ... nearly every evening, doing their best to win favor. At first they were either ignored or received very coldly; but after a while, met with better success." Eventually, some were even invited to share wine and cake with the girls, and—a detail that delighted Kimbell—this was at a house that had previously flown a rebel flag. This victory may have even made it to the social column of the battery's newspaper; Kimbell recalled that boys of the battery took over an abandoned print shop and put out a paper called the *Picket Guard*, which was a "very creditable sheet."[22]

If the young soldiers could put out of their minds that they were in the middle of a war, General Smith could never forget it. He fretted about railroad security. According to Lew Wallace's recollection, "I think he had a feeling that if he were Bishop Polk, and master of an advantage like that road, with rolling stock—the Confederates had been careful to secure every locomotive and car—he would not sleep until Paducah was repossessed." Wallace continued: "The surprise of a chief of General Smith's experience was difficult, if not impossible. The ordinary resorts of picket and videttes were not enough for him. He kept a correspondent in Columbus, and in the country between Paducah and Mayfield maintained an outlying detachment of mixed arms varying in strength from one to two thousand men."[23]

It was not only the NO&O that worried Smith. Before Paducah was a railroad town, it had been a river town, and Smith had to carefully guard the Ohio and Tennessee rivers, as well as the railroad. November was filled with rumors of General William Hardee and his plan to lead a force of eight thousand Confederates across the Ohio to invade the Old Northwest. Governor Richard Yates of Illinois was deeply concerned at the prospect of a Rebel invasion and insisted upon his own scheme of defense, which department commander General Halleck countered with a plan of his own. Halleck wrote to his Paducah subordinate: "The protection of the line of the Ohio between the mouths of the Wabash and the Tennessee against rebel force attempting to cross the river into Illinois to operate upon the rear of Cairo, to isolate you at Paducah or to obtain subsistence from that State, it seems to me will be better secured by concentrating your forces at Paducah, with your bridge-head on the Illinois side of the Ohio held by a strong guard, than by any dispersion of them in posts at Shawneetown, Cave-in-Rock, and Golconda, as has been strongly argued by the Governor of Illinois." Halleck said, "Against any apprehended danger from rebel gunboats descending the Tennessee or Cumberland your main reliance will be the activity of your flotilla and your own guns in position at Paducah."[24]

The war had barely touched Paducah, and the young volunteers who were posted there were happy in the bright days of autumn. It was different for General C.F. Smith, the professional, who was burdened with the knowledge that this was not the way that wars were won. The days were peaceful now, but a change would be coming.

8

Grant and Polk After the Battle of Columbus-Belmont
(November–December 1861)

After the Battle of Columbus-Belmont, General Grant was pilloried in the North for having led his army to defeat in a battle that was needless to begin with. There were a total of about 590 casualties, killed, wounded, and missing. One of the wounded was Colonel Dougherty, now a Confederate prisoner. The *Chicago Tribune* called the battle a "bad defeat," and moaned, "It may be said of these victims, they have fallen and to what end?"[1]

The soldiers, too, had a negative opinion of the expedition and its results. Private C.W. Wills of the 8th Illinois Infantry was especially sharp in his comments when he wrote, "General Grant tries to make out that there were about 150 or 175 men lost on our side, but I'll stake my life that we lost not less than 500.... Grant says that he achieved a victory and accomplished the object of his expedition. It may be so (the latter part of it) but almost everyone here doubts the story. He says his object was to threaten Columbus, to keep them from sending reinforcements to Price. Well, he has threatened them, had a fight, and why they can't send reinforcements now as well as before, is more than I know."[2] Wills went on: "Grant got whipped.... The retreat was a route, for our men that were in it say that every man took care of himself and hardly two men of a regiment were together."[3]

Grant insisted in private and in public that he had won a decisive victory. He wrote to his father on November 8: "Taking into account the object of the expedition the victory was most complete." The same day, he wrote to General C.F. Smith: "We drove the Rebels completely from Belmont, burned their tents and carried off their artillery, for want of horses to draw them, we had to leave all but two pieces on the field. The victory was complete. Our loss is not far from 250 Killed, Wounded, and Missing. The Rebel loss must have been from five to six hundred including 150 prisoners brought from the field."[4]

From headquarters, District of Southeast Missouri, Grant also issued a congratulatory order to his men on November 8:

> The general commanding this military district returns his thanks to the troops under his command at the battle of Belmont on yesterday.
> It has been his fortune to have been in all the battles fought in Mexico by Generals Scott and Taylor save Buena Vista, and he never saw one more hotly contested or where troops behaved with more gallantry.
> Such courage will insure victory wherever our flag may be borne and protected by such a class of men.
> To the many brave men who fell the sympathy of the country is due, and will be manifested in a manner unmistakable.[5]

Grant's second official report, the one that appears in the *Official Records*, is problematic. It was dated November 17, 1861, claimed the battle to be a victory and mildly criticized Napoleon Buford for pulling out of battle line during the retreat to the transports, but it is light on details. Belmont scholar Hughes says that this report "was actually written in 1864.... It is in this revised report that the mysterious 2:00 A.M. message from W.H.L. Wallace that Grant claimed 'determined me to attack' appears." Hughes also points out that Grant's post-battle actions gave lie to his loud confidence that he had handed the Rebels a significant defeat: "Grant, on the night of November 7 and the morning of November 8, pulled back the units he had deployed in Missouri and Kentucky. An Illinois soldier wrote, 'Well, Grant got whipped at Belmont, and that scared him so that he countermanded all our orders and took all the troops back to their old stations by forced marches.'"[6]

Nevertheless, Grant, and McClernand, too, said again and again that they had prevailed over the Confederates, and gradually they won the press over. It was easier for the correspondents to accept this version of events than to explain the complicated truth. The often repeated story of Grant, calmly riding over a gangplank to the transport, the last man off the battlefield, though false in at least some respects, resonated with the public. Lew Wallace, who was a keen judge of what made a good narrative, wrote that the story did Grant "great good."[7] Grant won over his superiors, too. On December 20, General Halleck in St. Louis rewarded Grant with command of an enlarged district. In Special Orders No. 78, Grant was put in charge of the District of Cairo, "including the southern part of Illinois, that part of Kentucky west of the Cumberland, and the southeastern counties of Missouri south of Cape Girardeau." The same order put General E.A. Paine in charge of the post of Cairo. Paine was a troublemaker, but he had a keen talent for survival.[8]

The navy men were not impressed by Grant's new hero status, no matter how adamant the propaganda. Commander Henry Walke, for one, felt aggrieved that the army was claiming too much of the credit for a victory at Columbus-Belmont and dismissing the navy's role, which was substantial. After all, "the protection afforded by the gunboats was of vital importance to Grant's army." One might reasonably argue that the gunboats *saved* Grant's army.[9]

Captain Andrew H. Foote was another who was exasperated with Grant. Their relationship had been a good one. Bruce Catton writes, "Foote and Grant understood one another from the start, and they made a harmonious team; in a command setup practically guaranteed to produce friction between Army and Navy commanders, Foote and Grant always got along perfectly."[10] Catton overstated the harmony in the relationship between Grant and Foote when he said "always." In fact, Foote was deeply upset with Grant after Belmont for the general's willful neglect in keeping him informed that an attack was about to be made. On November 8, Foote objected to secretary of the navy Welles and coupled his complaint with the realistic assertion that he ought to be promoted to the rank of flag officer:

> When last in Cairo I requested Brigadier-General Grant, the commanding officer of the army here, to inform me by telegram, at St. Louis, whenever an attack upon the enemy was made requiring the cooperation of the gunboats, that I might be here to take them into action. To this, the general assented, and, under the assurance, I returned to St. Louis, where my services were essential in fitting out the gun and mortar boats. But no telegram was sent me, nor any information given by General Grant when the movement upon Belmont was made; nor did he let Commander Walke, or Stembel, know his intention until he directed them to proceed with his force on the armed reconnaissance toward Belmont. I deeply regret the withholding of this information from me, as I ought not only to have been informed, in order that I might have commanded the gunboats, but it was a want of consideration toward the Navy, a cooperating force with the army on such expeditions. General Grant however, on my arrival early this morning, called upon me and expressed his regret that he had not telegraphed as he had promised, assigned as the cause that he had forgotten it, in the haste in which this expedition was prepared, until it was too late for me to arrive in time to take the command; still, in this instance ... it may be readily seen the importance of the naval officer commanding, whoever he may be, of having the appointment and rank of flag officer for the safety and efficiency of the gunboats, by giving him immunity from the orders of brigadier-general down to lieutenant-colonel, who are inexperienced in naval matters, claiming rank over naval captains of under five years date of commission.[11]

Foote got the promotion he asked for on November 11, 1861, when he was made flag officer, a rank equivalent to that of an army major general. The inland fleet would no longer be completely at the mercy of the army's whims. Now, anyone from the rank of brigadier general down had no authority over Foote at all. (The Brown Water Navy remained under the authority of the War Department, however, specifically the Quartermaster's Department, until

October of 1862, when an act of Congress put the inland fleet in Welles' department.)

The increase in rank solved one of Foote's potential future problems, but there were more immediate ones. Some of his responsibilities were of the ordinary sort, such as ordering armaments. On December 2, he wrote to the Allegheny Arsenal at Pittsburg, Pennsylvania, to order "3500 42-pounder rifle shell, also 150 x-inch Columbiad shell, for the flotilla." The same day, he ordered nine hundred barrels of gunpowder. A week later the *New York Times* reported from Cairo that there were "great quantities of ammunition and naval supplies lying about."[12]

By mid–December, seven ironclad gunboats had arrived from Carondelet, with three more on the ways at Mound City being fitted with their armor plating. The ironclads were found to have unexpected problems. They were underpowered and not easy to handle in the strong currents. Commander Walke added, "The construction of these western gunboats was so defective, that they were liable not only to be blown up in the ordinary wholesale casualties of war ... but owing to their furnaces being so near the bottom of the vessel, the occupants were actually placed 'between two fires,' as the vessels very frequently took fire." At least, they were being delivered.[13]

Not so the mortar barges, which almost became a casualty of the change of command at the St. Louis headquarters. They were begun on Frémont's order, but General Halleck saw no point in continuing to spend time and treasure on them. Generally, Foote had a low opinion of Halleck (he called him "a military imbecile" and said that the general "might make a good clerk"); however, in the matter of the barges he was inclined to agree. Real boats had sails and steam engines, whereas the unpowered mortar barges were practically cripples; they had to be tugged into position. Unpopular as they were in the West, though, they had a powerful advocate in the East, President Lincoln. Lincoln had always had a fascination with innovative machinery of all kinds. In the winter of 1861–1862 he requested a construction summary from assistant secretary of the navy Gustavus A. Fox. In January, Fox reported that not a one was completed. Geoffrey Perret says, "Lincoln was incensed." He went to the officer in charge of the Navy Bureau of Ordnance, Lieutenant Henry A. Wise, and told him to get the job done. "Now I am going to devote a part of every day to get these mortars," said Lincoln, "and I won't leave off until it fairly rains bombs!"[14] Lincoln did not "leave off." He was described as being "mad about mortars." By his insistence, the mortar barges were eventually completed and sent on their way to Grant. They were sixty feet long and twenty-five feet wide, and once in Cairo, they were each fitted with a 13-inch mortar capable of throwing a shell two miles or more. In campaigns to come, they would prove their worth. Frémont and Lincoln were right to have faith in them.[15]

Another of Foote's continuing problems, the major one, probably, was getting crews for his vessels. He had tried recruiting all over the Upper Midwest with little success. In Cleveland, for example, he had signed on only three men. He wrote secretary of the navy Welles on November 4: "I shall therefore close all rendezvous except the one at Chicago, from where we have received over one hundred men, and the one for shipping firemen and coal heavers at Pittsburg." As the end of the year approached, Foote had only shipped two hundred men and needed 1700 more.[16]

By this time, contrabands were making their way from slavery into Paducah and other Union camps. They appeared eager to serve on the gunboats, but they were not welcome. As strapped for men as he was, Foote turned the free blacks down. He and some others feared the effect on Southern populations of seeing whites and Negroes serving on the same crew. Foote said, "As there are objections or difficulties in the Southern country about colored people, we do not want any of that class shipped."[17] There were also worries about confining in the tight spaces of a gunboat black sailors and white Midwesterners, who were not refined, exactly. In fact, they were mostly the "offscourings" of the army. Foote was still one thousand men short at the end of December; he had written assistant secretary of the navy Fox that he would take soldiers "even if they are without brains, I only ask for muscle."[18]

Grant jumped at the chance to empty his guardhouses of men who were convicted of nothing more than minor offenses. Within weeks, Foote had reason to regret his open-handed appeal for manpower. He wrote Welles: "We have to keep two companies of soldiers to guard them, and are now disarming them of their revolvers.... I am pained and discouraged to have to take such men into action. We want no more from the Army. I prefer to go into the action only half manned than to go with such men."[19]

The undesirables who were transferred from the coastal blockading squadron were just as bad as the army jailbirds. Historian Michael J. Bennett included them with the group of Western sailors he called "unhinged," and writes, "As soon as some blockade rejects landed ... these recruits took to drinking in the many saloons that dotted Cairo. One night, 260 of them began brawling in the streets after oversampling the local spirits. Some men drank so much that they died from liquor overdoses."[20]

One problem in recruiting able-bodied brown water men was that they could earn more in civilian life than in the service. Not only did the navy pay less, the wages were also slow in coming. On November 22, 1861, Commander R.N. Stembel had to plead with Foote for pay for his men: "I have the honor to indicate duplicate requisitions for $1,250. I am induced to make the requisition, in addition to the $5,000 already received, in order to pay my crew the two-thirds of their wages faithfully promised them at the time of their enlistment."²¹ To stretch the initial $5,000, Stembel had already been forced to reduce the promised payment by 25 percent. The money problems besieged Foote from all sides. A few days after Stembel wrote, the flag officer received a complaint from James B. Eads: "After waiting four days I have had an interview with Meigs, presenting accounts for more than three hundred thousand dollars. I can obtain no assurance of receiving a dollar, and must return as I came."²²

On top of everything else, and at the bottom of everything else, too, was the Confederate threat. They still stood fast only a few miles down the Mississippi, more confident than before, and stronger, too. On December 7, six Confederate gunboats steamed up the Mississippi to Columbus, and it was reported that "the land batteries are being rapidly depressed, in order to get the range of our boats when they come down."²³

Manpower and money problems, underpowered ironclads and unfinished mortar barges, and a Confederate war effort with which the Federals could barely keep pace: it was all enough to make a man long again for the deep blue sea, a good ship, and a star above to guide her by.

On the morning after the Battle of Columbus-Belmont, a little boy in a Confederate uniform reported to General Gideon Pillow's headquarters. When an aide asked the urchin what he wanted, he said, "I belong to the army.... Yesterday I was on the battlefield and got down in a sinkhole, when I saw a Yankee with his gun pointed right at my Colonel, and I fired away and killed him." If the aide doubted him, the boy said, he would show him the dead Yank's watch. He had done his duty, the boy declared, and expected his reward. "Now I want a furlough to go home and see my father and mother," the little soldier said.²⁴ The twelve-year-old, who had run away from home to help Generals Polk and Pillow defend Dixie, was one of the lucky ones. After the Battle of Columbus-Belmont, there were 105 young Rebels who would never see their mothers and fathers again. There were another 420 or so who would go home bullet torn and scarred by shell, and about 120 who were in Federal custody, wondering if they would ever see home again.

On the night after the battle, surgeon Lunsford Yandell wandered the battlefield, tending the wounded. He wrote his parents in Louisville: "The wounded men groaned and moaned, yelled and shrieked with pain. I had opium, brandy, and water with which I alleviated their torture, and ... they were exceedingly grateful. I was out until two o'clock that night.... In the woods and the field the dead men were so thick that it required careful riding to keep from trampling their bodies." J.M. Cartmell of Co. H, 6th Tennessee Infantry, confirmed Yandell's impression of the carnage. He said, "There must have been eight hundred (killed and wounded) in that field."²⁵

Yandell went back to the battlefield the next morning. The burial parties were gathering the dead and taking them across the river to Kentucky for burial while other details were picking up rifles and overcoats discarded by reason of death, wounds, or panic, and taking them over to Polk's camp for distribution. Viewing the scene by morning light, Yandell realized that the tattered and littered countryside did not look a bit better than it had in the night. He spoke of the trees that were chewed up by rifle balls and he might have taken special notice of the same witness tree that attracted the attention of a *New York Times* reporter who described for his readers: "A large tree standing in the middle of the battleground [which] bore the marks of ten bullets and on one side its truck was spattered with human brains, where a bullet had sped true to its mark and destroyed a life." As a Kentuckian, Yandell was deeply affected by the mangled horses he saw, saying, "many horses lie upon the ground, some of them torn open by shells and others riddled by bullets. You can see innumerable stains of blood on the ground.... I wish the war would close."[26] Over the next few days, Yandell's distress grew, as did that of other former civilian doctors in many far-flung camps in the early months of the war. As he worked at the Confederate hospital, the Louisvillian realized that his civilian training had left him unprepared to deal with such injuries as were now before him. He wrote that he could not "amputate a limb or tie an artery." The doctors who survived would get better at this new facet of medicine; the school of war forced physicians into a steep learning curve.[27]

The Battle of Columbus-Belmont was considered a Confederate victory. General Polk congratulated his troops in General Orders No. 20, saying, "The major general commanding, with profound acknowledgment of the overruling providence of Almighty God, congratulates the army under his command in the glorious victory.... The battle began under disadvantages which would have discouraged veteran troops, yet the obstinate resistance offered by a handful of ones to an overwhelming force must be a lesson to them, and the closing scene of the day, in which a routed army was vigorously pursued, will ever be remembered in connection with that spirit of our people which has proclaimed in triumphant tones upon every battlefield: 'We are and will be free.'" If these words suggest Polk's style in the pulpit, his parishioners in Louisiana must have been prayerfully grateful that the bishop had traded his bishop's robes for the gray uniform. That aside, across the whole Confederacy, the people felt that their boys had delivered unto the Yankees a stinging and humiliating slap. The victory even inspired a popular song, "The Belmont Quickstep," written by Jo Benson and published in Nashville.[28]

When the Battle of Columbus-Belmont was fought, the matter of Polk's resignation was pending. On November 12, President Jefferson Davis wrote the general: "I think the present condition of the service imperiously demands your continuance in the Army.... You are master of the subjects involved in the defense of the Mississippi and its contiguous territory. You have just won a victory, which gives you fresh claim to the affection and confidence of your troops. How should I hope to replace you without injury to the cause which you beautifully and reverently described to me when you resolved to enter the military service.... I must ask of you, then, to postpone your resignation."[29] Polk replied on December 8. After thanking Davis for "the confidence you have been pleased to express in me," Polk said, "I have concluded to waive the pressing of my application for a release from further service, and have determined to retain my office so long as I may be of service to our cause." That he had waited a month to reply did not show any indecision on Polk's part, but rather was because on November 11 he had become one of the last casualties of the battle.[30]

That massive artillery piece, the Lady Polk, had performed admirable service during the contest of November 7. From its bluff-top parapet, it landed one "lamppost" after another among the Yankees who were first looting and then burning Colonel Tappan's camp across the river. On November 11, Polk was inspecting the circular parapet where the Lady Polk was "mounted *en barbette*," with "a temporary magazine or receptacle for cartridges being located in the parapet to the right and opposite the trunnions of the piece ... there were stored in this receptacle from sixty to eighty cartridges of ten pounds each."[31]

Polk had stopped to compliment Captain William Keiter, the chief of the artillery crew, and learned that, at battle's end, an unfired round had been left in the Lady Polk. The general asked that the mighty cannon be fired upstream so that he could see its range. Oddly, neither Polk nor the artillerymen nor any of the others gathered around foresaw any danger in the demonstration. The shells for Lady Polk had a slightly oversized flange around the bottom. They were difficult to cram in, even when the cannon was warm, and now the barrel had cooled and contracted tightly around the shell inside. When the big gun was fired, the barrel burst and detonated the nearby magazine. William D. Pickett, in his *Confederate Veteran* article, remembered, "The gun was found in four pieces—the breech found not to the line of recoil, but in a line not far from the direction of the blast of the magazine, showing the almost immediate ignition of the magazine on pulling the lanyard." The other three pieces of iron were found at varying distances, all of them in "the direction indicated by the explosion of the magazine."[32]

The number of men killed has been estimated to be as high as twenty-eight. Eleven were killed instantly. The head of one decapitated man was found three hundred feet away. Some who were not killed instantly died later of their wounds. One of these was a civilian named John Doublin of Mayfield, who had come to camp to visit his soldier son, Private E.J. "Jack" Doublin of Co. K, 5th Tennessee Infantry. Mr. Doublin's leg was destroyed by a heavy fragment. He survived the injury; the amputation that followed killed him. General Polk and three others who were standing directly behind the breech survived. However, the explosion blew Polk down and tore off most of his clothes. One member of the general's staff went to Polk as he was regaining consciousness and asked him, "General, isn't this hell?" Polk replied, "Rucker, it smells like it!" Polk's life was spared, along with his sense of humor, but he was weeks in recovery. During his recuperation, command of the 1st Division, Western Department, devolved to General Pillow, a situation that was not greeted with universal enthusiasm.[33]

Sam Tate, president of the Memphis and Charleston Railroad, wrote from his office in Memphis to General Albert Sidney Johnston's headquarters in Bowling Green: "Permit me to say to you that our people are very much exercised about General Pillow being in supreme command at Columbus.... No one here has the slightest confidence in Pillow's judgment or ability, and if the important command of defending this river is to be left to him, we feel perfectly in the enemy's power."[34]

If the people lacked confidence in Pillow, he had enough to cover the deficit. He tried to take care of such mundane matters as getting back pay for the men and issued orders that all stock and produce seized for army use and all damage to private property should be assessed and paid for. He arrested men who foraged too freely. However, the ordinary tasks of a regional military commander did not begin to satisfy Pillow. While in temporary command, he planned one of his elaborate operations, a move to sweep north and capture Bird's Point, Fort Holt, and Cairo, with the help of Commodore George N. Hollis' gunboats. This came from the man who had performed so poorly at Belmont and who now was outnumbered more than two to one by the Federal forces. Pillow asked for Polk's agreement, which the recovering general sensibly withheld. A failure, he pointed out to Pillow, would leave the river as far as Memphis, and Memphis itself, vulnerable.

Pillow was equally ineffective in continuing the prisoner exchanges that had begun between Grant and Polk shortly after the battle. Bruce Catton says, "There were several ... flag-of-truce boats" in the days after Columbus-Belmont. "Rival officers made a point of being very affable and courteous to one another on these occasions." Catton says that Colonel Napoleon Buford of the 27th Illinois hosted a gathering of Rebel officers, including Polk, who liked him very much, and it was said that Grant got drunk with the boisterous General Benjamin F. Cheatham on a different occasion. So many of these career officers knew each other from the Mexican War or frontier service or at least had the West Point experience in common that it was easy for them to forget between battles that there was a war going on at all, especially when the bourbon flowed. It was so very odd for them to be now on opposite sides.[35]

In these meetings, the exchange of between 250 and 300 men was arranged. However, when Pillow tried to continue the exchanges, the Federal officers who had known Pillow treated him with disdain. When, on November 24, Pillow tried to negotiate an exchange of eight prisoners with General C.F. Smith, the old Regular replied with icy formality, "To do this would imply that the Government of the United States admits the existing civil war to be one between independent nations. This I cannot admit and must therefore decline to make any terms or conditions in reference to those we mutually hold." Departmental commander General Henry W. Halleck upheld Smith and the prisoners remained in custody.[36]

While Polk recuperated, work continued at Fort Henry on the Tennessee and Fort Donelson on the Cumberland. The army was playing catch-up, for as Cooling points out, "very little construction actually took place on the twin rivers that summer." The situation was a microcosm of a problem the whole Confederacy faced: with a smaller population than the North, how could the South keep a sufficient number of soldiers in the field and at the same time have a domestic workforce large enough to perform the vital tasks of building defenses, repairing railroads, working in the mills and manufactories, and carrying on other heavy labors? Able-bodied whites were in short supply and slaves were, very naturally, recalcitrant and had to be constantly prodded and closely supervised. Cooling points out that there were never more than two hundred men "present for duty ... due to leave and sickness," and even the men who were present were not allowed to work uninterrupted on the forts. They were always being detailed for other service. So, the work went slowly until the fall, when a Federal incursion reminded the Confederates of the importance of completing their river defenses.[37]

In October 1861, the Federal gunboat *Conestoga* made a reconnaissance to Eddyville on the Cumberland River. Eddyville was central to a region where "a majority of the inhabitants are secessionists of a violent and desperate type." The area was notorious among the Federals for a vigorous black market trade in provisions for the Confederacy, flour especially. Also, reports indicated that the nearby Empire Furnace was casting cannon, shot, and shell for the Rebels. At the very least, it was sending pig iron to Nashville. The *Conestoga* was commanded by Lieutenant S. Ledyard Phelps, and he had on board several companies of Illinois cavalrymen when he landed at Eddyville. The boat disgorged the horse soldiers. Onshore, they fought a skirmish with the enemy, killing seven and capturing fifty-four. They captured two loads of flour, along with a quantity of weapons, and forty-two horses and mules with equipage. They also escorted seven blacks back to the *Conestoga* and carried them downstream into the Federal zone.[38]

A few weeks later, the *Conestoga* went back up the Tennessee to examine the Empire Furnace. Lieutenant Phelps found that "there was no evidence of their having been employed, as reported, in casting cannon and shot, or in any but legitimate business." He also found that local Unionist sentiments "were rapidly increasing" since the earlier Eddyville expedition. The Federal gunboats apparently had the ability to come and go at will for a certain distance up the Cumberland River. It encouraged their friends and concerned their enemies. The time would come when the gunboats would make bold to probe deeper into Dixie and when that day came the Confederate defenses had better be ready.[39]

Tennessee senator Gustavus A. Henry of the Confederate Congress was deeply worried about it. He wrote to General Polk on October 17: "I beg leave to draw your attention to the defenseless condition of the Cumberland River. From here to Smithland there are not 300 soldiers in arms.... We are in actual danger of being invaded and without any means of defense." If those prowling Yankee gunboats should push beyond the unfinished Fort Donelson, they would be able to inflict terrible damage. Henry wrote, "Wood, Lewis & Co. have very valuable property on the river a few miles above Fort Donelson—the Cumberland Rolling Mills—now engaged in manufacturing iron for the Confederate States, which could be destroyed any night. Its machinery could not be reinstated now, and the public loss would be irreparable. The bridge at Clarksville over the Cumberland River could also be destroyed, which would sever all connection with West Tennessee, and this loss could not be repaired at a cost of $200,000." The remedy to this peril? Henry wanted Polk to send an infantry regiment to Fort Donelson.[40]

A month later, Senator Henry wrote General Johnston in Bowling Green. "I hope you will not consider me importunate, but the condition of things at Fort Donelson demands immediate attention," Henry said. "There are there about 800 cavalry and 500 infantry, and a great want of organization and drill. They have not men enough to form a regiment, and no sort of order prevails.... The guns at Donelson are wholly unprotected, as they were at the date of my last letter, and will probably remain so till the regiment is organized and some one is in command who will push on the work to completion. Captain Dixon is ready and willing to work, but he is not sustained."[41]

As mentioned earlier, Johnston turned to General Lloyd Tilghman to take charge of finishing the river defenses. Though assigned in late October, Tilghman did not arrive until mid-December. He said, "I found at my disposal six undisciplined companies of infantry, an unorganized light battery, while a small water battery of two light guns constituted the available river defense." He immediately began pushing the work forward, using slaves, iron furnace workers, and mill hands as work gangs. Under Tilghman's guidance, "two water batteries ... began to take shape at Fort Donelson [and] on the Tennessee River,

Colonel Adolphus Heiman's 10th Tennessee (720 men armed with flintlocks) completed their organization and began work on Forts Henry and Heiman (across the river)."[42]

Fort Henry was nearer to completion than Fort Donelson. In mid–October Colonel Heiman described the works to General Polk: "It is a bastion fort, inclosing an area of a little over 3 acres. The ditch surrounding it is 20 feet in width, with an average depth of 10 feet, making the height of parapet from the bottom of the ditch about 18 feet. The line of parapet is 2,270 feet." The whole was defended by nine pieces of artillery. If adequately manned, Fort Henry would be a strong position. However, Heiman saw that there were two main problems with Fort Henry. First, the fort sat far too low, barely above river level, and would be subject to flooding when the winter rains set in. Old-timers in the neighborhood who had watched the river for years had tried to warn them about this and were paid no attention. Second, and perhaps worse for defensive purposes, Fort Henry sat in the shadow of some hills 150 feet high over on the Kentucky side of the Tennessee.[43]

Colonel Heiman had written, "These hills I consider really dangerous points, and proper batteries placed on them will certainly command the fort." For the sake of Fort Henry's security, it was vital for the Confederates to occupy the Kentucky palisade. It might have been done weeks earlier, except that it was politically impossible to build there and at the same time respect Kentucky neutrality. When neutrality collapsed under the Confederate and Union invasions, it was both possible and desirable to make use of the site, but by then there were too few hands to begin the work. It was not until fall that ground was broken for the works on the coveted Kentucky side of the Tennessee River. These works were named Fort Heiman. Chief engineer Lieutenant Colonel Jeremy F. Gilmer verified the many advantages of the site in a report to his superiors:

> On the left bank of the river there was a number of hills within cannon range that commanded the river batteries on the right bank. The necessity of occupying these hills was apparent to me at the time. I inspected Fort Henry early in November last [1861] and on the 21st of that month Lieutenant [Joseph] Dixon, the local engineer, was ordered from Fort Donelson to Fort Henry to make the necessary surveys and construct the works. He was at that time informed that a large force of slaves, with troops to protect them, from Alabama, would report to him for the work."[44]

Gilmer admired the site, but he did not admire the order that assigned Lieutenant Dixon to Fort Henry/Fort Heiman from Donelson. He objected so strenuously that Dixon was ultimately allowed to remain at Donelson and Captain Charles Hayden was assigned to complete the works on the Tennessee.

The 27th Alabama and the 15th Arkansas were detailed to help finish the work on the rifle pits and artillery platforms. Once the big Parrot guns arrived and were mounted, no Federal gunboat would be able to cruise past this deadly point on the Tennessee River. The 10th Tennessee was at Fort Henry, too, and this regiment, at least, did not have its mind entirely on work. Private Patrick M. Griffin (Co. E, 10th Tennessee Infantry) remembered, "At Fort Henry there was no whisky on our side of the river, but across the stretch of water was Madame Peggy's saloon. There was some mystery as to where the beverage she sold was obtained, but this only added to her popularity. Peggy did a land office business until Colonel Heiman ordered all the skiffs and smaller boats in the neighborhood smashed." The boys of the 10th were not willing to give up their whiskey ration so easily. After the boats were destroyed, Griffin just swam across the Tennessee River with empty canteens hanging around his neck and swam back with the canteens filled. Fueled and loosened by Madame Peggy's liquor, the boys had a nightly stag dance, "and there was an exchange of visits right and left and no time to think of the dark days ahead."[45]

While the Tennessee boys drank whiskey and capered the nights away, the officers had to think of the "dark days ahead." Time was of the essence now. They did their best to keep the men at work and not let them be detailed to unrelated tasks or distracted by alarms. To protect them while they worked, Nathan Bedford Forrest kept eight cavalry companies on the scout all around the forts. The officers might make the men work and Forrest's horsemen could guard the approaches, but no one could control the weather. In December, about the same time that General Tilghman arrived, the weather turned so foul that work on Fort Donelson had to cease while the men built four hundred log cabins to take the place of the shelter tents in which they had been living. By necessity, work would be intermittent now. The weather had become as much of an enemy as those devilish Yankee gunboats.

At the end of November 1861, Colonel John S. Bowen had 4,200 men present for duty at Camp Beauregard. They could hear the guns from the Battle of Columbus-Belmont, but had themselves seen no action. Even when they went out to confront General Paine's column during the demonstration, they failed to make contact, and they settled down in their hilltop camp again, watching the autumn colors develop in the treetops in the valley below. The nearest village was Feliciana, about a mile away. "There were four stores, two hotels, a Masonic lodge, a school, a druggist, four physicians, an attorney, a magistrate, two blacksmiths, a boot and shoemaker, a tanner, a painter, and two tailors," Captain Joseph Boyce of the 1st Missouri Infantry remembered. "The boys always found good Bourbon whiskey there."[46]

Private John Milton Hubbard of the 7th Tennessee Cavalry, remembered almost fifty years later that Camp Beauregard "was a charming place for holiday soldiering, situated near the village of Feliciana. As the cavalry was encamped outside the infantry lines and there was little fear of attack, the discipline was sufficiently lax to permit us to draw upon the surrounding country for luxuries. These consisted of such things as old hams, chickens and 'peach and honey.' The boys did not neglect their opportunities."[47]

There was "little fear of attack," Hubbard said. It must have rankled some of these energetic boys that they had joined to kill Yankees and yet all they seemed to do was camp out and make trips to Mayfield to pick up supplies or in response to the continual, ever-false alarms. On at least one occasion, their war fever, possibly fueled by alcohol, spilled over in an unexpected direction. In 1916, L.B. Wardlow, formerly of Company B, 22nd Mississippi, remembered the event. He said, "Our boys, on arriving at Mayfield, found a Union man that at the time ran a saloon, and they actually took him out and killed him; it was an act that I did not in any way approve of and did not participate in."[48]

The boys at Camp Beauregard felt that they were missing all of the action. The worst battle they fought was not at all of the type they expected. Autumn was pleasant until November 30, when three inches of snow fell. The men began to build log cabins to replace their tents. The weather continued to be ugly. Surgeon G.C. Phillips of the 22nd Mississippi remembered:

> The weather became cold and rainy, then sleet and snow.... Soon typhoid fever and pneumonia broke out among the men. There were 75 cases of typhoid fever and typhoid pneumonia in the hospital tent during one month. I speak only of our regiment. It was as bad or worse than other regiments. Then the most terrible disease, cerebro-spinal meningitis broke out, killing nearly every case attacked, and frequently in a few hours.... The drs. were all at sea. None of us had ever seen a case of this disease.... This was an epidemic more fatal that yellow fever.
> Col. Bonham sent for me and asked if nothing could be done to stop this high death rate among his men.... I advised the Col. to move his camp, if only half a mile, and to have his commissary issue corn meal, bacon, dry salty meat, turnips, potatoes, onions, and cow peas as rations to the men, that this was an experiment, but I could advise nothing else."[49]

The camp hospital was a group of over-sized tents, furnished with cots and kept dry by a layer of wheat straw on the floor. The floor-covering quickly became foul and was replaced every day or every other day. The doctors who labored there, combating the meningitis epidemic on top of the expected seasonal illnesses, were frazzled with frustration and overwork.

If there was no immediate relief for the sick and weary bodies, at least there was balm for their troubled souls. The patients and the orderlies, and perhaps the doctors, too, were ministered to by Father Arthur J. Durbin of Shawneetown, Illinois. It is said that the sixty-three-year-old priest made the

120-mile round-trip by horseback and "visited the camp three times" in the fall and winter of 1861. Captain Joseph Boyce said, "His coming was hailed with delight by the command, and it was a beautiful sight to see this worthy man escorted into camp by the men. He remained about three days at each visit." In December 1861, Father Durbin must have spent much of each visit in the hospital tents, murmuring the last rites over some and praying with others who hoped not to need them.[50]

Then, as mysteriously as it had come, the disease began to disappear. By mid–December, the doctors could see an encouraging decline in the number of deaths. Colonel Bonham had told Phillips that this was "worse than a battle," and so it was. Four hundred men died of the various diseases in this one regiment, the 22nd Mississippi; the Battle of Columbus-Belmont had cost fewer than two hundred lives, total. If one counts the combined casualties of the battle of November 7 (killed, wounded, and captured), the number is fewer than 1500. The total number of men who died during the five-month life of Camp Beauregard may have been even higher. Many of the dead were shipped home by rail, but at least 350 were buried on that Graves County hilltop, to be the garrison of Camp Beauregard forever.

In the end, it was transfers, not epidemic disease, that put an end to Camp Beauregard. On December 4, 1861, General Polk resumed command of the 1st Division, Western Department, and the calls from Johnston for him to diminish his command quickly resumed. Johnston was facing General Don Carlos Buell's Army of the Ohio, which was moving slowly down the line of the Louisville & Nashville Railroad toward Bowling Green. On December 24, Polk wrote to Johnston: "I have resolved to send you Bowen's command of infantry, about 5000 strong.... I can retain his cavalry and two batteries of artillery and will replace his forces at Feliciana by four regiments [of] sixty-days' men from Mississippi."[51]

On Christmas morning the men moved down to State Line Station, where they boarded cars on the Mobile & Ohio Railroad for the trip east to General Albert Sidney Johnston. It was ironic that, in Polk's impoverished command, the men of the 1st Missouri had received an issue of "new muskets, overcoats, and caps" just before their transfer order. With their shining arms, their new caps and coats, and their dark blue regimental flag with the bold legend "BEWARE," they presented "a very soldierly appearance" and made a good impression.[52] But it was General Johnston, not Polk, who got to admire them for it. Johnston was not satisfied. In no time at all, he asked for the two artillery batteries that Polk had mentioned. "If you can spare the artillery, send it," he said.[53]

On December 30, Polk informed Johnston that he had ordered Hudson's

8. Grant and Polk After the Battle of Columbus-Belmont

and Beltzhoover's batteries to Bowling Green. "I shall be obliged in consequence of this movement to break up Camp Beauregard, and remove the sixty-day troops from there to Union City. I shall substitute for this force a cavalry force on the Tennessee and Kentucky lines as the best and only thing left to me."[54] To make up for the transfers, Polk began accepting unarmed twelve-months men. Secretary of war Benjamin made him stop, as they were "immensely expensive and utterly useless." It was one of General Polk's manifold frustrations that his superiors seemed determined to bleed him white. He had no choice but to comply, but it did not matter much, finally. Columbus would not have to defend itself again; the war was about to shift east.[55]

9

The Federal Expedition
(January 1862)

General Grant had the usual problems within his command. There were too few of some things and too many of others. There were too few ambulances and too few serviceable uniforms and too few weapons. Grant complained to Halleck that he had eight companies of cavalry that were completely without weapons. There were too many runaway slaves and indignant masters, and too many bushwhackers taking potshots at the pickets and at the supply boats. And there were too many refugees. Many of them were from Cave-in-Rock, Illinois, where a whole colony of displaced Kentuckians had taken refuge, actually living in the cave. Grant had ordered them brought in and followed a precedent set by Halleck to support them. Believing that "justice demands that the class of persons who have caused their sufferings should bear the expense of the same," Grant ordered that funds be collected from Rebel sympathizers in the same manner followed by Halleck in St. Louis, i.e., well-to-do Rebels were made "to contribute" $10,000 to the charitable cause and if they resisted "their property would be seized and sold at auction." Grant added the provision that "a pro-secessionist who was liable to this assessment, and who happened to be of Northern birth and education, would be required to pay fifty percent more than a Southerner of the same class and means." It was a clever plan, designed to not only support the refugees, but also to punish the Secesh, with a little extra twist of the knife toward Northerners who had betrayed their own region.[1]

There was too much smuggling. A newspaper report said that "men professing to be Unionists ship goods marked for Union men at Cairo and other places, which are put off at Smithland and Paducah, and then shipped up the Tennessee River." Another black market route led through Jonesborough in southern Illinois, across the Mississippi River, and into Missouri. The crossing point was infested with desperadoes. In addition, a large business in salt and hogs "is being done by the rebels via Caseyville [Kentucky] and Cave-in-Rock.

It is known that vast quantities of good find their way to Nashville through that section of the country of which Caseyville is the leading point."²

Lieutenant S. Ledyard Phelps identified another smuggling operation during a cruise of the *Conestoga*. Phelps said, "There is entirely too much smuggling done between this point [Paducah] and Evansville, and as usual by Jews. Steamers still stop at all points along the Kentucky shore.... Steamers should only be permitted to land at fixed points along the north bank of the Ohio, where the Government has agents or a military force." He also pointed to the continuing mail delivery to towns on the Kentucky shore as "affording a constant means of communication and information to the rebel force at Bowling Green."³ It was Flag Officer Foote who addressed Phelps' concerns. He ordered Lieutenant J.W. Shirk and the *Lexington* to be added to Phelps' command on January 1, 1862: "With this additional vessel you will be able to guard the extensive interest intrusted to you along the margin of the Ohio, Tennessee, and Cumberland Rivers."⁴

Grant had a problem with too much corruption. On January 12, 1862, he wrote to General Halleck: "I have placed Captain Hatch, assistant quartermaster, in arrest, and directed him to turn over all public property to Capt. A.S. Baxter, assistant quartermaster.... Every day develops further evidences of corruption in the quartermaster's department, and that Mr. Dunton, chief clerk, if not [the] chief conspirator, is at least an accomplice. I have ordered his arrest in confinement." Also, he said, "I have directed the books and safe of Captain Hatch to be taken possession of and kept guarded until orders are received disposing of this matter."⁵

All of this was U.S. Grant's portion as head of the District of Cairo. In addition, he had to constantly guard against a Confederate attack on Fort Holt or Bird's Point, Cairo and Paducah were probably safe in and of themselves, but the land and river approaches had to be kept secure. Then came an extra and unwelcome assignment. As Grant told it,

> Early in January, 1862, I was directed by General McClellan through my department commander, to make a reconnaissance in favor of Brigadier General Don Carlos Buell, who commanded the Department of the Ohio, with headquarters at Louisville, and who was confronting General S.B. Buckner with a larger Confederate force at Bowling Green. It was supposed that Buell was about to make some move against the enemy, and my demonstration was intended to prevent the sending of troops from Columbus, Fort Henry or Donelson to Buckner.⁶

The demonstration was designed to cover a lot of territory. General C.F. Smith would move down the bank of the Tennessee River toward Forts Henry and Heiman. Foote's gunboats would ascend the river at the same time. General John A. McClernand would move down toward Columbus and threaten Camp Beauregard. Grant decided to accompany McClernand for at least part of the way. Halleck told Grant, "Make a great fuss about moving all your forces toward Nashville, and let it be so reported by the newspapers.... Let it be understood that 20,000 to 30,000 men are expected from Missouri, and that your force is merely the advanced guards to the main column of attack."[7]

Halleck wanted the demonstration to begin on January 8, but the heavens opened up and then a heavy fog descended to hang like a wet veil over the land. On January 9, Grant wrote Halleck: "The fog is so dense that it is impossible to cross the river." The first column to set out, McClernand's could not begin its march until the 11th and General Smith's did not step off until the 15th of January. General McClernand's column of 5200 men rendezvoused at the site of George Rogers Clark's old Fort Jefferson on January 10, 1861. Clark had tried in 1780 to plant a colony of soldiers and settlers here to defend the confluence of the Ohio River and the Mississippi. A combination of Chickasaw resistance and insufficient support from Virginia doomed Clark's far-flung outpost. Perhaps McClernand's soldiers of 1861 would have a better outcome to their efforts. They came from Cairo and from Fort Holt, and General E.A. Paine brought his troops from Bird's Point.[8]

McClernand was a Kentucky-born Illinoisan. He was a self-educated lawyer, a veteran of the Black Hawk War, and a former member of the U.S. Congress. When the Civil War began, the one-time militia private was named by President Lincoln as a brigadier general of volunteers. Yet, he was never quite able to shake his more natural persona as a politician. Dr. John H. Brinton accompanied McClernand as a member of his staff on the January 1862 expedition and had a good chance to observe the general. Brinton said that McClernand was "a fine, or rather let me say good, specimen of an active, bustling western politician.... Doubtless he was a clever lawyer and shrewd politician but he aspired to be something else,—a general." Brinton perceived that McClernand was jealous of Grant but said, "He was, however, kind to me."[9]

McClernand ordered a small cavalry reconnaissance to Blandville, thence to Weston, thence back to Fort Jefferson on January 11. A much stronger march of six cavalry companies and two regiments of infantry occurred the next day. The infantry simply marched to Elliott's Mill and camped, while the cavalry advanced to "within a mile and a half of the enemy's defenses, driving his pickets into camp and bringing away several prisoners and their horses." When no enemy appeared to oppose the Federal horsemen, McClernand concluded, "the rigor of the weather and the non-appearance of any considerable rebel force led to the belief that they were closely collected around camp fires within their intrenchments, and indisposed to take the field."[10]

The main force at Fort Jefferson remained in place until the 14th, when they moved to Blandville and encamped, and then on the 15th they advanced

9. *The Federal Expedition* 99

The Union timberclads *Conestoga* and *Lexington* (*Harper's Weekly*, September 7, 1861).

to Weston. A cavalry scout to Milburn resulted in the arrest and questioning of a man who had just come from Columbus. He talked quite freely and told his interrogators that the "demonstration toward Columbus had excited much alarm, and induced the enemy to call in his forces at Jackson, Beauregard, New Madrid, and other places."[11]

McClernand said that Milburn "is reproached as a Union town by the rebels." One wonders if the citizens were still pro–Union after the general's column passed through, for McClernand's soldiers were living off the land. It went harder on the Rebel property owners, of course, but even Unionists suffered when the army passed through. In his after-action report McClernand said,

> The unavoidable deficiency of transportation with which my command set out, aggravated by the bad condition of the roads, prevented me from taking ... the five days' supply of rations and forage directed by the commanding officer of this district; hence the necessity of an early resort to other sources of supply. None other presented but to quarter upon the enemy or to purchase from loyal citizens. I accordingly resorted to both expedients as I had opportunity. In some cases finding live stock, provision, forage, etc., the owners of which had abandoned it and gone into the rebel army, I took and appropriated it to the uses of the United States without hesitation. In other cases I purchased from loyal citizens such supplies as were indispensible, and caused certificates to be issued, charging the Government for the fair value of the certificates thus obtained. By these means of supply, resorted to from necessities of the case, substantial economy was practiced in saving to the Government in supplies and transportation more than their full value for the five days named.[12]

Though McClernand gave certificates to the citizens whose property he took, that did not mean they were honored when presented at headquarters by the holders. Across the state, Kentuckians were suspected of disloyalty and Yankee clerks, puffed up with responsibility and self-righteousness, would often deny the claims. To appeal was a waste of still more time and there was no guarantee of satisfaction even then. Many times, the property seized by the army was never paid for, and all the property owner got out of it was a humiliating and fruitless round-trip to the nearest Federal encampment. However, McClernand would not be meeting many Unionist Kentuckians during his January jaunt through the Jackson Purchase.

General Grant joined McClernand at Weston, and accompanied the main column as it moved the next day to Milburn. McClernand said, "I here maneuvered my forces so as to leave the enemy in doubt whether my purpose was to attack Columbus, march upon Camp Beauregard, or destroy the railroad leading from Columbus to Union City, and to awaken apprehension for the safety of each." McClernand did not yet know that Camp Beauregard was mostly abandoned, and Columbus was too strongly defended to attack, of course. A bit of railroad destruction on the Mobile & Ohio Railroad might have been a useful exercise for his men and an inconvenience for the Confederates, but McClernand decided instead to rest his men through the afternoon and night, except for a company of the hard-riding cavalry.[13]

The cavalry often had hours of duty ahead of them after the foot-soldiers were settled in and brewing coffee. On the night of January 16, the infantrymen might have for once willingly traded places with the cavalry, for their camp was not a comfortable one. D. Leib Ambrose of the 7th Illinois Infantry wrote, "Our camp is in the Mayfield Creek bottom. The water is standing all around us. The creek is rising very high, and it is still raining. Our subsistence is now running short and Fort Holt our nearest depot of supplies. Mud! Mud! everywhere, the situation looks critical."[14]

While Ambrose contended with the Mud! Mud!, the cavalrymen rode to Mayfield to open communication with General C.F. Smith, who was with his column farther east. From Smith, McClernand learned that the enemy troops had been removed from Camp Beauregard. It was not a result of the demonstration, for it had happened three weeks earlier, but it was a surprise to McClernand.

After a day of soggy rest, the column moved to Lovelaceville, and on the 18th proceeded westward. Only the head of the column had reached Blandville when an early halt was forced upon them by a torrential rain, which turned the road into a quagmire and delayed the arrival of the tail of the column and part of the baggage train. They did not catch up until the next day.

At Blandville, McClernand believed from reports received that he would be attacked. He deployed his troops and placed strong pickets on the approaches to town. He destroyed the bridges. He also sent a courier to Fort

Jefferson, ordering that a force be sent out to hold and keep open the return route through Elliott's Mill. McClernand was alarmed for nothing. General Polk at Columbus had no thought of attacking him. He saw this whole exercise as an attempt to draw his forces out of Fort De Russey. Once the Confederate works were weakened, the gunboats would come and the Federal column would turn to catch the Confederates in a double envelopment. The fighting bishop was too canny to fall for it. He wrote General Johnston that he was not going to take any risks; he was simply going to remain in his works, strengthen his position, and wait for the Yankees to come to him. Until they did, he was satisfied to send out cavalry patrols to keep a close watch on McClernand.

The Federals had a long, tense night at Blandville. No attack came, and the next morning McClernand pushed his main column toward Fort Jefferson. Still expecting that the Confederate cavalry might make a dash upon his left flank, he kept a strong cavalry presence and infantry flankers thrown out toward the west. Again, no attack came, and the column began to arrive at Fort Jefferson by midday, January 20. The rear came in on the 21st. Summarizing the march, McClernand said, "The reconnaissance thus made completed a march of 140 miles by the cavalry and 75 by the infantry over icy or miry roads during a most inclement season, and has led to the discovery of several important roads which did not appear upon our maps.... It has forcibly and deeply impressed the inhabitants of the district through which we passed with the superiority of our military preparations and of our ultimate ability to conquer the rebellion." Reading McClernand's overblown claims, one is left wondering why the Confederacy did not sue for peace before the end of January 1861.[15]

An ordinary soldier, Corporal Phineas Orlando Avery of Co. I, 4th Illinois Cavalry, had no such grandiose ideas about the effect of the march on the enemy, but had a very strong idea, indeed, of what it meant to the young Federals—it was hard. Avery wrote of his regiment's first excursion: "We started with five days' rations and were gone thirteen days. Besides short rations, the weather was stormy and the roads horrible. Upon the whole it was a rough introduction to soldiering."[16] Grant, too, had a more down-to-earth view of McClernand's short tour of the Jackson Purchase: "We were out more than a week splashing through the mud, snow and rain, the men suffering very much. The object of the expedition was accomplished."[17]

On January 9, 1862, Flag Officer Andrew H. Foote wrote Secretary Welles from Cairo: "I have received from General Grant, commanding this post, confidential communications in relation to an expedition of troops planned by General Halleck. On consultation with General Grant, I have ordered two gunboats up the Tennessee River, in charge of Lieutenant Commanding Phelps, a judicious officer."[18] The gunboats had been patrolling the river on their own reconnaissance missions, but not until now had they served as part of a major joint operation on either of the twin rivers. The *Lexington* and the *Conestoga* left Paducah on January 16, accompanying the troop transport *Wilson*. They moved quickly and anchored that night "near where the Tennessee line strikes the right bank of the river."[19] The next morning, the *Conestoga* steamed up toward Fort Henry and fired a few shells at the spot where a masked battery was reported to be. Lieutenant Phelps reported, "We also fired a few shells at Fort Henry, 2½ miles, too distant for effect." Neither attempt drew any return fire and the gunboat dropped downstream to Aurora, where the troops disembarked the transport vessel and marched for Murray, the seat of Calloway County.[20]

General Smith always took pains to preserve order and hoped his men would adopt his attitude toward good discipline. General Halleck wrote Adjutant General Lorenzo Thomas that Smith's command "is reported in the best discipline and order of any one in the department." However, the lesson seemed to have been forgotten on this short overland jaunt to Murray. Calloway County historians Dorothy and Kerby Jennings wrote that the soldiers "did a great deal of damage to the citizens of Murray and surrounding country. The detachment became disorganized on account of the bad condition of the roads, and the soldiers went unrestrained through the country, taking whatever property they saw fit."[21]

One likes to think that the men would have behaved better if General Smith himself had been along, but the evidence suggests otherwise. Smith was with a two-brigade column (practically his whole division except for the 40th Illinois, held at Paducah) which began its march on January 15. The cross-country men had gone down a route that took them over Hickory Creek on the 15th, Mayfield Creek (January 16), and Clark's River, where they bivouacked on the 17th. Private Thomas F. Miller, of Co. H, 29th Illinois Infantry, said, "We ruined every farm we camped on."[22] On January 18, it began to rain, and the marching became heavy work. Private Miller griped about "packing fifty pounds of gear" and said "it was a hard sight to see hundreds of stout young men sitting and crying along the roadside, many of them crying and weeping because they could not keep up with their comrades."[23]

General Smith bore the weather and the work as well as or better than the younger men. Lew Wallace was unsure of dates in his *Autobiography*, but he was firm in his memory "the country had become an ocean of mud, and there was rain and melting snow, and from the beginning to end no dry place to set a foot could be discovered.... General Smith could have had comfortable houses often as night overtook us; but such was not his habit when on the road. I remember finding him one fluvial midnight in a dog-tent half filled with straw. In such manner he silenced the croakers."[24]

9. *The Federal Expedition* 103

Mushy roads made progress slow on the return march to the Tennessee River, and it was not until January 21 that the column reached Calloway Landing, twenty miles downriver from Forts Henry and Heiman. Anticipating his arrival, Smith had sent a request for the *Lexington* and the *Wilson* to come up from Aurora. The vessels arrived at the landing about the same time as the troops. As Lieutenant Shirk of the *Lexington* remembered, "At the request of General Smith I then proceeded up the river for the purpose of ascertaining the truth of a report that the general had heard, which was to the effect that Fort Henry had been evacuated." En route, Shirk encountered the Rebel gunboat *Dunbar*, gave pursuit, and fired a round at her, which fell short. Continuing to Panther Island near the fort, the *Lexington* stopped for a half hour, fired shells into the same previously reported position of a masked battery (still no response), and fired a round into the Confederate camp. Drawing no return fire at all, the boat returned to Smith. Shirk had seen large numbers of Rebels and was able to report positively that Fort Henry had not been abandoned.[25]

The next day, January 22, General Smith asked Shirk to take him up to the fort. "I did so," said the lieutenant, "and threw several shot and shell at it. One of the shot fell in the water immediately at the foot of the works and several of the shell burst over them. The enemy fired one shot at this vessel, which fell short about half a mile." In response, the *Lexington* fired one more round, and turned about toward Calloway Landing. As Fort Henry dropped astern, a thought was forming in General Smith's mind.[26]

On the morning of January 23, the troops left the landing and the *Lexington* and the *Conestoga* steamed back toward Paducah. As the column marched back over the muddy countryside, their rear was harassed by "950 cavalry and some artillery" which General Lloyd Tilghman had sent after them. No serious action developed, though the Confederates pestered the bluecoats to within eleven miles of Paducah. Smith's men arrived at their post on January 25, having completed a round-trip march of 125 miles.[27]

Both McClernand's and Smith's expeditions were valuable in that they provided young soldiers with the experience they would need in campaigning, but there was a development that grew out of Smith's that made it the more important of the two. He had laid eyes on Fort Henry, had examined its defenses, and had come back to Paducah convinced that it could be taken. He wrote to General Grant on January 22: "I think two iron-clad gunboats would make short work of Fort Henry. There is no masked battery at the foot of the island, as was supposed, or, if so, it is now under water." Grant agreed with Smith's assessment. He asked for permission to travel to St. Louis to see Halleck.[28] Grant remembered, "The leave was granted, but not graciously.... I was received with so little cordiality that I perhaps stated the object of my visit with less clearness than I might have done, and I had not uttered many sentences before I was cut short as if my plan [to attack Fort Henry] was preposterous. I returned to Cairo very much crestfallen."[29]

Bruce Catton thinks the reason for Halleck's rude treatment of Grant was that he was offended by his junior's presumption in proposing such a campaign. Halleck was the head of the department; he was responsible for planning strategy. In fact, if General William T. Sherman's recollection was trustworthy, Halleck had already conceived of the very plan Grant was proposing and may have felt a little proprietary toward it. Sherman was in conversation with Halleck and his chief of staff, G.W. Cullum, when the department chief pointed to a map he had unrolled and asked,

> "Where is the rebel line?" Cullum drew the pencil through Bowling Green, Forts Donelson and Henry, and Columbus, Kentucky. "That is their line," said Halleck. "Now, where is the place to break it?" And either Cullum or I said, "Naturally the centre." Halleck drew a line perpendicular to the other, near its middle, and it coincided nearly with the general course of the Tennessee River; and he said, "That's the true line of operations." This occurred more than a month before General Grant began the movement, and, as he was subject to General Halleck's orders, I have always given Halleck the full credit for that movement.[30]

However aggrieved he might have felt about Grant's inadvertent trespass on his Tennessee River scheme, there were other factors at play that finally pushed Halleck to make an affirmative decision on the matter. For one, the man in Cairo had an influential ally in Flag Officer Foote. He and Grant conferred on the right approach to win Halleck's favor and seem to have agreed that they would each resubmit the proposed move to headquarters, this time in writing. Grant actually wrote twice. On January 28 his message read, "With permission, I will take Fort Henry on the Tennessee, and establish and hold a large camp there."[31] Grant's second letter, dated January 29, said, "I would respectfully suggest the propriety of subduing Fort Henry.... From Fort Henry it will be easy to operate either on the Cumberland, only 12 miles distant, Memphis, or Columbus. It will, besides, have a moral effect upon our troops to advance them toward the rebel States. The advantages of this move are as perceptible to the general commanding as to myself, therefore further statements are unnecessary."[32]

Another reason for Halleck's eventual decision is suggested by Shelby Foote. He says that Halleck overcame his ennui regarding the proposal to attack Fort Henry because of General George H. Thomas' victory over the Confederates at Mill Springs, Kentucky, on January 19. Thomas was one of General Don Carlos Buell's subordinates and Mill Springs was in his Department of the Ohio. Foote says that Halleck "saw that he must accomplish something to counterbalance the success his rival [Buell] had scored at the opposite end of the line" or risk losing overall command of the West to him.[33]

A third, and perhaps the most important, reason for Halleck's agreeing to the Smith-Grant-Foote suggestion was the startling news that Confederate general P.G.T. Beauregard was coming west with fifteen regiments. If a campaign were to commence with any hope of success, it would have to be before the ambitious Creole, one of the Confederacy's earliest heroes, came with such a massive infusion of fresh troops. Halleck himself said that this was the reason he decided to authorize the attack: "I had no idea of commencing this movement before the 15th or the 20th instant till I received General McClellan's telegram about the reinforcement sent to Kentucky or Tennessee with Beauregard. Although not ready, I deemed it important to move instantly."[34] Halleck responded to Grant's entreaties on January 30, 1862. He said, "Make your preparations to take and hold Fort Henry. I will send you written instructions by mail."[35]

10

The Attack on Fort Henry and Fort Heiman
(February 1862)

On the last day of January 1862, Lieutenant Colonel Jeremy F. Gilmer returned to examine Fort Henry on behalf of General Albert Sidney Johnston. Gilmer saw impressive changes since his earlier visit in November. He said, "By the exertions of the commanding general [Tilghman], aided by Lieut. Joseph Dixon, the main fort (a strong fixed work of fine bastion front) had been put in a good condition for defense, and seventeen guns mounted on substantial platforms, twelve of which were so placed as to bear well on the river." The gunners were being intensely trained by a very good man, Lieutenant Colonel Milton Andrew Haynes, who had written *The Confederate Artillerist: Instructions in Artillery, Horse, and Foot*. General Leonidas Polk had sent Haynes from Columbus.[1]

Gilmer continued: "In addition to placing the main work in good defensive order I found that extensive lines of infantry cover had been thrown up by the troops forming the garrison, with a view to hold commanding ground that would be dangerous to the fort if possessed by the enemy. These lines and the main work were on the right hand of the river and arranged with good defensive relations, making the place capable of offering a strong resistance against a land attack coming from the eastward." These lines, which defended the fort from the east, consisted specifically of a long line of rifle pits and an abatis both thick and wide.[2]

It was Gilmer who had insisted on fortifying the hills on the Kentucky side of the river. Lieutenant Dixon had made the survey and drawn the plans, and it was expected that five hundred slaves would be sent as a work gang. But Gilmer said, "By some unforeseen cause the negroes were not sent until after the 1st of January last. Much valuable time was thus lost but ... General Tilghman and his engineers pressed these defenses so rapidly, night and day, that when I reached the fort (January 31 last) they were far advanced, requiring only a few days' additional labor to put them in a state of defense." There were about 1000 men in the Fort Heiman garrison, commanded by Colonel Adolphus Heiman, plus a section of field artillery. Gilmer said that the "lines of infantry cover [at Fort Heiman] which had been thrown up were capable of making a strong resistance even without the desired artillery, should the attack be made on that (the left) bank of the river." Gilmer said "without the desired artillery." It worried him deeply that no heavy guns had been delivered to fully arm Fort Heiman, especially since there had been increasing signs of an impending attack: the gunboats had come up and fired their guns on January 17, 19, 21, and 22, and again on this very January 31.[3]

To bolster his defenses, General Tilghman had ordered torpedoes to be planted in the

General Lloyd Tilghman (Wikicommons).

river. These five-foot-long cylinders were anchored to the river bottom and floated invisibly just below the water surface. They "featured a hinged, iron arm to which were attached two sharp prongs designed to catch in the wooden bottom of a boat and activate a firing mechanism that would detonate seventy pounds of powder—enough to sink a gunboat."[4] It should also be said that Fort Henry was not isolated; it was connected to Fort Donelson and Cumberland City by a telegraph line, which allowed Tilghman to remain "in close relations with Bowling Green and Columbus."[5]

General Tilghman was an engineer by training. He was a numbers man, a detail man, and he found satisfaction in perfecting his defenses against the Yankees. There was no doubt that the Federals were coming. Their activities on the Tennessee River (even before the demonstration) were only the preliminaries. They repeatedly came up and fired and faded away again, but Tilghman was not deterred from his duties. On January 17, while receiving long-range fire from Federal gunboats, he reported, "I have not returned the fire, but proceed with my preparations. Men very cool." And on January 19, he said, "I have possession of the [Kentucky] hill and am fortifying hard. Can make it strong if time is allowed.... Have moved 600 men and three pieces field artillery from Donelson." He was calm and he kept his men calm during the demonstration, as well; he held his fire and only returned one artillery round to let the invaders know that he could.[6]

The Federal probes were a loud but harmless annoyance. They presaged something more serious, though. Confederate commanders at the sister forts on the Tennessee River knew it would only be a matter of days before the Yankees returned, and this time they would come to fight.

Lieutenant S. Ledyard Phelps returned from his January 31 scout up the Tennessee with some important intelligence. He told his superiors, "There is evidently a large force at Fort Henry, and the report everywhere is that an attack is anticipated by the rebels and that they are prepared to defend the post at all hazards."[7] The Federals at Cairo headquarters did not care if the Rebels expected them or not. They were overjoyed at Halleck's permission for them to make the attack. Catton says, "Staff officers stopped work at their desks.... [Captain John A.] Rawlins kicked over a couple of chairs and pounded the walls with his fists. Other officers threw their hats in the air and kicked them as they came down." The calmest man at headquarters seems to have been Grant. He described no such bedlam in his memoirs, but he was undoubtedly pleased that his idea (and Smith's and Foote's) had finally been approved. The campaign accorded perfectly with his simple philosophy of war as he explained it later to Dr. Brinton: "Find out where your enemy is, get at him as soon as you can, and strike him as hard as you can, and keep moving on."[8]

The same day that he received the terse approval of his plan, Grant was sent a detailed set of instructions from Halleck. The department commander told Grant to convoy by steamer rather than travel the miserable roads, to take supplies, to leave some gunboats behind to protect Cairo, and also enough men to defend Paducah, Fort Holt, etc. Flag Officer Foote would command the gunboats on the campaign. Halleck promised Grant eight infantry regiments and three companies of artillery from St. Louis before his departure, along with a supply of telegraph wire and a group of telegraphers so that he could string lines from Fort Henry to Paducah. Halleck was a commander who insisted on frequent communications. He warned Grant to completely invest the fort so as to prevent any escape and ordered him to send some cavalry to break the railroad between Paris and Dover. Finally, he urged him to move before P.G.T. Beauregard showed with his fifteen regiments from Virginia. Grant would command an army of 17,000 men divided into the 1st Division under McClernand and the 2nd Division under Smith. Lieutenant Colonel James B. McPherson would accompany as chief engineer, but there would be no role for E.A. Paine, who was to be left behind as the head of the Cairo garrison.

While Grant made his preparations, Flag Officer Foote attended to his own. He inspected his vessels and grouped them into two divisions. For their first battle, the ironclads *Carondelet, St. Louis, Essex,* and *Cincinnati* would be the 1st Division, and the timberclads *Conestoga, Tyler,* and *Lexington* would make up the 2nd Division. The flotilla boats were all to rendezvous at Paducah on February 2. Foote gave a little speech as he toured the gunboats, telling his short-handed crews (he had only about six hundred of the sixteen hundred he needed) "to be brave and courageous and above all to place their faith in Divine Providence." To the chiefs of the gun crews, he had a little more to say. The Connecticut-born Foote showed his parsimonious New England nature when he warned James Laning of the *Essex* "to make every shot count and ... to be sure you do not throw any ammunition away. Every charge you fire from one of these guns cost the government about eight dollars. If your shots fall short you encourage the enemy. If they reach home you demoralize him, and get the worth of your money."[9]

Lieutenant S. Ledyard Phelps had thought earlier that the mortar barges might be useful, if they were properly manned, but Foote decided not to use them. He wrote to Halleck from Cairo that "the difficulty of towing boats of their construction against the strong current, and for other reasons [including that they rode too low in the water when armed], I do not consider it feasible to attempt to take the mortar boats up these rivers."[10] Halleck had doubts that even the gunboats would perform. He wrote to General Don Carlos Buell on February 2: "It remains to be determined whether the gunboats are worth half the money spent on them." Halleck's skepticism may have been genuine; these were still the early days of amphibious operations. More likely, there was a little intra-service rivalry at work in Halleck's mind.[11]

By February 2, the plan was coming together. Grant issued General Orders No. 7 to the gathering forces:

> On the expedition now about starting from Smithland, Paducah, Cairo, Bird's Point, and Fort Holt the following orders will be observed:
>
> 1. No firing, except when ordered by proper authority, will be allowed.
> 2. Plundering and disturbing private property is positively prohibited.
> 3. Company officers will see that their men are kept within camp, except when on duty.
> 4. Rolls will be called evening and morning and every man accounted for, and absentees reported to regimental commanders.
> 5. Company commanders will have special care that rations and ammunition are not wasted or destroyed by carelessness.

6. Troops will take with them three days' rations and forage, all camp and garrison equipage, and not to exceed four teams to each regiment.

7. Regimental commanders will be held strictly accountable for the acts of their regiments, and will in turn hold company commanders accountable for the conduct of their companies.[12]

By the evening of February 3, the gunboats, the transports, McClernand's men from the Cairo area, and Smith's from the Paducah and Smithland area, had all rendezvoused at Paducah. McClernand, with Grant accompanying, departed first with his division, while Smith waited with his 2nd Division to follow in the second convoy. There was a mishap at the start. It was sleeting, and that may be why Sergeant Matthew Wallace, Co. E, 4th Illinois Cavalry (and the brother of Colonel W.H.L. Wallace), fell off the transport *D.A. January* and drowned.

The transports deposited McClernand's division at Itra's Landing, on the east bank of the Tennessee about eight miles below Fort Henry. When the troops were off, McClernand ordered an immediate reconnaissance in the direction of the Rebel works. The Federal cavalrymen had an exchange with the Confederate pickets—and with a cantankerous Secesh woman who screeched at them from her cabin door, "You think you're goin' to take that Fort, but you'll get fooled! There's a right smart heap of men thar!"[13]

While the cavalrymen scouted around on the east bank, Grant went forward on a scout of his own aboard the *Essex*. The gunboat did not try to approach quietly; it shelled both sides of the Tennessee River as it struggled upstream and received a shot in return. The Confederate shell tore "through the pantry and officers' quarters and visited the steerage." A bit to one side and the Federals might have lost their commander before the battle even began. Satisfied after a while at what he had seen, Grant asked to be taken back downstream to McClernand at Itra's Landing. The soldiers were ordered back onto the transports and were delivered another three miles or so closer to Fort Henry. They clambered off again at Bailey's Ferry and set up camp, which McClernand christened with the brown-nosey name of Camp Halleck. This done, Grant returned to Paducah to accompany General Smith's division forward. The leading elements of the 2nd Division arrived before sundown the next day, February 5, and the balance came up before midnight. Smith ordered them to set up camp at Pine Bluff, on the west bank of the Tennessee opposite McClernand.[14]

The plan for February 6, the day of battle, was for Smith to move forward from Pine Bluff and attack Fort Heiman with his 1st and 2nd brigades. Simultaneously, Engineer James B. McPherson would lead McClernand's division, augmented with a borrowed brigade (Smith's 3rd) on a great looping march from Camp Halleck to the rear of Fort Henry. Once there, the job was to

10. The Attack on Fort Henry and Fort Heiman

The ironclad U.S.S. *Essex* (Library of Congress).

throw a roadblock across the Confederate escape route and also to prevent reinforcements from coming from Fort Donelson. Each division would step off about 11:00 A.M., and each man would carry cooked rations in his haversack and forty rounds in his cartridge box. At the same time, Flag Officer Foote would steam forward with his gunboats, ironclads in front and timberclads behind. They would engage the fort's shore batteries. If it happened that McClernand needed support in his sector, Smith would stand ready to come over on transports after the fall of Fort Heiman.

That was the plan. The first battle of the young soldiers' and sailors' lives was nigh, and many of those who had been so eager for the adventure of war must have lain awake until late in the night wondering how they would behave when men were shooting at them, and trying to remember why it was, exactly, that they had signed up in the first place.

When the first Federals began landing, General Lloyd Tilghman was not at Fort Henry. He and Lieutenant Colonel Gilmer had gone to Fort Donelson on February 3 to work on the defenses there. When they heard artillery fire coming from the direction of the Tennessee River on February 5 (apparently the guns of the *Essex*), they were alarmed, and then came a rider from Colonel

Heiman, whom Tilghman had left in charge, confirming that Federal gunboats were on the Tennessee and that enemy troops were landing. Tilghman made ready to return to Fort Henry at once and persuaded Colonel Gilmer to accompany him.

They arrived about midnight with their cavalry escort and went into conference with Colonel Heiman. Heiman proposed evacuating Fort Heiman on the Kentucky side, and would have done so earlier except that Tilghman had ordered him to hold it, and at the start of the crisis had not been on hand to rescind the order. Now he did order the evacuation, somewhat sadly, considering the tactical advantages of the palisade, but certain in the belief that the mushy roads would prevent the Federals from dragging cannon there to threaten Fort Henry. At dawn on February 6, the Fort Heiman garrison was brought across the river. To offer the enemy resistance when they marched up the Kentucky bank, Tilghman left at Fort Heiman a cobbled-together force consisting of the 27th Alabama Infantry, 15th Arkansas, two companies of Alabama cavalry, an unorganized company of forty Kentucky cavalrymen, and a light artillery battery.

The situation at Fort Henry was bad. There had been recent heavy rains and the Tennessee was swelling out of its banks. Heiman had kept fatigue parties busy trying "to keep the water from the rapidly rising river out of the fort. Already the lower magazine had been flooded to a depth of two feet. The ammunition was moved and stored in a temporary magazine." Tilghman, Gilmer, and Heiman spent the day of February 5 making plans and Tilghman guided an artillery crew in gunnery practice. There was more heavy rain that night and the river rose to twenty-five feet.[15]

Februrary 6 dawned unusually mild for a late winter day and there was a nice breeze. The wind was welcome, for everyone knew that it would blow the smoke of battle away. The overnight rain had pushed the water level in the fort to waist deep. Early in the morning, Lieutenant Milton A. Haynes, the artillery instructor, came over from Fort Donelson. He could discover no way to get into Fort Henry by foot or horseback, so he found a small boat and rowed in. This convinced him "that the fort was untenable and ought to be forthwith abandoned." Looking at the dirty lake contained inside the bastion, Haynes' argument was difficult to refute.[16]

That did not mean, however, that no defense would be mounted. While Tilghman did decide to send Colonel Heiman and the bulk of the garrison west to the outerworks to await developments, he ordered Captain Jesse Taylor and fifty men of the 1st Tennessee Heavy Artillery to remain behind as the sole defenders of Fort Henry. Tilghman asked Taylor to hold the Yankees back for one hour. Then he went out with Heiman and the rest of the troops. Tilghman would come back to share the fate of the artillerymen, but the responsi-

10. The Attack on Fort Henry and Fort Heiman

bility was all on Captain Taylor's shoulders when Federal gunboats appeared at the head of Panther Island a bit after noon.

The gunboats had left Bailey's Ferry about 11:00 A.M. to begin their slow cruise upstream. Flag Officer Foote saw no reason to hurry. Though Smith's infantry was on the move on the Kentucky bank and McClernand had begun his wide loop to the east, Foote "doubted the infantry's ability to keep on schedule, marching on the heavy roads." He had tried to make Grant see the good sense in letting the infantry step off before his gunboats began their approach, but Grant refused. So Foote now ordered his fleet to ease forward slowly in order to give the foot soldiers more time to get into position.[17]

The boats moved in relative safety due to the good work already performed by the timberclads. On February 5, there had been an early morning fog, and Commander Walke saw some white objects floating on the river that he thought resembled polar bears. Of course, he knew they were not. They were underwater mines ("torpedoes," in the parlance of the day) that had been torn loose from their moorings by the heavy current and the debris in the flooded Tennessee River. It was safer for the Federals for the mines to be floating on the surface than lurking under it, but they were still a threat and they had to be removed. This was the job of the timberclads *Tyler* and *Conestoga*. Their crews spent the day grappling perhaps as many as twenty of them out of the river, clearing the way for the ironclads to proceed next morning in the vanguard of the attacking brown water fleet.

Andrew Hull Foote was fifty-five years old. He had been in the U.S. Navy for forty years and had held every kind of assignment from shore duty as director of the Navy Asylum (a combination of pension home for sailors and a school for midshipmen), to patrolling the Atlantic chasing slave traders. He was considered "one of the most level-headed men in the Navy ... practical and as free as possible from red tape foolishness." He had fought pirates off the coast of Mexico and the Chinese in Canton during the Second Opium War, but in all of his experience he had never fought a battle like the one that was about to commence in the Tennessee River. He commanded a fleet of a new style of vessel and was engaged in a new type of operation; this was the time to dispel the doubts of General Halleck and all other critics of the Brown Water Navy.[18]

The gunboats squeezed through the narrow chute between Panther Island and the riverbank and then stopped long enough to array themselves for the battle. The four ironclads, *Essex*, *Cincinnati*, *Carondelet*, and *St. Louis* (the 1st Division), were lined up abreast. The river was so narrow that the *Carondelet* and the *St. Louis* were "interlocked and remained so during the fight."[19] The timberclads, *Tyler*, *Conestoga*, and *Lexington* (the 2nd Division), steamed behind. Properly aligned for battle, the fleet crept forward. Commander Henry Walke remembered, "As we slowly passed up this narrow stream, not a sound could be heard nor a moving object seen in the dense woods which overhung the dark and swollen river. The gun-crews of the *Carondelet* stood silent at their posts, impressed with the serious and important character of the task before them."[20]

At a distance of 1700 yards, the flagship *Cincinnati* fired three rounds to test the range. They fell short. The other boats observed the test and their guns' elevation was adjusted. The *Essex* was invited to fire next. Her test round hit Fort Henry's parapet and "exploded handsomely."[21] The bow guns of the other vessels immediately opened up and the attack was on. The gun crews settled into their well-practiced routine. Coombe says,

> One man would drop a powder bag into the muzzle, and the second would ram it home with a long rammer equipped with a strip of rawhide with which to mark the depth of the rammer thrust. The first muzzle man would drop a round shot into the bore, and the second would ram it home. The chief gunner would pierce the bag through a hole in the top of the breech, using a vent pick, and insert a primer. The gun would be run out of the port, by a system of ropes and pulleys. The gunner would hook a lanyard to a flintlock-type hammer over the vent. On command to fire, he would yank the lanyard and the hammer would fall and strike the primer.[22]

There was a bright flash and an earth-shattering boom. The piece would recoil with a mighty lurch and the casemate would fill with clouds of gun smoke. The piece was drawn in, quickly sponged out, and the process would begin again. The effect was like a contained cataclysm, deafening, blinding, a concussive experience that was multiplied infinitely when enemy rounds began crashing against the iron plating outside.

The Rebel gunners were very good. Captain Taylor assigned a specific Yankee boat to each of his gun crews, and when the booming gunboats came within one mile, the batteries opened fire, and "as pretty and as simultaneous as a 'broadside' was delivered as I ever saw flash from the sides of a frigate." After a good beginning, the Rebels only got better. In the minutes that followed the opening shots, Captain Taylor said, the action "became general" and "was apparently inclined in favor of the fort."[23] Commander Walke had to agree that the Confederates were a worthy enemy. He wrote, "From the number of times the gun-boats were struck, it would appear that the Confederate artillery practice, at first, at least, was as good, if not better than ours." The *Carondelet* was hit thirty times and the *Cincinnati* was hit thirty-two times. Seven Rebel shells struck the *St. Louis*, and the *Essex* was hit in her boilers and had to drop downstream.[24]

The gunboats continued moving forward, however, and the battle began to turn. At six hundred yards, the ironclads fired shells with fuzes cut for only five seconds. The timberclads were dropping long-range shells into Fort Henry from their position a half-mile behind and close to the Kentucky bank of the river. Foote said that they did "good execution there during the action."[25] The fire of the gunboats was catastrophic. Captain Taylor said that the "Federal rifle shot and shell penetrated the earth-works as readily as a ball from a Navy Colt would pierce a pine board." Things began to go wrong. The Confederates' 42-pounder rifle was not properly swabbed, discharged prematurely, and killed or wounded all the men of its crew. Then, the best piece in the fort, the 10-inch Columbiad, was spiked by her own gunners when the vent pick broke off in the breech, plugging the hole. A blacksmith hurried forward and "labored with great coolness for a long time exposed to the warmest fire of the enemy." The unnamed blacksmith's bravery was unrewarded; he could not remove the plug from the vent and the gun was out of action.[26]

Bad luck continued for the Confederates. Two of the fort's 32-pounders were directly hit and "the flying fragments of the shattered guns and bursted shells disabled every man at the two guns." The men were growing tired and discouraged. The remaining 32-pounders seemed ineffective against the iron-armored boats of the enemy, and their crews quit loading and firing. Lieutenant Colonel Gilmer remembered that Tilghman, who had returned and was in the fort through the thick of the fight, "did everything that it was possible to do to encourage and urge his men to further efforts. He assisted to serve one of the pieces himself for at least fifteen minutes; but his men were exhausted, had lost all hope, and there were no others to replace them at the guns."[27]

Only two Confederate pieces were still firing. The ironclads had closed to within two hundred yards of the parapets, pumping one salvo after another into the fort. They were firing "in perfect security and with the coolness and precision of target practice, sweeping the entire fort." General Tilghman sent word out to Colonel Heiman to strike out for Fort Donelson, convened a quick council of war with Gilmer and Taylor, and in a moment ordered a white flag to be raised. A bit more of bad luck remained on this curséd day. The flag staff had been so badly damaged and the halyards so fouled that the Confederate colors could not be lowered. Now that the Confederates wanted to surrender, they could not. Meanwhile, the Union shells were still landing. Captain Taylor and an orderly sergeant named Jones climbed the staff, removed the flag under which they had fought and attached the white flag under which they would become prisoners of war. Taylor took a moment to appreciate the view from atop the staff, perhaps the last long look he would have as a free man for some time to come. He had nothing to be ashamed of. Tilghman had asked him to resist for only one hour, and the captain had given him two.[28]

Tilghman sent two messengers out in a small boat to the flagship *Cincinnati* to request a parley. In response, Foote "dispatched Commander Stembel [of the *Cincinnati*] and Lieutenant Commander Phelps [the *Conestoga*], with orders to hoist the American flag where the secessionist ensign had been flying, and to inform General Tilghman that I would see him on board the flag-ship."[29]

On the Kentucky bank, General Smith's men had been listening to the thunder of artillery and sometimes felt that they themselves were in the fight when an overshoot would crash among the surrounding trees. The men were cold and wet. They had waded across an arm of the Tennessee where the water came up to their armpits. One remembered, "We put the bayonets on our guns, hung the cartridge boxes from the bayonets and held our guns above our heads to keep the powder dry."[30] Nearing Fort Heiman, they heard the firing from the river stop. A moment later, a bluecoat cavalryman came riding from the direction of the fort and reported to General Smith that it was empty. Lew Wallace heard the exchange:

"How do you know?" asked Smith.

"I have been in," said the rider.

"The devil!" said Smith. He turned to Brigadier General Wallace and said, "It's just as well. Move in and take possession."

This Wallace did.[31]

The Alabamians and Kentuckians who had been posted to resist the Yankees if they approached had fled Fort Heiman so hurriedly that they had not even finished their breakfast. The 1st Illinois artilleryman Private Charles Kimbell wrote, "We found several of their camp fires burning and hot corn bread and pea coffee cooking on some of them. Their tents had not been disturbed, and as the boys were tired and hungry, the find was a great treat, and very acceptable and refreshing to them." The Confederates had left a full mailbag behind. The commanding officer had left behind his camp desk and a trove of papers, as well as his own breakfast of pork and cornbread. Smith and Wallace appointed themselves the man's proxies and ate his breakfast for him.[32]

Fort Heiman, located on the best defensive ground in the whole area, had fallen to the Federals without a single shot being fired.

On the Tennessee bank, McClernand's division struggled forward. A *Cincinnati Gazette* reporter who was on the march said, "Our route was along a rough cut path which twisted and turned about among the high wooded hills in a most perplexing manner." The bottoms were like "soft porridge," and at places the water was belt deep. The artillery had to be muscled through such low spots, a slow and exhausting process, followed by a steep, slick climb to the next ridgetop. Thigh muscles must have trembled under the unending and unaccustomed strain.[33]

At 2:00 P.M. the cannon fire from the river ceased. "We looked in each other's faces," said the Cincinnati correspondent, "and wonderingly asked, what does it mean? Is it possible that our gun-boats have been beaten back?" McClernand's men were practically lost in the woods, cold, muddy, exhausted, and entirely uninformed about the situation. If they went forward, they might march straight into a disaster. If they went back, McClernand would have failed to obey his orders, though unopposed, and the consequences would not be pleasant. There was really no good choice; McClernand ordered the column to press on.[34]

After a while, the 1st Division emerged onto the crest of a high ridge, and there before them were the Confederate fortifications. "An earthen breastwork defended by an immense, long rifle-pit stretched away on either side, until it was lost to sight in the thick woods. Outside of this the timber had been filled in a belt of several rods in width, forming a barrier very difficult for footmen and impossible for cavalry. This breastwork inclosed fully a square mile." There was a second barricaded line within, and a third, but the most interesting thing about the elaborate works was that they were completely empty. Abandoned. The Yankees marched through them until they could see Fort Henry proper. Above it flew the American flag.[35]

Benjamin Cooling writes, "Once the Confederate flag had been lowered pandemonium broke out in the flotilla. Even the old sailor [Foote] lost control of the men aboard his flagship as a 'cheer ran up from this ship, a yell in fact and I had to run among the men and knock them on the head to restore order.'" He told the hollering Surgeon John Lidlow "he ought to be ashamed of himself."[36]

The sailors had reason to celebrate. They had taken the fort with no help at all from the army. Moreover, though their gunboats had been battered and the *Essex* disabled by that shot through her boilers, the number of casualties had been minimal, at only thirty-nine killed or wounded. The men loved the day Fort Henry fell, and loved to remember it. In 1886, W.H.C. Michael told the Nebraska Chapter of the Military Order of the Loyal Legion of the United States that the Battle of Fort Henry "was a handsome fight.... The results were very encouraging to the officers and men of the flotilla, and the experience derived went a long way toward preparing them for the succession of fights in which they were soon to take part."[37]

While Phelps and Stembel were accepting the surrender of Fort Henry from Captain Taylor, General Tilghman was making his way to meet with Foote on the *Cincinnati*. There are two versions of what happened at their interview. Commander Walke recounted that Tilghman said to Foote, "I am glad to surrender to so gallant an officer." Foote replied, "You do perfectly right, sir, in surrendering, but you should have blown my boat out of the water before I should have surrendered to you."[38]

Foote biographer J.M. Hoppin says Foote "rarely, if ever, forgot that he was a gentleman, and especially with those who the fate of war had made prisoners." Keeping that in mind, and also remembering that Commander Walke wrote years rather than days after the event, one finds more verisimilitude in the account which Foote himself wrote of his exchange with Tilghman. In it, the Confederate general appeared before Foote highly agitated and saying, "'I am in despair; my reputation is gone forever.' I replied, 'General, there is no reason that you should feel thus. More than two-thirds of your battery is disabled, while I have lost less than one-third of mine. To continue the action would only involve a needless sacrifice of life, and, under the circumstances, you have done right in surrendering. Moreover, I shall always be ready to testify that you have defended your post like a brave man.' I then added, 'Come general, you have lost your dinner and the steward has just told me that mine is ready,' and taking him by the arm we walked together into the cabin. This is all that passed between us.'"[39]

Foote did praise the "determined gallantry" of the Confederate commander in his after-action report. But, whether he reassured Tilghman at their meeting or rubbed it in, the outcome was the same. The gunboats under his command had inflicted twenty-one casualties on the Rebels, killed, wounded, and missing; had taken seventy-eight prisoners in the fort and sixty patients in a hospital ship; and had captured quantities of supplies, twenty artillery pieces, and "tents capable of accommodating 15,000 men."[40]

An hour after the surrender, General Grant came up in his headquarters boat, the *New Uncle Sam*, to take possession of the fort. What he saw was a ruin. Dr. John H. Brinton visited Fort Henry shortly after Grant and said that "it was a dreadful sight. Great heavy columbiads were overthrown, some with their muzzles pointing in the air, their carriages were broken and stained with blood. Here and there, too, were masses of human flesh and hair adhering to the broken timbers. The interior of the fort was a mass of mud, the back water from the stream having flowed in from the rear."[41]

The Battle of Fort Henry was small by Civil War standards, but it brought big results. The first and most immediate result was that the gunboats had proven their worth. Also, combined with the Confederate defeat at Mill Spring on January 19, the fall of Fort Henry convinced department commander Albert Sidney Johnston that his defensive line in Southern Kentucky was untenable, and he began to fall back from Bowling Green toward Nashville. Troops under General Simon Bolivar Buckner were ordered from Russellville to reinforce Fort Donelson. In addition, the Tennessee River route was now open to the Deep South, that is, Northern Alabama and Mississippi. Finally, there was a psychological effect on the Confederacy. Fort Henry represented the first serious defeat that Dixie had suffered. The defensive shell was cracked, and suddenly the South did not seem so secure.

11

Between Two Battles
(February 1862)

Fort Henry had fallen in mid-afternoon, February 6, 1862. That left several hours of daylight, and there was still work to do. That same afternoon, General McClernand ordered a pursuit of Colonel Heiman's fleeing Confederates. They caught up with the rear guard of the grayback column, the 10th Tennessee Infantry, about three miles out, and skirmished with them. The Tennesseans were able to deliver a heavier fire than their pursuers expected, for they had picked up the guns of their retreating comrades who had tossed their rifles aside. Every man had several shots to fire before reloading. Nevertheless, McClernand's Federals made a spirited try. They killed two officers, and captured thirty-eight men before the Rebels lashed them back. The Federals returned to Fort Henry and the Confederates made it intact to Fort Donelson.

There was a more ambitious expedition that began that afternoon. Flag Officer Foote ordered Lieutenant S. Ledyard Phelps to take his own *Conestoga*, the *Tyler* (commanded by Lieutenant William Gwin), and the *Lexington* (Lieutenant James W. Shirk) on a cruise up the Tennessee River with the primary object of destroying the bridge on the Memphis & Ohio Railroad, twenty-five miles from Fort Henry. En route, the boats hoped to draw the Confederate gunboat *Dunbar* into a fight, but she could not be caught. She was thought to have escaped up a tributary. Phelps reported that the timberclad division came upon the railroad bridge after dark and destroyed the machinery for turning the bridge out of the way of river traffic. A party from the *Tyler* was landed "to destroy a portion of the railroad track and to secure such military stores as might be found," while the *Lexington* and *Conestoga* chased some Confederate transports they had spotted. Like the *Dunbar*, they preferred to run rather than engage. Their crews finally abandoned three of them and put them to the torch, their cargoes of military stores still in their hulls. One was carrying ammunition. When the fire reached the gunpowder, the resulting explosion broke the skylights on the Federal boats and sprang the locks on doors and blew them open, even at a distance of one thousand feet. Phelps wrote, "The whole river for half a mile around about was completely beaten up by the falling fragments and the shower of shot, grape, balls, etc. The house of a reported Union man was blown to pieces, and it is suspected there was a design in landing the boats in front of the doomed house."[1]

The next day, February 7, the three timberclads proceeded upstream to Cerro Gordo Landing, Tennessee, and found the docked Rebel steamer *Eastport* being refitted as a gunboat. Rebel snipers began to pepper the Northern boats, which dispersed them with some shell fire. A search of the *Eastport* turned up 25,000 feet of lumber. The *Tyler* was left behind to guard the *Eastport* and the lumber and other naval supplies, while the faster *Conestoga* and *Lexington* continued against the current to Florence, Alabama, 250 miles from the mouth of the river at Paducah. There, too, the Rebels burned some steamers before running off. A Union landing party rescued some cargo from the burning boats. What could not be loaded on board the two timberclads was destroyed.

The *New York Times* reported that all through Tennessee and Alabama, the gunboats were "received with astonishing welcome by numerous Union families ... and at times along the river the old flag was looked upon as a redeemer, and hailed with shouts of joy," and that "the people of Florence are so delighted at finding the Stars and Stripes once more giving protection to them that they were prepared to give a grand ball to the officers of the gunboats, but they could not remain to accept their courtesies."[2]

Perhaps it was so. Lieutenant Phelps did not mention any plans for a dance at Florence, but he did substantially agree with the New York reporter's story. Phelps said, "We have met with the most gratifying proofs of loyalty everywhere across Tennessee, and in the portions of Mississippi and Alabama we visited most affecting instances greeted us almost hourly. Men, women, and children several times gathered in crowds of hundreds, shouted their welcome and hailed their national flag with an enthusiasm there was no mistaking. It was genuine and heartfelt." He said that men and women alike cried at the sight of the flag they still honored, though out of fear of reprisal the people tended to be more guarded in their feelings the deeper into the South they penetrated.[3]

Phelps admitted that there were also towns where the citizens ran off when the timberclads appeared. The people of Florence were somewhere in between. "A deputation of citizens of Florence waited upon me, first desiring that they might be made able to quiet the fears of their wives and daughters with assurances from me that they would not be molested; and, secondly, praying that I would not destroy their railroad bridge." Phelps informed the worried citizens that the men of his command were "neither ruffians nor savages." As far as the bridge was concerned, he could not discern that it had any military value; it would be spared.[4]

Returning downstream, the *Lexington* and the *Conestoga* paused at Cerro Gordo Landing to pick up the *Tyler*. Lieutenant Gwin's crew had grown by the twenty-five men he had enlisted and they had made a good start at loading the lumber. The other two gunboat crews helped finish the job, along with securing some hardware from the boatyard, while a detail went to destroy the nearby sawmill. Gwin had also learned of a Confederate camp at Savannah, Tennessee. Phelps decided to destroy it. Gwin led the landing party of 130 riflemen and a 12-pounder howitzer only to find the camp abandoned. The sailors took the arms and equipment, some clothing and a mailbag, and destroyed everything else. Back at Cerro Gordo, they collected the *Eastport* and two other vessels, which they took in tow, and steamed toward home. They lost one of the boats en route due to an unstoppable leak, but arrived at Fort Henry with the other two prizes and the rest of their plunder on February 10.

General Grant wanted some action, too. He had been in two battles, so far. He had lost the first, which he would not admit, and the navy had won the second, which he could not deny. He wanted and needed to make his mark and he began making plans to march on Fort Donelson immediately after the fall of Fort Henry. He boasted, "I shall take and destroy Fort Donelson on the 8th, and return to Fort Henry with the forces employed." Details were sent out to repair roads and rebuild bridges in the rugged spine of land between the two rivers, and patrols were sent out to scout towards Fort Donelson. But unless Grant wanted to make the attack without the gunboat flotilla, he was going to have to wait. The timberclads were up the Tennessee River until the 10th and the ironclads had been so battered by the battle on the 6th that Foote had taken three of them back to Cairo for repairs. Only the *Carondelet* had been left at Fort Henry, as for a guard. The self-imposed deadline of February 8 came and went. Time was passing and Grant was impatient.[5]

The men, too, were basically twiddling their thumbs. There were frequent foraging details. Corporal Henry I. Smith (Co. B, 7th Iowa Infantry) remembered that the men "had very little to eat, so that the troops had to resort to foraging from the surrounding country, the most of which consisted of sheep, cattle, and hogs, all of which were spring poor."[6] Some of the boys seem to have gotten carried away, for Grant had to scold them. In Field Orders No. 5, he cautioned his soldiers that pilfering would not be tolerated and warned brigade commanders that they would be held accountable. Pilfering "has been done but to a very limited extent in this command so far, but too much for our credit has already occurred to be allowed to pass without admonition."[7]

Then there was the unauthorized discharging of firearms in camp. Sergeant William R. Akers, one of Smith's comrades in the 7th Iowa, remembered that the burden of driftwood and other objects floating in the flooded Tennessee River was irresistibly tempting, and the boys decided to use it for target practice one day while Grant was off on one of his scouts to the east. They were all firing at once and it sounded like "a regular fusillade." Grant came galloping up ahead of his staff to see that the racket was nothing more than a bunch of boys wasting ammunition. Still on horseback, he charged among them, and grabbed John Akers, the last boy who fired, "by the nape of the neck or the top of the head ... and commanded him to fork over the ... still smoking revolver." This the boy started to do, when the rightful owner of the pistol reached up and grabbed it just as the general took hold. The two grappled over it, until the general's horse became frightened and began whirling around. The gun's owner was flung down on the ground, leaving the pistol in the general's hand. Grant reared back and hurled it into in the river. The boy "proceeded to lavish upon the general some of his choicest bouquets of 'sass,' and was arrested." After the general rode away, the boys fished the revolver out. Young John Akers was released within the hour, and a comic but unbecoming episode was over.[8]

Grant was frustrated that all he could do was wait until Flag Officer Foote came back with the ironclads, and it showed.

Private George W. Driggs of Co. E, 8th Wisconsin Infantry, saw the battered ironclads arrive in Cairo and said that they "look rather worse for hard usage." Rough-looking though they were, they came in with style. The flagship *Cincinnati* was flying a captured Confederate flag beneath the Stars and Stripes. The *Cincinnati* had the Federal dead and wounded on board, as well as a number of prisoners. At the dock, the ironclads welcomed visitors aboard and displayed not only the secessionist flag but also some of the cannonballs that had blown through the casemates and come to rest inside.[9]

The Rebel prisoners did not remain in Cairo long. They were sent to Paducah under a guard from the 12th Iowa. At Paducah, they were placed in the custody of Colonel Davis Stewart, which did not mean that they were put into cells. Indeed, by the generosity of the victors the Confederate officers were allowed to move freely within the city limits. Grant had wired Halleck: "Can General Tilghman and other officers be placed on parole and confined to the limits of Paducah?" Halleck replied the same day: "They can be released as proposed."[10]

The Federals seem never to have considered that their arrangement might lead to controversy. Paducah was where General Tilghman made his home, and the reception that he and his fellow officers received—and their own unbowed behavior—offended the Unionists. On February 10, Grant wrote that he had "received such reports of their conduct as to make me believe it was not prudent to leave them within our lines so near the enemy. Paducah being the home of General Tilghman makes it particularly objectionable."[11] They were ordered back to Cairo. General E.A. Paine, and a guard of four hundred men of the 8th Wisconsin Infantry, went up to Paducah on the *Hannibal* and took the Rebels back into custody, and returned to Cairo on the 15th. At Cairo, the officers were given the choice of going to Cincinnati on parole or, refusing that, of going with the enlisted men to the prison camp at Alton, Illinois. Tilghman had chosen to share the fate of his artillerymen on February 6 at Fort Henry, and he decided to share it now. It would be Alton. Private Driggs said, "I had the pleasure of getting a 'squint' at the prisoners as they were going aboard the train [to Alton]. Gen. Tilghman is a smart, active man of medium height, with a keen eye; he wears a grey suit and a drab felt hat rolled up on one side, attached with three stars. The other officers were uniformed in grey, on which was an extensive amount of fancy trimming. They are all intelligent looking men, and seem to appear easy and indifferent about matters as you please. Their private soldiers were rough looking men, without uniforms, with ragged clothes, sheepish looking and silly in conversation."[12]

The brief exchange of messages between Grant and Halleck regarding the Confederate prisoners was one of the few contacts they had in the period immediately after the fall of Fort Henry. Grant did not know that while he waited in the mud at Fort Henry and the ironclads underwent their repairs at Cairo, Halleck in St. Louis was trying very hard to replace him. The reason for Halleck's dislike of Grant is something of a mystery, even 150 years later. Some suggest that it was a simple difference in styles. Halleck, McClellan, Buell, and other life-long professionals had a kind of majestic deliberation about them; Grant moved too quickly. He seemed impetuous. Some have suggested that Halleck, who was known to be a man given to envy, saw in Grant a rising star whose fame would soon outshine his own. It may be nothing more than that he simply did not like his scruffy junior. Grant has come down through history as an "aw, shucks" sort of fellow whose common touch was admired by all, but this is too shallow a view. Grant was a more complicated man than that; he had his ambitions, and he could have a temper. He sometimes became awfully proud of himself, he was not always perfectly forthright (especially in his reports he was not above telling falsehoods to show himself and his friends in a more heroic light, such as his accounts of the Battle of Columbus-Belmont) and he would exceed his orders if given half a chance. He appeared to be something of a hypocrite in that he was squeamish at the sight of blood; even rare beef on his plate made his stomach quiver and he could not stand to see a horse mistreated. Yet he was perfectly willing to throw men by the thousands against Confederate barricades to be slaughtered. There were those who did not like Grant, and Halleck, for whichever reason or reasons, was one of them.

The difference between Halleck and the others who disliked Grant was that Halleck was in a position to do something about it. He tried to persuade General Don Carlos Buell to come west and lead the advance on Fort Donelson, and he suggested that General William Tecumseh Sherman would be acceptable. But the man he really wanted for command was Brigadier General Ethan Allen Hitchcock, a sixty-four-year-old native of Vermont and an 1817 graduate of West Point. On February 8, Halleck wrote to secretary of war Edwin M. Stanton: "If Brig. Gen. E.A. Hitchcock could be made major-general of volunteers and assigned to this department it would satisfy all.... If it can be done there should be no delay as an experienced officer is wanted immediately on the Tennessee line."[13] Stanton replied the same day, "Your dispatch is received. I concur in your suggestion, and will urge its adoption by the President."[14]

Halleck took this as a sign that his plan would go through in its entirety. The next morning, he wired Brigadier General Sherman at Benton Barracks: "Hitchcock will be appointed tomorrow morning, and I am directed to assign officers accordingly. Make your preparations to take a column or division on the Tennessee or Cumberland." Halleck had jumped the gun. Hitchcock was promoted to major general, but he ultimately declined to take command of forces on the Tennessee, pleading poor health. The unsuspecting Grant would lead the attack on Fort Donelson.[15]

The question was: when? As of February 10, Foote's ironclads still were not ready to leave the Cairo boatyard. The damages from February 6 were serious, except in the case of the *St. Louis*, which had been hit only seven times. The *Essex* had been hit with that devastating shot that exploded her middle boiler, and the flagship *Cincinnati* had been hit thirty-two times. Walke remembered, "Her chimneys, after-cabin, and boats were completely riddled. Two of her guns were disabled." The extensive repairs just took time, which Grant was not willing to give.[16]

Halleck was methodically sending regiments to Paducah to be shuffled forward to Grant. The riverfront must have been a wasps' nest of activity during the second week in February. The 76th, and 78th Ohio had come to Paducah, closely followed by the 20th and the 56th and they were not all; more regiments were coming all the time for service with Grant. What they did not know was that Grant was done with waiting. On February 10, 1862, he convened a council of war aboard his new headquarters boat, the *Tigress*. The question Grant posed to the assembled officers was: should the army march on Fort Donelson or wait for the reinforcements. General C.F. Smith urged an immediate march. Next was General McClernand, who was becoming more insufferable all the time. On this occasion, too, he lived down to expectations. Lew Wallace said, "General McClernand ... drew out a paper and read it. He, too, was in favor of going at once. It had been better for him, probably, had he rested with a word to that effect; as it was, he entered into details of performance.... The proceeding smacked of a political caucus, and I thought both Grant and Smith grew restive before the paper was finished." As soon as McClernand finished, Grant quickly polled the junior officers present. All said "go," and Grant announced that the army would march. The officers were dismissed to ready their commands.[17]

Surprisingly, Grant got plenty of encouragement from St. Louis. Halleck wired on February 11: "Push forward the Cumberland expedition with all possible dispatch." Now that he was committed to Grant's plan, Halleck expected Foote to follow suit. The general ordered the flag officer to advance on Fort Donelson from Cairo. Foote agreed, with a definite lack of enthusiasm. As was his custom, he turned to secretary of the navy Welles with his complaints and said, "I leave again tonight with the *Louisville*, the *Pittsburg*, and *St. Louis* for the Cumberland River, to cooperate with the army in the attack on Fort Donelson. I go reluctantly, as we are very short of men.... I shall do all in my power to render the gunboats effective in the fight, although they are not properly manned, but I must go, as General Halleck wishes it." He regretted that he could not wait ten days, at which time he could double his force of ironclads and augment it with eight mortar barges.[18]

Grant ordered his troops to be ready to march as early as possible on the morning of February 12. McClernand's men moved a few miles out on the road on the night of the 11th so as to be out of the way and also to be in the first position when the army stepped off. Smith's division would follow. No tents or baggage were allowed except what the soldiers could carry. Each man took forty cartridges and two days' cooked rations. "Three days' additional rations may be put in wagons to follow the expedition, but will not impede the progress of the main column," said Grant.[19]

One brigade from the 2nd Division was to be left behind to protect Fort Henry and Fort Heiman. To Brigadier General Lew Wallace's disappointment, it was his brigade that was chosen. He watched with his staff from the hurricane deck of his headquarters steamboat as the columns assembled and marched away, "flags flying, drums beating." The old campgrounds were deserted by noon. Though the mood was "melancholy," Wallace expressed his belief to his staff that they would be summoned to the front within twelve hours. Grant's force of 15,000 could not handle the barricaded 18,000 Confederates at Donelson. To be ready when the call came, Wallace ordered four boats to raise steam and stand ready to cross the men over from Fort Heiman. "I want but one trip," he said.[20]

The resigned but brave demeanor which Wallace displayed before his staff fell away when he wrote to his wife about being left behind. He was bitter about it and said to her, "The whole force except my brigade marched this morning to attack Fort Donelson. Through old Smith, I am left behind in command of this Fort [Heiman] and Fort Henry. Nice arrangement! I have been sick from rage since yesterday."[21]

Two main roads connected Fort Henry with Fort Donelson. The Ridge Road was the southernmost; the Telegraph Road was roughly parallel and a few miles to the north. On the march to Fort Donelson, two of McClernand's brigades took the Ridge Road, while the other brigade moved eastward along the Telegraph Road, followed by C.F. Smith's division. Cavalry patrols watched the space in between. Grant and his staff rode with McClernand. Dr. John H. Brinton was in Grant's party, "near the General on my black horse, a strong powerful beast, which I had bought at Cairo. He was possessed of a fast walk, and moreover he would push in front of the other horses on the Staff. I could hardly keep him back; he particularly and persistently would pass the General who rode his old favorite stallion 'Jack.' Finally, he very good-naturedly said, to me, 'Doctor, I believe I command this army, and I think I'll go first.'"[22]

Everyone was in a celebratory mood. The drums and fifes were playing. It was good to be leaving old sickly Fort Henry and the threat of pneumonia and typhoid fever behind. The long rain had stopped, and the roads were firm. The day was lovely, so warm for mid-February that the men began throwing away their overcoats and blankets.

The columns began to approach the outer works of Fort Donelson in early afternoon and encountered Rebel skirmishers about two miles out. From the direction of the river, over the flat crack of musketry, they could hear the reverberation of navy guns. The *Carondelet* had preceded the other gunboats up the Cumberland and had arrived just before Grant's men. En route from Paducah, every sailor was busy preparing for the action to come. Coombe says, "Gunnery Officer Richard Adams was putting his crews through their paces.... Assistant Surgeon James McNeely was preparing his hutch for the expected casualties.... Chief Engineer Faulkner and his two assistants, Charles H. Cavin and Augustus Crowell, were busy checking the boilers and engines in preparation for the moment when the gunboat sallied forth on her own." Now was that moment. As Commander Walke told it, "At 12:50 P.M. to unmask the silent enemy, and to announce my arrival to General Grant, I ordered the bow-guns to be fired at the fort.... There was no response except the echo from the hills.... After firing ten shells into it, the *Carondelet* dropped down the river about three miles and anchored." It was all coming together. The first gunboat was already on the scene and more were coming, along with transports carrying thousands of reinforcements, those men from Paducah who had been too late to join the march. Grant had 15,000 men and the weather was beautiful. This was going to be a picnic.[23]

No part of the Fort Donelson defenses were in Kentucky, but if Kentucky's border had not taken that peculiar jog at the Cumberland River, it would have been very near, if not directly astride, the state boundary. It was only eleven miles from Kentucky to the west and ten miles from Kentucky to the north. The fort was both attacked and defended by Kentuckians, including two regiments of the famous Orphan Brigade (officially the 1st Kentucky Brigade, CSA), and the man who was arguably the best of the three generals in its clumsy tripartite command structure, Simon Bolivar Buckner. In the coming battle, the inevitable conclusion of the campaign that began at Forts Henry and Heiman, Buckner would have to help defend Fort Donelson against U.S. Grant, the man who had been his friend in what was now called the "Old Army." When Grant was leaving the army in drunken disgrace in 1854 and was without funds, it was Buckner who lent him the money to get home.

Fort Donelson was on the left bank of the Cumberland River, downstream from the town of Dover. The fort was flanked by two north-flowing streams. Just to the west was Hickman Creek, to the east was Indian Creek. These creeks and their tributaries, plus an intervening landscape of steep-sided hills, posed considerable difficulties for any attacking force and gave Fort Donelson's garrison a real defensive advantage. The fort itself contained fifteen acres surrounded by a six-foot high earthen bastion. Beyond that was a line of works that increased the size to one hundred acres. In the summer and fall of 1861, work there had lagged behind Fort Henry. General Tilghman had spurred the work forward when he took charge of the defenses on the rivers, and after the fall of Fort Henry the Confederates worked with a will to strengthen it before the Federals appeared. "This included digging rifle pits that reached out some two miles toward Fort Henry and clearing timber to secure unobstructed fields of fire and constructing entrenchments.... The defenders cut down trees about chest high, leaving them attached to their stumps with the tops pointed outward from the entrenchments to form a crude abatis in front of most of the line."[24]

Commander Walke, who was first to see the main works, said, "Fort Donelson occupied one of the best defensive positions on the river. It was built on a bald bluff about 120 feet in height, on the west side of the river, where it makes a slight bend to the eastward. It had three batteries, mounting in all fifteen guns: the lower, about twenty feet above the water; the second, about fifty feet above the water; the third, on the summit." The firepower was impressive. There were ten 32-pounders, an 8-inch howitzer, two 9-pounders, one rifled gun, and one 10-inch Columbiad. Captain Joseph Dixon was in command of the batteries.[25]

Colonel Adolphus Heiman, who had led two infantry brigades into the fort at midnight on February 6, directed the Donelson men in their work until the night of February 7, when the first of the generals began to arrive. That was Brigadier General Bushrod Johnson and he had been ordered there "to take instant command," by a rather dazed Albert Sidney Johnston. The fall of Fort Henry had been a terrible blow to General Johnston and shook his confidence to its foundations. He wrote on February 8, "Operations against Fort Donelson ... are about to be commenced, and that work will soon be attacked.... I think the gunboats of the enemy will probably take Fort Donelson without the necessity of employing their land force in co-operation, as seems to have been done at Fort Henry." Johnston had little faith in the fighting ability of the garrison at Donelson. He said that they "were not well armed or drilled, except Heiman's regiment and the regiments of Floyd's command."[26]

The Floyd to whom Johnston referred was Brigadier General John B. Floyd, former governor of Virginia and secretary of war under President James Buchanan. He was to become the ranking officer at Fort Donelson when he arrived on February 13. Floyd may not have been the wisest choice for a number of reasons, including the fact that he shared Johnston's pessimism. Floyd glumly observed, "If the best information I can gather about these iron-clad boats be true they are nearly invulnerable, and therefore they can probably go wherever sufficient fuel and depth of water can be found.... Unless I am misinformed as to these boats, the enemy will attempt to come up this river and destroy the towns upon its banks and every bridge across it. They can, to be sure, be kept confined to the river, but this will be done at heavy cost and inconvenience with the obstructed transportation we will have." He deplored the insufficient defenses upon which Colonel Heiman was laboring, and opined that the artillery batteries were badly placed.[27]

General Simon Bolivar Buckner (collection of the author).

Floyd was the last of the three commanders to appear,

and the only one of the three whom Grant did not know well, if at all. His prewar friendship with General Buckner (who arrived at Fort Donelson on February 11) has been alluded to. His acquaintance with General Gideon Pillow (who arrived on February 9, when he assumed command from General Bushrod Johnson) could hardly be called a friendship; in fact, Grant held Pillow in the same low esteem that did so many others did. Grant said, "I had known General Pillow in Mexico, and judged that with any force, no matter how small, I could march up to within gunshot of any intrenchments he was given to hold. I knew that Floyd was in command, but he was no soldier, and I judged that he would yield to Pillow's pretensions."[28]

The most forceful man at Fort Donelson may well have

General John B. Floyd in civilian clothes (Library of Congress).

been Colonel Nathan Bedford Forrest. He entered the fort on February 11 and assumed command of all the mounted forces there. In reality Forrest and his cavalry had been protecting Fort Donelson since October, when he was charged with patrolling the land along and between the Tennessee and Cumberland rivers. His men disrupted shipping on the river, shot up steamboats, and, more important, captured cargoes of precious supplies. In October, a detachment of Forrest's men led by Major David C. Kelley had made a major haul when they stopped a Federal transport near Smithland. It was loaded with coffee, bacon, blankets, and other supplies for the army. They forced the boat's crew to load the goods into wagons and delivered them to Hopkinsville, farther south. One of the greatest fights of the autumn came soon after the Smithland raid. It was against the timberclad *Conestoga*, which was steaming for Canton on the Cumberland to seize a store of Confederate uniforms. Forrest's eight cavalry regiments made a hard nighttime ride of thirty-two miles from Hopkinsville and reached Canton just moments before the *Conestoga* did. The boat anchored, but soon realized that something was not just right onshore. She reversed engines and moved downstream a short distance, and suddenly began to spray the bank with "a heavy fire of grapeshot and canister." Forrest's men fired back with small arms and also with a little 4-pounder they had lugged along. They "fired through the open ports, at close range, with such perfect accuracy and such deadly effect as to compel the vessel to close her ports and get away as fast as possible." The *Conestoga* suffered one of her few defeats and the CSA uniforms were saved. Forrest's reputation grew a little larger and he was soon able to recruit at Hopkinsville two more companies of horsemen, for a total of ten.[29]

It is odd that such a dynamic leader as Forrest did not resist Grant's approaching columns during the whole length of their eleven-mile march from Fort Henry on February 12. He did not. Instead, Forrest and his cavalry waited to strike until the bluecoats were within two miles of the Fort Donelson's outer works. This is not the only mystery. Joseph H. Parks says the whole list of command decisions pertaining to Fort Donelson showed a murkiness of thought. He writes, "The plan finally adopted defies explanation. There was to be no effective concentration at Donelson. Pillow, Buckner, and Floyd were ordered there, raising the total to about 15,000 men. Hardee, however, was to evacuate Bowling Green and fall back upon Nashville. Had Hardee's 14,000 men been added to the defense at Donelson, Grant might have been defeated." On the other hand, if headquarters decided "that Fort Donelson was either untenable or unworthy of concentrated effort (and the records show they had), it was poor generalship to send in thousands of men to be crushed or captured."[30] Moreover, as the Federals piled up outside their works, with Smith taking up his position on the Federal left and McClernand on the right, the Confederates continued to make mistakes. John Fiske observes that the Rebels "behaved as if paralyzed." He says, "It is seldom in history that a force behind intrenchments has allowed itself to be quietly invested by a force no greater than itself."[31]

Yet, it was all true. Departmental commanders had sent in thousands of men—but insufficient thousands—to hold this critical point, the gateway to Nashville, and the generals on the scene had allowed the Yankees to surround them unopposed. From Johnston on down, the Rebel commanders had squandered every advantage and allowed the Northerners to even the odds. The entire Confederacy would pay for their lack of foresight, beginning on February 13. Before it was done, the price would be very steep indeed.

12

The Battle of Fort Donelson
(February 1862)

On Wednesday, February 11, 1862, the Maury County Tennessee Artillery, Captain Reuben Ross commanding, arrived at Fort Donelson. Though they were a light artillery unit, Captain Ross and his men were assigned to man the upper river battery, plus the 10-inch Columbiad of the lower battery. These batteries were strong but rough, consisting of "natural earthen traverses, mostly revetted with hurdles of sapwood, capped between embrasures with sandbags, the embrasures lined as usual with rawhide." The men saw that "there were no bomb proofs or roofs of any kind" to shelter them. They knew that they would be facing the dreaded ironclads and exposed as they would be, they expected to lose three-fourths of their numbers. General Pillow told them that "it was the post of danger, but the post of honor."[1]

Ross and his men spent the rest of that day drilling, learning the management and use of heavy artillery pieces. They resumed their training the next morning and got some practical experience when the *Carondelet* came steaming around the bend. The boat anchored at more than two miles out and fired a few rounds at the batteries. Captain Ross's men fired about a dozen shots in return before the gunboat pulled back.

At about 11:00 the next morning, February 13, the *Carondelet* again pulled into view and began firing. She threw "139 70-pound and 64-pound shells at the fort," Commander Walke remembered. "We received in return the fire of all the enemy's guns that could be brought to bear." Walke was careful to stay out of range of most of the Confederate guns. In the case of the Maury County artillerists, there were only two cannon that were practical to the occasion, the "Columbiad and the 6.5-inch rifle—the only pieces capable of responding to Walke's long range fire."[2]

The Rebel batteries had little luck until one of their big guns sent a 128-pound solid shot crashing through the side of the boat into the engine room, bouncing around, breaking steam pipes, and filling the air with "an immense quantity of splinters.... Some of them as fine as needles shot through the clothes of the men." A dozen crewmen were wounded. Walke decided that this was enough for the morning, and the *Carondelet* retired. Though the Maury County boys had come through their first fight in good condition, not everyone was so lucky. One of the *Carondelet*'s shots killed the energetic engineer Captain Joseph Dixon. He had done valuable work at Fort Henry, Fort Heiman, and Fort Donelson, but now his labors were ended.[3]

During the early afternoon lull, the *Carondelet* crew ate their lunch and the wounded men were transferred to the *Alps*, which had towed the underpowered ironclad upstream the day before. The damages to the *Carondelet* were given a quick field repair and she steamed back into the fight. The firing lasted all afternoon. At dusk, the ironclad retired. She replenished her ammunition when Flag Officer Foote arrived about midnight, with the *St. Louis*, *Louisville*, and *Pittsburg*, and the timberclads *Tyler* and *Conestoga*.

If the attack of the *Carondelet* was indecisive in its outcome, it did at least help to cover the arrival of reinforcements by transport boat. Steaming toward their first battle, the men made the river cruise a frolic. Private John H. Beadle (Co. A, 31st Indiana) remembered that the soldiers "paraded on the upper deck, and arms and ammunition thoroughly inspected. Our magnificent band played inspiring tunes and all the soldiers danced and sang and shouted till they were hoarse." The surgeons, though, did not take part in the hilarity. Smith continued, "I came down into the cabin, and there the surgeons had their instruments laid out for inspection on the long table—knives, saws, tourniquets, everything indicating dreadful work at hand. A sudden revulsion of feeling overcame me. I turned cold around the heart at the thought of a dreadful wound and possible amputation."[4]

The *Carondelet* fight also helped cover the advance of General Smith's division on the left and General McClernand's on the right toward Fort Donelson's outer works. The line was a serpentine mess. It "stretched away over hills, down hollows, and through thickets, making it impossible for even colonels to see their regiments from flank to flank." Not only that, the Federal commanders could not see the enemy lines before them with any clarity. General Smith was facing Simon Bolivar Buckner; the question was, where were his batteries? Smith sent his two brigades forward to find out. Colonel Jacob Lauman and Colonel John Cook advanced, covered by the fire of Battery D, 1st Missouri Light Artillery. They did not get far. The abatis slowed them down and the Confederates poured combined rifle and cannon fire into them. One hundred Northern men lost their lives. The two brigade commanders backed out of the fight by late afternoon, having accomplished nothing.[5]

McClernand was facing Pillow. The two had traded cannon fire the night before and McClernand had somehow concluded that his artillery had quieted the enemy's guns and scattered his infantry. On the morning of the 13th, the general ordered his brigades to slide to the right and take position upstream of the Rebels. During the shift, McClernand's men had to cross open ground; in doing so, they discovered that the enemy was still in their front. Colonel Heiman's artillery fired into them. This angered McClernand, who ordered the two regiments of his undersized 3rd Brigade (the 17th and the 49th Illinois) to charge the Rebels and silence those guns. The 3rd Brigade started forward under the command of Colonel William E. Morrison and supported by the 48th Illinois Infantry under Colonel I.N. Haynie. At the last moment, Morrison and Haynie got into a little discussion about who ranked whom and, consequently, whose charge this really was. What might have become an unseemly incident in the face of enemy fire ended amicably when the two colonels agreed to take the Rebel redoubt together. They stepped off toward the point where Heiman's brigade of General Bushrod Johnson's wing met Colonel William D. Baldwin's brigade of General Simon Bolivar Buckner's wing.

Morrison and Haynie had not gone far when Morrison was shot, and Haynie ended up leading the charge, after all. It was, however, as unsuccessful as General Smith's had been. Some of the Federal attackers lost their nerve and pulled out of the fight to make their way back to Dr. Brinton's hospital tent, which was behind their sector. Brinton was offended that it was "not only the wounded, but many, a great many faint-hearted ones, who disgracefully sought the hospital precinct as a shelter."[6]

Meanwhile, the more stout-hearted pressed on to the abatis. Many were snagged in its tangles and struggled to get free while the Rebel bullets cut them down. Fifteen minutes was all it took to cost 150 Yankees their lives. The grass and leaves caught fire from the spray of sparks exploding from the mouths of the Confederate cannon, and as the Northerners withdrew, dozens of their wounded were in danger of being burned alive. The Rebels, who had been trying to kill them a short time before, now leaped from behind their barricades to save as many as they could from the flames. The little battle wound down.

Back at the hospital, the men continued to crowd around, and Dr. Brinton began to fear that the Rebels, seeing the stragglers, would be encouraged to launch a counterattack. The men would all be captured, along with the bulk of the hospital stores. When Brinton went to Grant to voice his concerns, the general calmly promised that the hospital would not be captured. The skulkers kept coming, though, and Brinton went to see Grant a second time, and a third, asking on the last visit, "Am I exaggerating the risk, or the consequences of the loss of the medical stores of your army, removed as we now are from fresh sources of supply?"[7] Grant said that Brinton was not exaggerating the peril, and he agreed that the hospital could be easily captured *if* the enemy came. But the enemy was not going to come: "They are not thinking of anything except holding their position, so make yourself easy. The enemy are thinking more of staying in than getting out, I know him."[8]

Grant was right; the Confederates did not come to capture the hospital. That was one bright spot in what had otherwise been a miserable day for the Federals. And they had a worse night. General Lew Wallace said, "From suggestions of spring it turned to intensified winter [and] the wind whisked suddenly around to the north and struck both armies with a storm of mixed rain, snow, and sleet. All night the tempest blew mercilessly upon the unsheltered, fireless soldier, making sleep impossible." Three inches of snow fell that night, and the mercury dropped to only a few degrees above zero. Those men who had jokingly thrown away their bulky encumbrances, their overcoats and woolen blankets, on the march over did not think themselves so clever now, in the blowing snow of that arctic night.[9]

Across the way, the Confederates were keeping busy, scouting and extending their earthworks. The gunners in the river batteries periodically fired rounds in the direction of the Federal gunboats to keep the Union sailors awake and to show that they were awake, too. Reports were coming in to General Floyd's headquarters of the Union transport boats bringing thousands of men to reinforce Grant, of the appearance of Foote's gunboat flotilla, and of McClernand's partial slide to their left. A council of war convened, and the three Confederate generals began to consider the wisdom of a breakout attempt.

That night in his cabin headquarters, thinking over his rough day, General Grant sent word to Brigadier General Lew Wallace on the Tennessee River to come forward.

The next morning, on the Federal front, General McClernand continued with great difficulty to ease to his right. Finally, Colonel John McArthur's all-Illinois brigade was detached from Smith's division and sent around behind McClernand to the extreme right, where they took up position as the easternmost brigade of Grant's battle line. The Federals still did not quite reach to the Cumberland, so a cavalry detachment was assigned to patrol the interval.

About 11:00 A.M. on February 14, Wallace's 2nd Brigade came marching in from the west. Wallace reported to General Grant at his headquarters, the humble Crisp family cabin. The brigadier described it as "a poor, little, unpainted, clap-boarded affair of the 'white-trash' variety, of logs, and a story and a half, with a lean-to on the side of our approach, half-room and half-porch." Wallace had been disappointed and bitter at being left behind at Forts Henry and Heiman two days before. Now he was elated when he heard Grant's plan. His brigade was going back to General Smith's division, but he was not. Grant was going to take some of the reinforcements that had come up the

Cumberland on transports and form a third division. The young Hoosier would command it. His first assignment was to take position in the center of the Union line, in the gap between Smith and McClernand.[10]

Grant's adjutant-general, John A. Rawlins, guided Wallace's division to his position. They came under long-range artillery fire as soon as they were spotted. To embolden his green troopers, Wallace ordered the fifers and drummers to play, and they continued to the front with no casualties sustained. Filing into place after their warm reception, Wallace was surprised at the width of the gap between Smith and McClernand and asked Rawlins, "Why hasn't the enemy come in here and cut you in two?"

Rawlins laughed and said, "Because there's but one soldier among them, and he is third in rank."

"What's his name?"

"Buckner," Rawlins said. Wallace was surprised again—he knew the man.[11]

These were all side shows to the main event of the day, Flag Officer Foote's attack. If things went well, that is, as they had gone at Fort Henry, this ought to be the last day of investment at Fort Donelson. The Confederates would be battered into surrendering and everyone could get out of this dismal weather. Personally, Foote was disinclined to attack. The flotilla was not prepared, there were no mortar boats, and he had not had the chance to reconnoiter the enemy's defenses, though Walke had. He expressed his concerns to Grant in a conference aboard the flagship *St. Louis*, but Grant would not hear of them. He insisted that the gunboats could silence the shore batteries, run past the fort, and gain the Rebel rear. Roughed-up and surrounded, the Rebels would surely surrender. Foote reluctantly agreed to try.

Now Foote met with his seven captains. He explained his worries once again, but said that Grant had ordered the attack and it must come off. The captains went back to their vessels to prepare. Walke said that "all the hard materials on the vessels, such as chains, lumber, and bags of coal, were laid on the upper decks to protect them from the plunging shots of the enemy."[12]

The Confederate batteries had already been busy that morning. Captain Ross said that he did not "resist the temptation" to fire on the Federal boats downstream. He gave the proper elevations and his crew opened fire with the Columbiad and the rifled gun. He later learned the results of the barrage from a somewhat reliable source: "Peter Casey, of Kentucky, brother-in-law of General Grant, a citizen with the gunboat fleet, stated afterwards to Mr. Comstock, a friend, that one of our shots tore off the prow of a transport and that we never missed their gunboats at all; that not infrequently would a ball take their gunboats lengthwise, ripping it badly, and carrying away in some cases a whole tier of bunks, bedding, etc.; that he often saw the surface of the water covered with those wrecks, intermingled with arms, legs, and fragments of every form. This is what he stated, but I am satisfied he much overestimated these things."[13]

However much or little the gunboats might have been damaged, the attack commenced on schedule. They raised steam about 1:30 P.M. and a little before 3:00 moved forward in two ranks against the shore batteries of Fort Donelson. The ironclads were in front: the *Louisville* on the west, then the *St. Louis*, *Pittsburgh*, and the *Carondelet*. About a half-mile behind were the timberclads, and behind them the complement of hospital boats and tugboats. At a mile out, the *St. Louis* fired, and the whole front division opened up with their big bow-guns. The shouts and cheers from Grant's infantrymen echoed down from the snow-covered hills. The boats closed to about nine hundred yards, and their rate of fire was ferocious. Even the fearless Nathan Bedford Forrest became rattled. He was watching the contest from the outer works when he suddenly cried out to Major David C. Kelley (a peacetime preacher), "Parson! For God's Sake, pray; nothing but God Almighty can save that fort!"[14]

General Pillow, second in command at Fort Donelson, became worse than rattled, if an (unauthenticated) telegram quoted by J.M. Hoppin is true. Pillow panicked. During the river battle, he is said to have wired his friend Governor Isham Harris saying, "The Federal gun-boats are destroying us. For God's sake, send us all the help you can immediately. I don't care for the land force of the enemy; they can't hurt us if you can keep those hell-hounds in check."[15] Nothing seemed to be going right for the Confederates. Captain Reuben Ross remembered:

> One of our balls refused to go down, stopping halfway in the bore; and all efforts to drive it down with rammers had proven unavailing. The boats were advancing, and things were looking serious. Ten or twelve men were ordered to leave the batteries and find a log large enough to fit the rifle. This they soon succeeded in doing, and in the midst of the fire they mounted the parapet and drove the ball home. After firing this load, these same men took the sponge, swabbed out the bore with copious water sufficient to soften the dirt already dried and stiffened by the heat; and then applying the rifler, cut the dirt from each of the six grooves until loose; then sponged ... and ended by greasing the sponge well and applying the same thoroughly to the entire bore.[16]

When the Federals approached to between six and eight hundred yards, the battle began to turn in the Rebels' favor. This was due, first, to the fact that the gunboats were overfiring. The closer they got, the worse their aim was. Confederate Captain B.G. Bidwell wrote that the Federal flotilla's fire "was more destructive to our works at two miles than at two hundred yards. They fired over us from that distance." Second, the elevation of Fort Donelson worked against the Federals. At Fort Henry, because of the flooded Tennessee River, the ironclad's guns were about on a level with those in the shore batteries.

At Donelson, the batteries were higher and could deliver plunging fire onto the gunboats. Their armor was designed to repulse lateral fire, not fire from above, and the "hard materials" piled on deck offered but little protection. A third factor which should not be discounted was the discipline of the Confederate gunners. Things had gone badly for them at the start of the engagement, but they had kept to their work coolly and skillfully until the scale tipped. They could feel the momentum beginning to turn.[17]

The Yankee ironclads were taking terrible punishment as they came nearer. Walke said that the enemy's "heavy shot and shell penetrated the gunboats with deadly effect."[18] The *Louisville*'s tiller cables were severed and a shell from a 32-pounder crashed into the pilothouse of the flagship *St. Louis*, carrying away the wheel. The shell mortally wounded the pilot, F.A. Riley, and inflicted a serious wound to Flag Officer Foote's left ankle and a lesser one in the arm. Compounding the injury, the *Tyler* rammed the *St. Louis* and wrecked her steering gear. With no ability to steer, both boats drifted down with the current. The fire from the Confederate bluff was bad enough, though not as insulting to the ironclad men as the fire from the timberclads behind them. They were so far back that their shells were falling short, right into the ironclad formation or exploding overhead and raining shrapnel down over them. Walke said that a "64-pound shell exploded over the *Carondelet* and the fragments penetrated her stern casemate."[19]

The *Carondelet* and the *Pittsburg* were left fighting, but the latter was taking on water and decided to retire. As she tried to execute her too-tight turn in the narrow river, she struck the *Carondelet* and broke her rudder. With no way to maneuver, the *Carondelet*, too, drifted downstream stern first, her three bow-guns still pounding the Rebels with shells for as long as they were within range. The Rebels were taunting them with reminders that this was not Fort Henry and they were still firing, too, skipping their rounds off the river's surface so that the balls would strike the boat low. Walke said the Rebels "soon succeeded in planting two 32-pound shots in her bow, between wind and water, which made her leak badly, but her compartments kept her from sinking until we could plug up the shot-holes."[20] Before she was out of range, sixteen more Confederate shots hit the *Carondelet*. The last one beheaded two men and cut another one in two. Commander Walke, who wrote so much, and at times so bitterly, about his war experiences, mourned the condition of his gunboat. He said that the *Carondelet* "was terribly cut up, not a mast or spar was standing. All our barges, boats, stanchions and hammock nettings, had been cut to pieces, with the pilot house and smoke pipes riddles; port side cut open fifteen feet, and decks ripped up, in many places plowed up; rifled guns and anchors in fragments; with four men killed and fifteen wounds, two mortally, and two solid shots in her bow between wind and water." Some of the wounded men mentioned by Walke were laid low by one of the *Carondelet*'s own guns. It exploded, split into three pieces, and took its crew out of the fight.[21]

The *Carondelet* was a mess. She was first in, last out, had been hit thirty-five times, and had twice the number of men killed and wounded of any other boat. Walke said, "Our decks were so slippery with the blood of the brave men who had fallen, that we could hardly stand until we covered them with sand." The *St. Louis* had been hit fifty-nine times, the *Louisville* thirty-six times, and the *Pittsburg* thirty times. The *Pittsburg* was taking on so much water that she could not make it back to the landing and tied up instead to a stout tree onshore to keep from going under before she could be patched up.[22]

The Rebel boys of the upper battery had been sure that they would take devastating losses in their fight with the Union gunboats, but they had not. Captain Ross wrote of the Valentine's Day fight with the Yankees: "There was one remarkable circumstance: though the air was full of their projectiles, smoke, and noise, not one man was hurt at our batteries. I am unable to account for so remarkable a circumstance, except that our always prompt and vigorous firing at long ranges had intimidated them and destroyed their capacity to take aim."[23]

However, the men in the batteries expected to the fight to resume the next morning. When it did, the Maury County artillery boys were determined to sink a gunboat. They spent a busy night preparing. Captain Ross said, "For this purpose, the artificers were set to work to make what we called disports—long, triangular pieces of thick plank, which, placed on the line of sight and lashed on the pieces with cord, make the thickness at the muzzle equal to that at the breech, and therefore at short ranges enable us to aim exactly at the object. Ordnance-Sergeant Stone then filled some shells with melted lead to give them great weight and strength, and on the next day, when they had reached their nearest range, we intended to lash on our disports and fire them at great depression, so as to go through the hulls."[24]

It was not to be. The gunboats had fought their last fight at Fort Donelson. Foote tried to put the best face possible on his effort, saying in his report that another fifteen minutes would have made all the difference and that his boats had frightened the Confederates away from their shore batteries, until the *St. Louis* and the *Louisville* were forced out of action. The facts were otherwise; the foot officer's flotilla had suffered a terrible defeat.

Foote began making preparations to take two of the ironclads (the *Pittsburg* and the *Carondelet*) back to Cairo for repairs. He would leave behind the other two ironclads and the two timberclads. If Grant was still fighting, Foote would come back in ten days with his boats, plus the *Benton* and some mortar scows. He did render one last service by sending the timberclad *Tyler* back around to the Tennessee River to destroy the rebuilt Memphis and Ohio

12. The Battle of Fort Donelson

Railroad bridge over the Tennessee River, "so as to prevent the rebels at Columbus re-enforcing their army at Fort Donelson."[25]

General Gideon Pillow regained his usual bluster after the gunboats withdrew. He wired Albert Sidney Johnston: "We have just had the fiercest fight on record between our guns and six gunboats, which lasted two hours. We drove them back, damaged two of them badly, and crippled a third very badly. No damage done to our battery and not a man killed." A similar wire went to General Polk at Columbus.[26]

Pillow was still in his chest-beating mood late that night when another council of war met. The question up for discussion was not retreat; that had been agreed to at the previous morning's council. Had it not been for the gunboat attack, the Confederates might have already been on their way south. The matter before them now was how best to accomplish the breakout. The final form of the plan called for General Pillow to attack the Federal right flank (McClernand's sector) at daylight. A successful assault would crack open the doorway to Nashville. Buckner would attack the Union center right to pry the door open even more and the army would rush through. Buckner's division would cover the retreat and follow as rear guard. The attack would pivot on Colonel Heiman's brigade. Pillow would hurl his own division, to be commanded during the attack by General Bushrod Johnson, at McClernand, and he wanted to augment it with the 2nd Kentucky Infantry of the "Orphan Brigade." Buckner was going to have work of his own to do and refused to give up any of his Kentuckians. Buckner did, however, see the necessity of the breakout attempt. He said, "The movement had become imperatively necessary in consequence of vastly superior and constantly increasing force of the enemy, who had already completely enveloped our position." The meeting broke up, and the commanders went to issue orders and prepare their men. The rest of the long winter's night was spent in massing regiments and batteries in front of the Federal right.[27]

They had prepared for almost any dire eventuality, including failure, by selecting a rendezvous point out in the open country for the troops, if they should become scattered. Incredibly, what they had not prepared for was victory. As Cooling tells it, "Every participant left the meeting with a different notion as to what would happen after the successful attack. Pillow held that his troops would return to the defenses and that victory would be so complete that time would permit retrieval of equipment, rations, and the units guarding the trenches and main fort.... Buckner and his subordinates thought that nobody would return to the trenches after the battle." It is unbelievable that such a critical matter was left murky. The responsibility for that, and for the consequences, was General Floyd's.[28]

Through the wee hours of February 15, the Federals huddled together, trying to survive another winter gale. They had the wind in their ears and did not hear anything of the Confederates stacking up in front of McClernand.

Grant went to meet with Foote early on the morning of February 15. The flag officer could not come to Grant because of his ankle wound. It was a distance of several miles, and Grant would be gone for hours. Still, he did not assign anyone to command on the battle line while he was absent, for, as he said, "I had no idea there would be any engagement on land unless I brought it on myself." He did leave orders that none of his division commanders were to make an attack while he was gone.[29]

The men were getting up from their snowy beds in their fireless camps when a crackle of rifle fire erupted on the far right, where Colonel John McArthur's brigade of Smith's division was posted. They had arrived in position after dark the night before, "without instructions, and, as I regret to add, without adequate knowledge of the nature of the ground in front and on our right."[30] Colonel McArthur's all–Illinois brigade had left Fort Heiman on February 12 and had brought up the rear of Smith's column on the march to Donelson. Last on the march, they were now first in the fight of February 15, as the Rebels burst out of the woods around them. The Confederates outflanked them by one regiment, but McArthur remained cool. He threw the 9th Illinois Infantry forward, and the 41st Illinois to the right, and two companies of skirmishers still farther to the right. These defenders did well for their colonel; the Rebels did not blow through them. McArthur said, "This ground was steadily maintained until exposed to a flanking fire upon the right from fresh troops of the enemy." The flanking fire drove them back.[31]

A new line was formed three hundred yards to the rear, and then another one behind that. The Illinoisans' retrograde movement had uncovered the right of Colonel Richard J. Oglesby's 1st Brigade of McClernand's division. The butternuts were bringing their fieldpieces forward and they began to exchange volleys with Oglesby's two-gun section. Oglesby later said, "The enemy did not spare their grape and canister, and occasionally sent a shell or round shot from the six or eight guns bearing on our lines."[32]

The infantry engaged. The Confederate attack was so determined as to be almost irresistible. The earth was churned into snow and mud and blood by the charging Rebels. Oglesby rotated new regiments forward as his men fell by the scores and the survivors ran low on ammunition. In this way, he was able to hold on for an hour despite the "galling fire," but he was using up regiments fast. Oglesby said, "I was tempted to use the bayonet, but the risk of breaking my lines in an effort to go through the thick brush, when the result under the most favorable circumstances could only be to drive them into their lines and expose my command to a raking fire of artillery and musketry upon emerging in broken files from the thick woods, determined me to hold my line to the last."³³

The Rebels pressed their attack and drove back 1st Division's right and center regiments. Colonel John A. Logan, commanding the 31st Illinois Infantry on the extreme left of Oglesby's brigade, described his dilemma: "Hour after hour passed, and still the battle raged. The Ninth, the Twelfth, and the Forty-first Illinois regiments, comprising McArthur's brigade ... had long since retired for more ammunition. The Eighth, the Eighteenth, the Twenty-ninth, and the Thirtieth, one after the other, were forced back by the terrible cross-fire of the enemy, when the last regiment of the brigade—the Thirty-first Illinois—was almost reached." Colonel Oglesby ordered Colonel Logan to bend his regiment's right wing back at a ninety-degree angle to its own center. The 31st was one of the crack units in this army and its leader one of the most promising volunteer officers. They were the ones who had opened a way through the Confederates during the afternoon fight at Belmont, allowing the Federals to reach the transport boats. Now the 31st Illinois Infantrymen were the very end of the line, and the situation was reversed—they were trying to stop the Rebels from plowing a gap through *them*. By refusing its own right, the regiment presented a broad front to the Rebels and simultaneously helped protect Captain Adolph Schwartz's Missouri artillery battery.³⁴

At the critical moment, Colonel Charles Cruft of Lew Wallace's division came forward with reinforcements, the 17th Kentucky, the 31st Indiana, and the 25th Kentucky. General McClernand had been on the field all morning and had made a smart move at the beginning of the attack by dispatching a courier to Grant with news of the attack, but now he made an unaccountable error. Instead of throwing Cruft's reinforcements straight into the fight, McClernand held them in reserve.

It seems to have been a call for help from Oglesby's rapidly crumbling right that put the men in motion again. On the way over, the guide they had been assigned lost his nerve and abandoned them. Unguided and confused, the 25th Kentucky saw what they thought were enemy soldiers ahead. They fired, only to learn that they were shooting into the 8th and 29th Illinois of Oglesby's brigade, who had turned from the fight to make their way to the rear and who may have fired first. It was a tragedy which there was no time to lament. Cruft reported: "A well-directed fire was opened on the Twenty-fifth Kentucky and Thirty-first Indiana before they could form to resist it. The line of battle, however, was formed rapidly and steadily under continued volleys of the enemy's musketry. The Seventeenth Kentucky and Forty-fourth Indiana were shortly brought up in good order and entered the action." The enemy pressed to within twenty feet of the Federal line and after only a couple of hours, during which time Oglesby fell back, Cruft's men had to retire.³⁵

Colonel W.H.L. Wallace's 2nd, Brigade was next in line and became engaged while Oglesby was fighting. At Pillow's request, Buckner had committed the 2nd Kentucky Infantry and the 3rd, 18th, and 32nd Tennessee Infantry to the battle. Nathan Bedford Forrest's cavalry cooperated with the foot soldiers, but Forrest had not just come on line; attack dog that he was, he had been on the field since early morning. Buckner's attacking Rebels gained the road in front of the 2nd Brigade, and then found that they could not hold it. Wallace reported: "The moment the rebel flag appeared above the crest of the hill a storm of shot from the 11th Illinois and 20th Illinois drove them back in confusion." This was a temporary setback for the Confederates.[36]

Wallace was aware that the right, Oglesby, was crumbling. Soon, the 2nd Brigade would be fighting on the front again and on the flank, as well. It was not long before his fears became fact. The Rebels were pressing him hard, and more were piling in. He called for reinforcements from General McClernand, but none were to be had and there was no way to hold on without them. Seeing that the entire right had melted away except for Colonel Logan's 31st Illinois, Wallace ordered his men to retire. Of his four infantry regiments, only the 11th Illinois, supporting Logan's regiment as it made its stubborn stand, remained on the battle line. When the 31st fell back for lack of ammunition, the 11th found itself inside a deadly box, and they too retired to join their comrades a half mile back. The 11th Illinois suffered the highest casualty rate of any Federal regiment in the battle that day, over 60 percent.

Now the attack was coming toward the 3rd Division of Brigadier General Lew Wallace. He moved his men forward to meet their attackers, and reported a semi-comic encounter with Colonel W.H.L. Wallace. General Wallace said, "It happened also that Colonel W.H.L. Wallace had dropped into the same road with such of his command as staid by their colors. He came up riding and at a walk, his leg thrown over the horn of his saddle. He was perfectly cool and looked like a farmer from a hard day's plowing. 'Good-morning,' I said. 'Good-morning,' was the reply. 'Are they pursuing you?' 'Yes.' 'How far are they behind?' That instant the head of my command appeared on the road. The colonel calculated, then answered: 'You will have about time to form line of battle right here.'"[37]

Wallace ordered his Battery A to hurry forward and ordered Colonel John A. Thayer to deploy the 2nd and 3rd brigades into battle line. The artillery arrived just a moment before the Rebels appeared. "The woods rang with musketry and artillery," said Wallace. The Rebels tried twice to overrun Wallace's (Thayer's) position and were twice repulsed. They had reached the limit, it seems. They had done an exhausting job that morning and needed a breather and the chance to regroup. It must be remembered, too, that most of these men had never had such an experience in their lives and that this was something far more intense than a chilly coon hunt or the dusty weariness after a hard day in the tobacco field. They were colder, hungrier, and more afraid than they had ever expected to be, and yet they had pressed on, with one-ounce slugs of lead and chunks of jagged iron flying at them in swarms. It is little wonder that a lull occurred in the fighting.[38]

General Wallace and General McClernand were taking a moment to confer when General Grant appeared. Of that moment, Grant wrote, "I saw men standing in knots talking in the most excited manner. No officer seemed to be giving any directions.... I heard some of the men say that the enemy had come out with knapsacks, and haversacks filled with rations." Grant interpreted this to mean that the Rebs were attempting a breakout. For some reason, they had fallen back, and now was the time to counterattack. "The one who attacks first now will be victorious and the enemy will have to be in a hurry if he gets ahead of me," he said.[39] He reasoned that the enemy right flank must be pretty thin, and so decided to attack with his left, General Smith. He ordered the men around him to refill their cartridge boxes and prepare to counter-attack. He sent a courier to Flag Officer Foote with a request to have his gunboats fire. "Make an appearance and throw a few shells at long range," he urged. Then he rode off to see Smith and explain to him what was wanted. Grant biographer Bruce Catton writes, "In this moment of crisis at Fort Donelson, Grant met one of the supreme tests of his career as a soldier."[40]

When Grant found Smith, he said to him, "General Smith, all has failed on our right—you must take Fort Donelson." Smith's reply was simple and forceful. "I will do it," he said. He mounted his horse, rode to the front of the 2nd Iowa Infantry, and pointed toward Fort Donelson. "Second Iowa, you must take that fort. Take the caps off your guns, fix bayonets, and I will support you." It was an odd final phrase; what he meant was that he would lead them.[41]

The Iowans stepped off, the other regiments fell in behind them, and they surged toward the works where the enemy would oppose them with everything from the siege guns in the main works to double-barrel shotguns. The way was steep. Smith was leading them on horseback when he saw men beginning to falter. He is said to have shouted, "Damn you, gentlemen. I see skulkers. I'll have none here. Come on, you volunteers, come on. This is your chance. You volunteered to be killed for love of your country and now you can be. You are only damned volunteers. I am only a solider and I don't want to be killed, but you came to be killed and now you can be." It seems like an awful lot to say in the face of buckshot and cannonballs, but that it what Smith is said to have said. No one denies that he was fearless, and the very sight of the dignified old warrior was an inspiration.[42]

Smith's men took the first line easily when its defenders ran off. The second line was tougher because Buckner's men had returned from the front. The fight hardened into a real contest, and they fought until dark. Over on the right flank, McClernand and General Wallace planned their counter-attack. There was not much light left on this short winter's day, and McClernand, who had endured a very hard ten hours, was perfectly happy to let Wallace lead the charge.

General Bushrod Johnson's men had not yet returned to their first position. They were still on the field, tending to their wounded and gathering dropped and abandoned weapons from the fight when Wallace ordered his men forward. They were led by the 8th Missouri and the 11th Indiana. The butternuts stopped what they were doing to pick up their rifles and resist the late-day attack. The Federals advanced by rushes, back over the ground that had been lost that morning. The Confederates did not fight with the same spirit they had shown earlier, and they must certainly have been dispirited even more when shells from the *St. Louis* and the *Louisville* began to fall among them, although Cooling points out that few of the Confederate reports "mentioned any naval fire on the fifteenth." He concludes that it is possible that "by then this stage of the fighting, none of the tired Confederates could distinguish between naval and field artillery gunfire." The dying sun put an end to the fighting on the right. Wallace had recovered the lost ground, had closed the door to Nashville, and that was enough. Like Smith on the distant left, he settled down for another cold night, but in position to finish the attack in the morning.[43]

The battlefield was busy that night with men wandering the field. Some were just walking over the bloody ground where they had fought, striving to understand all that had happened. Other men were prowling for plunder, looking for missing friends, or hoping for a chance to perform some humanitarian service after a day of murder. Rice Graves, the captain of an artillery battery belonging to the Orphan Brigade, went searching the field that night. He discovered a severely wounded Federal and brought him into Confederate lines. Oliver Steele, one of Graves' gunners, happened to be nearby. He looked at the wounded Yankee, and saw his own brother. The Steele boys had left their Henderson County home to go into different armies and now one, still ablebodied, was given the gift of tending his enemy, his brother, in the final moments before he died. Historian of the Orphan Brigade William C. Davis writes, "Here for the first time, though certainly not the last in this war, the Orphans discovered the horror of what was, for Kentucky, truly a 'brothers' war.'"[44]

There was another wanderer that night. General Grant was out, and he saw a "wounded Union lieutenant feebly attempting to give a drink from his canteen to a Rebel private lying beside him. Borrowing a flask of brandy from a staff officer, Grant gave each man a swallow." He ordered some stretcher bearers to come over and take both men to the hospital and then continued his tour. The horses were hard to control because of the smell of blood, and it began to get to Grant, too. He said to his aide, "Let's get away from this dreadful place."[45] The battlefield of February 15 was sickening, but Steven Woodworth points out that the horror of the scene did not shake Grant's resolve: "Back at headquarters, before turning in, Grant issued his orders for the next morning: all-out assaults on both sides of the fort."[46]

13

The Surrender of Fort Donelson
(February 1862)

What had happened? The Confederate attack had worked perfectly. The door to Nashville was forced wide open and then the Confederates had paused and allowed the Federals to slam it in their faces. What had happened was exactly what General Pillow understood to be the plan: open the way, return to the trenches for equipage, and move out when it was quite convenient for everyone.

This was not Buckner's understanding at all. In his view, the victory was won, the road was clear, and the breakout should immediately follow. He raged when he received Pillow's order to retire, and was still raging when General Floyd arrived on the front for the first time that day. The Kentuckian argued his point and believed that he had persuaded Floyd, who rode off to find Pillow. Pillow persuaded Floyd back again. There was time, Pillow argued. Phase one had been a complete victory and the demoralized Yankees would not be able to stop the men later, after they had rested, eaten their rations, and secured their gear. Then they would start for Nashville. So, Floyd upheld Pillow, and the Confederate effort of February 15 guttered out like the flame of a dying candle. For no good reason, the commanding officers had surrendered the initiative and had subjected their fighting men to a stinging counterattack from Smith and Wallace. The Rebel soldiers in the ranks were as bitter as Buckner that their morning victory had been squandered.

That night, the three generals met again in council. Pillow still maintained that an overland breakout was possible. Buckner disagreed. He reported that Smith had broken through his first line and was ready to continue the assault come morning. The enemy had been reinforced through the day, and his men would not be able to resist them for more than thirty minutes when they were attacked. They were suffering from frostbite and had not received a regular issue of rations in several days. Their ammunition was almost gone. They were now in too-weakened condition to make a forced march. Even if they tried, they would come under attack by the enemy's gunboats as well as his cavalry as soon as they began their march. It looked as if there were no alternative but to surrender.

Nathan Bedford Forrest was at the meeting. He had been scouting between the river and the enemy's right flank and he assured the generals that the Federal investment was not complete: "I said that I would agree to cut my way through the enemy's lines at any point the general might designate and stated that I could keep back their cavalry."[1] Someone pointed out that the enemy would not have to chase them; they could simply bombard them with artillery fire. At this point, Forrest said he "went out of the room." Considering the way he went out of other rooms at other times when his instinct to fight was rebuffed, he probably stomped out in heavy-booted fury.[2]

The generals continued their discussion. Floyd was as indecisive as ever and General Pillow wavered. As he listened to Buckner's grim assessment of the Confederate predicament, he lost faith in the plan for an overland breakout. He now argued that they should remain in their works and hold on for one more day until the steamboats which had been evacuating the wounded to Nashville could return. The river packets could take the army onboard and in that way the men could escape. Buckner disagreed. He said that he could not hold on for another twenty-four hours; he repeated that his command was "weakened and exhausted" and "could not successfully resist the assault which would be made at daylight by a vastly superior force." He did say, however, that he was willing to continue the fight, if General Johnston's retrograde movement from Bowling Green had not yet been completed. He would fight "even at the risk of destruction of our entire force, as the delay even of a few hours might gain the safety of General Johnston's force." Floyd said that Johnston's force had safely reached Nashville. Buckner replied that if that was the case a sacrifice of more lives was needless and that they should "obtain the best terms of capitulation possible." The other two generals agreed.[3]

The decision had been made, leaving only a final, unflattering dénouement to be played out. After agreeing to the surrender, Pillow remarked "that he thought there were no two persons in the Confederacy who the Yankees would prefer to capture than himself and General Floyd." This was a typically self-aggrandizing statement, considering that former Vice President John C. Breckinridge was now wearing a Confederate uniform, but Floyd was quick to accept the compliment and the serious threat that accompanied it. It was agreed between them that, whatever else happened, Generals Floyd and Pillow would try to escape. Forrest came back in while this was going on. He asked "if they were going to surrender the command." General Buckner told him that that was the decision. Forrest "then stated that I had not come out for the purpose of surrendering my command, and would not do it ... that I intended to go out if I saved but one man." He left the room a second time.[4]

(Pillow and Floyd seemed to struggle briefly with the decision to abandon their responsibilities. They wanted Buckner to vindicate them. Buckner sidestepped a bit when he said that it "was a question for every officer to decide for himself." Their way was not Buckner's though. He told them "that in my own case I regarded it as my duty to remain with my men and share their fate, whatever it might be." Pillow and Floyd were perfectly willing for responsibility to devolve on the Kentuckian, and so Simon Bolivar Buckner was handed command of Fort Donelson after every opportunity had been lost and there was nothing left to do except surrender it.[5])

No man at Fort Donelson had been busier than Nathan Bedford Forrest. He had scouted for long hours in the saddle and had lost a horse in the morning fighting of February 15. Between times he had taken his turn with the rifle and plinked Yankee sharpshooters from their perches in the trees. Forrest had given a supreme effort at Fort Donelson, and he was not going to end his career there by surrendering. He had left the council chamber and hurried back to his waiting horse soldiers. "Boys," he said to them, "these people are talking about surrendering, and I am going out of this place before they do or bust hell wide open." At 4:00 A.M. on February 16, five hundred men of Forrest's cavalry, and as many as two hundred infantrymen who had asked to join them, rode out of Fort Donelson.[6]

They had barely begun their ride out when a report came that Federals blocked their way. Forrest rode ahead with his brother Jeffrey to investigate and found that the ominous Federals were no more than a split-rail fence. The only Federals that Forrest encountered that night were wounded men, which the cavalry rode past on their way to freedom. About a mile out, the riders found that a long stretch of the road ahead was underwater; no one knew how deeply until Forrest nudged his horse forward into the muddy swill. He found that it came no higher than his saddle skirts, hardly an obstacle at all. The men crossed and continued to higher ground and the Cumberland Iron Works Road. Forrest wrote, "More than two hours had been occupied in passing. Not a gun had been fired into us. Not an enemy had been seen or heard."[7]

By nightfall on February 16, Forrest's cavalry was twenty miles away from Fort Donelson. The column arrived safely in Nashville on February 18. In his after-action report, Forrest fired a double-barreled reproach at his superiors. He said, "I am clearly of the opinion that two-thirds of our army could have marched out without loss, and that, had we continued the fight the next day, we should have gained a glorious victory." The war was young, but Forrest was already learning that there were not many officers in the Confederate service who had his reserves of energy and fighting spirit.[8]

There were men of honor, though, and Simon Bolivar Buckner was one of them. He may have been too pessimistic about the ability of the men to hold out. That point is still argued. However, after command devolved on him, his duty was clear and his resolve was firm. He called for a pen and paper and wrote to General Grant:

> Sir:—In consideration of all the circumstances governing the present situation of affairs at this station, I propose to the Commanding Officer of the Federal forces the appointment of Commissioners to agree upon terms of capitulation of the forces and post under my command, and in that view suggest an armistice until 12 o'clock today.

At the Crisp cabin, Grant read the note, conferred briefly with General C.F. Smith, and replied with one of the most famous passages of the Civil War:

> Sir:—Yours of this date proposing armistice and appointment of commissioners to settle terms of capitulation is just received. No terms except an unconditional and immediate surrender can be accepted. I propose to move immediately upon your works.

Buckner was stunned and his reply showed it:

> Sir:—The distribution of the forces under my command incident to an unexpected change of commanders and the overwhelming force under your command compel me, notwithstanding the brilliant success of the Confederate arms yesterday, to accept the ungenerous and unchivalrous terms which you propose.[9]

    Buckner got word to his brigade commanders to send white flag couriers out to the enemy forces on their front to prevent the outbreak of another battle. The white flags appeared none too soon. Brigadier General Wallace was already deploying his troops. The Southern officers and men in the works were shocked when they learned what was happening. General Bushrod Johnson, for example, was not even sent the white flag order. In his report, Johnson said that his men came out of their trenches between 1:00 and 2:00 A.M. and prepared to cut their way out through the Yankee right flank, as had been directed the day before. As they waited for the order to advance, Johnson noticed that the Virginia regiments were moving off toward Dover, by order of General Floyd. More waiting followed. Finally Johnson sent an aide to report that his men were ready to move and was informed that command had fallen to General Buckner, who ordered Johnson to wait for instructions. After a while, Johnson personally went to headquarters. There, he learned that Buckner had asked Grant for terms and was ordered to communicate the fact to the Yankee pickets in his front.

    The men who were arraying themselves for battle showed no lack of spirit in the pre-dawn hours of February 16. They believed that they had won on the 15th and had expected to win the fight this morning. Now it was plain that their generals had failed them. Two of their generals even fled. About daylight, General Floyd commandeered two transport boats. It was an irony that one of them, the

General Anderson, was delivering about four hundred reinforcements to Fort Donelson, just in time to become prisoners. Floyd got the reinforcements off, got some of his own men on board, and steamed away. One of those who escaped with Floyd was Colonel Henry C. Burnett, the secessionist firebrand from the Jackson Purchase. He had helped recruit the 8th Kentucky Infantry in November 1861 and was with his regiment at Fort Donelson. His close call at Fort Donelson persuaded Burnett that he preferred politics to soldiering. He subsequently traveled to Richmond to represent the provisional (that is to say, imaginary) Confederate state of Kentucky in the upper legislative house.

Floyd left behind hundreds of frantic soldiers at the wharf. Some of them quietly accepted their fate, stacked their arms, and sat down to wait for the Yankees. Others threw their guns into the Tennessee River and went to share the storehouse whiskey that the commissary officers had made available. The abandoned men who gathered at the wharf needed something to dull their feelings. They were astonished at the turn of their fortunes. Private J.J. Montgomery of the 53rd Tennessee wrote, "I could not believe it, as we had been successful for three days, both on land and water.... I hastened to the river where I found the steamer Gen. Anderson waiting to carry off Pillow—horses, negroes, and baggage. I went to headquarters and made every effort to get aboard, but appealed in vain, as they were afraid the boat would sink. However, I saw three horses and two negroes with baggage taken on afterwards.[10]

General Pillow and his staff escaped across the Cumberland River on a small flatboat, waited until their horses were ferried over, and rode to Clarksville, where they joined Floyd in his underloaded transport. Together, they traveled to Nashville, arriving on February 17.

Grant issued a number of orders after he received Buckner's second note. He forbade looting and pilfering, he assigned a captain in the quartermaster corps to be responsible for securing surrendered property, ordered the quick disarming of the Rebel soldiers, and authorized the issue of two days' rations to every man who surrendered before they began their journey to prison camp. They would keep their property, if it was on them, and officers could keep their sidearms. Colonel Jacob Lauman's 2nd Iowa Infantry of General Smith's division was awarded the honor of being the first Federal unit to enter the Confederate works.

Lauman's regiment might have been that, but General Lew Wallace was the first Federal officer to go to Confederate headquarters. He wanted to see his friend Buckner. They exchanged pleasantries and Buckner offered Wallace breakfast. They chatted, with Buckner's staff present, about various topics, until Buckner asked what must have been on every gray-clad officers' mind: "What will Grant do with us?" "I can't say," answered Wallace, "But I know General

Grant, and I know President Lincoln better than General Grant, and I am free to say that it is not in the nature of either of them to treat you, or these gentlemen, or the soldiers you have surrendered, other than prisoners of war."[11]

Wallace was there when Commander Benjamin M. Dove of the *Louisville* came into Confederate headquarters. Commander Dove had rushed upstream at Commander Walke's orders, stopped briefly at the shore batteries, then hurried to find Buckner. Walke hoped that his representative would secure the Confederate surrender for the navy. Seeing that General Wallace had beaten him to the symbolic victory, Dove stayed long enough to save face and left. The gunboats returned to Cairo later that day. About an hour after Dove left, Grant came. He chatted with Buckner, "very kind and civil and polite," and even stated his regret, in a mocking way, that Pillow had run away. "If I had captured him, I would have turned him loose. I would rather have him in command of you fellows than as a prisoner," he said.[12]

Before the day was done, Grant informed headquarters that Fort Donelson was in Union hands: "I am pleased to announce to you the unconditional surrender this morning of Fort Donelson, with twelve to fifteen thousand prisoners, at least forty pieces of Artillery and a large amount of stores, horses, mules and other public property."[13] News of the surrender was a wonderful curative for the men in the Union hospitals. Surgeon Horace Wardner of the 12th Illinois Infantry remembered, "Every demoralized soldier about the hospital rendezvous at once became brave and started for the fort. Every wounded man who could walk hastened to the scene of victory." Perhaps they wanted to get in on the plunder before it was all gone.[14]

Grant did not have perfect control over his men. Despite his orders forbidding looting, there was some of that, both in the Confederate supply rooms and in the stores and shops of Dover. In a few cases, it was claimed, Confederate officers' sidearms were taken from them. And despite the continuing presence of pickets on the perimeter, the guards were inattentive and quite a few Confederates passed through to freedom after the surrender. Some were members of burial details who simply wandered through the porous Yankee picket line. Others made their way out individually. One of these latter was General Bushrod Johnson. Johnson is considered by some to have been the forgotten general at Donelson. He was largely ignored by his superiors in February 1862, was not even invited to sit in on their councils, and he is often overlooked in modern histories of the battle. Perhaps the fact that Johnson was a native of Ohio had something to do with the other generals' apparent bias against him. However, he deserves better. He had commanded Fort Donelson briefly before General Pillow arrived and, more important, he had been in the field directing the men of Pillow's division during their morning victory of February 15. He had won *his* fight. When the end came, he did not surrender and he did not passively wait to be sent to a prison camp. Of his escape, Johnson said, "In the afternoon, towards sunset, of February 18 I walked out with a Confederate officer and took my course towards the rifle pits on the hill, formerly occupied by Colonel Heiman, and finding no sentinel to obstruct me, I passed on and was soon beyond the Federal encampments. I had taken no part in the surrender; had received no orders or instructions from the Federal authorities; had not been recognized or even seen by any of the general officers; had been given no paroles, and had made no promises."[15] Besides all of that, the men of Johnson's command had been taken away by steamers that morning; he was responsible for no one who remained at Dover save himself. So he left. He said, "If my escape involves any question of military law, duty, or honor, I desire it may be thoroughly investigated, and I shall submit with pleasure to any decision of the proper authorities."[16]

By the time of General Johnson's escape, eleven thousand prisoners had been loaded on steamers and sent past Smithland and Paducah to Cairo. Nine thousand of them had gone on to St. Louis. The vast number of prisoners taken at Fort Donelson presented problems for the authorities. There were too many of them for any one town. General Halleck ordered that three thousand should go to Springfield, Illinois, three thousand more to Indianapolis, and the rest to Chicago. The officers would be paroled to Camp Chase in Columbus, Ohio. This was the original plan, but there were several changes made as to the dispersal of the grayback POWs, and in the end seven thousand went to Camp Douglas in Chicago, about 4200 to Camp Morton in Indianapolis, and "smaller groups of enlisted men were held at Alton, and Camp Butler, Illinois, and Terre Haute and Lafayette, Indiana."[17]

Some officers did go to Camp Chase, as originally proposed. One of them was the well-traveled J.F. Melton, former town marshal of Murray, Kentucky. It will be recalled that Captain Melton had fought at first Bull Run with the company he recruited, and had returned afterward to Calloway County to recruit another company, which he led to Fort Henry. When the fort fell, he escaped with Colonel Heiman to Fort Donelson. He fought there until February 16, when he was among those who were included in the surrender. It appeared that his luck had run out. Camp Chase would be his home for the foreseeable future—but there was an epilogue. Captain Melton escaped his captors at Camp Chase and made his way to Canada. He eventually was recaptured and taken to Alton, Illinois. He escaped again and briefly returned to his roost at Calloway County before joining Nathan Bedford Forrest's cavalry.

Buckner of Fort Donelson and Tilghman of Fort Henry and their field officers were too valuable and the authorities would not risk imprisoning them in a camp too close to Dixie. They were sent deep behind enemy lines for confinement at Fort Warren, in Boston, Massachusetts.

As for Grant, his victory at Fort Donelson did not win him much additional favor with his enemy General Halleck. Halleck did recommend to the War Department that Grant be promoted to major general (so long as he himself was promoted at the same time and remained Grant's superior), and he informed him that his command had been enlarged; he would now be in charge of the District of Western Tennessee. What Halleck did not do was congratulate Grant personally or in his dispatches to Washington. In truth, it seemed that Halleck went out of his way to diminish Grant's role in the victory. He sent an effusive thanks to General David Hunter, who had supplied Grant with reinforcements, saying, "To you more than to any other man out of this department are we indebted for our success at Fort Donelson," and he sent a message to the War Department in which he praised General C.F. Smith for his role in the victory. "Make him a major general," Halleck urged. "You can't get a better one. Honor him for this victory and the whole country will applaud."[18]

All the while, Halleck ignored Grant except for a formal order issued from headquarters that thanked him and Flag Officer Foote jointly for their services. Grant noticed the personal slight, and complained in his *Memoirs*: "I received no other recognition whatever from General Halleck."[19]

Grant was not so inconsiderate to his subordinates. On February 17, he issued General Orders No. 2, which said in part, "The general commanding takes great pleasure in congratulating the troops of this command.... For four successive nights, without shelter, during the most inclement weather known in this latitude, they faced an enemy in large force in a position chosen by himself.... Without a murmur this was borne, prepared at all times to receive an attack, and with continuous skirmishing by day, resulting ultimately in forcing the enemy to surrender without conditions ... the men who fought the battle will live in the memory of a grateful people."[20]

The long February campaign that had commenced when the gunboats and transports steamed out of Paducah on February 3 was concluded. Fort Donelson had cost the Union army about 2600 men killed and wounded and another two hundred missing. The navy had lost fifty-eight killed and wounded. Confederate figures are harder to determine, but the best estimates place the number of killed and wounded at 1500 to two thousand.

Sometimes, men seemed to die for nothing in battle. The families of the Confederate dead might certainly have been excused for feeling that their sons' lives had been wasted, considering the betrayal of their gallant efforts by Floyd and Pillow. This was not so for the mothers and fathers of the Union dead. The important effects of their sons' sacrifice were immediately recognized. The fall of Fort Donelson forced the evacuation of not only Nashville, Tennessee, but also Columbus, Kentucky, "The Gibraltar of the West." The Confederacy had suffered a deep and gaping wound that would never close.

14

Reconnoiters and Evacuations
(February-March 1862)

The fall of Fort Donelson may have upended the fondest hopes of the Jackson Purchase, but most of the rest of Kentucky celebrated. The House of Representatives in Frankfort passed a comprehensive resolution of gratitude that named a long list of prominent Union officers, ending with General Grant and Flag Officer Foote and thanking them for their victories that drove the Rebels from the borders of the Bluegrass State.

While the legislators sweated over the precise phrasing of their resolution, the men in uniform worked to tighten their hold over Western Tennessee and Kentucky. The 40th Illinois Infantry, which was stationed at Smithland and missed the battles at Fort Henry and Fort Donelson, was assigned to string telegraph lines. Sergeant John McLean of Co. A wrote, "Soon after the surrender of the latter my company was ordered back to Paducah, and was detailed to string a line of telegraph wire from Paducah to Fort Henry, from thence to Fort Donelson, and from thence to Clarksville.... The telegraph line was constructed through Kentucky on the high ground between the Tennessee and Cumberland rivers." McLean was fascinated with the handful of residents he found in the rugged land between the rivers, "primitive, uneducated people, few of whom could read or write. There were no school houses, and only occasionally a church, which the natives invariably called a 'meeting house.'" McLean found that slavery was uncommon in this area, but that it was "generally approved."[1] Like many impoverished people, they had, by some alchemy, been swindled by the rich into thinking that what was good for those at the top of the social pyramid was also in the interest of those at the bottom. It was not called a "rich man's war, poor man's fight" for nothing. McLean said that the telegraph line he and his fellows constructed "was the first in the country and served to inspire the natives with fear, awe, and wonder."[2]

Surgeons worked to mend the broken bodies shipped from the Tennessee battlefields downstream to Paducah and Cairo. General William T. Sherman, now in command of the Post of Paducah, wrote to his wife on February 17,

1862: "A great many wounded have come here and are in our Hospitals. The sick [and] wounded and prisoners are coming down from Fort Donelson and I am very busy." They came in groups of 150 at a time aboard the steamer *Minnehaha* and others. The Marine Hospital had once seemed so large; now it was barely adequate. After the next big battle, Shiloh, it would not come close to accommodating all the wounded. A few weeks hence, the churches, the McCracken County Courthouse, and even the female seminary would be requisitioned for use as hospitals.[3]

Another of Sherman's burdens was protecting Paducah against counterattack. Halleck was always fearful of an attack and transmitted that worry to his nervous subordinate. In the same letter in which he mentioned the many wounded arriving in Paducah, Sherman told his wife, "I have about 3000 men here, and there is an apprehension that Beauregard will come over to this place from Columbus and attack." Columbus continued to be a stone in the Federal boot. By their works there, the Confederates commanded the northern approach to the lower Mississippi River, and the Mississippi was considered by many of Lincoln's strategists to be the key to ultimate victory. Once it fell into Union hands, the Confederacy would be split.[4]

It was the navy's job to keep watch on Columbus. On February 23, only a week after the fall of Fort Donelson, Flag Officer Foote led five gunboats, two mortar barges, and four transports in a reconnaissance in force to Columbus. Foote was still hurting from the wounds he had received in the fight of February 14. He wrote his wife: "I am still on crutches and may be for a week, but my foot is rapidly improving. I have no objection to the wound either in the foot or in the arm, as they are honorable wounds, but I tell you the last was a bad fight."[5]

When the Federal armada came into view, General Polk's guns opened on them. Before the Union gunboats could respond, they saw a river packet steaming toward them, white flag flying. They could also see that there were women on board. Pulling alongside Foote's flagship, the *Cincinnati*, a courier handed over a note from Polk. It was addressed to General Halleck and it requested permission for the ladies to visit their prisoner-of-war husbands. Obviously, the action was over. Foote returned to Cairo, disgusted. He wrote his wife of the incident, saying that when they saw the white flag of the Confederates, "we hoped it was to surrender, but instead it was a mean artifice to discover our strength. We shall write a withering letter to the right reverend general to-morrow, charging him with violating all military rule of propriety by his unwarrantable act."[6] He added, "We were glad it [the reconnaissance] was done, however ... still we will give the bishop a hit."[7]

Foote could not know that at the very moment he was preparing more mortar boats in order to "give the bishop a hit" the bishop was making plans to evacuate Columbus. The fall of Fort Donelson had doomed Columbus. Never successfully attacked itself, the "Gibraltar of the West" had been outflanked.

On February 18, 1862, General P.G.T. Beauregard sat down to write to Confederate adjutant and inspector general Samuel Cooper. Beauregard had come west as second in command to Albert Sidney Johnston in the Western Department and had established his headquarters at Jackson, Tennessee. However, he had been too ill since arriving to assume active command. He merely corresponded with his officers in the field, offered them advice, and served as a conduit between them and the government in Richmond. Beauregard was writing Cooper to say that the fall of Fort Donelson made a decision about Columbus imperative. It must be decided to either defend it to the last or evacuate it. Cooper chose to evacuate Columbus and secretary of war Judah P. Benjamin ordered it done. Beauregard was informed on February 19 and conveyed the order to Polk.

Polk began by ordering the evacuation of Camp Beauregard. It had been only lightly manned by rotating units of short-term enlistees and cavalry since December, when its regular garrison was stripped and sent to General Johnston in Bowling Green. Captain R.A. Pinson of the 1st Mississippi Cavalry was now in command of Camp Beauregard, but it was Lieutenant Colonel Thomas H. Logwood who was in charge of destroying the camp. On February 21 he was able to report to Polk, "I have destroyed the railroad as well as possible from within 5 miles south of Mayfield back to Fulton Station. All the bridges are destroyed as far as Viola." He said that he had destroyed a locomotive and some of the rolling stock. Those rail cars he had spared were filled with supplies. Logwood continued: "I had a large lot of flour and other provisions, some wagons, etc., moved from Camp Beauregard to Fulton Station, and there, as directed by you, I set fire to that camp."[8]

Polk's next concern was the sick. He ordered their evacuation from Columbus on February 25. Next came the commissary and quartermaster's stores and the ordnance stores. Farmers in all of the surrounding area were made to give up their wagons for the army's use in moving supplies to the Mobile & Ohio Railroad depot for the short trip to Union City, Tennessee. The siege guns were moved by transport to Island Number Ten, where Brigadier General John P. McCown was taking charge. He went there with his division of three thousand men on February 27.

Most of the heavy work having been done, Polk ordered the remaining infantry to begin moving. General B.F. Cheatham's men moved south to Union City, Tennessee, on March 1. The same day, General A.P. Stewart's men took a steamer to New Madrid, Missouri. Lieutenant Edwin H. Rennolds, Co. K, 5th Tennessee Infantry, recalled the steamboat trip south as presenting a final, potentially tragic danger to his regiment's stay at Columbus. He wrote, "In passing Hickman, Kentucky, where Company 'M' had been enlisted, the people lined the shore and by waving handkerchiefs and cheering us, so excited the soldiers that they ran to that side of the boat and tilted it so much as to cause the water in the boilers to cover their red-hot sides and thus risked the danger of an explosion that would have sent a thousand men into the water and most of them into eternity. Lieutenant-Colonel C.D. Venable hurried the men back to their proper places and the equilibrium was restored and disaster averted."[9]

Polk and the cavalry remained behind to finish the light work. On the afternoon of Sunday March 2, 1862, Polk sent the last dispatch from Columbus. He wired secretary of war Benjamin: "The work is done. Columbus gone. Self and staff move in half an hour. Everything secured." To his daughter, General Polk revealed a more sentimental reaction to abandoning Columbus. A week after the event, he confessed to her, "I felt in leaving it as if I was leaving home."[10]

Federals observed much of the Confederates' activity as they prepared to abandon their Gibraltar. Lieutenant S. Ledyard Phelps had led a gunboat reconnaissance down to Columbus on March 1 and on his return to Cairo he informed Flag Officer Foote, who informed Secretary Welles, "Columbus is being evacuated ... saw the rebels burning their winter quarters and removing their heavy guns on the bluff, but the guns in the water batteries remain intact.... Large fires were visible in the town of Columbus and upon the river banks below, indicating the destruction of the town, military stores, and equipments."[11]

Perhaps in response to Phelps' report, General Sherman ordered Lieutenant Colonel Harvey Hogg to lead a battalion of the 2nd Illinois Cavalry to scout in the direction of Columbus. It was an easy ride down from Paducah, but they slowed down and moved cautiously when they came in sight of the Rebel stronghold. Seeing no signs of activity, they entered the Confederate works at 6:00 P.M. on March 3 and occupied them without ever having to fire a shot. They were the first Federals, other than prisoners, who got a close look at the massive fortification that had blocked them for so many months.

The same day, Foote made an armed reconnaissance to Columbus. The expedition was not as productive as it might have been, for, as he wrote, "the rain and dense fog prevented us from ascertaining whether or not the water battery had been removed, although we saw fires at Columbus and in rear of the bluff upon which heavy guns had been mounted, indicating an evacuation." Foote did not report seeing any sign of Lieutenant Colonel Hogg's cavalry in the former Confederate camp. Thinking that it was still up for grabs, Foote said that he planned to propose to Brigadier General G.W. Cullum (Halleck's chief-of-staff) that "a land force, together with several gun and mortar boats, return to Columbus and take possession of that place."[12]

On the morning of the next day, March 4, Foote's proposed excursion got under way. It included six gunboats, four mortar scows, and three transport boats that carried the 27th Illinois and battalions of the 54th and 71st Ohio and the 55th Illinois. General William T. Sherman was in command. Brigadier General Cullum wrote a detailed account of the successful expedition which said in part:

> Columbus, the Gibraltar of the West, is ours, and Kentucky is free, thanks to the brilliant strategy of the campaign, by which the enemy's center was pierced at Forts Henry and Donelson, his wings isolated from each other and turned, compelling thus the evacuation of his strongholds of Bowling Green first and now Columbus.
>
> On arriving at Columbus it was difficult to say whether the fortifications were occupied by our own cavalry on a scout from Paducah or by the enemy. Every preparation was made for opening fire and landing the infantry when General Sherman and Captain [sic] Phelps, with 30 soldiers, made a dashing reconnaissance with a tug, steaming directly under the water batteries. Satisfied that our troops had possession, they landed, ascended to the summit of the bluff, and together planted the stars and stripes amid the heartiest cheers of our brave tars and soldiers....
>
> The fortifications appear to have been evacuated hastily, considerable quantity of ordnance and ordnance stores, a number of anchors, and the remnant of the chain which was once stretched over the river, and a large supply of torpedoes remaining. Desolation was visible everywhere; huts, tents, barracks presented nothing but their blackened remains. Though the town was spared, I discovered a large magazine smoking from both extremities and caused the train to be cut. A garrison was left in the work of nearly 2,000 infantry and 400 cavalry, which I will strengthen immediately.[13]

Cullum's report of the large quantity of Confederate supplies left behind at Columbus was widely broadcast. General Polk, now established in Humboldt, Tennessee, and in charge of all CSA forces north of Jackson, read the accounts of his waste and inefficiency in evacuating Columbus, and he took time out from his duties to defend himself. He wrote to his friend President Jefferson Davis: "In pursuance to instructions received from the Department I evacuated Columbus, as I informed Mr. Benjamin by telegraph on the 3d. The work was done promptly and thoroughly, though under the pressure of the enemy's boats. The operation was effectually masked, and I retired all my military stores of every description, ammunition and guns all being removed. I fired the buildings of every description erected by the army, and with my staff brought up the rear.... The necessity compelling its abandonment was a trying one, but it was not as described."[14]

Polk was even more adamant in his letter to secretary of war Benjamin

14. Reconnoiters and Evacuations

a week later. He said, "I perceive that General Halleck and General Cullum have made their reports of the evacuation of Columbus to their Government, and that they have been published to the world. These reports are inflated, do injustice to the truth, and are intended to act upon and influence the world's mind.... I have sent forward to the Adjutant and Inspector General's office my official report of that evacuation, which differs very materially from the reports of the gentlemen above named. I hope it will be promptly published."[15] It is ironic that one supporting witness to Polk's claims was General William T. Sherman, at least in private. Sherman wrote to his wife: "The place must have been very formidable, but they carried off nearly all their guns, and materiels, burned their huts and some corn and provisions. I placed a garrison there, staid one day and came back to this my post [Paducah]."[16] Sherman told a different story for public consumption. He reported that large amounts of "guns, shot, shell, and stores" were left behind by General Polk. It appears that there was an officially approved version of events that differed somewhat from what was insisted on by the Confederates and privately admitted by the Federals.[17]

The Union garrison retired the old Rebel name of Fort De Russey and dubbed their new post Fort Halleck. As they policed the works, they found only a small amount of military supplies amid the debris and down along the river's edge. The most amusing thing the Federals found in the deserted stronghold was " a great number of humorous Valentines ... which the men had sent each other," as well as stuffed dolls of Union personalities such as Lincoln and McClellan "represented in grotesque form [and] always associated in some way with gallows and with negroes, had bottles in their hands, and invariably had ascribed to them some 'ultra-Abolitionist' sentiment."[18]

And the men found time to make their own amusements, including the ever-popular pastime of publishing a regimental newspaper. On March 15, 1862, the *Louisville Daily Journal* reported the first edition of a rival publication: "We have received the first number of the *Federal Scout*, by the 2nd Ill. Cav., the gallant boys who took possession of that place."[19] However, the days of leisure were soon at an end. There were said to be four thousand Rebel soldiers at Union City and defenses needed to be readied to meet them should they attempt a strike. Before the end of the month, General Halleck ordered "the columbiads and rifled guns, with carriages and ammunition, now at Fort Donelson, will be immediately removed to Columbus, and mounted in position best for iron-clad gunboats; also heavy guns, if any, to be removed to same place. Several columbiads and rifled guns are on the way from Pittsburg to Cairo. They will be sent to Columbus and mounted."[20]

The War Department was in complete accord with Halleck's thinking and supported him fully in arming and manning the works at Columbus. By the first of April, Halleck received a report that "fortifications at Columbus [were] going on expeditiously." An additional battalion of cavalry was ordered there, and another infantry regiment was requested. In addition, Colonel Napoleon B. Buford at Paducah was ordered to keep his Illinois regiment prepared to march at a moment's notice in response to an emergency at Columbus.[21]

The effectiveness of the Confederate effort at Columbus is hard to judge. Understanding the vital importance of the Mississippi River, the Confederates had moved decisively to defend it against invaders, and in this they were eminently successful. The post was continually probed for weakness and frequently came under fire from prowling Federal gunboats, but it never came close to being reduced by assault. Yet, the Confederates may have damaged the larger war effort by their obsession with the Iron Bluffs. Jay Carlton Mullen proposes the interesting theory that the strength of the Confederate works at Columbus was itself the cause of its ultimate failure to keep the Yankees off: "The outer works alone required a garrison of 13,000 men, while there were only 15,000 in the whole district. Employing so great a number to hold a single position left no forces to operate in the field. A modest garrison of 3,000 to 5,000 men in a well constructed fort could have defended the river. Such an arrangement would have availed reserves for emergencies. With rail connections extending from Columbus, Kentucky to Humboldt, Tennessee, and thence to Bowling Green, Kentucky, swift transfers of reserves would have been possible."[22]

Mullen's point is well taken. However, it was easier to see the strategic weakness inherent in such a massive buildup of manpower at Columbus from the vantage point of one hundred years later than it was in 1861. At that time, the Confederates knew only that they *must* defend the lower Mississippi and that Columbus was the best point to make their stand. It was worth any cost, and looking at the matter in light of what was known at the time, the Confederate high command did right. Once Columbus fell, the enemy made swift progress down the Mississippi, gouging the Confederates out of their lesser defenses, beginning with Island Number Ten.

15

Island Number Ten
(March–April 1862)

On February 26, 1862, Brigadier General John P. McCown arrived at New Madrid, Missouri, a few hours after leaving General Polk. McCown was a West Point graduate, a veteran of General Winfield Scott's Mexican Campaign, and a career U.S. Army artillerist, until he resigned in 1861 to become a Confederate. McCown had been a general for only four months when he was ordered to the area of New Madrid and Island Number Ten. His assignment was to examine the state of preparedness of the next line of CSA defenses below Columbus, which was being evacuated.

At New Madrid, McCown found the 11th and 12th regiments of Arkansas infantry in possession, along with two artillery batteries, all under the command of Colonel E.W. Gantt. They called their works Fort Thompson. Before the day was done, McCown ordered two additional regiments to be sent up from Fort Pillow, Tennessee. When they arrived he posted them slightly upstream from New Madrid and set them to erecting a second set of works, which they named Fort Bankhead. The other main point of defense in McCown's sector was Island Number Ten. Though there were some defensive shore batteries protecting it, the island itself was, as yet, completely undefended.

This was earthquake country, and the geography was a nightmare. Begin with the course of the Mississippi River. Mark Twain, who knew the area well, said, "In this region the river passes from Kentucky into Tennessee, back into Missouri, then back into Kentucky, and thence into Tennessee again." Imagine a capital letter "Z" lying on its back, so that the top bar points north and the bottom bar points south. This letter represents the river. Island Number Ten lies in the first angle of the "Z" and New Madrid lies on the north bank at the point of the second angle. Thus, even though it was *north* of Island Number Ten, New Madrid was *downstream*. These bends in the Mississippi were low-lying and so tight that they made perfect chokepoints to defend against Yankee invaders.[1]

These points were difficult to reach by land. Below Island Number Ten was a narrow strip of land between the Mississippi River on the west and Reelfoot Lake on the east. The only town in this swampy isthmus was Tiptonville, and only one north-south road connected the town with the outside world. North of Island Number Ten was a delta-shaped region of swamps that not only prevented an approach by southbound land forces, but also protected the eastern flank of New Madrid. In addition to the normal difficulties of the region, in February and March 1862 the Mississippi was in flood, at its highest level in four years.

Nature could hardly have designed a more confusing land- and waterscape, but man's scribbling on the map made it worse, for three states came together there. Directly to the north of Island Number Ten, that inundated delta mentioned above was Missouri. Flanking this on the east and west (that is, northeast and northwest of Island Number Ten) was Kentucky. The northwestern portion, called Madrid Bend, was the westernmost point of the Jackson Purchase, and it was completely detached from Kentucky by the river. However, it was attached to Tennessee on the south. Tennessee lay southwest, south, and southeast of Island Number Ten. The island belonged to Tennessee, though it was within two hundred yards of Kentucky on the east and approximately the same distance from Missouri on the north. Island Number Ten was an ovoid plug of land about three miles long and a quarter mile wide. It was sandy and heavily timbered, and there was not a gun or a man on it. There were two partially completed shore batteries protecting it: Battery Number One, which was slightly northeast of the island on the Kentucky bank, and Battery Number Five, south of the island on the Tennessee bank.

McCown returned briefly to Columbus to report to General Polk, and then returned to New Madrid with his division on February 27. The reinforcements were welcome additions, now that it was certain that the Federals would be coming, but there was still a great deal of work to be done, especially on Island Number Ten. When Brigadier General A.P. Stewart arrived from Columbus, McCown left him in charge of New Madrid, and he went to the island to conduct the work. When he was finished, McCown had cleared timber in a wide band back from the north face of the island and established in the clearing five new batteries mounting nineteen guns. He also had five batteries on the "mainland" (including the two original ones on the Kentucky and Tennessee shore), mounting twenty-four guns. In addition, he had a floating battery of nine guns. It was named the *New Orleans*, and it was under the command Commodore George N. Hollins.[2]

To scout the approaches, man the works, and work the guns, McCown had an aggregate of about 7500 men. The work to one side, theirs was a miserable assignment. Lieutenant Edwin H. Rennolds of the 5th Tennessee Infantry remembered that the troops camped near the shore batteries (at least

Island Number Ten
Theater of Operations
March-April 1862

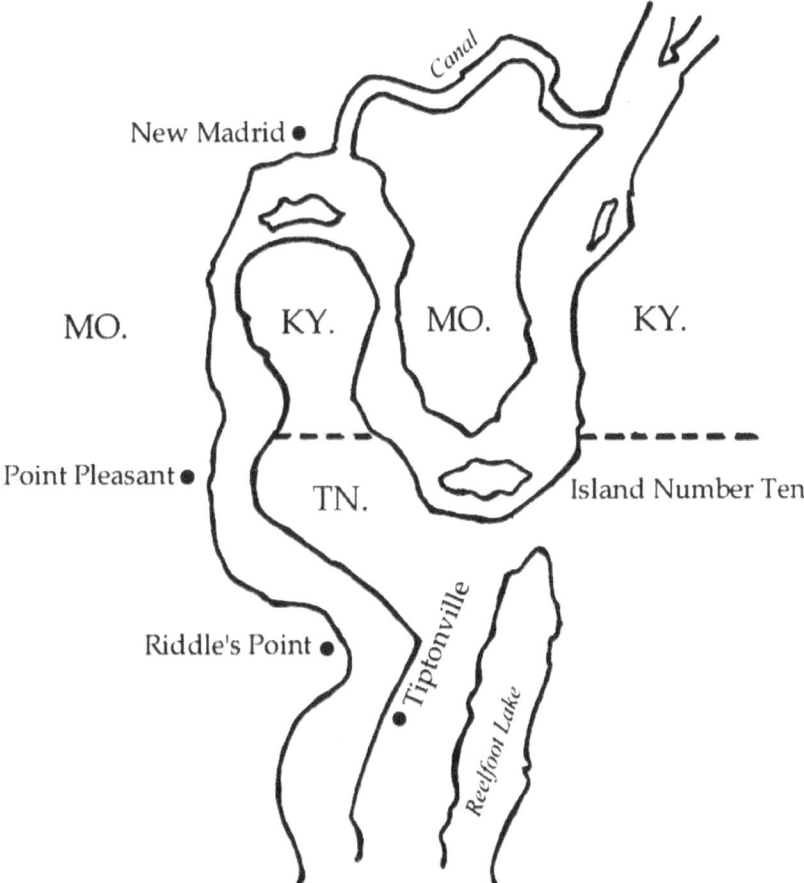

Island Number Ten, Theater of Operations, March—April 1862 (by the author).

on the Tennessee bank) found it necessary when pitching their tents "to floor them with rails and carpet them with cornstalks to elevate their blankets above the water, with which the rains had covered the river bottom." In the inescapable chilly dampness, sickness naturally took hold in the camps, reducing the number of General McCown's effectives. Many of the worst cases were sent to Hickman, Kentucky, the nearest hospital. There was nothing that General McCown could do about the weather. All he could do was place his men as well as possible, to arm and supply them, and wait for the Yankees to make their appearance.[3]

General John Pope was not yet forty years old. He was a Kentuckian by birth, a West Point graduate, and a veteran of the Mexican War. Pope was primarily an engineer, but he did not shy away from action. In Mexico, he was on General Zachary Taylor's staff and was twice promoted for gallantry in action. He was a man of some talent and undoubted courage. Major Manning F. Force of the 20th Ohio Infantry (and future Medal of Honor winner) spoke of Pope's "large ability and great acquirements," and said that he was "a positive man born to command." And yet, his boastful, fault-finding personality unraveled any deep admiration his fellow officers might otherwise have felt for him and they tended to dislike him. After the war with Mexico ended, Pope spent years helping to survey a route for a railroad to the Pacific across a southern route. In 1861, he was appointed to brigadier general and was given command of the District of Northern Missouri. In late winter 1862, his assignment was to take Island Number Ten away from the Rebels. He planned his campaign at Commerce, Missouri.[4]

There were two divisions under his command, the 1st under Brigadier General Schuyler Hamilton and the 2nd under Brigadier General John M. Palmer. The cavalry was commanded by Colonel Gordon Granger. In this campaign there would be a leading role for the engineers; they were commanded by Colonel Joshua W. Bissell. Pope's force was augmented by regiments from all over the Old Northwest and Missouri. These men, "the nucleus of the army corps afterward designated the 'Army of the Mississippi,'" stepped off for New Madrid on a wet and cold February 28, 1862. Their subsequent march along a corduroy road was later remembered by General Pope as "three of the most disagreeable days I ever passed."[5]

On March 3, a small force of M. Jeff Thompson's partisans tried unsuccessfully to block Pope's way. All that came from the Rebels' puny effort was nine casualties and the loss of their two small cannon to the Yankees, who arrived near New Madrid later that day. Normally, New Madrid had about one thousand residents. Now the citizens were gone. Only Confederates lived there and no one would find it an attractive place to live. All of its shade trees had been cut and some of the houses had been burned by the occupying Rebels to clear fields of fire. Other homes stood open to the weather, ransacked, their contents looted. New Madrid was ruined. What had been a pleasant riverside community was transformed completely by the five infantry regiments who occupied the two forts and the artillery crews who manned the twenty-one artillery pieces.

There were fourteen guns in Fort Bankhead and seven in Fort Thompson. Confederate firepower was supplemented by six gunboats that were anchored between the forts. All told, New Madrid was defended by sixty pieces of artillery, but the gunboats were especially worrisome. Pope remembered that the Mississippi River was so high that "the gunboats looked easily over the banks and completely commanded the [table-flat] country within their reach."[6] Rather than storm the Rebel forts and risk the wrath of their gunboats, Pope decided to wait for some heavy artillery wearing the Federal brand. He instructed Colonel Bissell to go to Cairo and take charge of delivering the heavy artillery pieces. Until they arrived, Pope ordered "forced reconnaissances" that "pushed over the whole ground and into several parts of the town." If it had not been for the gunboats the Federals would have attempted to take the enemy's entrenchments; as it was, the effort "would have been attended with heavy loss, and we should not have been able to hold the place half an hour exposed to the destructive fire of the gunboats."[7]

Meanwhile, Pope did receive reinforcements which increased his strength to 18,000 men. It forced him to reorganize his army into five divisions: the 1st under General David S. Stanley; the 2nd under General Schuyler Hamilton; the 3rd under General John M. Palmer; the 4th under the bad penny General Eleazer A. Paine; and the 5th under Colonel (soon to be General) Joseph B. Plummer. Pope's army outnumbered the enemy two to one, but the Rebels were getting reinforcements, too. General McCown was pouring soldiers into New Madrid by steamer. Since Pope had no gunboats to stop them—the Rebels controlled the river—he decided to try to close the Mississippi from below by use of land forces. To that end, General Pope handed Plummer and the 5th Division a special assignment on March 5. Plummer was to lead three infantry regiments, a squadron of cavalry, and a four-gun battery down to Point Pleasant to seal off the river below New Madrid.

Plummer reported: "The march was made by a circuitous route, for the purpose of avoiding 5 miles of road upon the river bank, upon which we would have been exposed to a fire from the enemy's gunboats. My object was to reach Point Pleasant about dark, take possession of the town, and establish my batteries and rifle pits during the night. But at dark, I was between 3 and 4 miles from the town, my men extremely fatigued by a march of 14 miles over a very bad road, and unfitted for labor." The infantry and artillery bivouacked for the night while the cavalry rode on ahead to reconnoiter the town. They discovered no enemy there, and Plummer marched in and took possession early the next morning.[8]

Fired upon by the Confederate gunboats, Plummer had to pull back for a few hours, but that night he returned to place his guns and dig rifle pits. The men settled into their occupation, their dull work enlivened by daily fire from the gunboats and by the two-gun battery of heavy guns the Confederates established on the opposite riverbank. For all that firepower, the enemy fire was singularly ineffective. Plummer wrote, "It is very remarkable that the enemy have thrown into this town since it has been occupied by me several hundred shots and shells without killing or wounding a man of my division. The only injury they have done me is the killing of one artillery horse."[9]

Pope continued to shuffle regiments forward to Plummer while he waited for Colonel Bissell to deliver the siege guns. They arrived about dusk on March 12, having been delivered from Cairo to Sikeston and dragged over the terrible roads from there. Pope ordered the guns—three 24-pounders and an 8-inch howitzer—to be placed that same night. The redoubts were completed by 3:00 A.M. and the guns opened fire from a distance of eight hundred yards at daylight on March 13. The enemy responded, and their fire was slightly more accurate here than at Point Pleasant. Pope only had four siege guns and a Confederate round shot disabled one of them, a 24-pounder, in the first contest. No other damage was done during the day-long duel.

That night, there was a terrible storm. When daylight came on March 14, two CSA deserters came into the Union lines and announced that the Rebels had abandoned New Madrid in the night. The Federals soon occupied the town and the works. Pope wrote of it:

> A brief examination of them disclosed how hasty and precipitate had been the flight of the enemy. Their dead were found unburied; their suppers untouched, standing on the tables; candles burning in the tents, and every other evidence of a disgraceful panic. Private baggage of officers and knapsacks of men were left behind. Neither provisions nor ammunition were carried off. Some attempt was made to carry ammunition, as boxes without number were found on the bank of the river where the steamers had been loaded.
>
> It is almost impossible to give any exact account of the immense quantities of property and supplies left in our hands. All their artillery, field-batteries and siege guns, amounting to thirty-three pieces, magazines full of fixed ammunition of the best character, several thousand stand of superior small-arms, with hundreds of boxes of musket cartridges, tents for an army of 10,000 men, horses, mules, wagons, intrenching tools, etc., are among the spoils. Nothing except the men escaped, and they only with what they wore.[10]

The Rebels tried spiking the cannon with rat-tail files, but they were in too much of a hurry and did an imperfect job. They were in so much of a hurry, in fact, that they left the body of an officer in its coffin in one of the tents, with the deceased's name only partially painted on the lid. They even left some of their sleeping men behind. Lieutenant Edwin H. Rennolds of the 5th Tennessee wrote the following in his memoirs: "The close proximity of the enemy made it imperative for us to omit the use of lights, and two men, Privates Thomas J. Dumas and Spence Hunt were overlooked and left asleep in one of the tents, many of which we left standing and when they awoke next morning they found the camp full of Federal soldiers and were captured."[11]

General A.P. Stewart, who commanded the defenses at New Madrid, left a lengthy report about the evacuation on the night of March 13. He admitted that he had little control over the men "to whom I was personally a comparative stranger," and he laid the blame for the haste and waste of the evacuation on the naval officers, primarily.[12] They were determined to save their boats and told the evacuees that they must hurry or be left behind that if the Federals opened fire with their siege guns, the boats would not hesitate to leave the men to fend for themselves. Stewart's cover letter to his report summarized its main points:

General John Pope (collection of the author).

> Allow me to say that I believe, though I am not positively certain, the evacuation was proposed and insisted on by the naval officers, who seemed to have little confidence in the ability of their gunboats to withstand the fire of the enemy's heavy guns; also that while I felt perfectly willing myself to remain and endeavor to hold the place as long as my superiors required or deemed proper, I felt that if we remained a day or two longer surrender was inevitable.
>
> The character of the weather the night of the evacuation was such as to render the removal of the guns impossible. I presume the water was a foot in depth over Fort Thompson and the soil a perfect mush.[13]

All of the captures from New Madrid added significantly to the Federal strength. The artillery was turned around toward the river, which was becoming increasingly difficult for Rebel traffic below Island Number Ten. However, that important outpost could not be reduced until Flag Officer Foote arrived with his gunboat flotilla, and Foote was proving to be obstinate.

Men are just men and battle changes them. It wrecks their bodies and sometimes their spirits. This is as true of the men who wear stars and gold braid as it is of the men who wear the single chevron of the private, and it is as true of sailors as soldiers. In the case of Flag Officer Andrew H. Foote, the physical wound that he had suffered at Fort Donelson was obvious to all, for it was not healing. The report of Dr. Geoffrey Aiguer, dated March 8, 1862, described considerable swelling in the left foot and concluded, "Judging from the present aspects of the case, and the length of time elapsed since the infliction of the injury, I must suppose that it was either of a very serious character from the first, or that very little, if any, improvement has taken place in consequence of neglect of the main [requirements] of a cure, *viz.*, absolute rest and horizontal position of the whole extremity."[14] In addition, there seem to have been multiple psychological factors working on Foote. For one, his gunboats had taken a terrific pounding in its defeat at Fort Donelson. It had, in the words of one biographer, "shaken his confidence and he was now cautious to the point of being reluctant."[15]

Furthermore, Foote was dragged down by pain and exhaustion into a deep trough of depression. He was dissatisfied with commanding the Brown Water Navy. He was a deep-sea man and said frankly, "I would this moment give all I am worth could I have been on the Atlantic, a captain of a good frigate, instead of out here." Besides a dread of battle and an ennui born of depression, there was a very practical reason that Foote stonewalled General Halleck and his chief-of-staff, General Cullum, as they bullyragged him to steam away south. That is, he had necessary repairs and desirable improvements to make to his vessels, and he was determined not to advance until the flotilla was, in his opinion, in fighting trim.[16]

On March 4, Halleck ordered Foote not to wait for repairs, but to make an "immediate demonstration" against Island Number Ten. "This is of vital importance, and there should be no delay," Halleck said. "I have much better information than you have of the condition of affairs, and, where possible, my instructions should be carried out." Foote ignored Halleck, but he forwarded a copy of the order to assistant secretary of the navy Gustavus A. Fox and commented, "I shall not again see my brave comrades fall around me, when by waiting a few days, I can move with almost a certainty of victory."[17]

On March 6, General Cullum tried his hand at influencing Foote to advance; Foote refused on the grounds that his vessels were not ready. Cullum had to inform Halleck, "Have urged Foote again and again to go down with gun and mortar boats, but can not induce him to move before Wednesday."[18] Foote admitted as much. On March 8, he wrote a telegram to Lieutenant Henry A. Wise in Washington, saying, "I am importuned daily by Genl Halleck to go on Monday to Attack Island No. ten (10) & New Madrid I shall not be ready till Wednesday to leave here I have said if asst Secy. Scott orders me to go I will try to do it but under a strong remonstrance that as the pilot houses are unsafe & we are not ready I believe that it would prove disastrous utterly demoralizing my command if I am responsible to the Gov't for the flotilla ought I not have the free exercise of my judgment of its ability when to perform the service required?"[19] On March 10, Halleck asked General Cullum why Foote could not advance the next day: "By delay he spoils all my plans." Cullum approached Foote with Halleck's question, and received in reply a heated note dated March 12. "I have repeatedly told you," scolded Foote, "that I shall not be ready with the flotilla, to move on Island No. Ten and New Madrid until Wednesday."[20]

That same day, Halleck tried another tack. He asked Foote "to go only as far as he could without engaging the Confederate batteries." Foote did not respond to Halleck; he wrote instead to President Lincoln. He sent a telegram in cipher in which he addressed a new concern. The note, dated March 13, read, "The iron-clad boats cannot be held when anchored by the stern in this current on account of the rods between the fantails forming the stern which yaws them about; and as the stern of the boats are not clad and have but two 32-pounders astern, you will see our difficulty of fighting downstream effectually. Neither is their power enough in any of them to back upstream, we must therefore, tie up to the shore the best way we can, and help the mortar boats." Foote implied yet another worry in his telegram to the president, namely that if a boat became disabled, the current would carry it toward the enemy, not away, as had been the case at Forts Henry and Donelson.[21]

There was one more worry that plagued Foote, and he confided it to his wife. He wrote that "if disaster occurs to my boats, the rebels could retake Columbus, capture St. Louis, and command the Mississippi River." He has been mocked by some for his fear, but there was more than a grain of truth in what he said. What was blocking the Rebels' own gunboat fleet from proceeding up the Mississippi River, if not the Union ironclads? Certainly, the small collection of bluecoat land troops could not be expected to successfully oppose them. Besides that, Foote's fear of Confederate invasion was no more ridiculous than Halleck's perpetual bug-a-boo that the Rebels were about to attack Cairo—and that was when there *were* ironclads in place to block them.[22]

By the morning of March 14, the flag officer had done all he could do to prepare. There was no more reason to delay the inevitable. His boats raised steam and turned their bows south. This was the biggest fleet that Foote had commanded since the war commenced. Behind his flagship, the *Benton*, were the ironclads *Carondelet, Louisville, Pittsburgh, Cincinnati, St. Louis,* and *Mound City*. Then came the timberclad *Conestoga*. Behind her were six transport boats towing ten mortar barges and farther back were the ammunition boats and other support vessels.

This would be the first test of the mortar scows. They were under the command of army Captain Henry B. Maynadier. Each vessel carried a 13-inch mortar capable of throwing a 220-pound shell over a distance of three miles. Since the barges were unpowered, they had to be tugged into position and tied up to the bank before going into action. A bag of powder weighing twenty-three pounds was rammed into the muzzle. A portable derrick was erected onshore to hoist the huge shells into the mortar's mouth. When it was ready to fire, the men hunkered down behind a wooden bulwark to protect them from the concussion. The gun roared, and thirty seconds later the shell dropped on or near its target and detonated with a force that seemed to crack the very footers of the earth. When the shells were fired at night, they arched through the sky with their burning fuzes visible and it was considered a pretty sight.

About noon on the 14th, Foote's armada anchored at Columbus. Colonel Napoleon B. Buford's 27th Illinois Infantry boarded and the cruise continued down to Hickman. The arrival of the Federal boats alarmed the Rebels who happened to be in town. A company of Confederate cavalry was observed galloping out of town and a train on the Nashville & Northwest Railroad pulled out from the station. It appeared suspicious to Foote and he ordered one of the *Benton*'s guns to fire a round. A 42-pound shell punched a hole completely through one of the cars behind the locomotive, but the train picked up speed and escaped.

Hickman was a prosperous little town. Though only thirty-two years old, it had paved streets lined with sidewalks and a brick business district. It also had a sizeable population of Northern sympathizers who welcomed some of the officers and men into their homes for the night. They had a warning for the Union men. In the words of a war correspondent who was traveling with the fleet,

> The citizens of Hickman seemed to be strongly impressed with an idea of the rebel force which awaited us at Island No. 10 and New-Madrid. They estimated the number of the enemy at not less than 20,000, while their guns and the strength and extent of their fortifications were beyond compulsion. The worst feature, however, in the powers which awaited us, was said to be the New-Orleans battering ram, the "Turtle."
>
> According to their account, the Turtle was more formidable than all the balance of the rebel engines put together. She was iron-clad, impervious to the heaviest missiles known to gunnery; could be sunk till level with the water, or raised at pleasure; was armed forward with two sharp steel plows; carried one heavy gun, which was fired from a bow-port that closed with a water-tight sliding panel—in short, could, and they feared would, sink our whole fleet in less time than one could swallow as many oysters.[23]

The fleet raised steam and continued south on the rainy dawn of March 15. They had gone about twenty miles when they encountered a Confederate supply barge guarded by the CSA gunboat *Grampus*. The *Benton* opened fire with her bow guns. Instead of firing back, the *Grampus* turned and raced down river, blowing four shrill blasts of her steam whistle as a warning to Island Number Ten, four miles farther on. The time for caution had come. The troop transports and mortar barges were secured to the Kentucky shore, while the ironclads eased forward for a look at what lay around the big river bend a mile below.

What they saw was the island and "a forest of steamers and hundreds of gleaming tents." There was no sign of the dreaded *Turtle*. What Commander Henry Walke noticed was the crazy geography of this region and the condition of the river. Walke wrote, "The twists and turns of the river near Island Number Ten are certainly remarkable. Within a radius of eight miles from the island it crosses the boundary line of Kentucky three times, running on almost every point of the compass." It concerned Walke that the river was high and the current fierce. It "carried away every movable thing. Houses, trees, fences, and wrecks of all kinds were being swept rapidly downstream."[24]

The current was a worry to Flag Officer Foote, too. He had warned that the boats could not fire accurately when anchored by the stern, which they would have to be when firing downstream. He had warned that neither could they turn about and attack with their stern guns, as the guns were too light and the stern was not armored. Now here he was facing the very trials which he had feared. If his boats were disabled they would float down toward the enemy and if they were destroyed, Federal positions as far north as Halleck's own St. Louis would be imperiled. Though he had come to fight, he decided it would be prudent to hold back some distance.

That did not mean he would be idle. The dangers posed by the powerful current notwithstanding, Foote decided to test the Confederate batteries from long range. Through the rest of the afternoon, "the six iron boats manoeuvered at this distance, carefully examining the prospect in front, and now and then varying the performance by sending a shell here and there on either shore, where appearances indicated that a rebel battery might be hidden." After a while, two mortar boats were towed forward and added their fire to that of the ironclads. At sunset the Federal bombardment ended. It had been more noisy than destructive, but the dance had begun.[25]

That night, the rest of the fleet was brought closer. The crews were issued pikes and sidearms, and pickets from the army were sent ashore to guard against a Confederate surprise. They traded fire with the Southerners all night, and in the morning six of them did not return.

On March 14, 1862, Confederate brigadier general James Trudeau, chief of artillery, conducted a "careful and complete" inspection of the defenses on Island Number Ten and the supporting batteries on shore. He was able to report that "our guns were all well mounted; that the implements for each were perfect and complete; that the men work their pieces with ease and facility; that they have an unbounded confidence in their new batteries, and, in short, that everything is as complete as our limited means would allow."[26]

Island Number Ten was stronger than ever. The garrison from New Madrid had been added to its number of defenders, and Flag Officer George N. Hollins was there with six gunboats. The observers who had escaped Hickman (and undoubtedly those from other points along the river) had given General McCown ample warning of the Yankee flotilla that was about to descend on them, and Trudeau had his gun crews at their pieces when the first hostile shots were fired. General Trudeau had ordered his men to fire "in case of attack only," and so as the Federals dropped shells among them, the Confederates remained silent.[27] That evening, they did throw a few long-range shots at some Union tugboats that came forward on a reconnaissance. The distance proved to be too great and the shooting had no effect. Of much more potential value was the intentional sinking of the steamboat *Winchester* in the channel north of the island. General Trudeau reported: "All went on quietly that night, and the obstruction of the channel was successfully performed without attracting the enemy's notice."[28]

The Rebel gunners had been at their stations all night, when the Federals came into view the next morning, March 16. The gunners watched with interest as the Yankees brought two mortar boats up and anchored one on the Missouri shore and one on the Kentucky shore. Between these two powerful flanks, the ironclads *Benton*, *Cincinnati*, and *St. Louis* steamed forward and lined up abreast. In the afternoon, when all were in place, they opened fire. It is uncertain how many total rounds the ironclads sent roaring in the direction of the Rebel stronghold, but upwards of three hundred mortar shells were fired before the day was done.

The navy resumed its attack the next day. Ammunition was distributed to the mortar barges and they opened fire, all eight of them, shortly after nine o'clock. The gloomy sky of early morning had cleared and the day seemed promising. A bit before noon, Flag Officer Foote moved to the front. The *Benton* was tied by lines between the *Cincinnati* and the *St. Louis* to keep the large but underpowered flagship from being carried by the current closer than intended to the enemy batteries and also so that unison volleys could be fired from the three ironclads' bowguns. At two thousand yards' distance, the gunboats' shelling began. It was difficult at that range to see what damage they might be inflicting on their target, Battery Number One. It was not hard to see the damages the Rebel gunners were inflicting on the gunboats. The *St. Louis* took a round through her casemate, the *Cincinnati* took a plunging shot through its deck, and the *Benton* was hit three times in her forward armor but was undamaged until a plunging shot penetrated her, bounded belowdecks nearly the whole length of the vessel, and demolished the lid of Foote's desk. The worst injury of the day, however, was of a different sort.

Foote had distinguished guests on board this day. Grant's patron, Congressman Elihu B. Washburne, and James B. Eads were on board the *Benton*. Eads was standing beside Foote when an officer came up with a packet of letters. As Eads recalled it, "While still conversing with me, his eye glanced over them ... and he selected one which he proceeded to open. Before reading probably four lines, he turned to me with great coolness and composure, and said, 'Mr. Eads, I must ask you to excuse me for a few minutes while I go down to my cabin. This letter brings me news of the death of my son, about thirteen years old, who I hoped would live to be the stay and support of his mother.'"[29] Young William Foote had died in New Haven on March 14, the day the flag officer steamed south from Cairo. Eads said that Foote returned to the deck after about a quarter of an hour, "perfectly composed." The flag officer's flinty self-control masked the terrible grief he felt and only raised higher the gloom that was swamping his soul at the start of this campaign he never wanted to fight at all.[30]

The Federal flotilla withdrew at dusk, the mortars continuing to fire at thirty minute intervals through the night.

Since the capture of New Madrid, the Federals at Point Pleasant had been in a sort of backwater. They maneuvered against M. Jeff Thompson, a bit, but mostly their time hung heavy and that always led to mischief. Not a farmhouse, smokehouse, chicken coop, or root cellar was safe from stragglers, the worst elements in the ranks. Private C.W. Wills wrote:

> Some of our soldiers impose on the natives pretty badly.... Whenever there is an army, for 10 or 15 miles around it, there will be hundreds of stragglers. Some out of curiosity, some to see the natives and talk with them, but the majority to pick up what they can to eat. There is not a farm house within ten miles of camp, notwithstanding the positive orders against straggling, that has not, at least, 50 soldier visitors a day, and they are the poorest soldiers and the meanest men that do all the straggling, or nearly all. They will go into a house, and beg what they can and then steal what is left. Rough, dirty, coarse brutes, if they were all shot our army would be better off. Most of these fellows are bullies at home, and that class makes plunderers in war.... The greatest objection and the only one I have to being in the army, is the idea of being associated, in the minds of the people of this country, as well as the home folks, with such brutes.[31]

Other Federals, however, had been busy with the legitimate work of extending their control farther south. At each desirable point along the way, they stopped to build gun emplacements. Because the Confederate gunboats were on the prowl and quick to open fire at any sight of the Yankees, Pope's men had to work by night. Their goal was Riddle's Point, a spot on the Missouri bank directly across from Tiptonville, Tennessee. Tiptonville was in that isthmus of land below Island Number Ten. Any guns that were placed to command it would also command the river and the only road by which the Rebels might escape. The Riddle's Point operation had been assigned to General John M. Palmer, commanding the 3rd Division. Palmer wrote, "We left New Madrid on the evening of March 16th and hauled with us a twenty-four pound iron gun and ammunition wagon, and reached Point Pleasant in the evening of the 17th, soon after sunrise [?], after wading half the distance."[32]

Though he knew that his move south was supposed to be clandestine, the sight of the CSA gunboats on the Mississippi almost overwhelmed Palmer's good judgment during the single day at Point Pleasant, and Pope had to send him a sharp warning. The general wrote his overeager subordinate: "On no account permit the 24-pounder gun to be fired at Point Pleasant. You will defeat my whole object by letting the enemy know the gun is there. I was surprised to learn from Colonel Bissell that you had thought even of firing it at gunboats or any other boats."[33]

The next day, Palmer continued south. A short five-mile march brought him to his destination of Riddle's Point. That night, his men "constructed an earthwork on the bank of the river for the protection of the gun, and flanked the works with rifle-pits in the sand, sufficient for the protection of a regiment." The topography offered some natural protection as well, irregularities in the lay of the land from the great earthquakes of a half century earlier. Palmer wrote, "The narrow elevations with corresponding depressions formed a natural protection for troops at supporting distances from the earthworks and the rifle pits."[34]

At daylight on the 19th, the CSA gunboats observed the new intrusion into their territory, and five of them approached and opened fire. A shot from Palmer's 24-pounder ricocheted off the water toward Tiptonville, the gunboats fired again, and the fight, such as it was, was on. The 24-pounder was well served. Two of the Confederate boats were soon crippled and forced to drop out of the fight. The others kept firing. The Federal 24-pounder was struck about the muzzle but was only lightly damaged. The boats fired a few more rounds, then fell back, ending the small engagement having inflicted no casualties at all and, so far as Palmer knew, suffering none.

In his report of the action to Halleck, General Pope made much more grandiose claims. He claimed that the Rebels had lost one gunboat sunk and many men killed on deck by the Yankee sharpshooters. It was typical of Pope to embroider his successes with inflated details, and was one of the reasons that he was unpopular among many of his fellow officers. Notwithstanding his boasts, Pope's larger point was true. The Federals now commanded the important point across from Tiptonville and could blockade the river "to any supplies and re-enforcements for the enemy at and around Island No. 10." Another benefit was derived from Palmer's occupation of Riddle's Point. Flag Officer Hollins ordered his gunboat flotilla to fall downriver below Tiptonville. He "was unwilling to risk his vulnerable wooden vessels to the heavy Union guns; after that his squadron was not a factor in the battle." The island and its shore batteries had lost much of their firepower and were now invested.[35]

An investment would not necessarily bring a quick conclusion to the campaign, however. Pope needed gunboats and transports below Island Number Ten to effect his crossing of the river, an operation he would have to complete before launching an infantry attack on the Tennessee side. In the meantime, he intended to tighten the noose around the Confederates. Both of these objects were on Pope's mind on March 16 when he sent engineer Colonel J.W. Bissell to see if a road could be cut through the Missouri peninsula north of the island so that batteries could be placed there. If a road proved to be impossible, Bissell was ordered "to ascertain whether it were possible to dig a canal across the peninsula from some point above Island No. 10 to New Madrid, in order that steam transports might be brought to me, which would enable my command to cross the river." Pope later admitted that the idea of a canal was suggested to him by General Schuyler Hamilton.[36]

Bissell discovered that, while building a road through the flooded delta was impossible, a canal could be made. In fact, he said he could "have the boats through in fourteen days."[37] Pope ordered him to begin the work immediately. In his article for *Battles and Leaders of the Civil War*, Bissell wrote, "The term 'canal,' as used in all the letters and reports relating to the opening of this waterway conveys an entirely wrong idea. No digging was done except by way of slightly widening a large break in the levee, and those who speak of 'working waist-deep in the water' know nothing of it."[38]

What it was, primarily, was a job of sawing. Proceeding west, the canal would first go through a levee upriver from Island Number Ten, cross a flooded cornfield, and would end in the St. Johns Bayou, which drained into the Mississippi at New Madrid, below the Confederate island. In between lay Cypress Swamp, a two-mile wide belt of timber so tight that the boats could not get through. This was where the heaviest work was required. Two shifts of men were put on rafts. The first would row out and cut the trees along the route the engineers had selected, leaving stumps that stuck up above the waterline. Then, as they moved forward, the second crew would come up on a raft fitted out with a timber frame that resembled a modern child's swing set. It was hinged at the top so that the whole frame could swing in an arc like a clock's pendulum. A cross cut saw forty feet long or more was attached to the bottom legs of the frame so that it described a half-circle and would cut as the frame swung forward and backward. The bow of the saw was below the water surface. The second raft with the timber cutters would be made fast to the stump, and four men pulling in rhythm on each end of the saw would thus cut off the stumps 4 1/2 feet below the water line, plenty deep for the shallow-draft troop transports. If the saw did not pinch, a two-foot thick tree could be cut in fourteen minutes. The debris the sawyers created, and the earlier debris deposited by nature, had to be cleared away, and in this manner a fifty-foot wide channel would be carved across the peninsula, yard by yard.

This was the job facing Bissell and his crews. They breached the levee on March 23 and began cutting their way through Cypress Swamp on the 29th.

On March 17, Pope had written to Flag Officer Foote, asking if he could run past Island Number Ten with one of his gunboats. If he could, the troops in Missouri could be transported across the Mississippi to Tennessee in safety. The channel around Island Number Ten being so narrow, the enemy's guns so numerous, and the ironclads' stern armor so inadequate, Foote declined.

In the meantime, the daily naval bombardment continued. It was so constant that it became the background noise of daily life and, like the people who endured other bombardments (most famously, the citizens of Vicksburg in 1863), the defenders of Island Number Ten grew used to it. It lost its terror. Philip B. Spence admitted that he "was kept busy running for bombproof positions, which had been constructed on every part of the island," but others were more nonchalant. Tennessee cavalryman John Milton Hubbard wrote that the gunboats would overshoot the gun emplacements and "send an occasional shot clear into the timber, and there was no telling when one might land right in camp. Our nervousness on this account soon wore off, as we were exposed thus for seventeen days." The Rebels were not particularly interested in wasting their ammunition firing back at a threat that was more clamor than calamity. There were days when they did not fire at all. In some ways, the danger was greater from firing their own guns than enduring the ineffective fire of the Federals. On March 19, the best gun the Confederates had, called "Lady Polk, Jr.," exploded while returning enemy fire. It was now a demonstrable fact that naming a cannon after General Polk's wife was simply reckless, an invitation to disaster. On this occasion, no one was injured, though the quality of the Confederate defense certainly was.[39]

Pope was bitter that the gunboats and mortars were satisfied merely to stand off and fire ineffective salvos from a distance of several hundred yards. He continued, unsuccessfully, to urge Foote to run the gauntlet of Confederate guns. He telegraphed Halleck: "As Commodore Foote is unable to reduce and unwilling to run his gunboats past the island, I would ask, as they belong to the United States, that he be directed to remove his crew from two of them and turn over the boats to me. I will bring them here."⁴⁰

In this, Pope and his department commander disagreed. It is true that Halleck had been seriously annoyed at Foote for his long delay in commencing the naval part of the programme. At one point Halleck was ready to call off the campaign entirely and send Pope's divisions to join the Army of the Tennessee (as it would soon be designated) at Pittsburg Landing, Tennessee. However, he seems to have approved of the flag officer's performance once the flotilla arrived at Island Number Ten. Halleck wrote to Foote: "I am very glad that you have not unnecessarily exposed your gun-boats. If they had been disabled, it would have been a most serious loss to us in the future operations of the campaign; whereas the reduction of these batteries, this week or next, is a matter of very little importance indeed."⁴¹

Pope never came around to this way of thinking. Convinced that he could not count on Foote for any meaningful support, he ordered construction to begin on his own squadron of gunboats, improvised from eighty-foot-long coal barges and capable of mounting one Columbiad and three 32-pounders. The work on these boats coincided with that on the canal and was ongoing when the principle work on the canal was done on March 31. All that remained was to clear the overhead limbs out of the way and haul some woodland rubbish out of the channel. By the next day, all was ready. Pope moved his unfinished boats into the canal and expected to complete the work on them by the night of April 3. "I have no hope of Commodore Foote," he wrote Halleck. "He has postponed trying to run any of his gunboats past Island No. 10 until some foggy or rainy night. The moon is beginning to make the nights light, and there is no prospect of fogs during this sort of weather. We must do without him."⁴²

On March 30, 1862, Colonel Napoleon B. Buford took the gunboat *Louisville* to Hickman. Traveling with him were his own 27th Illinois Infantry and the 15th Wisconsin. With little role for the army so far, Buford was trying to find useful ways to contribute. He had a novel adventure on March 25, when he ascended in the balloon of Captain John H. Steiner of the aeronautics corps. From an altitude of six hundred feet, they could see for miles over the flooded countryside and Island Number Ten. They observed the island and onshore gun emplacements, whose location was already known, and also saw that the enemy's camp of tents had been moved farther toward the interior, which was an encouraging sign that the mortar and gunboat fire was intimidating the Rebels, if nothing else.

The balloon ascent was interesting, but the expedition of March 30 promised to be more productive. At Hickman, Buford summoned Lieutenant Colonel Harvey Hogg and two companies of the 2nd Illinois Cavalry, a company of cavalry led by Captain William D. Hutchens, and a four-gun battery commanded by Captain Frederick Sparrestrom. Buford shared with these assembled officers and Captain Dove of the *Louisville* that he was going on a raid against Union City, Tennessee. A Rebel brigade was there, commanded by Colonel Edward Pickett, and they sat astride the Mobile and Ohio Railroad, which the defenders of Island Number Ten might use in the final eventuality to escape capture. This would be an undesirable outcome to the Federal campaign, and Buford was going to take preemptive action.

Buford's column moved out in mid-afternoon. He ordered four companies of the 22nd Missouri, under Lieutenant Colonel John D. Foster to remain behind as a reserve and to make sure than no one left Hickman. It was an unusually warm afternoon; the mercury stood at 80°, but the column made good time until it reached Reelfoot Lake. There, all of the bridges had been destroyed. When the men finally got across, they found that the road on the other side was bad and led through a heavy woods where it paid to be watchful. Buford called a halt at nightfall, four miles from Union City, near the home of a Rebel sympathizer named Lawson. Buford allowed no one in the house to leave, only to learn that there had already been a breach of security. Buford said, "I learned [Lawson] had been apprised of our advance by one of his neighbors, and apprehended information had reached Union City."[43]

The march resumed at sunrise, March 31, and by 7:00 A.M. the men had arrived at their target. It was a quick march because Buford had denied his men their breakfast. They could see the Rebel camp and the town beyond. As they began to form their battle line, the Confederates opened fire. Sparrestrom placed his artillery in a wheat field on the right, on a small hill that commanded the Secesh camp.

It might have turned into a sizeable fight, except that at the moment Sparrestrom's guns began to fire, the loud whistle of a train was heard, coming from the direction of the M & O station. The train was pulling out, which gave the defending Rebels an idea. As Buford reported it, "The whistle of the departing engine was heard ... and the stampede of infantry, cavalry, loose horses, and citizens was complete. The artillery moved forward, and the cavalry and infantry marched into the camp."[44]

Fourteen prisoners were caught by Captain Hutchens' cavalry company, while Lieutenant Colonel Hogg took charge of the nearly deserted town. "Our work was accomplished," said Buford. He ordered the enemy camp to be destroyed, along with the telegraph line, all uniforms, provisions, many weapons, and three railcars near the depot. The depot was full of useful supplies and was spared. A hundred horses and mules, some weapons, the mailbag, three battle flags, and two guidons were claimed as prizes by Buford's men.[45]

In the aftermath of the hasty Confederate retreat, the African American population of Union City came out of hiding. They visited with the Yankees "in great numbers, and seemed mightily pleased at the pageantry afforded by the military gathering."[46] One of the females declared that the Northern men looked better than the Southern boys, and announced that she was going to have a dress made up in red, white, and blue. The blacks did not have long to visit with their new friends. As quickly as they had come, the Federals turned back toward Hickman. "As my place was in front of Island No. 10, to cooperate with our gallant Navy and its war commander, Flag Officer Foote, I felt compelled to return as soon as the main object was accomplished," Colonel Buford explained. He was back with the fleet in time to write his report on the evening of March 31.[47]

The same day of Buford's raid, Confederate brigadier general William W. Mackall assumed command at Island Number Ten. General McCown had been on General Beauregard's short list for early replacement ever since the fall of New Madrid. Being relieved was not career-ending for McCown. He was sent to Fort Pillow and went on to fight with mixed success in some of the major battles of the war in the West.

Mackall was a Marylander, a West Point classmate of Braxton Bragg, and a Mexican War veteran. He lately had been on the staff of General Albert Sidney Johnston. He was a solid, if not spectacular, soldier, and by accepting command of Island Number Ten, he proved that he was not intimidated by a difficult assignment. He could scarcely have come at a worse time. As he reported,

> The concurring testimony of the commanders of regiments was to the effect that their men were broken down by hard labor, dispirited by two recent evacuations, and impressed with the idea that the post was untenable and its defense hopeless. Examination by Captain [Victor] Sheliha, my engineer, on April 1 and 2, showed that the works of defense consisted of a naval floating battery, and of water batteries mounting about fifty guns, on a coast of 25 miles in extent, without a single magazine, and the guns of far less range than those of the enemy. Satisfied that the post was only tenable so long as the forces of the enemy could not cross, and that with the troops at my disposal I could not secure the batteries from a land force, I devoted myself to increasing my batteries and establishing order among the troops and system in the staff department.[48]

General Mackall realized that maintaining the defenses of Island Number Ten was a herculean task and was probably rendered hopeless before he assumed command. The news was bad, and it was soon to become much worse.

Pope was ungenerous in his opinion of Foote, condemning him for his supposed lethargy. The flag officer authorized for the night of April 1 one of the memorable events of the campaign, a nighttime raid to silence the guns of the Kentucky Battery once and for all. The Kentucky Battery (also called by the names Battery Number One and Redan Number One) was two miles upriver from the island. It was the most advanced Confederate position and, though partially flooded, had shown itself to be a formidable obstacle to any naval advance.

Since the first full day of battle, the Kentucky Battery had been the fleet's greatest challenge. It was commanded by Captain Edward W. Rucker. In the fight of March 17, it had sustained the most intense fire from the Federal gunboats and mortar barges simply because it was closer to the invading fleet and because it continued to resist after the other batteries, too far away to be effective, quit firing. Captain Rucker reported: "The enemy turned their whole force on my little forts, pouring an incessant fire from the mortars and broadsides from rifled cannon of the heaviest caliber."[49]

The shells plowed deep furrows through the parapets, but the Rebel gunners remained at their posts and continued firing with their three heaviest guns, 8-inch Columbiads. Their smooth-bore 32-pounders were useless at that range. When the Federal flotilla withdrew at sundown, the Rebels assessed the damage they had sustained: one gun had been dismounted, one man had been killed, and seven more were slightly wounded. The battery had survived with remarkably little damage, considering the intensity of the day-long Federal fire. Artillery chief Trudeau had nothing but praise for the defenders and particularly for Captain Rucker. Trudeau said, "Captain Rucker behaved throughout the day with cool judgment and discretion. I say nothing of the bravery he displayed on that day. Captain Rucker is a hero and behaved like one."[50]

The Kentucky Battery continued to offer stubborn resistance through the rest of March. Rucker wrote that, since the 17th the Yankees had "not returned to the close position occupied by them on that day, although they have kept up a continual fire with heavy shell and shot at a greater distance, fortunately doing but little damage to us." Since direct assault had proved ineffective, Foote decided to reduce the battery by sabotage.[51]

The night of April 1 was stormy. The noise and the darkness covered the movement of Colonel George W. Roberts and forty men of the 42nd Illinois and the fifty sailors who rowed them forward to the Kentucky battery. They were unobserved until they had closed to within a few yards. A lightning flash spotlighted them. Two Rebel sentries fired once and then ran, never delivering a second volley. Colonel Roberts and his raiders scrambled ashore and spiked all six Rebel pieces. The work was done in thirty minutes and the men returned across a choppy river to the flotilla, their mission a success.

Incidentally, the storm that covered Colonel Roberts and his men on the night of April 1 preceded a tornado that struck New Madrid, careened upriver, uprooted a tree that crashed down on a tent in the camp of the 7th Illinois Cavalry and killed three men. Others were hurt and some horses were killed.

The twister tore across Island Number Ten, where it killed two men of the 1st Alabama, before it headed toward the Federal flotilla, costing two boats their chimneys. Before the storm blew itself out, it killed five people in Cairo and tore the roofs off of thirty houses in Paducah. Men might fire their cannon and scar the face of the earth with their canals and fortifications and think that they had done a mighty thing, but Yankees and Rebels alike were reminded on the night of April 1–2 that there was a greater force still which showed how little their efforts really were.

Since March 17, General Pope had been putting pressure on Flag Officer Foote to run one or two gunboats past the gauntlet of Rebel guns on and around Island Number Ten. Though Foote had stubbornly refused, the thought of it had been planted in his imagination. He believed that it could not be done, but he wanted to poll his gunboat commanders, so on March 20, as he wrote to Welles, "for the first time since I have been in command of the flotilla, I called a council of war, with the view of ascertaining the opinion of the officer with reference to sending, or attempting to send, aid to General Pope. The officers, with one exception were decidedly opposed to running the blockade, believing it would result in the almost certain destruction of the vessels." The one officer who believed that he could safely run past Island Number Ten was Commander Henry Walke of the *Carondelet*.[52]

A week later, Foote convened a second council of war. Not a man had changed his opinion, including Walke, still the only officer present who insisted that he could make the run in his gunboat. Foote was reluctantly persuaded. As the council ended, he gave Walke verbal permission to run the gauntlet and followed up with written orders to that effect on March 30. Walke began immediately to prepare and he wrote of it:

> All the loose material at hand was collected, and on the 4th of April the decks were covered with it, to protect them against plunging shot. Hawser and chain cables were placed around the pilothouse and other vulnerable parts of the vessel, and every preparation was adopted to prevent disaster. A coal-barge laden with hay and coal was lashed to the part of the port side on which there was no iron plating to protect the magazine. It was truly said that the *Carondelet* at that time resembled a farmer's wagon prepared for market. The engineers led the escape-steam, through the pipes aft, into the wheel-house, to avoid the puffing sound it made when blown through the smoke stacks.[53]

On the morning of April 4, Walke was about ready. He issued "pistols, cutlasses, muskets, boarding pikes, and hand grenades" to his crewmen and "attached hoses to the boilers for throwing scalding water over any who might attempt to board." If it appeared that capture was inevitable, orders were for the *Carondelet* to be scuttled.[54]

Shortly before launch time, Colonel Napoleon B. Buford came onboard with a complement of twenty-three sharpshooters (42nd Illinois Infantry), which the army was lending to the navy for this enterprise. They were commanded on this special mission by Captain John A. Hottenstein. The *Carondelet* and her crew were as ready as Walke could make them. Walke's hopes for an overcast night were dashed. The weather was calm and the moon was, unfortunately, bright. All unnecessary lights onboard were shut off and the ports all closed, and at 10:00 P.M. the *Carondelet* cast off. At the wheel was Pilot William R. Hoel, a riverman of twenty years' experience who had volunteered for the duty.

Spring is a variable season in the land where the rivers come together. About the time the *Carondelet* slipped into the main channel, a sudden storm front blew in. The sky clouded over. The rain began to fall and the lightning flashed. The *Carondelet* was slow, and the barge lashed to her side made her move even more sluggishly, but the current was with her and the sudden storm gave her a chance to succeed in a mission that no other gunboat commander had even thought possible. Walke wrote, "All speed was given to the vessel to drive her through the tempest."[55]

Battery Number One was no longer a threat; shore Battery Number Two was where the danger would really begin. The *Carondelet* had just drawn abreast of the battery when her smokestacks suddenly blazed up like signal flares. "It was caused by the soot becoming dry, as the escape-steam, which usually kept the stacks wet, had been sent into the wheel house, as already mentioned, to prevent noise." The timing could not have been worse. The *Carondelet* was a lighted target until the flame was smothered. Too late. Confederate sentries on shore spotted the gunboat and the guns of shore Batteries Two, Three, and Four began to roar.[56]

Though it happened repeatedly through the run past the shore batteries, Walke always thought that the danger posed by the flaring smokestacks was exaggerated. He felt that the lightning illuminated the *Carondelet* enough that the Rebels would have seen her, even without the ersatz torches her smokestacks made. Perhaps he was right, but it is hard to believe that the torches did not pinpoint the location of the boat better than the pulsating light of the storm would have done.

In any case, the Rebel artillerists on shore tended to overshoot. The Union gunboats and mortar barges upstream began to fire into the shore batteries to distract the enemy gunners, at least, and perhaps to disable their pieces entirely. The *Carondelet* ran safely through the shell fire to the island, and veered close in, hugging its north shore. The sunken wreck of the *Winchester* proved to be no obstacle at all. The muzzles of the Confederate guns on the island had been depressed to keep the rain out and now the gunners hurried to elevate them in order to fire. The *Carondelet* got past them and steamed toward the enemy's floating battery, the *New Orleans*, three miles below the foot of the island. The battery had been closer until long-range Federal fire on April 2 had cut her cables, causing her to drift down freely until she could be stopped and made fast. In her new location, she was unable to deliver effective fire. "As we passed her she fired six or eight shots at us, but without effect," said Walke. One round did strike the coal-barge and was discovered later buried in a bale of hay.[57]

It had been prearranged that when approaching New Madrid, the *Carondelet* would fire signal guns to let General Pope's artillerists know that she had made a successful run and was coming in. The storm was so furious that Walke feared the sound of thunder would blend with that of the guns and the signal would go unnoticed. To give the storm time to pass, the *Carondelet* paused in midstream. After a time, "orders were given to get the guns in readiness and fire three times at intervals of one minute, and after a lapse of five minutes to fire three guns." When no answer signal came from New Madrid, the gunboat crept forward and Walke shouted through a speaking trumpet that the *Carondelet* was below Island Number Ten and was approaching. The message was received and the gunboat moved forward with no opposition. She did run aground, but backed off and docked about 1:00 A.M. The soldiers cheered and General Pope rewarded the sailing men of the *Carondelet* with a barrel of grog (a fact that would have upset Flag Officer Foote, a teetotaler who had spent years fighting Demon Rum and had, in fact, succeeded in making it against regulations to issue rum rations in the navy).[58]

The next morning, assistant secretary of war Thomas A. Scott and General Pope came on board the *Carondelet*. Pope was delighted with the previous night's events and with Commander Walke. He said, "A more gallant, zealous and capable officer I do not know." Pope was not yet satisfied, however. If one ironclad was good, two would be better, and he wanted it soon. On April 5 he wrote Foote: "I have not a doubt but that one of them could run the batteries to-night without any serious injury.... My best artillerists, officers of the Regular Army, of many years' service, state positively that it is impossible in the night to fire with any kind of certainty the large guns, 32s, of our batteries, especially at a moving object." Besides, said Pope, even if it was a dangerous undertaking, "certainly the risk to a gunboat moving down in the night is not nearly so great and involves no such consequences as the risk to 10,000 men crossing a great river in the presence of the enemy."[59]

While waiting, Pope had work for the *Carondelet*. On the 6th, he sent some officers and the 43rd Ohio Infantry on a reconnaissance to Tipton. They were to count the number of enemy gun emplacements and determine their location. The enemy artillerists accommodated them by firing at the gunboat as it passed by. Pope reported: "The whole day was spent in this reconnaissance, the *Carondelet* steaming down the river in the midst of a heavy fire from the enemy's batteries along the shore. The whole bank for 15 miles was lined with heavy guns at intervals, in no case exceeding 1 mile."[60]

Walke returned the Rebels' compliments. He fired on their batteries on the way down and said that, according to reports, one round from the *Carondelet* "killed and wounded four men at a battery; and a shell which fell in the midst of their encampment, in the rear of these batteries, exploding as it struck, killed and wounded others." At Point Pleasant, Walke had his midday meal, took General John M. Palmer on board, and turned about for New Madrid. "Our shot and shell struck the enemy's guns or breast-works at nearly every fire of our now experienced and well trained gunners," he said. At the last Confederate battery before the end of the cruise, the officers decided to send a group ashore to spike the guns. The landing party was opposed by a remarkably tall Confederate marksman who had taken position behind a cottonwood tree. He was armed with two rifles and he calmly peppered the Yankees with fire, until combined fire of grape and canister from the gunboat and the rifle fire of the Federal sharpshooters drove him away from his sniper's nest. There was no more trouble. The guns were successfully spiked and the men returned to the *Carondelet*.[61]

General Pope's request for a second gunboat did not sit well with Foote. For one thing, the flag officer could not understand why Pope had not made his wishes known earlier. The night of April 4, when the *Carondelet* ran past the Confederate guns, turned out to be ideal for the effort and it would have been as easy to send one as two. The element of surprise was now lost. Besides that, wrote Foote, it was "too late to obtain the hay and other necessary articles for the protection of the gunboats to-night; to say nothing of the clear atmosphere rendering a boat as visible or as good an object to sight as in the daytime."[62]

Foote also had something to say about Pope's feeling—acquired from his New Madrid gunners—that running the gauntlet of Confederate guns should be an easy thing for the gunboats. "I can not consider the running of your blockade, where the river is nearly a mile wide and only exposed to a few light guns, at all comparable to running it here, where a boat has not only to pass seven batteries, but has to be kept 'head on' to a battery of eleven heavy guns at the head of Island No. 10, and to pass within 300 yards of thirty strong fortifications. If it did not sink the gunboat, we would, in the Navy, consider the gunners totally unfit for employment in the service." In spite of all of his grumbling, however, Foote agreed to prepare a second gunboat for a perilous run past Island Number Ten.[63]

Luck was with them. There was another storm blowing when the *Pitts-*

burg began her run, about 2:00 A.M. on April 7. She arrived undamaged at New Madrid at 5:00 A.M. Everything was coming into place. On the night of the 6th, four transport steamers were brought through Colonel Bissell's canal and were ready to ferry troops across the river when the order came. The gunboats were now there to cover them, and there was every reason to expect success. After the arrival of the *Pittsburg*, Pope sent Foote a note saying, "I shall cross the river if possible to-day, and shall probably be prepared to assault the works near Island No. 10 by 2 P.M. to-morrow. May I beg that you will have a careful watch kept for us, that we may suffer no injury from your boats as we approach the rear of the enemy's batteries?"[64]

Preparations of a different kind were taking place in the Rebel camps. Mackall knew that the second gunboat had made it past his gunners and he could anticipate what that would mean. He ordered the evacuation of the island, and while his men crossed the river to the Tennessee shore, he sent emissaries under a flag of truce to surrender the post to Flag Officer Foote. From the *Benton*, Foote informed secretary of navy Welles by telegram at 3:25 A.M. on April 7: "Two officers have this instant boarded us from Island No. 10, stating that by order of their commanding officer they are ordered to surrender Island No. 10 to the Commodore commanding the gunboats.... I will telegraph when further information is received. With Gen. Pope now advancing from New Madrid in strong force to attack in rear, I am with the gun and mortar boats ready to attack in front while Gen. Buford here is ready to cooperate with the land forces, but it seems the place is to be surrendered without further defense." He directed General Buford to be ready to occupy the works on the island after daylight. This Buford did about 6:00 A.M. His prize was 385 army officers and men (one hundred of them sick), one hundred sailors, and several tons of supplies.[65]

It is unclear whether or not Pope knew of the surrender. Foote wrote that he was in communication with the general, and it *is* hard to imagine that there would have been no possible way for the flag officer to get this important bit of intelligence to Pope, but in his *Military Memoirs* the general made no mention of receiving word of the surrender before he began his attack on the morning of the 7th. Of course, there may have been a very good reason for his not mentioning it: if the surrender had already been arranged, then the importance of his own role on the climactic day of battle was reduced to a mopping-up operation. In any event, whether he did not know or simply chose to ignore the surrender, Pope plowed ahead as if nothing had changed. He ordered the *Carondelet* and the *Pittsburg* to attack the battery at Watson's Landing on the Tennessee shore below New Madrid. This was where he intended to cross the troops. The *Pittsburg* was not ready at the appointed hour of 7:00 A.M., so the *Carondelet* made the attack alone, firing shells burning a ten-second fuze.

When the Confederates seemed to have been driven away from the gun emplacements, Walke sent a landing crew to spike the guns; they found them already disabled by the *Carondelet*'s fire. There was no enemy to be seen. The sailors proceeded up the bank, disabling the guns as they came to each battery, four in all.

While the *Carondelet* was making the attack, Pope put General E.A. Paine's division into the transports. When they landed, Paine's three thousand men, the first to hit the beach, were expected to push inland as fast as they could toward Tiptonville. General David Stanley's division would follow close behind. Pope believed that the Rebels would be trying to escape the deadly geographical and military trap in which they found themselves. The idea was for Paine and Stanley to bag the entire garrison as it tried to escape from Island Number Ten.

General Mackall's Rebels *were* trying to escape. He had "left a force of a few hundred men on the island, without specific instruction, and with the bulk of his force moved toward Tiptonville."[66] Many of them abandoned the main (and only) road and scattered into the swamps at the edge of Reelfoot Lake. The others continued toward the town. Three times they turned and formed a battle line, but each time when the Yankees appeared, they fell back. Mackall's column arrived in Tiptonville only to find the Federal gunboats waiting. Paine's division was coming up from behind. The swamps and Reelfoot Lake on their east appeared to be impassable. So, with no way out, Mackall made the unavoidable decision. He wrote, "In my judgment, resistance and escape were alike hopeless, and the next morning I surrendered the column under my immediate command."[67] As General Paine reported it, "At 2 o'clock A.M. of the 8th a flag of truce borne by the adjutant general of Brig. Gen. W.W. Mackall, was conducted to my headquarters. He brought a written communication from General Mackall tendering the unconditional surrender of his entire force, which was accepted, and during the day was surrendered about 3,000 men, besides the prisoners taken during the day before and straggling parties picked up by scouts. The whole force captured exceeded 5,000 men." In addition, Mackall surrendered a number of artillery pieces and sizeable quantities of small arms and supplies.[68]

It was finished. The congratulatory messages flew. Welles congratulated Foote in response to his 3:25 wire, saying, "A nation's thanks are due you and the brave officers and men of the flotilla on the Mississippi whose labors and gallantry at Island No. 10, which surrendered to you yesterday, have been watched with intense interest. Your triumph is not the less appreciated because it was protracted and finally bloodless." Welles remembered the army, too. He said, "Let the congratulations to yourself and your command be also extended to the officers and soldiers who cooperated with you."[69]

Pope wired Halleck multiple times on April 8 to keep him apprised of the unfolding events. The last message, sent at 7:00 P.M. said, "Everything is ours. Few, if any, of the enemy escaped. Three generals, 6,000 prisoners, an immense quantity of ammunition and supplies, 100 pieces of siege and several batteries of field artillery, great numbers of small arms, tents, wagons, horses, etc., have fallen into our hands." Halleck replied effusively the same night: "I congratulate you and your command on your splendid achievement. It exceeds in boldness and brilliancy all other operations of the war." Halleck did not mention at all the role the navy had played. It became another source of hard feelings on the part of the officers of the Brown Water Navy.[70]

If Foote congratulated his officers and men, as he must certainly have done, the message has not come to light. Pope's has survived. On April 10, in General Orders No. 30, he quoted to his forces Halleck's entire message and said, "The general commanding has but little to add to this dispatch. The conduct of the troops was splendid throughout. It was precisely what was expected. To such an army nothing is impossible, and the general commanding hopes yet to lead them to some field where superiority of numbers and position will tempt the enemy to give them the opportunity to win the glory which they are so capable of achieving. The regiments and battalions of this command will inscribe on their flags New Madrid and Island 10."[71]

On the Confederate side, Jefferson Davis read General Mackall's report. He marked it "Read. Unsatisfactory."[72]

A hard year was over. Months before, the North and South alike had begun a campaign to defend the Jackson Purchase from invasion by their nations' enemies. Now, for one side, it was finished. The political effort had failed first, then the military. With the fall of Island Number Ten, the main armies moved far away from the Purchase to pursue their aims on other fields, and they would not return in strength. There was no need. Control of the Jackson Purchase had been won by the Federals, and against their powerful presence the ever-weakening Confederacy could make no impression. Small garrisons would be enough to hold the Purchase.

The Federals controlled the land where the rivers came together. This was not to say, however, that they controlled the unhappy citizens who resented the bad turn of fortune that had left the bluecoats at their door. They hated the Yankees with undiminished ferocity, and the flame of Confederate loyalty never flickered in their hearts. For the rest of the war, with every small Confederate incursion into the Purchase, the people found renewed reason to hope.

16

Rebel Incursions and Yankee Injustices
(1862–1865)

In February 1862, after the fall of Fort Henry, the 5th Iowa Cavalry was assigned to garrison Fort Heiman on the Kentucky shore. The 5th Iowa included men from Iowa, as would be expected, and also from Minnesota, Missouri, and the Territory of Nebraska. The regiment was commanded by Colonel W.W. Lowe. Before they had come to their new post, the men were vaccinated against smallpox. For some, this was an unexpected and sickening introduction to soldiering. The method was gruesome. A few incisions were made on the soldier's arm, then a vaccine made from the scabs of an earlier patient was rubbed in the cuts. At the very least, the soldiers ended up with sore arms, though the consequences could be much worse. Doctors' fingers, the instruments they used, and the skin surface of the man being vaccinated were all so dirty that infection was often the result.

Sometimes it took several attempts for the smallpox vaccination to take. In the case of Bugler Lorenzo P. Roe of Co. C, 5th Iowa Cavalry, it took three tries. When it did take, Roe developed a very light case of the virus and was able to reassure his mother: "It has left scarcely a mark on me; and you could not tell that I ever had it."[1] After he recovered at the hospital in Paducah, they kept Roe working as an orderly for nearly two months. When he was at last released from his hospital duties and rejoined his regiment at Fort Heiman, Roe wrote home: "I never enjoyed better [health] in my life. I am as fat and hearty as a pig; and weigh a hundred and forty pounds, to a notch. That is more than I ever weighed before." He went on to answer their question about his "situation." He said, "We are encamped in a beautiful grove, situated among gently sloping hills on the west side of the Tennessee River and about three miles from it directly opposite Ft. Henry. We live in tents (Ours is a large one *taken from "The Secesh"* and accommodates twelve men) and sleep on a blanket spread on the ground (for straw or hay is very scarce here at present.)"[2]

He continued: "It would make you laugh to see us cooking and taking our repast, for we are a jolly set of fellows, and enjoy ourselves as well as we can." The food was satisfactory, especially since they had gotten away from the hard crackers they called "pilot bread," which were "so hard that you could hardly bite them with[out] breaking your teeth." Now the men had flour and could make griddle cakes and biscuits. They got issues of fresh beef, rice, beans, and coffee. Sugar was available, if not plentiful. The diet was basic and hard to embellish, for "nick nacks are out of the question, even if we had money, everything is so high. Butter is from thirty to forty cents per pound, eggs from twenty to thirty cents per dozen, milk ten to fifteen cts per quart, and other things in proportion." Roe said that he and his mess mates did skimp on their coffee a little so that they could have some to trade for dried fruit. "We can get six pounds of dried peaches for a pound of coffee," he said.[3]

Roe reassured his mother throughout his letter that life was good at Fort Heiman. He focused on such homey topics as food and shelter and did not mention that his regiment had occasional brushes with the Confederates. Just a few weeks earlier, in mid–February, they had had a small fight with two battalions of Mississippi Cavalry led by Lieutenant Colonel J.H. Miller. Miller had crossed the border into Kentucky because, as he said, he had "learned that the enemy were committing terrible depredations on the citizens between Concord and Fort Heiman." The citizens had requested a Southern force "to check the depredations of the enemy and to force them to draw in their foraging parties." Miller led his horsemen toward Fort Heiman on February 13 only to find that the Federals were expecting him; they had their pickets and skirmishers out. The ground was unsuited to cavalry, so he veered off to the west in order to find flat ground where horse soldiers could maneuver. There, too, Miller found the enemy prepared. He sent forward a company under a Captain Stock, who was "soon engaged in a skirmish with the enemy, but seeing their whole force, about 200, before him, he fell back, having 2 men wounded slightly, and 1 I fear mortally, who was left on the field." Stock reported that he had killed "2 or 3" of the Federals. That was the conclusion of one small Confederate incursion into the Jackson Purchase.[4]

Two days later, at Mt. Carmel Church, a company from Fort Heiman had a firefight with two brigades of Confederates who had ventured to within a mile and a half of the camp. Yankee fire initially forced the Rebels to fall back, but when they regrouped and charged, the Federals turned about and made their escape to Fort Heiman.

At other times, the Federals from Fort Heiman went looking for a fight. On March 11, 1862, four companies of the 5th Iowa Cavalry joined the 52nd Indiana Infantry and Battery I of the 1st Missouri Light Artillery on an expedition to Paris, Tennessee. The column was commanded by Iowan Captain

J.T. Croft, and it was going south at the request of some Tennessee Union men who were about to be forcibly drafted into Confederate service. The Confederates who had come to Paris to enforce the conscription law were Major Henry Clay King's "Hell Hounds," a battalion of mounted Kentucky, Tennessee, and Alabama riflemen. They were camped about a quarter mile on the other side of town, and they must have known the Federals were coming, for the bluecoat column made no secret of their approach. They marched straight through the center of town, flags flying.

Late in the afternoon of the 11th the Federals drew near the Rebel camp. Captain Robert E. Bulliss' artillery deployed right, where they unlimbered on a high hill and opened fire. After the big guns had shelled the Confederate works for a while with no responding fire, Companies A and B of the Iowa horse soldiers charged forward. The men had not ridden far when they "discovered the ambuscade." The enemy "opened a terrible fire" on them. The cavalrymen answered with their pistols and carbines, but they were finally forced back with five killed and three wounded. The Union fieldpieces opened fire again on the Confederates, "causing a sad havoc among them." After about an hour, the Hell Hounds had had all they wanted, and they began to retire. Just before the end of the fight, Captain Bulliss suffered a mortal wound. The Federals returned to Paris, cut the telegraph wires, and "took possession of the court house and a large hotel for our sick and wounded." The action had cost the Federals five men killed and five men wounded. The next morning the column returned to Fort Heiman, taking eight prisoners with them. They had to halt repeatedly en route to douse the bridges that had been set ablaze by Confederate soldiers. There was no more fighting, though.[5]

This is the way the Federals guarding Kentucky's southwestern border spent 1862 and 1863. While their comrades were marching on Shiloh and Corinth, and trying and failing and trying again to make inroads against the Rebel stronghold of Vicksburg, the Jackson Purchase Federals fought skirmishes not only with small, regularly enrolled units of the enemy but also with the guerrilla bands that rose up to attack Grant's communications and to try to hold the region for the Confederacy until General P.G.T. Beauregard or Sterling Price or Earl Van Dorn or *somebody* could march north and redeem it.

The guerrillas were a particular problem. They stole horses, killed furloughed soldiers at their homes, and hanged known Unionists from their own shade trees. In July 1863 a guerrilla band numbering as many as three hundred men occupied Hickman, "ransacking local unionist property and hunting down unionists who were to be liquidated." The pursuing Federals were a day behind them, and the bushwhackers left weeping Hickman behind, never having been challenged at all. There was an even more extensive raid in November of 1863. A gang of no less than five hundred bushwhackers moved into the area of Mayfield and Paducah. They stole $18,000 from the home of Lucien Anderson, who was a member-elect of Congress, and detained him; they burned railroad bridges, derailed and burned trains, and robbed the passengers of their money, watches, and jewelry. The Federals seemed to be powerless against them, and they operated with impunity until they themselves decided that it was time to go.[6]

Knowing that the marauders lived off the land and would take what they wanted from Southern sympathizers as quickly as they would Yankees, farmers resorted to several cunning practices. They buried their foodstuffs in cleverly disguised caches and staked out their cattle "in hollows and fence rows at night, the hours when marauders scourged the countryside." They lived in fear on these isolated farms. "Women folks would bar doors and windows against feared attacks while fathers and sons who were left behind would stalk the shadows of homes and barns at night as protective sentinels. Arson, rape, thieving and murder were commonplace."[7]

Yet, so deep was hatred for the Yankees that many citizens who never carried a pistol or stole a horse were willing to work with the partisan rangers. In May 1862 the Federals discovered an espionage cell in Paducah which involved as many as six hundred Southern sympathizers. The existence of the group was revealed by an informer, and the Federals took the threat seriously enough that the 64-pounders mounted at Fort Anderson (on the grounds of the Marine Hospital), were trained on the town in case of an incident.

The Marine Hospital had been as busy as an anthill, not only in handling the volume of sick and wounded from New Madrid and Shiloh (which sent as many as seven hundred patients through Paducah), but also in the transformation of its campus into a fortified site. The earthworks of Fort Anderson were not tall—only about as high as a man's belt buckle—but they were extensive and the artillery platforms were numerous and well-served with 64-pounders. Gunboats often lay offshore directly behind the fort, adding their firepower to the defenses.

On the night of November 17, 1862, the Marine Hospital, pride of Paducah, burned down. The patients and most of the furniture were rescued; the building itself was a total loss. Although the fire seems to have been a pure accident, the suspicion that it was a case of arson gripped the town. The *New York Times* reported: "Great consternation prevailed, owing to an impression that this was the herald of a rebel attack. Double pickets were placed around the town."[8]

Paducah existed in a deepening swill of mutual suspicion. Federal attempts to contain the undeniably strong current of sympathy for the Confederates included mandating a round of loyalty oaths. Citizens who refused to take it were arrested and made to give a bond in the amount of $10,000 to the United

States court in Paducah. The people thought of such measures as abusive, and yet there *was* a great deal of support for the Rebels and there continued to be a vigorous black market trade in livestock, tobacco, salt, and other consumables between the Purchase and areas farther south. Patricia Ann Hoskins observes, "The Jackson Purchase's geographic location ... made the area rife for illegal commerce with the South. The vast amounts of trade led Federal authorities to pass trade restrictions and impose harsh fines on the civilian population. These restrictions and the ever increasing number of Federal garrisons at Paducah, Columbus, Mayfield, Benton, Murray, and Hickman led to a rise in guerrilla warfare between fall 1862 and winter 1863." Every action led to a reaction in an endless cycle of escalation.[9]

The illicit trade was the excuse the Federals used to target one group, the Jews, for extraordinary measures. As early as 1861 a rumor that the Federals hated Jews had caused a substantial number to flee to Illinois. Lieutenant S. Ledyard Phelps' identification of the Jews as being behind the black market trade in January 1862 seemed to support the reputation of anti–Semitism among the western forces. General William T. Sherman, Grant's good friend, was one of several army officers who complained about the practices of Jewish traders. Another was E.A. Paine, who claimed that the Jews were secessionists, and worse, that they supported the guerrillas. Even those Jews who were licensed to trade legally (in cotton, for instance, or as sutlers) were not exempt from suspicion. It was widely charged that they carried military intelligence to the enemy.

Anti-Semitism was apparently endemic in both branches of the service, and the fiction of universal Jewish disloyalty was a new expression of a preexisting bias, easily believed, eagerly repeated. Patriotism could not be defined within the framework of religious belief, yet the Jews were condemned as a traitorous sect, while Gentile traders were never classed together in the same way. There undoubtedly were some Jews who, just like the Baptists, Methodists, and Catholics, reached for the chance to make some black market dollars. Conversely, just as with the Gentiles, there were also many loyalists in the Jewish population. The Kaskel brothers, for example, were very public in their support for the Union. Cesar Kaskel was vice president of the Paducah Union League Club, and Julius was a Union army recruiter. Nevertheless, the charges of Jewish disloyalty in Paducah and throughout the Department of the Tennessee persisted. They prompted Major General U.S. Grant to issue General Orders No. 11, one of the most singular documents in American history. Dated December 17, 1862:

> The Jews, as a class violating every regulation of trade established by the Treasury Department and also department orders, are hereby expelled from the department within twenty-four hours from the receipt of this order.

16. Rebel Incursions and Yankee Injustices 193

Fort Anderson and the Marine Hospital, Paducah (Library of Congress).

Post commanders will see that all of this class of people be furnished passes and required to leave, and any one returning after such notification will be arrested and held in confinement until an opportunity occurs of sending them out as prisoners, unless furnished with permit from headquarters.

No passes will be given these people to visit headquarters for the purpose of making personal application for trade permits.

By order of Maj. Gen. U.S. Grant.[10]

If the language were not outrageous enough, the idea behind the order was against the very American principles that Grant, Sherman, et al., were presumably fighting to preserve. All through Grant's department, post commanders began to round up and expel the Jews. Very few resisted. For some of the soon-to-be refugees, it was a long journey to Illinois from the Tennessee and Mississippi towns, and they were not allowed time to sell or secure their property before their exile began. The property they took with them was sometimes vandalized during their trip. They wondered what they had done to deserve such callous treatment. To one young couple, it was explained in blunt and hateful terms by Brigadier General James Tuttle in Cairo. "You are Jews," Tuttle said, "and they are neither a benefit to the Union or Confederacy."[11]

Cesar Kaskel was ordered out of Paducah on December 28, 1862, one of nearly thirty local men who were ordered to leave with their families. Kaskel was not a man to accept this injustice lightly. He, his brother Julius, and three others sent a telegram to President Lincoln, describing the situation and appealing for justice. And when the time to leave Paducah came, Kaskel traveled not to some dreary exile in Illinois, but to Washington, D.C., to plead his case in person. He was not alone; groups from Louisville and Cincinnati were on their way to see Lincoln, as well.

In Washington, Kaskel met with Ohio congressman John Addison Gurley and together they went to see the president. Lincoln had not received Kaskel's telegram and he had not seen Grant's order. Kaskel told him of what had happened, and in an exchange (which historian Jonathan D. Sarna thinks is apochryphal), Lincoln is said to have said, "And so the children of Israel were driven from the happy land of Canaan?"

"Yes," said Kaskel, "and that is why we have come unto Father Abraham's bosom, asking protection."

"And this protection they shall have at once," said Lincoln.[12]

Sarna says that Lincoln "did instantly command the general in chief of the army, Henry Halleck, to countermand General Orders No. 11." His work done, Kaskel returned home to Paducah with Lincoln's promise that he had nothing more to fear. Approached by an officer at Paducah after his arrival and challenged to name the person who had given the order allowing his return, Kaskel said, "By order of the President of the United States."[13] General Halleck's order to Grant to rescind General Orders No. 11 was firm. Halleck sent Grant a wire on January 4, 1863, that said, "A paper purporting to be General Orders No. 11, issued by you December 17, has been presented here. By its terms it expels all Jews from your department. If such an order has been issued, it will be immediately revoked."[14]

The issue had started as an in-house army matter, but it inevitably became widely known, taken up by the politicians, and the battle lines drawn. Senator Lazarus Powell of Kentucky sponsored a resolution in the upper house condemning General Orders No. 11. A similar resolution in the House of Representatives was blocked by Grant's patron and defender in all situations, Elihu Washburne. Washburne also sent Lincoln a letter regarding the administration's response to the order. The congressman wrote on January 6: "I see a report that you have revoked Grant's order touching the Jews—I hope not. I consider it the wisest order yet made by a Military Command, and from my own personal observations, I believe it was necessary. As the friend of that distinguished Soldier, Gen'l Grant, I want to be heard before the final order of revocation goes out, if it be contemplated to issue such an order. There are two sides to this question."[15]

Lincoln did not see two sides to the question. His decision stood, and two days later, January 7, Grant rescinded the order. The same day, the Board of Delegates, American Israelites, meeting in special session in New York City, passed a resolution deploring the order. The Jewish leaders' thinking was clearer than Grant's in regards to the American principle of fairness. In part, the resolution said that "if an individual be guilty of an infraction of discipline or offence against military law or treasury regulations, punishment should be visited upon him alone, and the religious community to which he is presumed to be attached, should not be subjected to insult, obloquy or disregard of its constitutional rights as a penalty for individual offences." They also voted a resolution of thanks to General Halleck for the "promptitude with which he revoked General Grant's unjust and outrageous order."[16]

Not every member of the Jewish community was in favor of the Board's resolution. The *New York Times* picked up the story and reported that "against the conduct of this committee the bulk of the Jews vehemently protest. They say they have no thanks for an act of simple and imperative justice—but grounds for deep and just complaint against the Government, that Gen. Grant has not been dismissed from the service on account of the unrighteous act."[17] The *Times* went on call Grant's order "odious," and "contrary to common sense and common justice." It said that it was "a humiliating reflection that after the progress of liberal ideas even in the most despotic countries has restored the Jews to civil and social rights, as members of a common humanity, it remained for the freest Government on earth to witness a momentary revival of the sprit of the medieval ages," and concluded: "Men cannot be condemned and punished as a class without gross violence to our free institutions. The immediate and preemptory abrogation of Grant's order by the President saved the Government from a blot, and redeemed us from the disgrace of a military assault upon a people whose equal rights and immunities are as sacred under the Constitution as those of any other sect, class or race."[18]

Though the public might howl, the army and the administration could not spare one of the country's fightingest generals. Grant had threatened to resign at various times before this and might do so again unless his feelings were soothed. To reassure Grant that his authority was not being eroded and to help him understand the nuances of such all-inclusive actions, Halleck wrote to the Union hero of the West. In a letter dated January 21, Halleck said, "The President has no objection to your expelling traitors and Jew peddlers, which, I suppose, was the object of your order; but, as it in terms proscribed an entire religious class, some of whom are fighting in our ranks, the President deemed it necessary to revoke it."[19]

Historical memory is selective, and General Orders No. 11 was soon forgotten in light of Grant's victories at Vicksburg and Chattanooga. In Paducah, Kentucky, though, there was a group of loyal citizens who did not easily forget how casually their constitutional rights had been stripped away as the war entered its middle phase.

Civil rights abuses did not end with the revocation of Grant's Jewish policy. They continued on a smaller scale throughout the Purchase. The Federals from Fort Anderson seemed especially angered by Calloway County, which had sent nine hundred of its sons to fight for the Confederacy and only forty-seven to Federal service.

The situation was somewhat different out in the country than in Paducah. The farmers were trying their best to survive the loss of their sons, who were in the service or in the ground, their slaves, many of whom had run away, and also a new revenue bill that levied a tax of $3 on every hundred pounds of tobacco. The *Louisville Democrat* decried this as "a virtual prohibition of the culture." Tobacco farmers generally expected to sell their crops for no more than $5 per hundred pounds; under the new tax, 60 percent of that would go to the state. When other costs were deducted from the remaining profit, the farmer was practically growing his crop for nothing.[20]

While Purchase farmers were too distracted by their daily struggles to give *very* active support to the Confederacy or consider the nuances of the era's politics, there were some whose lives had become so bitterly intolerable that their solution was to wage individual war. Making war became their primary occupation. One such man was Jack Hinson, who became a local legend. Late in the war, Hinson haunted the rugged land between the rivers. Colonel W.W. Lowe had hanged two of Hinson's sons—perhaps for no more serious crime than being found hunting in the woods, guns in hand—and the old man became a specter of retribution. He killed from hiding places in the underbrush. Young soldiers on the picket line, riverboat pilots, anyone who appeared in the sights of his long rifle soon became a corpse. Hinson evaded capture, and before he was done he could count thirty-six notches on the stock of his well-worn gun.

Hinson was an obsessed killer, but he and his kind were the exceptions. If other farmers who lived near the rivers liked to take a casual potshot at passing gunboats from time to time, it was because the gunboats would sometimes shell the riverbank, and their crews would sometimes swarm ashore to empty farmers' corncribs and kill their cattle for fresh meat. Against gangs of rough Yankee sailors or whole regiments of Federal horse soldiers, the people were mostly defenseless, and their defenselessness made them easy targets. The Yankees took advantage of the civilians' powerlessness, striking not only the lonely farms but also the seat of local government.

Murray was the county seat of Calloway. It was a pretty little market town of ten general stores and a pharmacy, situated on top of a picturesque hill. One quiet morning in 1863 a squad of Federals from Fort Anderson rode into Murray and removed at bayonet point a whole slate of office holders from their positions. The county judge, county clerk, circuit court clerk, sheriff, and jailer were all turned out and Unionists installed in their places. In addition, county clerk P.M. Ellison and others "were arrested by the soldiers and carried to Paducah and put in prison because they would not take the oath of allegiance to the Union."[21]

The Yankees' malevolent interest in Murray continued. They built a fortified outpost on the outskirts of town from which they went out to plunder at will. A group of their fellows, two hundred Home Guards who were no doubt emboldened by the presence of the Fort Anderson detachment in Calloway County, prowled the backroads and swooped down on lonely homesteads in the night and "captured a great many Confederates at home on furlough." As a capper, in one three-day span late in the year, the Federals burned two sides of the courthouse square. They burned the east side of the square on Friday night and the following Monday night they burned the north side.[22]

Blacks, too, suffered under Federal rule. They had been running away from their masters ever since the Yankees came in 1861. In May 1863, the Union War Department increased the incentive to do so by General Orders No. 143, which created the Bureau of Colored Troops. African Americans could now fight for the Union. The next month, the 1st Regiment, United States Colored Troops, were enlisted, and there would be more to come, for "the recruitment of colored troops was going on all over the country." This included areas under Union control, such as the Purchase.[23]

When Purchase blacks enlisted (almost entirely in artillery units) at Fort Anderson, their wives and children tended to follow them. It was natural. They had neither shelter nor means of support, they were unwilling to return to their masters, and they hoped that the Federals would give them succor while their men wore the blue uniform. In this, they were disappointed. Marion B. Lucas, the recognized authority of Kentucky African-American history, says that, with few exceptions, the Federal authorities were hostile to the refugees. Lucas writes, "Federal authorities were generally as unprepared as unwilling to receive refugees after 1863 as they had been in 1861 and 1862. When hundreds of relatives followed recruits to Fort Anderson in Paducah, they soon encountered starvation and hostile military commanders who ordered that women, children, the ill, infirm, and aged be 'returned to their masters.'" It was a ham-handed and callous response to the plight of suffering civilians, but it was perfectly in keeping with the general mistreatment of Jackson Purchase citizens as the Federal grip tightened in the middle years of the war.[24]

In March 1864, General Abraham Buford's division (two brigades) of Nathan Bedford Forrest's cavalry came north from Mississippi to disrupt Union communications and to gather supplies and horses. Their own mounts were in terrible condition, "old hacks, and so weak that for many days we walked fifteen minutes of every hour to give them rest," remembered trooper J.V. Greif. As they came north, the overall quality of their horses improved by the traditional method—acquisition.[25]

On or about March 24, the graycoat cavalry crossed into Kentucky, which many of the men called home. It *looked* like home. It was said that "shout after shout went up" with each tobacco barn they passed. One of the riders was Captain J.F. Melton, the former town marshal of Murray, who had fought in three battles and escaped from two prisoner of war camps before joining Forrest. On the morning of March 25, the Rebels approached Paducah. Federal scouts warned the town about noon that Forrest was coming, and the Unionists began to flee. An estimated three thousand citizens crossed the river into Illinois. One of them was the baker George M. Oehlschlaeger, who was enjoying himself counting money when the alarm was given. He had just been paid $2,628 in silver for supplies provided to the Federals. Oehlschlaeger threw a newspaper over the table where the silver was stacked and ran out. He did not even take time to pull on his coat. He fled his 3rd Street shop in his shirtsleeves and made for the north bank of the Ohio.[26]

About three miles out, Forrest's men ran into Federal patrols and began a running skirmish that continued through early afternoon and took them all the way into town. At 2:00 P.M. they came within sight of Fort Anderson on the western edge of the city. They saw before them an earthen fortification hard beside the river, where two Union gunboats, the *PawPaw* and the *Peosta*, rested at anchor. There was a moat on three sides of the fort and inside were 665 men commanded by Colonel S.G. Hicks. The Federals were escaping into the safety of the fort and Greif said, "The men clamored to be led against them while outside but as the object of the raid was for medical supplies, and not fight or prisoners, no movement was permitted." The men inside the fort had to be pinned down while the raiders were in Paducah, though, so Forrest ordered General Buford to deploy the two brigades of his division, Colonel Tyree Bell on the south and Colonel A.P. Thompson on the west.[27]

Not every Yankee had gotten into the fort. The raiders encountered groups of them and a street fight developed. It is surprising how many civilians were in the street as the bullets flew. This was a more exciting spectacle than Dan Rice's Circus and some people, even children, could not resist taking a ringside seat. A boy named George A. Fisher, who lived on the corner of 7th and Broadway, remembered seeing "a Confederate officer and a Yankee [who] came out Broadway fighting; both were mounted; the Confederate shot at the 'Yank,' missing him, and just after passing 7th Street the 'Yank' turned across an open lot and the Confederate threw his pistol at him. I walked over to the lot; the Confederate was riding about looking for his pistol, which I picked up and handed to him."[28]

After an hour of fighting, Forrest sent in to Colonel Hicks a demand for surrender. He said, "Colonel: Having a force amply sufficient to carry your works and reduce the place, and in order to avoid the unnecessary effusion of blood, I demand the surrender of the fort and troops, with all public property. If you surrender, you shall be treated as prisoners of war; but if I have to storm your works, you may expect no quarter." Hicks answered, "I can answer that I have been placed here by my Government to defend this post, and in this, as well as all other orders from my superiors, I feel it to be my duty as an honorable officer to obey. I must, therefore, respectfully decline surrendering as you may require."[29]

With Hicks' refusal to surrender, the fight resumed. Colonel A.P. Thompson decided to exceed his orders and charge the fort. He led the 3rd and the 7th Kentucky Mounted Infantry forward. They had gone only a short distance when Colonel Thompson was hit in the body by an artillery round. He was "cut entirely in two," and two of his staffers were instantly killed. Greif remembered, "I was within ten feet of him when he was struck, and my old gray Confederate hat was covered with his blood." Others who were nearby were sprayed with gore and struck by pieces of Thompson's shattered body. Colonel Ed Crossland of the 7th Kentucky took charge and ordered the men to take shelter in the surrounding houses. Not only did they find shelter in the houses; those who took position in the upper floors were also able to continue the fight by firing down inside the fort.[30]

Some of the cavalrymen-turned-marksmen found a warm welcome inside. William R. St. Clair remembered the he and a dozen or so Kentucky boys occupied the upper story of Dr. Bassett's brick home. Mrs. Bassett was "delighted with the visit" and considered it her duty as a Southern hostess to offer the finest hospitality. She had her big dining room table carried upstairs to the snipers' nest and "heaped [it] with all the delicacies and good things that the house, cellar, or pantry offered." The boys feasted and fired, keeping the artillery crews (who were either of the 1st Kentucky Artillery or the 8th United States Colored Heavy Artillery) away from the 32-pounders inside Fort Anderson's walls. An artillery round finally was fired from one of the big guns at the house, but it did no harm. A second round was better aimed. It "hit the edge of the table and made a promiscuous mingling of china, wood, meat, iron, vegetables, glassware and pie." The walls of the room were "plastered with pie, and the blackberry jam and preserves [were] dripping mournfully for the ceiling." Their picnic over, the sharpshooters thanked Mrs. Bassett and left, and her home, now unprotected, was pounded into rubble by a Federal storm of solid shot and grape.[31]

As the afternoon dragged on, the gunboats on the Ohio cast off, began cruising from the upper end of Paducah to the lower end, and added the fire of their guns to that coming from the fort. They demolished some of the buildings along Front Street where snipers hid. A man and a little girl in the town were killed by the sweeping fire. After three hours, Forrest began to fall back. The men who were not fighting had spent the time gathering the medical supplies and other stores for which they had come. They found a lot of nice saddle mounts and mules, about four hundred in all, and had burned the steamer *Dacotah* in dry dock, a few dozen bales of cotton, and also some rolling stock on the New Orleans & Ohio Railroad. They had in custody fifty prisoners, which they took with them when they retired from Paducah shortly before midnight. The Rebels left behind an undetermined number of dead. Colonel Hicks reported that Forrest had lost three hundred killed and upwards of 1200 wounded, a ridiculous claim. Forrest reported twenty-five killed and wounded. Major J.F. Chapman, of the 122nd Illinois, said that the Confederates failed to recover fifteen lifeless bodies near the fort. The dead Rebels were gathered up and buried in a common grave on the north side of Trimble Street. For their part, the Federals reported fourteen killed and forty-six wounded.

Early the next morning, the Rebels appeared again. Hicks still felt the sting of the sharpshooters from the day before and did not want to endure it again. He "ordered Major [George F.] Barnes, of the Sixteenth Kentucky Cavalry, to send out squads to burn all the houses within musket range of the fort." He also ordered Lieutenant Shirk of the navy to be ready to "protect the fort and let the town go to hell." The town soon looked like hell. Twenty-five homes were put to the torch. While the houses burned, Forrest sent forward a white-flag messenger. The note he carried proposed a prisoner exchange, man for man. Hicks refused the offer, saying, "I have no power to make the exchange. If I had, I would most cheerfully do it." With this, Forrest fell back to Mayfield. He gave the Kentucky boys in Buford's division a leave of absence to visit their homes. They were ordered to rendezvous at Trenton, Tennessee, on April 3.[32]

Forrest's Paducah raid was over. The civilians who had been refugees across the Ohio returned to their homes and shops. Some were heartbroken to find their property battered to pieces or burned. Coatless George M. Oehlschlaeger was luckier than most. He came back to his 3rd Street bakery to find that the store had been ransacked, but the $2,628 in silver was still under the newspaper on the table, right where he had left it.

Colonel Abraham Buford was forty-four years old. He was a West Point graduate and a Mexican War veteran. He left the service in the mid–1850s to raise stock on his fine Bluegrass region farm near Versailles, and it was with real reluctance that he left civilian life to put on the gray uniform. After General Braxton Bragg invaded Central Kentucky in the fall of 1862, Buford joined the Confederate service with a brigadier's commission. Despite his initial hesitation to reenter the service, he was, like his cousins John and Napoleon B. Buford, a natural-born soldier, had a certain zeal for it, and was noted for his buoyant sense of humor. Private Mercer Otey, who served with the 7th Kentucky Mounted Infantry in Buford's "Kentucky Brigade," later remembered him as "a genial and jovial companion" and said that "he weighed something over three hundred pounds, of powerful frame, a round, ruddy face, covered with a short stubby red beard, dressed in brown butternut Kentucky jeans, his pants invariably stuck in his boots, he was the most perfect picture of the Jack of Clubs, as displayed on the packs of cards made [in] those times." Buford's bulk did not make him sluggish, though. Otey said, "With all his weight he was the most graceful dancer I ever saw swing a lady."[33]

At Trenton, Tennessee, in April 1864, Buford read a mocking item in a captured Yankee paper that Forrest's cavalry had missed a lot of horses at Paducah during their March raid. He carried it to Forrest, who gave him permission to take the eight hundred men of his Bluegrass State brigade and go get them. Besides the horses to be had, there was an added advantage: Forrest was about to begin another small campaign and Buford's raid would draw Yankee attention away from the main Confederate target, Fort Pillow, Tennessee. Buford set out on April 8 with the 3rd, 7th, and 8th Kentucky Mounted Infantry, and the 12th Kentucky Cavalry. Riding north, Buford ordered Captain H.A. Tyler to take 150 men and threaten Columbus, Kentucky, while the main column proceeded to Paducah. He arrived on April 14, drove the Federal pickets back into Fort Anderson and then sent in a white flag. Buford's message to Colonel Hicks read, "Reluctant to endanger the lives of women and children and non-combatants, I respectfully request that you order all such out of the town. They will be allowed to pass through my lines, and will be allowed one hour to get out."

Hicks replied, "Your notice of one hour to let the women and children out exhibits an act of humanity on your part, but do not allow your men to sack the city during that time, nor attempt to take possession, or I will fire on you. After that time, come ahead; I am ready for you."[34]

An hour was not long. The navy began hurriedly ferrying citizens over to Illinois, a state that was becoming very familiar to Paducahans. Colonel Hicks later claimed that Buford took unfair advantage during the one-hour truce. He said that Buford's men "were going through the upper part of the city, under protection of white flags, breaking into homes and robbing and plundering." To put an end to the looting, Hicks sent Lieutenant Colonel Charles G. Eaton and two hundred men of the 72nd Ohio from Fort Anderson. The guns of the fort and the gunboats covered them as they moved. When the Rebels saw Eaton coming, they did not make a stand. They rejoined their main body and fell back. When Hicks' guns and those of the gunboats began lobbing shells among them, they hurriedly escaped with whatever loot they could carry and 140 government horses. W.W. Faulkner and the 12th Kentucky Cavalry lagged behind to intimidate possible pursuers, but they need not have bothered. No enemy was coming to fight them.[35]

That is, no enemy from Fort Anderson. That night, the 7th Kentucky's Colonel Ed Crossland, who had been wounded in the day's fighting, and some others stopped to spend the night at the house of a citizen named Bill Pryor a few miles south of Mayfield. An hour before midnight, as the Confederates lay sleeping, the door to their bedroom burst open and a party of twenty-five Home Guards led by a man named Gregory rushed in. Gregory's band was "a terror to the whole community. It was said that they boasted of the fact that they never took a prisoner—if a Confederate fell into their hands he was murdered; and they were guilty of as brutal conduct as any gang of cutthroats who roamed those sections."[36]

One of Crossland's companions was killed and the other crawled under the bed. Crossland was caught. Gregory is reported to have said to him, "You damn son-of-a-bitch in that bed, surrender." Crossland told Gregory, "I am wounded and helpless, and of course I surrender." Then Gregory shot him. It was only a flesh wound, but the quick-thinking Crossland cried out, "I am killed!" and he lay there, playing dead.[37]

In an adjoining room, four other Confederates were set upon with sabers. Two who survived the attack were taken outside and ordered to kneel down. One refused and was shot dead. The other ran. According to Henry George, the historian of Forrest's Kentucky Brigade, "He was fired upon by a fusillade from Gregory's gang ... and as he ran by the guard he fired upon him, but he was not struck in the legs, and kept running and escaped. On the next morning he was brought to Mayfield and was found to be riddled with bullets; the surgeons cut twenty-eight bullets out of his body."[38]

After the shooting, the Home Guards went into the stable, perhaps to have a drink, for it was a cold night. Crossland took the opportunity to try to escape. He crawled out of the house to a chicken coop, which he rejected as a hiding place, and continued until he was stopped by a rail fence that he could not get over. Two of his men who had escaped the Gregory gang found him there and got him into the woods. There they stayed until the next morning, when some of their cavalry comrades found them and took them into Mayfield.

Most of the men with Buford's raiding party escaped such harrowing incidents during their retreat from Kentucky. Back in Tennessee, they rejoined Forrest's main column coming back from Fort Pillow. Swapping stories with their comrades, the men of the Kentucky Brigade must have been quietly thankful that they had been with Buford. They had plundered private homes,

16. Rebel Incursions and Yankee Injustices 203

an act unbecoming to Southern chivalry, but by their raid on Paducah, they had been spared the guilt of participating in an event that would have marked them for life, one of the war's most notorious atrocities, the Fort Pillow Massacre.

The Federal grip on the Jackson Purchase tightened. The signs of the Yankee presence were everywhere. In Smithland, for instance, they had built a two-story brick commissary with arched windows looking out over the rivers. Inside were stored quantities of salt pork and beef, hardtack, flour, and cornmeal, beans and rice, coffee, sugar, molasses, and the infamous desiccated vegetables. It was enough to feed a good number of men their average rations of three pounds' weight (cost per soldier per diem: twenty cents). The commissary was a handsome building, but it was for the *Yankees*.

The Yankees liked the Purchase better than the Purchase liked the Yankees. Even as late at 1864, surrounded though they were by an embittered population, the soldiers seemed to like Western Kentucky. Hawley V. Needham of the 134th Illinois wrote of battered old Paducah: "I am very much pleased with the place, nice people, beautiful scenery, good water, and a splendid bathing place." He added, "John Thomas and I procured passes and did up Paducah. Along the levee the buildings show the effects of war, they being full of shotholes. At the end of town near the Fort a number of fine buildings have been blown up. But I was so much pleased with the place some pretty nice houses and tasty grounds surrounding them. In good times it must be a thriving place."[39]

One who did not like either the place or the people was General Eleazer A. Paine, who was assigned to command the District of Western Kentucky, headquartered at Paducah on July 19, 1864. Paine was a familiar face in Paducah. He had made himself an anathema to the citizens there during his two brief tenures in command, the first as post commander immediately following Grant's occupation of the city, and the second during his sixty-day tenure as the commander at Cairo (including its dependencies) in February and March 1862. Just before he returned to Paducah for the third time, Paine had been serving in the Department of the Cumberland, where Grant had sent him in August 1862. His conduct there while commander of the post of Gallatin, Tennessee was typically troublesome, and no one wanted him or knew quite what to do with him. On January 15, 1864, Grant wrote General George H. Thomas: "Can you not order Gen. Paine to the command of a Brigade in the front. He is entirely unfit to command a Post. General [Lovell H.] Rousseau will send you by mail some statements of, his administration of affairs. If nothing better can be done I advise that you send a Staff Officer to investigate fully and report upon his administration, and if then found advisable, I will relieve him." General Thomas did not want Paine. He replied to General Grant's query the same day he received it: "I do not think it advisable for Genl. Paine to come to the front. His rank will entitle him to a division, and if not placed in command according to his rank I should have constant trouble with him. I think it better to have his conduct enquired into and his position fixed according to his deserts."[40]

Paine was a spiteful, conniving, avaricious, and ambitious volunteer with a creative talent for cruelty—and someone thought he would be perfect to keep the lid on western Kentucky. To be sure, Paine did have his supporters in Paducah. The chief officers of the Union League of America, members of the merchant class who were anxious to reestablish a healthy business climate in the city, said, on July 11, about a week before Paine's assignment, "We have heard with pleasure the probability of our old and true friend, General Paine, being assigned to command here and to have his headquarters in Paducah, and from him we hope and expect to obtain relief."[41]

One wonders how long the entrepreneurs of the Union League remained confident that Paine would bring them relief, for he landed in Paducah with vengeful enthusiasm. Within days, Paine began banishing citizens from his district to Windsor, Canada. They included Mrs. Robert Woolfolk, her six children, and their African-American nurse; Mr. Robert Shanklin; Miss Kate Sanders; and eventually over forty others who in some way offended Paine's sensibilities. They were taken to Cairo by boat where they were joined by a party of deportees from Columbus. At Cairo, they were put on a northbound train and traveled under guard. For a long time afterward it was remembered that "Captain B.H. Norton and twenty black soldiers from the Eighth Kentucky (Colored) Heavy Artillery escorted the prisoners.... In their journey to Canada the prisoners were packed into the traveling car with their black escorts, apparently to humiliate them."[42]

Paine imposed a tax of $100,000 on the 1st Congressional District and an additional $95,000 tax on the citizens of McCracken County. He imposed a tax of $10 on every hogshead of tobacco "as well as a 25% ad valorem duty on all cotton." He levied a tax of fifty cents on every check cashed in a bank, and an equivalent tax on the mail sent by his own troops. He seized the rents paid to non-Unionist property owners and searched private homes. At the wave of Paine's hand, warehouses and their contents were seized and all workers arrested, and he refused to issue business licenses to any whose loyalty he found suspect. To any and all who protested, Paine had a standard response: "You are a God-damned scoundrel; God-damn you. I'll dig a hole, shoot you, and put you in it."[43]

They had reason to fear that he would do just that. Within days of assuming command, Paine began a round of executions that eventually totaled forty-three victims, many of them taking place at the new Federal works in Mayfield.

Paine had ordered the building of a gigantic fort on the Graves County Public Square. Hundreds of men from Graves, McCracken, and Hickman counties, even "cripples, sick, and infirm old men," were made to do the work under the guns of black guards. Men died from overwork, but there was a way to secure an exemption—a personal tribute to Paine of from $50 to $300.[44]

The soldiers in the ranks modeled their behavior after General Paine's. There was a breakdown of discipline in the troops occupying Mayfield, a state of affairs which the diarist Needham unashamedly admitted. He said, "The boys have been in the foraging business. I got soap, rice, peppers and peppermint, a lot of utensils, glassware, woodenware, razor strop, books, etc. Some got books and other articles of considerable value." Needham commented, too, on the field of little craters in the courthouse wall, showing where executions had been carried out.[45]

For fifty-one days, the people of the Jackson Purchase suffered under Paine's "Reign of Terror." Protests began to be heard, and not only from the citizens. Officers in the military hierarchy and editors in the civilian press came to be among Paine's loudest critics. Brigadier General Henry Prince at Columbus wrote to U.S. Grant that the new commander had instituted the following:

> [A] policy calculated, in my belief, to spread ruin and devastation, and having no good in it, is being pursued at the moment that an improvement in the feeling of the citizens toward the Government was making itself apparent to me. They were getting tired of the rebel reign of terror, propagated by guerrillas, and were meditating on the comfort of being relieved from them and of having a government. The new policy propagates a new reign of terror by means of soldiers and hired assassins and unsettles every nook of society. The facts which I shall state to illustrate the move of proceeding are only some which are well and thoroughly known by me. The new commander took from my custody at Columbus, Ky., a man named Kesterson, whom I had captured and whom I was holding in prison for trial, conducted him to Paducah, Ky., and publicly killed him there, in semblance of an execution, without authority of law or any proper justification. One Gregory, a citizen heading a gang employed by the new commander and acting under his orders, took a man named Bryant from his bed, near Dublin, in the district conducted him to Mayfield, and there publicly killed him in semblance of an execution, without authority of law or any proper justification. The first of these acts was committed on the 27th day of July, 1864; the second on the 2d day of this present month. He has sent under guard from this neighborhood quiet and peaceable citizens, who had taken the oath of allegiance, and actually banished them to Canada.[46]

Prince wanted it clearly understood that he had taken no part in these actions and concluded by asking to be relieved.

The *New York Times* did not fault Paine so much on the immorality of his behavior, as the indirect and inadvertent acceptance of the Confederate point of view in his banishment doctrine. An August 10, 1864, editorial explained:

> To banish them either to Dixie or to Canada does not prevent their doing mischief. On the contrary, it gives many of them an opportunity for doing vastly more harm to the national cause than the worst of them could do at home. Banishment, even as a military punishment, resolves itself practically into a confession by those that employ it; that the person subjected to it are not citizens, but aliens. Foreigners who become nuisances—without committing any positive breach of public law—may be ordered to leave the country. It is a wholesome right which every civilized State reserves to itself. But the citizens of this Republic can only be so treated by accepting the very doctrine that Davis and his minions proclaim—that the United States no longer constitute one, but two countries.[47]

Furthermore, said the *Times*, the practice engendered sympathy for the Confederacy in distant quarters: "Every one of them becomes a 'victim' of military oppression among those they take refuge with."[48]

By early September, the tide of official opinion was running strongly against Paine. On September 2, 1864, Kentucky governor Thomas E. Bramlette requested an investigation into Paine's command. A commission gathered "enough evidence to charge Paine with extreme misconduct." On September 4, General Grant wrote to General Halleck in familiar language: "General Paine must be removed from Paducah. He is not fit to have a command where there is a solitary family within his reach favorable to the Government. His administration will result in large and just claims against the Government for destruction of private property taken from our friends. He would do to put in an entirely disloyal district to scourge the people, but even then it is doubtful whether it comes within the bounds of civilized warfare to use him."[49]

On September 6, 1864, Paine was relieved and instructed to "turn over all his books and papers." Instead, he bolted and "promptly fled Paducah for Illinois, taking with him the majority of the records detailing his administration."[50] The story was told that after Paine left Paducah, letters were found in his desk saying, "Don't send any more pianos or plated silver or pictures; all the kin are supplied. But you can send bed linen and solid silverware." If not true, it did at least capture the spirit of Paine's larcenous character, to which Grant himself alluded.[51]

A court-martial in the case of General Eleazer A. Paine met in March 1865. The disgraced general resigned his commission the following month, on April 5. Other, more important, matters soon occupied the attention of the government's prosecutors. It was November before the board handed down its decision, which reflected the nation's war-weariness. For a career of murder, theft, graft, extortion, disobedience of orders, and perversion of the Bill of Rights, Paine received a reprimand.

16. Rebel Incursions and Yankee Injustices

The Federals abandoned Fort Heiman in early March 1863. Within days, they heard that the Confederates had moved in. Lieutenant Commander Le Roy Fitch of the USS *Moose* led an expedition from Smithland up the Tennessee River to investigate. In addition to Fitch's own vessel, there were the *Lexington*, the *Fairplay*, and the *Brilliant*. En route, Fitch overtook Lieutenant Commander James W. Shirk and the *Tuscumbia*. Fitch was going to cooperate with General Alexander S. Asboth, who had been ordered to recapture the fort. The alarm turned out to be false. Fitch said, "Finding the fort perfectly quiet and free from rebels, the boats returned to Smithland." Five gunboats and a land force dispatched in response to a rumor—the Federals obviously took seriously the possibility of a Rebel reoccupation of Fort Heiman—and they kept an eye on it for the rest of the war. It was not difficult to do, for boats were always cruising by. The Tennessee River remained a heavily traveled supply route.[52]

Even so, in late October 1864, General Abraham Buford moved into the fort with two Confederate brigades and began placing batteries, one two-gun section in the fort itself and another a bit downstream. His goal was to disrupt shipping to Johnsonville, the great Yankee supply depot in Humphreys County, Tennessee. That same evening, October 28, four small steamers passed Fort Heiman, headed downstream toward Smithland. Since they were going from Johnsonville, they were empty and were not too tempting. They posed no threat and carried no valuable plunder. Buford wanted to hit steamers headed *upstream*. He would not have to wait long.

The next morning, a Yankee riverboat called the *Mazeppa* hove into view. She was towing a barge. This was a prize worth taking. The Rebel guns barked when she pulled into range, and a round slammed into her machinery. The pilot immediately steered the drifting boat for the opposite shore. Coming to rest on a sandbar, the crew piled off the wounded boat and scurried into the woods. The *Mazeppa* was stopped, but on the wrong side of the Tennessee River. Captain Frank P. Gracey and two others built a raft, which fell apart in the water, and the captain finally just swam across, clinging to a log for buoyancy. He found some of the *Mazeppa*'s crewmen hiding among the trees on the Tennessee side. He brandished his two waterlogged pistols, captured the frightened deckhands, and ordered them to take one of the *Mazeppa*'s lifeboats over to get more men. General Buford was one of them. A cable was attached to the *Mazeppa*, and she was hauled over. General Buford climbed up to the hurricane deck and cut capers while the men muscled the *Mazeppa* across. He "rang the bell, gave orders to imaginary crews, and exhibited many evidences of delight." Approaching the Kentucky shore Buford shouted, "Boys, there is plenty to eat and plenty to wear for every soldier, but only enough whiskey for the General." The *Mazeppa* had seven tons of supplies onboard, worth an estimated $20,000. They included winter uniforms, blankets, hardtack and a thousand barrels of flour. The vessel was unloaded and the stores piled onshore, and then Buford's men burned her.[53]

The next day, the *Anna* was seen passing downstream. Knowing that her captain would see the burned wreck of the *Mazeppa* and make a report to the Federals, Buford ordered his men to immediately fire on her. The captain hoisted a white flag and promised to stop. It was a ruse to quiet the Rebel cannon fire. The *Anna* drifted slowly down, presumably to an anchorage at the lower landing, but then she leaped forward in the water and made her escape amidst the renewed gunfire. As feared, she made it to Paducah and a report was filed with post commander General Solomon Meredith of the new danger at Fort Heiman.

Paducah was thrown into a panic. If Forrest's men were at Fort Heiman, they must be planning an attack on Paducah. It was reported that "every business house in Paducah is closed and the goods in them are being removed to a place of safety.... Everything is prepared to give Forrest a warm reception."[54]

Paducah was not in danger, but no more supply boats were sent upstream until the situation at Fort Heiman was resolved. Meanwhile, more boats did come down the Tennessee River from Johnsonville and were attacked. The *J.W. Cheeseman* was badly damaged (and later burned) and her crew taken prisoner. The gunboat *Undine* traded fire with the Confederate batteries until her crew abandoned ship and escaped on the far bank. She was captured, along with the *Venus*.

Buford's men did not burn these last two steamers. Instead, they began to repair them for Confederate service. Forrest was planning an attack on the Johnsonville depot and adding a river-borne element to his offensive would greatly enhance his chances of success. Forrest came to Fort Heiman on October 31, and on November 1 the Confederates marched—and steamed—south to commence their new campaign. Buford's Fort Heiman operation had been a success. In three days, the Confederates had taken over forty prisoners, killed eight and wounded eleven. They had captured tons of supplies, had struck a blow against Federal shipping, and had captured two vessels as the genesis of their own fleet.

After the Confederates moved off toward Johnsonville, a Federal flotilla came steaming up the Tennessee River, blasting the bank with artillery fire. When they drew abreast Fort Heiman, one of the gunboats shelled the shore for two hours, continuing until its ammunition chests were empty. Part of the crew went ashore and burned the remnants of the cargo from the *Mazeppa*, which the Rebels had piled up and then left behind.

In the attack on Johnsonville, both the *Venus* and the *Undine* were lost. Forrest repaid the Yankees by destroying $2,200,000 worth of U.S. government stores.

The end of Buford's operation at Fort Heiman also marked the end of the war in the Jackson Purchase. Federal patrols still crisscrossed the region, the dark gunboats still plied her rivers, and guerrilla bands continued to be active into the last weeks of the war; but there were no more long columns of men marching to give battle. The largest groups seen were in the last days of the war, when bunches of men in gray and butternut came riding into Paducah to surrender. The Jackson Purchase had given her sons, her treasure, and her heart to the Confederacy, and it had lost all.

There was one final moment of joy for the Rebel-hearted citizens of western Kentucky. On April 15, 1865, President Lincoln died in Washington, D.C., and the Jackson Purchase celebrated the news. As late as 1955, Jennie Billings Moore, a native of Calloway County, remembered the "celebrations that were held following the death of the martyred president." She was only six years old at the time, but her memory was distinct of the festive mood. "In our ignorance we celebrated the occasion," she said.[55]

Afterword

The world moved on after the fall of the Confederacy in April 1865. The people of the Jackson Purchase were occupied with spring planting, the eternal first task of the year in an agricultural society. The farmers worked to replace their fences and replenish their livestock. As the growing season advanced, they found time to help regrade and resurface the county roads that had been so cut up by the movements of the armies. Downed bridges had to be rebuilt. All manner of debris needed to be carried away and the land restored. Whole city blocks in Paducah had to be cleared of the rubble of half-demolished buildings and Mayfield had to remove all traces of General Paine's massive earthworks on the courthouse square. Murray had to rebuild the half of the town square the Yankees had burned. The people had to adjust to a world without slavery. They had to get used to the absence of those who would never return from the distant fields where they had died. They had to grow accustomed to the sight of young men who were missing arms and legs and who were lacking something of the joy that young men should feel when they are in the prime of life. Their youth had been spent.

The decades passed and the people had other hardships to endure: periodic agricultural depressions brought on by America's boom and bust economy, drought, corrupt politicians, the Spanish-American War, and the decade-long effort of the Planters' Protective Association to break the monopolistic power of James Buchanan "Buck" Duke (head of the American Tobacco Company) and his tobacco trust. Duke's trust had driven tobacco prices to as low as three cents a pound for prime leaf. These were starvation prices and brought on what was a small civil war in its own right. In both Tennessee and Kentucky, some members of the protective association organized themselves into squads of night riders. They borrowed their methods from the Ku Klux Klan and used violence against those dark leaf tobacco farmers who refused to join the association. They burned barns, scraped plant beds, and dragged men out of bed to bull-whip them for their recalcitrance. Even the towns were threatened. Warehouses and a distillery were burned in Princeton. A large gang of night riders surrounded Murray. If Judge A.J.G. Wells had not had the foresight to post guards about the town and in the upstairs windows of the buildings surrounding the courthouse square, the riders might have occupied Murray as they did Hopkinsville. The situation in western Kentucky was growing desperate. The state militia had to be called out to restore order.

Several factors brought the disturbances to an end. The rising level of violence and a growing autocratic attitude on the part of their leaders disgusted the members of the rank and file, who began to abandon the association. There were several successful civil suits brought against the night riders; one jury ordered that a group of convicted arsonists pay $35,000 in damages. Most important, perhaps, was a 1911 decision of the U.S. Supreme Court that Duke's trust was a violation of federal law. He was ordered to break up his operation. With that, tobacco prices finally began to rise and the Planters' Protective Association blinked out of existence.

To a large extent, the Black Patch War was fought by the sons of men who had worn butternut and gray in the 1860s. The night riders and their leaders were too young to have served the Confederacy, but they were weaned on stories of the war and of the brave deeds of the men who had faced the oppressive foe, even when the odds were long.

The daughters of the former Rebels were inspired, too, by the stories their fathers told. In the final decade of the 19th century, the women of the South organized into the United Daughters of the Confederacy (UDC). Kentucky had never left the Union and was not included in Reconstruction in the same way that the former Confederate states were. However, martial law had continued in Kentucky for months after the war ended, and Federal troops had occupied Kentucky into the 1870s. Resentment toward the federal government grew strong during these years, accompanied by a longing for the way life was before the war. The Klan took root in the state and violence against blacks was widespread. The commonwealth's voters developed the habit of electing former Confederates as governor. Simon Bolivar Buckner was one of them. Across the state, nostalgia for the Old South was running high. In the Jackson Purchase, of course, this was not so much a shift in attitude as a continuation of the old loyalties.

The spirit of the age was conducive for the Daughters to emerge as a powerful social group. They were determined to honor their fathers by making the South a shrine to the memory of the "Lost Cause" and those who had served it. In the Purchase, the Daughters began their efforts with a monument in Fulton, a memorial arch topped by a statue of a Rebel soldier. It was erected in 1902. A Confederate monument in Paducah was next in 1907. It was followed by a heroic statue of General Lloyd Tilghman (partially financed by his surviving sons) in 1909. Thousands turned out to pay homage to Paducah's favorite adopted son at the statue's dedication. That same year, the UDC began the effort to erect a monument to commemorate Camp Beauregard. It took over a decade to raise the necessary funds, but by 1920 the Daughters had done so, and a handsome marker dedicated to the memory of the men who served and died at Camp Beauregard was the result. By that time there was a monument in Hickman, one in Mayfield (followed by a second in 1924), and a really fine statue of Robert E. Lee erected on the Murray town square in 1917. General Lee faces defiantly north, his hand on his sword, ever ready to defend the South.

The UDC intended that no one should ever forget which side the Jackson Purchase had favored in the War Between the States. No one would ever forget that the Purchase was part of Dixie.

Chapter Notes

Introduction

1. Patricia Ann Hoskins, "'The Old First Is with the South': The Civil War, Reconstruction, and Memory in the Jackson Purchase Region of Kentucky," PhD diss., Auburn University, 2008, 9, www.jacksonpurchasehistory.org/jackson-purchase-during-the-civil-war (accessed March 9, 2012).
2. Benjamin Franklin Cooling, *Forts Henry and Donelson: The Key to the Confederate Heartland* (Knoxville: University of Tennessee Press, 1989), 71.
3. Cooling, *Forts Henry and Donelson,* 45 (first quote); Dorothy Jennings and Kerby Jennings, *The Story of Calloway County, 1822–1976* (self-published, 1980), 9.
4. Lon Carter Barton, "A History of Graves County, Kentucky, 1818–1865," Master's thesis, University of Kentucky, 1960, 61.
5. Barton, 69 (first quote); Hoskins, 47 (second quote).
6. Barton, 69.
7. Pearl Handley, quoted in Barton, 67.
8. Robert C. Black, *The Railroads of the Confederacy* (Chapel Hill: University of North Carolina Press, 1952), 50. The completion of the M&O Railroad was in April 1861. If it had been planned by some malevolent, profit-hating deity, it could scarcely have come at a more unfortunate time. Black notes that the very next month, May 1861, the "Annual Report of the Mobile & Ohio ruefully noted the 'complete prostration of business'" (71).
9. Charles H. Bogart, "Kentucky's Railroad Network, 1861," in *Kentucky's Civil War, 1861–1865,* ed. Jerlene Rose (Clay City: Back Home in Kentucky, 2005), 54.
10. Hoskins, 59.
11. Hico, "Letter from Western Kentucky," *New York Times*, August 25, 1855.
12. Hoskins, 54, 55.
13. Richard G. Wood, "Construction of the Louisville and Paducah Marine Hospitals," *Register of the Kentucky Historical Society* (January 1958), 28.
14. Ibid., 29.
15. "Great Fire in Paducah, Ky.," *New York Times*, April 5, 1852.
16. "Telegraph Under the Ohio," *New York Times*, August 18, 1853 (first and second quotes); Quintus Quincy Quigley, *The Life and Times of Quintus Quincy Quigley, 1828–1910: His Personal Journal, 1859–1908,* ed. George Quigley Langstaff, Jr. (self-published, 1999), 60 (third quote).
17. Hoskins, 77.
18. Alan Bearman, "'The South Carolina of Kentucky': How Evangelical Religion Influenced the Jackson Purchase of Kentucky to Support Secession," LD 3571 M5 2000 B43, Forrest C. Pogue Special Collections Library, Murray State University, Murray, Kentucky, 40 (first quote); 47 (second quote). Bearman says that "evidence points to the Iron Banks Baptist Church, possibly founded in 1810, as the first church in the region" (40).
19. Quigley, 62.

Chapter 1

1. Hoskins, 99–100.
2. Berry F. Craig, "Henry Cornelius Burnett: Champion of Southern Rights," *Register of the Kentucky Historical Society* (Autumn 1979), 266.
3. R.E. Banta, *The Ohio* (New York: Rinehart, 1949), 469.
4. Craig, "Burnett," 267.
5. Ibid., 268.
6. Lowell H. Harrison, *The Civil War in*

Kentucky (Lexington: University Press of Kentucky, 1975), 26.
7. Craig, "Burnett," 267 (first quote); Berry F. Craig, "Kentucky's Rebel Press: The Jackson Purchase Newspapers in 1861," *Register of the Kentucky Historical Society* (January 1977), 21 (second quote).
8. Lowell H. Harrison and James C. Klotter, *A New History of Kentucky* (Lexington: University Press of Kentucky, 1997), 187. A week after his defiant answer to President Lincoln, Governor Magoffin also refused the Confederate secretary of war's (L.P. Walker) request to send troops to the Confederacy.
9. Ibid., 188–189.
10. Harrison, *Civil War in Kentucky*, 9.
11. Quigley, 69.
12. Ibid.
13. Ibid.
14. United States War Department, *The War of the Rebellion: A Compilation of the Official Records of the Union and Confederate Armies*, 129 volumes (Washington, D.C.: Government Printing Office, 1880–1901), Vol. 52, Part II, 61–62 (hereafter referred to as *ORA*).
15. Steven L. Wright, "'Oh, God, What Is in Store for Us!': Kentucky's Illusion of Neutrality," unpublished ms. p. 24.
16. Ibid.
17. George B. McClellan, letter to Abraham Lincoln, May 30, 1861, "The Abraham Lincoln Papers at the Library of Congress," http://memory.loc.gov/ammem/alhtml/malcap.html (accessed September 19, 2012) (hereafter cited as Lincoln Papers).

Chapter 2

1. William Howard Russell, *My Diary North and South* (Boston: T.O.H.P. Burnham, 1863), 334–335.
2. Jay Carlton Mullen, "The Turning of Columbus," *Register of the Kentucky Historical Society* (July 1966), 213–214.
3. "The Camp at Cairo," *New York Times*, May 8, 1861.
4. Charles Wright Wills, *Army Life of an Illinois Soldier* (Washington, D.C.: Globe, 1906), 17.
5. John M. Adair, *Historical Sketch of the Forty-Fifth Illinois Regiment* (Lanark, IL: Carroll County Gazette Print, 1869), 3.
6. Benjamin Prentiss, et al., letter to Abraham Lincoln, May 24, 1861, Lincoln Papers.

7. George B. McClellan, letter to Abraham Lincoln, May 30, 1861, Lincoln Papers.
8. Leslie Combs, letter to Abraham Lincoln, August 14, 1861, Lincoln Papers.
9. *ORA*, Vol. 12, p. 678.
10. Ibid., Vol. 4, p. 254.
11. Hoskins, 86; Craig, "Kentucky's Rebel Press," 23.
12. United States Naval War Records Office, *Official Records of the Union and Confederate Navies in the War of the Rebellion*, Series I, 27 Volumes (Washington, D.C.: Government Printing Office, 1894–1917), Vol. 22, p. 788 (hereafter cited as *ORN*).
13. *ORA*, Vol. 52, Part II, 95–96.
14. Frank Moore, ed., *The Rebellion Record: A Diary of American Events, with Documents, Narratives, Illustrative Incidents, Poetry, Etc.*, vol. 1 (New York: G.P. Putnam, 1862), 76.
15. Ibid.
16. Ibid.
17. Hoskins, 88.
18. Moore, 76.
19. Wright, "Oh, God!," 12.
20. Steven L. Wright., ed., *Kentucky Soldiers and Their Regiments in the Civil War, 1861* (self-published, 2009), 11.
21. Benjamin Franklin Cooling, *Forts Henry and Donelson: The Key to the Confederate Heartland* (Knoxville: University of Tennessee Press, 1989), 14.
22. Ibid., 46.
23. *ORA*, Vol. 52, Part II, 100–101.
24. Jack Calbert, "The Jackson Purchase and the End of the Neutrality Policy in Kentucky," *Filson Club History Quarterly*, July 1964.
25. Wright, "Oh, God!," 52–53.
26. "Outrages in Southern Kentucky," *New York Times*, August 27, 1861.
27. "Some Stories Around Town," *Paducah Sun*, October 2, 1909.
28. Wright, *Kentucky Soldiers and Their Regiments*, vol. 1, p. 14.
29. Ibid., 31.
30. *ORA*, Vol. 4, p. 374.
31. Wright, *Kentucky Soldiers and Their Regiments*, vol. 1, p. 38.

Chapter 3

1. Wills, 11 (first quote), 13 (second quote). Cairo was then, and is still, pronounced "Kay-roe" by the people of the region. Only the un-

informed call the southern Illinois town "Kye-roe."
  2. Ibid., 13, 17.
  3. Ibid., 15, 23.
  4. Russell, 330.
  5. John H. Brinton, *Personal Memoirs of John H. Brinton, Civil War Surgeon, 1861–1865* (Carbondale: Southern Illinois University Press, 1996), 49.
  6. Ibid., 67.
  7. Russell, 306–307.
  8. Nathaniel Cheairs Hughes, Jr., *The Battle of Belmont: Grant Strikes South* (Chapel Hill: University of North Carolina Press, 1991), 53. Sedgwick became a corps commander in the Army of the Potomac. He was shot and killed May 9, 1864, at the Battle of Spotsylvania.
  9. Ibid.
  10. Russell, 321.
  11. *ORA*, Vol. 3, 619.
  12. Charles W. Davis, "New Madrid and Island No. 10," in *Military Essays and Recollections: Papers Read Before the Commandery of the State of Illinois, Order of the Loyal Legion of the United States*, vol.1 (Chicago: A.C. McClurg, 1891), 77; "The War in Missouri," *New York Times*, August 28, 1861.
  13. *ORA*, Vol. 3, 390.
  14. Tom Chaffin, *Pathfinder: John Charles Frémont and the Course of American Empire* (New York: Hill and Wang, 2002), 460.
  15. Brinton, 32–33.
  16. Thomas Ewing, letter to Abraham Lincoln, September 17, 1861, Lincoln Papers.
  17. James B. Eads, "Recollections of Foote and the Gun-Boats," in *Battles and Leaders of the Civil War: The Opening Battles*, ed. Robert Underwood Johnson and Clarence Clough Buel (Edison, NJ: Castle Books, 1995), 338.
  18. Myron J. Smith, Jr., *The* Carondelet: *A Civil War Ironclad on Western Waters* (Jefferson, NC: McFarland, 2010), 7.
  19. William Garrett Piston and Thomas P. Sweeney, "Missourians and the War on the Western Rivers," *North and South*, August 2009, p. 45.
  20. J.M. Hoppin, *Life of Andrew Hull Foote, Rear-Admiral, United States Navy* (New York: Harper and Brothers, 1874), 165.
  21. Michael J. Bennett, *Union Jacks: Yankee Sailors in the Civil War* (Chapel Hill: University of North Carolina Press, 2004), 82; Jack D. Coomb, *Thunder Along the Mississippi: The River Battles That Split the Confederacy* (Edison, NJ: Castle Books, 2005), 22.
  22. *ORN*, Vol. 22, 302.
  23. Ibid., 299.
  24. Eads, "Recollections," 339.
  25. Cooling, 24.
  26. Ibid.
  27. *ORN*, Vol. 22, 313.
  28. Coombe, 20.
  29. Spencer C. Tucker, *Andrew Foote: Civil War Admiral on Western Water* (Annapolis: Naval Institute Press, 2000), 114.
  30. *ORN*, Vol. 22, 320.
  31. Eads, "Recollections," 346.
  32. *ORN*, Vol. 22, 493 (first quote), 314 (second quote); Tucker, 114 (third quote).

Chapter 4

  1. *ORA*, Vol. 4, 183. If the Columbus Rangers were like the militia company from Hickman, the Federals had little to fear. In "History and Other Facts Relating to Fulton County" (*Hickman Courier*, February 4, 1909), the pitifully inadequate armaments of the weekend soldiers were listed as "rifles, flintlock muskets, pitchforks, battle-axes, spears, [and] spades."
  2. Wills, 18–19 (first quote); Russell, 335 (second quote).
  3. *ORA*, Vol. 4, 178 (first quote); 177 (second quote).
  4. Ibid., 177.
  5. Ibid., 176–177.
  6. Berry F. Craig, "Northern Conquerors and Southern Deliverers: The Civil War Comes to the Jackson Purchase," *Register of the Kentucky Historical Society* (January 1975), 21.
  7. "Miscellaneous Washington News," *New York Times*, August 30, 1861.
  8. Augustus L. Chetlain, "Recollections of General U.S. Grant," in *Military Essays and Recollections: Papers Read Before the Commandery of the State of Illinois, Order of the Loyal Legion of the United States*, vol. 1 (Chicago: A.C. McClurg, 1891), 12.
  9. Frémont, "In Command in Missouri," 284.
  10. *ORA*, Vol. 4, p. 179.
  11. James A. Ramage, "Grant's Occupation of Paducah," in *Kentucky's Civil War, 1861–1865*, ed. Jerlene Rose (Clay City: Back Home in Kentucky, 2005), 33.
  12. U.S. Grant, *Personal Memoirs of U.S.*

Grant (New York: Library of America, 1990), 175.

13. Fred G. Neuman, *The Story of Paducah* (N.p.: Young, 1927), 146–147. In *The Tennessee: Civil War to TVA*, David Donaldson adds that thirty years or more after the war Mrs. Jarrett's controversial and never discovered Rebel banner was put to its final use: it covered Mrs. Jarrett's casket. Paducahans had a long memory.

14. *ORA*, Vol. 4, p. 196 (first quote); Ramage, 33 (second quote); Charles B. Kimbell, *History of Battery "A," First Illinois Light Artillery Volunteers* (Chicago: Cushing, 1899), 35.

15. *ORA*, Series II, Vol. 2, p. 55.

16. John McLean, *One Hundred Years in Illinois, 1818–1918* (Chicago: Paterson, 1919), 138.

17. *ORA*, Vol. 4, p. 198.

18. Hoskins, 117–118.

19. U.S. Grant, "The Papers of U.S. Grant, April–September, 1861," vol. 2, Mississippi State University, U.S.Grant Digital Collection, http://digital.library.msstate.edu/collections/document.ph?CISOROOT=%2FUSG_volume&CISOPTR=16321&REC=17&CISOBOX, 191n (accessed March 5, 2012) (hereafter cited as Grant Papers).

20. Ibid.

Chapter 5

1. *ORA*, Vol. 4, pp. 181–184.

2. Joseph H. Parks, *General Leonidas Polk, C.S.A.: The Fighting Bishop* (Baton Rouge: Louisiana State University Press, 1962), 70.

3. Ibid., 157–158.

4. Ibid., 169.

5. Philip B. Spence, "Service for the Confederacy," *Confederate Veteran*, August 1900, p. 373. General Polk never quite gave up his bishop's robes. He preached a sermon in Harrodsburg, Kentucky, after the Battle of Perryville and performed the marriage ceremony of John Hunt Morgan and his second wife in Murfreesboro in December 1862. Before the war was done, Polk would also baptize two of the best known Confederate generals, Joseph E. Johnston and John Bell Hood.

6. *ORA*, Vol. 4, p. 179.

7. Ibid., 180.

8. Ibid., 287.

9. Ibid., 179 (first quote), 191 (second quote).

10. Ibid., 180.

11. *ORA*, Vol. 52, Part II, 141–142. Much has been written about the phrase "the necessity justified the action." Some modern scholars are sure that Polk rephrased to his own advantage the words President Davis actually used. Bryan Bush, for example, says in *Lloyd Tilghman: Confederate General in the Western Theatre* that Davis really said, "The necessity must justify the action." Bush points out, "It is of some interest to note that this statement can have several interpretations. It can mean the necessity does justify the action or the necessity had better justify the action" (p. 50). Davis may or may not have said those exact words to Polk, but he did say something very similar regarding Polk's advance to Governor Harris in a letter dated September 13, 1861. Davis said, "As a necessity it was sanctioned" (*ORA*, Vol. 4, p. 190).

12. *ORA*, Vol. 4, pp. 185–187.

13. John Milton Hubbard, *Notes of a Private* (Memphis: E.H. Clarke & Brother, 1909), 12.

14. Hughes, 40.

15. Nancy D. Baird, "There Is No Sunday in the Army: Civil War Letters of Lunsford P. Yandell, 1861–1862," *Filson Club History Quarterly*, July 1979, p. 319.

16. Bell Irvin Wiley, *The Life of Johnny Reb: The Common Soldier of the Confederacy* (Baton Rouge: Louisiana State University Press, 1990), 62.

17. Henry Morton Stanley, *The Autobiography of Sir Henry Morton Stanley* (Boston: Houghton Mifflin, 1909), 178–179.

18. Ibid., 177.

19. Ibid., 176.

20. Mark Twain, *Life on the Mississippi* (New York: Harper and Brothers, 1917), 215. Columbus was originally at river level, but it was moved to higher ground after the 1927 Flood. The U.S. Corps of Engineers planned and directed the work. Now the town is behind the CSA works and the nice state park that preserves them.

21. Kentucky Department of Parks, "Columbus-Belmont: 'The Gibraltar of the West,'" in *Kentucky's Civil War, 1861–1865*, ed. Jerlene Rose (Clay City: Back Home in Kentucky, 2005), 28–29.

22. *ORA*, Vol. 4, pp. 491–492 (first quote), 560 (second quote).

23. William C. Winter, ed., *Captain Joseph Boyce and the 1st Missouri Infantry, C.S.A.*

(St. Louis: Missouri History Museum, 2011), 46.
24. Dieter C. Ullrich, "Confederate Operations in the Jackson Purchase: A History of Camp Beauregard, Kentucky," *Filson Club History Quarterly*, October 2002, p. 471.
25. *ORA*, Vol. 4, pp. 446 (first quote), 455 (second quote), 551 (third quote), 448 (fourth quote).
26. Ibid., 513.
27. Ibid., 522.

Chapter 6

1. Geoffrey Perret, *Lincoln's War: The Untold Story of America's Greatest President as Commander in Chief* (New York: Random House, 2004), 89.
2. Chaffin, 465.
3. Grant, 177.
4. Benjamin Henry Grierson and Bruce J. Dinges, *A Just and Righteous Cause: Benjamin H. Grierson's Civil War Memoir* (Carbondale: Southern Illinois University Press, 2008), 60.
5. Jay Carlton Mullen, "The Turning of Columbus," *Register of the Kentucky Historical Society* (July 1966), 221.
6. "The Rebellion," *New York Times*, November 29, 1861.
7. Grant Papers, Vol. 3: October 1, 1861–January 7, 1862, p. 25.
8. Ibid., 10. Many of the soldiers felt the same way as Grant about Paducah. Private Charles W. Wills wrote, "I fell in love with Paducah while I was there, and I think I will settle there when the war is over. I never saw so many pretty women in my life. All fat, smooth-skinned, small-boned, highbred looking women. They hollered 'Hurrah for Jeff Davis' at us, some of them, but that's all right. I could write until to-morrow morning about Paducah" (Wills, 29).
9. McLean, 146.
10. Grant, *Memoirs*, 178.
11. William S. McFeely, *Grant: A Biography* (New York: W.W. Norton, 2002), 92.
12. Brinton, 72. The shot that Dr. Brinton paid the black youths to excavate for him turned out to be a conical shell about eighteen inches long. It had been filled with lead and was "fired as a solid shot." The heavy souvenir became such a burden to lug around that Brinton later left it behind in Cairo. "What became of it I never knew," he said in 1891. "I daresay it is a household ornament somewhere at this moment" (*Personal Memoirs*, 72–73).
13. Ibid., 74.
14. *ORN*, Vol. 22, 792.
15. Henry Walke, "The Gun-Boats at Belmont and Fort Henry," in *Battles and Leaders of the Civil War: The Opening Battles*, ed. Robert Underwood Johnson and Clarence Clough Buel (Edison, NJ: Castle Books, 1995), 360.
16. Henry Walke, *Naval Scenes and Reminiscences of the Civil War* (New York: F.R. Reed, 1877), 34.
17. Don Singletary, "The Battle of Belmont," *Confederate Veteran*, November 1915, p. 506.
18. William M. Polk, "General Polk and the Battle of Belmont," *Battles and Leaders of the Civil War: The Opening Battles*, ed. Robert Underwood Johnson and Clarence Clough Buel (Edison, NJ: Castle Books, 1995), 355.
19. *ORN*, Vol. 22, 401.
20. Ibid., 409 (first quote), 426 (second quote).
21. Ibid., 426.
22. John A. Logan, *The Volunteer Soldier of America* (Chicago: R.S. Peale , 1887), 64 (first quote), Hughes, 130 (second quote).
23. Brinton, 75.
24. Robert E. Denney, *Civil War Medicine: Care and Comfort of the Wounded* (New York: Sterling, 1994), 55.
25. Hughes, 131.
26. Brinton, 77
27. Grant, *Memoirs*, 180.
28. Brinton, 78.
29. Twain, 217.
30. *ORN*, Vol. 22, p. 418 (first quote); Singletary, 507 (second and third quotes).
31. *ORN*, Vol. 22, p. 419.
32. Ibid., 410.
33. Ibid., 414.
34. Ibid., 410.
35. Ibid.
36. Grant, *Memoirs*, 183.
37. Hughes, 149.
38. Brinton, 80–82. Dr. Brinton later learned that the major had survived long enough to be carried to Columbus, where he died.
39. Walke, *Naval Scenes and Reminiscences*, 36–37.
40. Ibid., 38.
41. Ibid.
42. Grant, *Memoirs*, 184.

43. James D. Porter, letter to John S. Mosby, *Confederate Veteran*, May 1910, p. 202.
44. Hughes, 171.
45. Brinton, 82–86.
46. Hughes, 175.

Chapter 7

1. Chetlain, 22.
2. Lew Wallace, *An Autobiography* (New York: Harper & Bros., 1906), 339.
3. *ORA*, Vol. 4, p. 302.
4. Ibid.
5. *ORA*, Vol. 3, p. 301.
6. Ibid., 302.
7. Bruce Catton, *Grant Moves South* (Boston: Little, Brown, 1960), 80.
8. *ORA*, Vol. 3, p. 303.
9. Steven E. Woodworth, *Nothing But Victory: The Army of the Tennessee, 1861–1865* (New York: Alfred A. Knopf, 2005), 57 (first quote); Winter, 45 (second quote).
10. *ORA*, Vol. 3, p. 303.
11. Marion Morrison, *A History of the Ninth Regiment, Illinois Volunteer Infantry* (Monmouth: J.S. Clark, 1864), 16.
12. Chetlain, 83–84.
13. Hall Allen, *Center of Conflict: A Factual Story of the War Between the States in Western Kentucky and Tennessee* (Paducah: Paducah Sun-Democrat, 1961), 29. Robert Woolfolk had every right to be in the Tilghman house shouting insults at the Yankees from an open window, for he was the actual owner of the property. The house was new when Lloyd Tilghman and his family moved in and was leased for them, either by the railroad or by the city of Paducah.
14. Ibid.
15. John B. Day, "Gen. Lew Wallace in Paducah," *Paducah Sun*, February 23, 1905.
16. Wallace, *Autobiography*, 351.
17. Ibid.
18. Catton, 88.
19. Ibid., 89.
20. "Our War Correspondence," *New York Times*, December 12, 1861.
21. Day, "Gen. Lew Wallace in Paducah."
22. Ibid. (first quote); Charles B. Kimbell, *History of Battery "A," First Illinois Light Artillery Volunteers* (Chicago: Cushing, 1899), 36–37 (second and third quotes).
23. Wallace, *Autobiography*, 354.
24. *ORA*, Vol. 7, 448–449.

Chapter 8

1. Lonnie E. Maness, "Columbus: Gibraltar of the West." *Journal of the Jackson Purchase Historical Society*, June 1982, www.jacksonpurchasehistory.org/jackson-purchase-during-the-civil-war (accessed April 4, 2012).
2. Wills, 40.
3. Ibid.
4. Grant Papers, Vol. 3, p. 138 (first quote); *OR*, Vol. 4, p. 346 (second quote).
5. *ORA*, Vol. 3, p. 274.
6. Hughes, 193. Historians have continued to try to shine the light on Grant's performance at Belmont. Steven Woodworth writes, "In his first engagement as a general officer, he had come about as close to ultimate disaster as it was possible to imagine without actually experiencing utter defeat. He had lost control of his army, been surrounded by the enemy, and returned to the transports in inglorious rout.... There would be other low points in his career, but never, not even at Shiloh, would he feel the hot breath of complete disaster this close on his neck" (Woodworth, 55–56).
7. Lew Wallace, "The Capture of Fort Donelson," in *Battles and Leaders of the Civil War: The Opening Battles*, ed. Robert Underwood Johnson and Clarence Clough Buel (Edison, NJ: Castle Books, 1995), 404.
8. *ORA*, Vol. 52, Part I, 201.
9. Walke, *Naval Scenes and Reminiscences*, 49.
10. Catton, 82.
11. *ORN*, Vol. 22, 399–400.
12. Ibid., 450 (first quote); "The Mississippi Expedition," *New York Times*, December 14, 1861.
13. Walke, *Naval Scenes and Reminiscences*, 95.
14. Tucker, 122 (first quote); Perret, 134 (second quote).
15. Perret, 135.
16. *ORN*, Vol. 22, p. 933.
17. Ibid., 337.
18. Ibid., 632 (first quote); Bennett, 81 (second quote).
19. *ORN*, Vol. 22, p. 632.
20. Bennett, 80.
21. Hoppin, 180.
22. Ibid., 163.
23. "The Mississippi Expedition," *New York Times*, December 14, 1861.
24. "Reminiscences: Mother of the Confederacy," *Confederate Veteran*, April 1894, p. 106.

25. Baird, 323 (first quote); J.M. Cartmell, "Witness to the Battle of Belmont," *Confederate Veteran*, April 1908 (second quote).
26. "The Battle of Belmont," *New York Times*, November 19, 1861 (first quote); Baird, 323 (second quote).
27. Baird, 323.
28. *ORA*, Vol. 3, p. 310.
29. *ORA*, Vol. 4, p. 522.
30. *ORA*, Vol. 7, p. 746.
31. William D. Pickett, "The Bursting of the 'Lady Polk,'" *Confederate Veteran*, June 1904, p. 277.
32. Ibid., 278.
33. Philip B. Spence, "Service for the Confederacy," *Confederate Veteran*, August 1900, p. 373. Incidentally, Jack Doublin, whose father died as a result of the amputation of his leg, was soon after given a mercy discharge from the army so that he could go home and care for his mother and siblings.
34. *ORA*, Vol. 53, Part II, 222.
35. Catton, 84.
36. *ORA*, Series II, Part I, 523.
37. Cooling, *Forts Henry and Donelson*, 60 (first quote), 48 (second quote).
38. *ORN*, Vol. 22, p. 383.
39. Ibid., 394.
40. *ORA*, Vol. 4, p. 458, first and second quotes. Henry's home, Emerald Hill, still stands in Clarksville.
41. *ORA*, Vol. 4, p. 526.
42. *ORA*, Vol. 7, p. 144 (first quote); Cooling, 48 (second quote).
43. *ORA*, Vol. 4, p. 460.
44. Ibid., 461 (first quote); *ORA*, Vol. 7, p. 132 (second quote).
45. Pat Griffin, "The Famous Tenth Tennessee," *Confederate Veteran*, December 1905, p. 553.
46. Phillip M. Shelton, "Camp Beauregard, Graves County, Kentucky," *Register of the Kentucky Historical Society* (April 1963), 150 (first quote); See also: Mrs. George T. Fuller, comp., *A History of Camp Beauregard in Graves County, Ky.* (Mayfield: Tilghman-Beauregard Camp No. 16, SCV, 1988), 27.
47. John Milton Hubbard, *Notes of a Private* (Memphis: E.H. Clarke and Brother, 1909), 18.
48. Fuller, 17.
49. Ibid., 21–22.
50. Winter, 46–47.
51. *ORA*, Vol. 7, p. 790.
52. Winter, 47.
53. *ORA*, Vol. 7, p. 790.
54. Ibid.
55. Ibid., 807.

Chapter 9

1. Catton, 127–128.
2. "Southern News Through Louisville," *New York Times*, June 12, 1861.
3. *ORN*, Vol. 22, 479. Phelps' bigotry toward Jewish citizens was not an individual quirk. Anti-Semitism was a dark line running through the story of Grant's relationship of the Jackson Purchase, as will be seen.
4. Ibid., 480.
5. *ORA*, Vol. 7, p. 546.
6. Grant, *Memoirs*, 189.
7. *ORA*, Vol. 7, pp. 533–534.
8. Ibid., 540.
9. Brinton, 103.
10. *ORA*, Vol. 7, p. 69.
11. Ibid.
12. Ibid., 69 (first quote), 71 (second quote).
13. Ibid., 70.
14. D. Lieb Ambrose, *History of the Seventh Regiment Illinois Volunteer Infantry* (Springfield: Illinois Journal, 1868), 22.
15. *ORA*, Vol. 7, p. 71.
16. Phineas Orlando Avery, *History of the Fourth Illinois Cavalry Regiment* (Humboldt, NE: Enterprise, 1903), 48.
17. Grant, *Memoirs*, 180. At another time, Grant expressed a much harder opinion of the January expedition. He considered it a useless expenditure of time and energy. He is reported to have said, "This sloshing about in mud, sleet, rain, and snow for a week without striking the enemy, only exposing the men to great hardships and suffering in mid-winter, is not war" (Catton, *Grant Moves South*, 121).
18. *ORN*, Vol. 22, p. 489.
19. Ibid., 507.
20. Ibid.
21. *ORA*, Vol. 7, p. 929 (first quote); Dorothy Jennings and Kerby Jennings, *The Story of Calloway County, 1822–1976* (self-published, 1980), 31 (second quote). In the same dispatch in which he praised General Smith to Lorenzo Thomas, General Halleck said, without confiding a name, that the man who spread rumors about Smith was "totally unfit for any command" (*ORA*, Vol. 7, p. 929). He was talking about E.A. Paine.
22. Cooling, 71.

23. Ibid., 70.
24. Wallace, *Autobiography*, 356.
25. *ORN*, Vol. 22, p. 520.
26. Ibid., 521.
27. *ORA*, Vol. 7, p. 75.
28. Ibid., 561.
29. Grant, *Memoirs*, 190.
30. William T. Sherman, *Memoirs of General W.T. Sherman* (New York: Library of America, 1990), 238.
31. *ORA*, Vol. 7, p. 121.
32. Ibid.
33. Shelby Foote, *The Civil War, A Narrative: Fort Sumter to Perryville* (New York: Vintage, 1986), 182.
34. *ORA*, Vol. 7, p. 593.
35. Ibid., 121.

Chapter 10

1. *ORA*, Vol. 7, pp. 131–132.
2. Ibid., 132.
3. Ibid.
4. Coombs, 47.
5. *ORA*, Vol. 7, p. 145.
6. Ibid., 835 (first quote); 74 (second quote).
7. *ORN*, Vol. 22, 528.
8. Catton, 136 (first quote); Brinton, 239 (second quote).
9. Tucker, 141.
10. *ORN*, Vol. 22, p. 514.
11. *ORA*, Vol. 7, p. 578.
12. Ibid., 579.
13. "The Capture of Fort Henry," *New York Times*, February 12, 1862.
14. Walke, "The Gun-Boats at Belmont and Fort Henry," 362.
15. Edwin C. Bearss, *The Fall of Fort Henry* (Dover: Fort Donelson National Military Park, 1999), 10.
16. Cooling, 101.
17. Bearss, 13.
18. W.H.C. Michael, "The Mississippi Flotilla," War Papers, Military Order of the Loyal Legion of the United States, http://suvcw.org/mollus/warpapers/NEv1p21.htm (accessed July 23, 2012).
19. Walke, "The Gun-Boats at Belmont and Fort Henry," 362.
20. Ibid., 363.
21. Bearss, 15.
22. Coombe, 49.
23. Jesse Taylor, "The Defense of Fort Henry," in *Battles and Leaders of the Civil War: The Opening Battles*, ed. Robert Underwood Johnson and Clarence Clough Buel (Edison, NJ: Castle Books, 1995), 370.
24. Walke, "The Gun-Boats at Belmont and Fort Henry," 365.
25. *ORA*, Vol. 7, p. 122.
26. Taylor, 371 (first quote); *ORA*, Vol. 7, p. 134 (second quote).
27. Ibid.
28. Taylor, 371.
29. *ORA*, Vol. 7, 123.
30. Thomas Wise Durham, *Three Years With Wallace's Zouaves: The Civil War Memoirs of Thomas Wise Durham*, ed. Jeffrey L. Patrick (Macon: Mercer University Press, 2003), 64.
31. Wallace, *Autobiography*, 370.
32. Kimbell, 37–38.
33. Logan, 631.
34. Ibid., 632.
35. Ibid., 632–633.
36. Cooling, 108.
37. Michael, "The Mississippi Flotilla."
38. Walke, "The Gun-Boats at Belmont and Fort Henry," 366.
39. Hoppin, 204.
40. *ORA*, Vol. 7, p. 123.
41. Brinton, 114.

Chapter 11

1. Early in the Civil War, citizens of the Deep South—especially in the backwoods—had no understanding of what a threat the Federal gunboats posed to them. In his fine book, Michael J. Bennett explains, "Gunboats and river sailors penetrated areas of the Confederacy thought unreachable because of a lack of good roads. Union river sailors, not soldiers, were often the first ones to penetrate the key areas of the Western Confederacy. The quickness with which sailors and their boats arrived as well as the little amount of water they needed to sail amazed Southerners.... The unexpected vulnerability created in Southerners an almost 'pathological fear' of gunboats" (Bennett, *Union Jacks*, 85).
2. "Operations in Tennessee." *New York Times*, February 13, 1862.
3. *ORA*, Vol. 7, p. 155.
4. Ibid., 154.
5. Ibid., 125. Though this was early in the war, Grant had already come to realize the

value of the gunboats in these Western operations. Time did not alter his opinion. In 1880, long after he had seen them in action at Fort Henry, Fort Donelson, Shiloh, Vicksburg, and elsewhere, Grant told W.H.C. Michael that "without the gunboats on the Mississippi and its tributaries any attempt of the army to wrest from the Confederacy the Mississippi valley must have proved futile; indeed, the Confederate states could have prolonged the war indefinitely but for the services of the Mississippi Squadron." It was a truthful and generous observation from a man who could be very territorial when assigning credit (W.H.C. Michael, "The Mississippi Flotilla," *Military Order of the Loyal Legion of the United States*, also referred to as MOLLUS, 1902, n.p. Available online at http://suvcw.org/mollus/warpapers/NEv1p21.htm).

6. Henry I. Smith, *History of the Seventh Iowa Veteran Volunteer Infantry* (Mason City, IA: E. Hitchcock, 1903), 35.

7. *ORA*, Vol. 7, p. 599.

8. Smith, *History of the Seventh Iowa*, 36–38.

9. George W. Driggs, *Opening the Mississippi; or, Two Years' Campaigning in the Southwest* (Madison: Wm. J. Park, 1864), 70.

10. *ORA*, Series II, Vol. 3, p. 247.

11. Ibid. General Tilghman was later transferred to Fort Warren, Boston, Massachusetts. He was exchanged in the fall of 1862 and returned to Confederate service. Tilghman was killed on May 16, 1863, at the Battle of Champion's Hill. He was buried in Woodlawn Cemetery, New York City, but he was not forgotten in his adopted hometown. His home on Kentucky Avenue in Paducah was preserved and is now a Civil War museum. There is a heroic statue of him in the city, and Paducah Tilghman High School is named in honor of his wife, Augusta.

12. Driggs, 71.

13. *ORA*, Vol. 7, p. 594.

14. *ORA*, Vol. 52, Part I, p. 208.

15. Ibid.

16. Walke, "The Gun-Boats at Belmont and Fort Henry," 365.

17. Wallace, *Autobiography*, 377.

18. *ORA*, Vol. 7, p. 603 (first quote); *ORN*, Vol. 22, p. 550 (second quote).

19. *ORA*, Vol. 7, 601.

20. Wallace, *Autobiography*, 378 (first quote), 380 (second quote).

21. Grant Papers, Vol. 4: January 8–March 31, 1862, 192.

22. Brinton, 115.

23. Coombe, 61 (first quote); Henry A. Walke, "The Western Flotilla at Fort Donelson, Island Number Ten, Fort Pillow, and Memphis," in *Battles and Leaders of the Civil War: The Opening Battles*, ed. Robert Underwood Johnson and Clarence Clough Buel (Edison, NJ: Castle Books, 1995), 431 (second quote).

24. Tucker, 146–147.

25. Walke, "The Western Flotilla," 430.

26. *ORA*, Vol. 7, pp. 358 (first quote), 130 (second and third quotes).

27. *ORA*, Vol. 7, p. 865.

28. Grant, *Memoirs*, 196.

29. Works Progress Administration, *Military History of Kentucky* (Frankfort: State Journal, 1939), 170–171.

30. Parks, 209–210.

31. John Fiske, *The Mississippi Valley in the Civil War* (Cambridge: Riverside Press, 1902), 59.

Chapter 12

1. "River Batteries at Fort Donelson," *Confederate Veteran*, November 1896, p. 393.

2. Walke, "The Western Flotilla," 431 (first quote); Cooling, 142 (second quote).

3. Walke, "The Western Flotilla," 431.

4. John T. Smith, *A History of the Thirty-First Regiment of Indiana Volunteer Infantry in the War of the Rebellion* (Cincinnati: Western Methodist, 1900), 199–200.

5. Lew Wallace, "The Capture of Fort Donelson," in *Battles and Leaders of the Civil War: The Opening Battles*, ed. Robert Underwood Johnson and Clarence Clough Buel (Edison, NJ: Castle Books, 1995), 406.

6. Brinton, 117.

7. Ibid., 117–118.

8. Ibid., 118. This is the last we shall hear from Dr. Brinton, though he remained with Grant's army through the Battle of Fort Donelson and traveled with the soldiers—hardened veterans now—up the Tennessee River to their rendezvous with General Albert Sidney Johnston's Confederates at Shiloh. Brinton missed that battle, having been sent by Grant to St. Louis to try to procure supplies. Returning south, he was detained at Cairo to serve on a panel investigating conditions at the Mound City Hospital. He rejoined the army in time to accompany it on its march to Corinth, but

left the Western Theater in May when he was ordered to report to Washington, D.C. He saw some service at the front with the Army of the Potomac, but his main duties were in the surgeon general's office. He was assigned to collect specimens for the Pathological Museum and material for a volume called *The Surgical History of the War*. He also served on various examining boards. Brinton returned to the West in October 1864 and joined General William S. Rosecrans in the Department of the Missouri. New orders two months later sent him to Nashville and service with General George H. Thomas. Brinton's resignation from the service was accepted in March 1865 and he returned to his surgical practice in Philadelphia. He served as an official with several medical museums and wrote his *Personal Memoirs*, which is among the best of Civil War recollections. Dr. Brinton died in 1907 and was buried in Philadelphia.
    9. Wallace, "The Capture of Fort Donelson," 410.
    10. Wallace, *Autobiography*, 385.
    11. Ibid., 392.
    12. Walke, "The Western Flotilla," 433.
    13. *ORA*, Vol. 7, p. 399.
    14. Brian Steel Wills, *A Battle from the Start: The Life of Nathan Bedford Forrest* (New York: HarperCollins, 1992), 60.
    15. Hoppin, 223.
    16. "River Batteries at Fort Donelson," *Confederate Veteran*, November 1896, p. 395.
    17. Tucker, 157.
    18. Walke, *Naval Scenes and Reminiscences*, 77.
    19. Walke, "The Western Flotilla," 434.
    20. Ibid.
    21. Walke, *Naval Scenes and Reminiscences*, 78.
    22. Ibid.
    23. *ORA*, Vol. 7, p. 400.
    24. Ibid., 400–401.
    25. Ibid., 167.
    26. Ibid., 255.
    27. Ibid., 331.
    28. Cooling, 165–165.
    29. Grant, *Memoirs*, 204.
    30. *ORA*, Vol. 7, p. 215.
    31. Ibid., 216.
    32. Ibid., 186.
    33. Ibid.
    34. Logan, 655.
    35. *ORA*, Vol. 7, p. 243.
    36. Ibid., 195.
    37. Wallace, "The Capture of Fort Donelson," 420.
    38. Ibid., 421.
    39. Grant, *Memoirs*, 205.
    40. *ORA*, Vol. 7, p. 618 (first quote); Catton, 168 (second quote).
    41. Catton, 169–170.
    42. Ibid., 170.
    43. Cooling, 195.
    44. William C. Davis, *The Orphan Brigade: The Kentucky Confederates Who Couldn't Go Home* (Garden City: Doubleday, 1980), 68.
    45. Woodworth, 115.
    46. Ibid.

Chapter 13

    1. *ORA*, Vol. 7, p. 295.
    2. Ibid.
    3. Ibid., 335.
    4. Ibid., 334 (first quote), 295 (second quote).
    5. Ibid., 334.
    6. Wills, 64.
    7. *ORA*, Vol. 7, p. 386.
    8. Ibid.
    9. Ibid., 596–597.
    10. J.J. Montgomery, "Daring Deeds of a Confederate Soldier," *Confederate Veteran*, January 1899, pp. 10–11.
    11. Edwin C. Bearss, *Unconditional Surrender: The Fall of Fort Donelson*, reprinted from *Tennessee Historical Quarterly*, March-June 1962, p. 33.
    12. Ibid., 35.
    13. U.S. Grant, letter to General G.W. Cullum, February 16, 1862, reprinted in Grant, *Memoirs*, 982.
    14. Horace Wardner, "Reminiscences of a Surgeon," War Papers, Military Order of the Loyal Legion of the United States, http://suvcw.org/mollus/warpapers/ILv3p173.htm (accessed July 22, 2012).
    15. *ORA*, Vol. 7, pp. 364–365.
    16. Ibid., 365.
    17. Bearss, *Unconditional Surrender*, 43.
    18. *ORA*, Vol. 7, pp. 636 (first quote), 637 (second quote).
    19. Grant, *Memoirs*, 214. In the weeks subsequent to the victory at Fort Donelson, Grant's behavior irritated General Halleck so grievously that Grant was not allowed to lead the advance up the Tennessee River. The assignment was given to General C.F. Smith.

Eventually, Grant was allowed to follow. He assumed command of the army once more after General Smith was injured in what at first seemed a minor mishap: he scraped his shin while getting into a rowboat. The abrasion became infected and Smith was bedridden. Thus it was Grant, not Smith, who was in charge of the Federal forces against General Albert Sidney Johnston at the Battle of Shiloh. General Smith died the last week of April 1862.
20. *ORA*, Vol. 7, p. 629. Grant's victorious men would soon be given the name by which they are remembered to history: The Army of the Tennessee.

Chapter 14

1. McLean, 145–146.
2. Ibid., 146.
3. William T. Sherman, letter to Ellen Sherman, February 17, 1862, reprinted in William T. Sherman, *Sherman's Civil War: Selected Correspondence of William T. Sherman, 1860–1865*, ed. Brooks D. Simpson and Jean V. Berlin (Chapel Hill: University of North Carolina Press, 1999), 191.
4. Ibid.
5. *ORN*, Vol. 22, p. 626.
6. Ibid. General Halleck received Polk's note when Foote returned to Cairo, and he did grant the Southern ladies the privilege of visiting their husbands while they were in custody.
7. Ibid.
8. *ORA*, Vol. 7, p. 898.
9. Edwin H. Rennolds, *History of the Henry County Commands* (Jacksonville: Sun, 1904), 28–29.
10. *ORA*, Vol. 7, p. 437 (first quote); Parks, 215 (second quote).
11. *ORN*, Vol. 22, pp. 650–651.
12. Ibid., 651.
13. Ibid., 653–654.
14. *ORA*, Vol. 10, Part II, 311.
15. *ORA*, Vol. 52, Part II, 288.
16. William T. Sherman, letter to Ellen Sherman, March 6, 1862, reprinted in *Sherman's Civil War*, Simpson and Berlin, eds., 195.
17. *ORA*, Vol. 7, p. 682.
18. Robert D. Whitesell, "Military and Naval Activity Between Cairo and Columbus," *Register of the Kentucky Historical Society* (April 1963), 144.
19. Steven L.Wright, ed., *Kentucky Soldiers and Their Regiments in the Civil War, 1862*, vol. 2 (Utica, KY: McDowell, 2009), 34.
20. *ORA*, Vol. 10, Part II, 72.
21. Ibid., 80–81.
22. Jay Carlton Mullen, "The Turning of Columbus," *Register of the Kentucky Historical Society* (July 1966), 218.

Chapter 15

1. Twain, 223.
2. *ORA*, Vol. 8, pp. 800–801.
3. Rennolds, 180–181.
4. Manning F. Force, "John Pope, Major General, U.S.A.," in *Sketches of War History, 1861–1865: Papers Prepared for the Ohio Commandery of the Military Order of the Loyal Legion of the United States*, vol. 4, ed. W.H. Chamberlain (Cincinnati: Robert Clarke, 1896), 355.
5. John Pope, *The Military Memoirs of General John Pope*, ed. Peter Cozzens and Robert I. Girardi (Chapel Hill: University of North Carolina Press, 1998), 47–48.
6. Ibid., 49.
7. *ORA*, Vol. 8, p. 81.
8. Ibid., 113.
9. Ibid., 114.
10. Ibid., 83.
11. Rennolds, 29.
12. *ORA*, Vol. 8, p. 165.
13. Ibid., 162.
14. *ORN*, Vol. 22, p. 660.
15. Larry J. Daniel and Lynn N. Bock, *Island No. 10: Struggle for the Mississippi Valley* (Tuscaloosa: University of Alabama Press, 1996), 68.
16. Ibid., 71.
17. *ORA*, Vol. 8, p. 588 (first and second quotes); Tucker, 175.
18. *ORN*, Vol. 22, p. 661.
19. Andrew H. Foote, telegram to Henry A. Wise, March 8, 1862, Lincoln Papers.
20. Tucker, 176 (first quote); Hoppin, 265 (second quote).
21. Tucker, 177 (first quote); Andrew H. Foote, telegram to Abraham Lincoln, March 13, 1862, Lincoln Papers (second quote).
22. Hoppin, 262.
23. "Operations in the West," *New York Times*, March 28, 1862.
24. Ibid. (first quote); Walke, "Western Flotilla," 439 (second quote).
25. "Operations in the West," *New York Times*, March 28, 1862.

26. *ORA*, Vol. 8, pp. 152–153.
27. Ibid., 153.
28. Ibid.
29. Eads, 345.
30. Ibid.
31. Wills, 73–74.
32. John M. Palmer, *Personal Recollections of John M. Palmer: The Story of an Earnest Life* (Cincinnati: Robert Clarke, 1901), 97.
33. *ORA*, Vol. 8, p. 620.
34. Palmer, 97.
35. *ORA*, Vol. 8, p. 86 (first quote); Tucker, 180 (second quote).
36. Ibid.
37. J.W. Bissell, "Sawing Out the Channel Above Island Number Ten," in *Battles and Leaders of the Civil War: The Opening Battles*, ed. Robert Underwood Johnson and Clarence Clough Buel (Edison, NJ: Castle Books, 1995), 460.
38. Ibid.
39. Spence, 374 (first quote); Hubbard, 19 (second quote).
40. Davis, 87.
41. Hoppin, 275.
42. *ORA*, Vol. 8, p. 657. Pope constantly referred to his "boats," while others insist that there was only one boat.
43. Ibid., 117.
44. Ibid.
45. Ibid., 118.
46. "The Clearing Out of Union City," *New York Times*, March 31, 1862.
47. *ORA*, Vol. 8, p. 118.
48. Ibid., 132.
49. Ibid., 160.
50. Ibid., 157.
51. Ibid., 161.
52. Hoppin, 273.
53. Walke, "The Western Flotilla," 442.
54. Ibid., 443.
55. Ibid.
56. Ibid., 444.
57. Ibid., 445.
58. Walke, *Naval Scenes and Reminiscences*, 133.
59. Pope, 55 (first quote); *ORA*, Vol. 8, p. 660 (second and third quotes).
60. *ORA*, Vol. 8, p. 88.
61. Walke, *Naval Scenes and Reminiscences*, 144 (first quote), 145 (second quote).
62. *ORN*, Vol. 22, p. 714.
63. Ibid., 715.
64. *ORA*, Vol. 8, p. 669.
65. Andrew H. Foote, telegram to Gideon Welles, April 7, 1862, Lincoln Papers.
66. Davis, 90–91.
67. *ORA*, Vol. 8, p. 183.
68. Ibid., 110.
69. *ORN*, Vol. 22, p. 724.
70. *ORA*, p. 675. In his official report, dated May 2, Pope played fast and loose with the sequence of events to make it appear that the surrender of Island Number Ten to Foote came after Paine landed and was pursuing the Rebels to Tiptonville. He wrote, "At 8 or 9 o'clock that night (the 7th) the small force abandoned on the island ... sent a message to Commodore Foote, surrendering to him" (*ORA*, Vol. 8, p. 89). By moving the event back by about sixteen hours, Pope was making a grab at the credit for forcing the enemy's capitulation.
71. Ibid., 681–682. The Island Number Ten operation was Foote's last. He did begin the joint navy-army effort against Fort Pillow, but he was not well. Secretary Welles granted him a sick leave, beginning on May 9. Foote later explained that "the inflammation arising from my wound, long neglected, had produced a fever and great prostration of physical and nervous energy to such a degree as led the surgeons to decide that my life was in imminent danger, unless I left the command when, by authority of the Navy Department, I transferred the command to Captain Charles H. Davis and retired from further active service in the Western Flotilla" (*ORN*, Vol. 22, 136). He made his way to New Haven and then to Washington, D.C. He was promoted to admiral on July 30 (backdated to July 16), and on August 7 reported for duty as head of the Bureau of Equipment and Recruiting. Anxious for a sea command, Foote was assigned on June 4, 1863, to the South Atlantic Blockading Squadron. Two weeks later he developed Bright's disease. On June 25, Welles relieved Foote of the assignment he had never really assumed, and the next night, June 26, Admiral Andrew H. Foote died.
72. Davis, 91.

Chapter 16

1. L.P. Roe, letter to mother, April 27, 1862, collection of the author.
2. Ibid.
3. Ibid.
4. *ORA*, Vol. 7, p. 416.
5. *ORA*, Vol. 10, Part I, 18.

6. Cooling, *Fort Donelson's Legacy*, 54.
7. Jennings and Jennings, 36.
8. "The War in the Southwest," *New York Times*, November 21, 1862.
9. Hoskins, 12–13.
10. *ORA*, Vol. 17, Part II, 424.
11. "Domestic Intelligence: How General Grant's Order Did Work Before It Was Revoked," *The Jewish Record*, January 13, 1863, http://www.jewish-history.com/civilwar/go11.htm (accessed October 26, 2012).
12. Jonathan D. Sarna, *When General Grant Expelled the Jews* (New York: Schocken, 2012), 21.
13. Ibid., 21 (first quote), 22 (second quote).
14. *ORA*, Vol. 17, Part II, 530.
15. Elihua B. Washburne, letter to Abraham Lincoln, January 6, 1863, Lincoln Papers.
16. Resolution of the Board of Delegates, American Israelites, January 8, 1863, Lincoln Papers.
17. "Gen. Grant and the Jews," *New York Times*, January 18, 1863.
18. Ibid.
19. *ORA*, Vol. 24, Part I, 9. In later years, Grant's actions showed that he felt some shame over his banishment of the Jews. He spoke of it only with the greatest reluctance, even to family members, and he did not refer to it at all in his *Memoirs*. It was used against him as a campaign issue in the 1868 presidential election. He won the presidency, nevertheless, and began with his first term to make amends. He appointed a number of Jews to important offices in the Western territories, the District of Columbia, and in the diplomatic corps. There were political benefits to be gained—he had much stronger Jewish support in his 1872 re-election bid—but his efforts on behalf of the Jews seem to have been motivated by a genuine sense of remorse for the appalling Orders No. 11.
20. "Tobacco versus Treason," *New York Times*, May 4, 1862.
21. Jennings and Jennings, 35–36.
22. John McElroth Meloan, "Murray and Calloway County Closely Linked with Kentucky History, Tradition," *History of Calloway County, Kentucky* (Murray: Murray Ledger and Times, 1931), 9.
23. *ORA*, Series III, Vol. 5, p. 661. Kentucky had more black soldiers than any other state except Louisiana.
24. Marion Brunson Lucas, *A History of Blacks in Kentucky: From Slavery to Segregation, 1760–1891* (Lexington: University Press of Kentucky, 2003), 160.
25. J.V. Greif, "Forrest's Raid on Paducah," *Confederate Veteran*, May 1897, p. 212.
26. John C. Waters, "A Civil War General," *Murray Ledger and Times*, no date, John C. Waters Papers, MS 88–01, Box 7, Forrest C. Pogue Special Collections Library, Murray State University, Murray, Kentucky.
27. Greif, 212.
28. "An Old Veteran, Confederate," *Confederate Veteran*, January 1897, 4.
29. *ORA*, Vol. 32, Part I, 547.
30. *Paducah Sun*, "More About General Forrest's Raid," March 28, 1902 (first quote); Greif, 212 (second quote).
31. William R. St. Clair, "Feasting and Fighting," *Confederate Veteran*, January 1894, p. 14.
32. *ORN*, Vol. 26, p. 198 (first quote); *ORA*, Vol. 32, Part I, 548 (second quote).
33. Mercer Otey, "Story of Our Great War," *Confederate Veteran*, March 1901, p. 110.
34. *ORA*, Vol. 32, Part I, 549–550.
35. Ibid., 550.
36. Henry George, *History of the 3rd, 7th, 8th, and 12th Kentucky, CSA* (Lyndon, KY: Mull-Wathen, 1970), 79.
37. Ibid.
38. Ibid., 80.
39. Hawley V. Needham, *Journal of Private Hawley V. Needham, 134th Illinois Volunteer Infantry Regt., Company G*, www.jacksonpurchasehistory.org/jackson-purchase-during-the-civil-war (accessed April 4, 2012).
40. Grant Papers, Vol. 10: January 1–May 31, 1864, p. 24.
41. *ORA*, Vol. 39, Part II, 171.
42. Hoskins, 207.
43. Lon Carter Barton, "The 'Reign of Terror' in Graves County, 1864," in *Kentucky's Civil War, 1861–1865*, ed. Jerlene Rose (Clay City: Back Home in Kentucky, 2005), 141 (first quote); E.L. Robertson, *Paducah, 1830–1980: A Sesquicentennial History* (Paducah: self-published, 1980), 64 (second quote).
44. Barton, "Reign of Terror," 142.
45. Needham, 14.
46. *ORA*, Vol. 39, Part II, 261. It is not surprising that as late as 1900 Confederate critics were still discussing Paine's conduct. One wrote, "Nero in his prime did not exceed him in heartless cruelty" ("United Daughters of the Confederacy," *Confederate Veteran*, December 1900, p. 521).

47. "The Banishment of Disloyal Citizens," *New York Times*, August 10, 1864.
48. Ibid.
49. Barton, "Reign of Terror," 142 (first quote); *ORA*, Vol. 39, Part II, 342 (second quote).
50. Hoskin, 213.
51. *Confederate Veteran*, "United Daughters of the Confederacy," December 1900, p. 523.
52. *ORN*, Vol. 23, p. 315.
53. "Capture of the Mazeppa," *Confederate Veteran*, December 1905, p. 567 (first quote); E. B. Ross, untitled item, *Confederate Veteran*, August 1895, p. 250 (second quote).
54. "The War in Kentucky," *New York Times*, November 1, 1864.
55. *Murray Sunday Democrat*, "History of Calloway County Related in Death of Pioneer Hico Lady in Athens, Tex., by her Son," Civil War Folder, John C. Waters, Papers, MS 88–01, Box 7, Forrest C. Pogue Special Collections Library, Murray State University, Murray, Kentucky.

Bibliography

Abraham Lincoln Papers at the Library of Congress. http://memory.loc.gov/ammem/alhtml/malcap.html (accessed September 19, 2012).

Adair, John M. *Historical Sketch of the Forty-Fifth Illinois Regiment.* Lanark, IL: Carroll County Gazette, 1869.

Allen, Hall. *Center of Conflict: A Factual Story of the War Between the States in Western Kentucky and Tennessee.* Paducah: Paducah Sun-Democrat, 1961.

Ambrose, D. Leib. *History of the Seventh Regiment Illinois Volunteer Infantry.* Springfield: Illinois Journal, 1868.

Ambrose, Stephen E. *Halleck: Lincoln's Chief of Staff.* Baton Rouge: Louisiana State University Press, 1990.

Anderson, Bern. *By Sea and By River: The Naval History of the Civil War.* Cambridge: Da Capo, 1962.

Ash, Stephen V. "Civil War Exodus: The Jews and Grant's General Orders No. 11." *The Historian*, August 1982.

Avery, Phineas Orlando. *History of the Fourth Illinois Cavalry Regiment.* Humboldt, NE: Enterprise, 1903.

Axton, W.F. *Tobacco and Kentucky.* Lexington: University Press of Kentucky, 1975.

Baird, Nancy D. "There Is No Sunday in the Army: Civil War Letters of Lunsford P. Yandell, 1861–1862." *Filson Club History Quarterly*, July 1979.

"The Banishment of Disloyal Citizens." *New York Times*, August 10, 1864.

Banta, R.E. *The Ohio.* New York: Rinehart, 1949.

Barton, Lon Carter. "The Civil War in the Purchase." *Journal of the Jackson Purchase Historical Society*, June 1989. www.jacksonpurchasehistory.org/jackson-purchase-during-the-civil-war (accessed March 9, 2012).

———. "A History of Graves County, Kentucky, 1818–1865." Master's thesis, University of Kentucky, 1960.

———. "The 'Reign of Terror' in Graves County, 1864." In *Kentucky's Civil War, 1861–1865.* Edited by Jerlene Rose. Clay City: Back Home in Kentucky, 2005.

"The Battle of Belmont." *New York Times*, November 19, 1861.

Bearman, Alan. "'The South Carolina of Kentucky': How Evangelical Religion Influenced the Jackson Purchase Region of Kentucky to Support Secession." LD 3571 M5 2000 B43. Forrest C. Pogue Special Collections Library, Murray State University, Murray, Kentucky.

Bearss, Edwin C. *The Fall of Fort Henry.* Dover: Fort Donelson National Military Park, 1999.

———. "Unconditional Surrender: The Fall of Fort Donelson." *Tennessee Historical Quarterly*, March-June 1962.

Bennett, Michael J. "Dissenters from the American Mood: Why Men Became Yankee Sailors During the Civil War." *North and South*, March 2005.

———. *Union Jacks: Yankee Sailors in the Civil War.* Chapel Hill: University of North Carolina Press, 2004.

Bissell, J.W. "Sawing Out the Channel Above Island Number Ten." In *Battles and Leaders of the Civil War: The Opening Battles.* Edited by Robert Underwood Johnson and Clarence Clough Buel. Edison, NJ: Castle, 1995.

Black, Robert C. *The Railroads of the Confederacy*. Chapel Hill: University of North Carolina Press, 1952.

Bogart, Charles H. "Kentucky's Railroad Network, 1861." In *Kentucky's Civil War, 1861–1865*. Edited by Jerlene Rose. Clay City: Back Home in Kentucky, 2005.

Brinton, John H. *Personal Memoirs of John H. Brinton, Civil War Surgeon, 1861–1865*. Carbondale: Southern Illinois University Press, 1996.

Bush, Bryan. *Lloyd Tilghman: Confederate General in the Western Theatre*. Morely, MO: Acclaim, 2006.

Button, Charles W. "Early Engagements with Forrest." *Confederate Veteran*, September 1897.

Calbert, Jack. "The Jackson Purchase and the End of the Neutrality Policy in Kentucky." *Filson Club History Quarterly*, July 1964.

Caldwell, Robert W. "The Civil War in Murray, Calloway County, Kentucky." *Journal of the Jackson Purchase Historical Society*, June 1989. www.jacksonpurchasehistory.org/jackson-purchase-during-the-civil-war (accessed March 10, 2012).

Callender, Eliot. "What a Boy Saw on the Mississippi." In *Military Essays and Recollections: Papers Read Before the Commandery of the State of Illinois, Order of the Loyal Legion of the United States*. Vol. 1. Chicago: A.C. McClurg, 1891.

"The Camp at Cairo." *New York Times*, May 8, 1861.

"Capture of the *Mazeppa*." *Confederate Veteran*, December 1905.

"The Capture of Fort Henry." *New York Times*, February 12, 1862.

"Career of Gen. Gideon J. Pillow." *Confederate Veteran*, November 1893.

Carstens, Kenneth C. "Fort Jefferson, 1780–1781: A Summary of Its History." In *Selected Papers from the 1991 and 1992 George Rogers Clark Trans-Appalachian Frontier History Conferences*. http://www.nps.gov/history/historyonline_books/gero/papers/1991–1992/sec3.htm (accessed September 12, 2012).

Cartmell, J.M. "Witness to the Battle of Belmont." *Confederate Veteran*, April 1908.

Catton, Bruce. *Grant Moves South*. Boston: Little, Brown, 1960.

Chaffin, Tom. *Pathfinder: John Charles Frémont and the Course of American Empire*. New York: Hill and Wang, 2002.

Chetlain, Augustus L. "Recollections of General U.S. Grant." In *Military Essays and Recollections: Papers Read Before the Commandery of the State of Illinois, Order of the Loyal Legion of the United States*. Vol. 1. Chicago: A.C. McClurg, 1891.

_____. *Recollections of Seventy Years*. Galena, IL: Gazette, 1899.

Clark, George Rogers. *George Rogers Clark Papers, 1771–1781*. Edited by James Alton James. Springfield: Illinois Historical Society, 1912.

Clark, Thomas D. "The Jackson Purchase: A Dramatic Chapter in Southern Indian Policies and Relations." *Filson Club History Quarterly*, July 1976.

"The Clearing Out of Union City." *New York Times*, 3 March 1862.

"Concerning Battle of Belmont." *Confederate Veteran*, January 1901.

"Confederate Soldiers from Southern Illinois." *Confederate Veteran*, March 1901.

Connelley, William McElroy, and E.M. Coulter. *History of Kentucky*. Vol. 2. Chicago: American Historical Society, 1922.

Cooling, Benjamin Franklin. *Fort Donelson's Legacy: War and Society in Kentucky and Tennessee, 1862–1863*. Knoxville: University of Tennessee Press, 1997.

_____. *Forts Henry and Donelson: The Key to the Confederate Heartland*. Knoxville: University of Tennessee Press, 1989.

Coombe, Jack D. *Thunder Along the Mississippi: The River Battles that Split the Confederacy*. Edison, NJ: Castle, 2005.

Cope, Alexis. *The Fifteenth Ohio Volunteers and Its Campaigns*. Columbus: self-published, 1916.

Craig, Berry F. "Henry Cornelius Burnett: Champion of Southern Rights." *Register of the Kentucky Historical Society*, Autumn 1979.

———. "Jackson Purchase Confederate Troops in the Civil War." *Journal of the Jackson Purchase Historical Society*, June 1974. www.jacksonpurchasehistory.org/jackson-purchase-during-the-civil-war (accessed March 10, 2012).

———. "The Jackson Purchase Considers Secession: The 1861 Mayfield Convention." *Register of the Kentucky Historical Society*, Autumn 2001.

———. "Kentucky's Rebel Press: The Jackson Purchase Newspapers in 1861." *Register of the Kentucky Historical Society*, January 1977.

———. "Northern Conquerors and Southern Deliverers: The Civil War Comes to the Jackson Purchase." *Register of the Kentucky Historical Society*, January 1975.

Crutcher, T.E. "Witness to the Capture of the *Mazeppa*." *Confederate Veteran*, February 1906.

Daniel, Larry J., and Lynn N. Bock. *Island No. 10: Struggle for the Mississippi Valley*. Tuscaloosa: University of Alabama Press, 1996.

Davidson, Donald. *The Tennessee: Civil War to TVA*. New York: Rinehart, 1948.

Davis, Charles W. "New Madrid and Island No. 10." In *Military Essays and Recollections: Papers Read Before the Commandery of the State of Illinois, Order of the Loyal Legion of the United States, Volume I*. Chicago: A.C. McClurg, 1891.

Davis, D. Trabue. *Story of Mayfield Through a Century, 1823–1923*. Paducah: Billings, 1923.

Davis, William C. *The Orphan Brigade: The Kentucky Confederates Who Couldn't Go Home*. Garden City: Doubleday, 1980.

Dawes, E.C. "The Army of the Tennessee." In *Sketches of War History, 1861–1865: Papers Prepared for the Ohio Commandery of the Military Order of the Loyal Legion of the United States*. Vol. 4. Edited by W.H. Chamberlain. Cincinnati: Robert Clarke, 1896.

Day, John B. "Gen. Lew Wallace in Paducah." *Paducah Sun*, February 23, 1905.

———. "Gen. Lew Wallace in Paducah." Letter to *Paducah Sun*, February 23, 1905.

Denney, Robert E. *Civil War Medicine: Care and Comfort of the Wounded*. New York: Sterling, 1994.

"Domestic Intelligence: How General Grant's Order Did Work Before It Was Revoked." *The Jewish Record*, January 13, 1863. http://www.jewish-history.com/civilwar/go11.htm (accessed October 26, 2012).

Driggs, George W. *Opening the Mississippi; or, Two Years' Campaigning in the Southwest*. Madison: Wm. J. Park, 1864.

Durham, Thomas Wise. *Three Years with Wallace's Zouaves: The Civil War Memoirs of Thomas Wise Durham*. Edited by Jeffrey L. Patrick. Macon: Mercer University Press, 2003.

Dyer, Frederick H. *A Compendium of the War of the Rebellion*. Dayton, OH: Broadfoot, 1994.

Eads, James B. "Recollections of Foote and the Gun-Boats." In *Battles and Leaders of the Civil War: The Opening Battles*. Edited by Robert Underwood Johnson and Clarence Clough Buel. Edison, NJ: Castle, 1995.

Eckerman, Nancy Pippen. *Indiana in the Civil War: Doctors, Hospitals, and Medical Care*. Charleston: Arcadia Press, 2001.

Eisterhold, John A. "Fort Heiman: Forgotten Fortress." *West Tennessee Historical Society Papers* 28 (1974). www.jacksonpurchasehistory.org/jackson-purchase-during-the-civil-war (accessed March 9, 2012).

Esposito, Vincent J., Jr., ed. *The West Point Atlas of American Wars*. New York: Praeger, 1978.

"Fight on the Tennessee River, A." *New York Times*, November 6, 1861.

Fiske, John. *The Mississippi Valley in the Civil War*. Cambridge: Riverside, 1902.

Fletcher, Samuel H. *The History of Company A, Second Illinois Cavalry*. Chicago: Unknown Publisher, 1912.

Foote, Shelby. *The Civil War: A Narrative; Fort Sumter to Perryville*. New York: Vintage, 1986.

Force, Manning F. "John Pope, Major General, U.S.A." In *Sketches of War History, 1861–1865: Papers Prepared for the Ohio*

Commandery of the Military Order of the Loyal Legion of the United States. Vol. 4. Edited by W.H. Chamberlain. Cincinnati: Robert Clarke, 1896.
Fowler, William M., Jr. *Under Two Flags: The American Navy in the Civil War.* Annapolis: Naval Institute Press, 2001.
Franklin, John Hope. *From Slavery to Freedom: A History of Negro Americans.* New York: Alfred A. Knopf, 1974.
Fraser, Kathryn M. "Fort Jefferson: George Rogers Clark's Fort at the Mouth of the Ohio River, 1780–1781." *Register of the Kentucky Historical Society*, Winter 1983.
Frémont, John C. "In Command in Missouri." In *Battles and Leaders of the Civil War: The Opening Battles.* Edited by Robert Underwood Johnson and Clarence Clough Buel. Edison, NJ: Castle, 1995.
"From Kentucky." *New York Times*, May 26, 1862.
Fuller, Mrs. George T. *A History of Camp Beauregard.* Mayfield: Tilghman-Beauregard Camp No. 16, SCV, 1988.
"Gen. Grant and the Jews." *New York Times*, January 18, 1863.
George, Henry. *History of the 3,rd 7,th 8,th and 12th Kentucky, CSA.* Lyndon, KY: Mull-Wathen, 1970.
Gleeson, Ed. *Illinois Rebels: A Civil War Unit History of G Company 15th Tennessee Regiment Volunteer Infantry.* Cincinnati: Emmis, 1996.
Goodheart, Adam. *1861: The Civil War Awakening.* New York: Alfred A. Knopf, 2011.
Grant, U.S. *The Papers of U.S. Grant.* Vol. 4 (January 8–March 31, 1862). Mississippi State University. U.S. Grant Digital Collection. http://digital.library.msstate.edu/collections/document.ph?CISOROOT=%2FUSG_volume&CISOPTR=16321&REC=17&CISOBOX (a)ccessed March 5, 2012.
_____. *The Papers of U.S. Grant.* Vol. 10 (January 1–May 31, 1864). Mississippi State University. U.S. Grant Digital Collection. http://digital.library.msstate.edu/collections/document.ph?CISOROOT=%2FUSG_volume&CISOPTR=16321&REC=17&CISOBOX (accessed March 5, 2012).
_____. *The Papers of U.S. Grant.* Vol. 3 (October 1, 1861–January 7, 1862). Mississippi State University. U.S. Grant Digital Collection. http://digital.library.msstate.edu/collections/document.ph?CISOROOT=%2FUSG_volume&CISOPTR=16321&REC=17&CISOBOX (accessed March 5, 2012).
_____. *The Papers of U.S. Grant.* Vol. 2 (April-September 1861). Mississippi State University. U.S. Grant Digital Collection. http://digital.library.msstate.edu/collections/document.ph?CISOROOT=%2FUSG_volume&CISOPTR=16321&REC=17&CISOBOX (accessed March 5, 2012).
_____. *Personal Memoirs of U.S. Grant.* New York: Library of America, 1990.
"Great Fire in Paducah, Ky." *New York Times*, April 5, 1852.
Greif, J.V. "Forrest's Raid on Paducah." *Confederate Veteran*, May 1897.
Grierson, Benjamin Henry, and Bruce J. Dinges. *A Just and Righteous Cause: Benjamin H. Grierson's Civil War Memoir.* Carbondale: Southern Illinois University Press, 2008.
Griffin, Pat. "The Famous Tenth Tennessee." *Confederate Veteran*, December 1905.
Groom, Winston. "Grant's 'Obnoxious Order.'" *America's Civil War*, November 2012.
"Guerrilla Raid in Northwestern Kentucky." *New York Times*, November 15, 1863.
Hancock, Richard R. *Hancock's Diary; or, a History of the Second Tennessee Confederate Cavalry.* Nashville: Brandon, 1887.
Harrison, Lowell H., and James C. Klotter. *A New History of Kentucky.* Lexington: University Press of Kentucky, 1997.
Harrison, Lowell H. "Beriah Magoffin, 1815–1885." In *Kentucky's Civil War, 1861–1865.* Edited by Jerlene Rose. Clay City: Back Home in Kentucky, 2005.
_____. *The Civil War in Kentucky.* Lexington: University Press of Kentucky, 1975.
Havighurst, Walter. *Voices on the River: The Story of the Mississippi Waterways.* New York: McMillan, 1967.

Hawkins, Susan. "Forts Henry, Heiman, and Donelson: The African-American Experience." Master's thesis, Murray State University, no date. www.nps.gov/history/history/online_books/fodo/hawkins.pdf (accessed March 4, 2012).

Hico. "Letter from Western Kentucky." *New York Times*, August 25, 1855.

Hill, Sarah Jane Full. *Mrs. Hill's Journal: Civil War Reminiscences*. Edited by Mark M. Krug. Chicago: R. Donnelley & Sons, 1980.

"History of Calloway County Related in Death of Pioneer Hico Lady in Athens, Tex., by Son." *Murray Sunday Democrat*, June 26, 1955.

Hoppin, J.M. *Life of Andrew Hull Foote, Rear-Admiral, United States Navy*. New York: Harper, 1874.

Hoskins, Patricia Ann. "'The Old First Is with the South': The Civil War, Reconstruction, and Memory in the Jackson Purchase Region of Kentucky." PhD diss., Auburn University, 2008. www.jacksonpurchasehistory.org/jackson-purchase-during-the-civil-war (accessed March 9, 2012).

Hubbard, John Milton. *Notes of a Private*. Memphis: E.H. Clarke & Brother, 1909.

Hughes, Nathaniel Cheairs, Jr. *The Battle of Belmont: Grant Strikes South*. Chapel Hill: University of North Carolina Press, 1991.

Hunt, John T. "Civil War Memoirs of Dr. John T. Hunt." http://civilwar.ilgenweb.net/scrapbk/huntdiary (accessed June 11, 2012).

"Important From Kentucky; Paducah Captured by the Rebel Gen. Forrest." *New York Times*, March 28, 1864.

James, James Alton. *The Life of George Rogers Clark*. New York: Greenwood, 1969.

Jennings, Dorothy, and Kerby Jennings. *The Story of Calloway County, 1822–1976*. Self-published, 1980.

Jewell, Ouida. *Backward Glance: A History of Fulton County and Surrounding Area*. Vol. 1. Fulton: Fulton, 1973.

Johnson, Adam R. "Fort Donelson." In *The Partisan Rangers of the Confederate States Army*. Edited by William J. Davis. Louisville: Geo. G. Fetter, 1904.

_____. "In Federal Camps." In *The Partisan Rangers of the Confederate States Army*. Edited by William J. Davis. Louisville: Geo. G. Fetter, 1904.

Joiner, Gary D. *Mr. Lincoln's Brown Water Navy: The Mississippi Squadron*. Lanham, MD: Rowman & Littlefield, 2007.

Kelly, R.M. "Holding Kentucky for the Union." In *Battles and Leaders of the Civil War: The Opening Battles*. Edited by Robert Underwood Johnson and Clarence Clough Buel. Edison, NJ: Castle, 1995.

Kentucky Department of Parks. "Columbus-Belmont: 'The Gibraltar of the West.'" In *Kentucky's Civil War, 1861–1865*. Edited by Jerlene Rose. Clay City: Back Home in Kentucky, 2005.

Kimbell, Charles B. *History of Battery "A," First Illinois Light Artillery Volunteers*. Chicago: Cushing, 1899.

Kleber, John E., ed. *The Kentucky Encyclopedia*. Lexington: University Press of Kentucky, 1992.

Klotter, James C. "The Echoes of the Civil War in Kentucky." In *Kentucky's Civil War, 1861–1865*. Edited by Jerlene Rose. Clay City: Back Home in Kentucky, 2005.

Kreiser, Christine M. "Grant's Atonement." *America's Civil War*, November 2012.

"Lathan-Tyler Controversy." *Paducah Daily Register*, July 26, 1907.

Lavonis, Sister Margaret Mary. "Sisters' Nursing Ministry Begins with Civil War." http://www.cscsisters.org/aboutus/media/features/Pages/CivilWar.aspx (accessed June 7, 2012).

Logan, John A. *The Volunteer Soldier of America*. Chicago: R.S. Peale, 1887.

Long, E.B. "The Paducah Affair: Bloodless Action that Altered the Civil War in the Mississippi Valley." *Register of the Kentucky Historical Society*, October 1972.

Longacre, Edward G. *General John Buford: A Military Biography*. Cambridge: Da Capo, 2003.

Lucas, Marion Brunson. *A History of Blacks in Kentucky: From Slavery to Segregation, 1760–1891*. Lexington: University Press of Kentucky, 2003.

Mackey, Thomas C. "Kentucky and Secession." In *Sister States, Enemy States: The Civil War in Kentucky and Tennessee*. Edited by Kent T. Dollar, Larry Howard Whiteaker, and W. Calvin Dickinson. Lexington: University Press of Kentucky, 2009.

Magdeburg, F.H. "Capture of Fort Donelson." In *War Papers Read Before the Commandery of the State of Wisconsin, Military Order of the Loyal Legion of the United States*. Vol. 3. Milwaukee: Burdick and Allen, 1903.

Maness, Lonnie E. "Columbus: Gibraltar of the West." *Journal of the Jackson Purchase Historical Society*, June 1982. www.jacksonpurchasehistory.org/jackson-purchase-during-the-civil-war (accessed April 4, 2012).

Marshall, Anne E. *Creating a Confederate Kentucky: The Lost Cause and Civil War Memory in a Border State*. Chapel Hill: University of North Carolina Press, 2010.

Matthews, Lisa Gaines. "Reluctant Unionists: Kentucky During the Civil War." In *Kentucky's Civil War, 1861–1865*. Edited by Jerlene Rose. Clay City: Back Home in Kentucky, 2005.

McFeely, William S. *Grant: A Biography*. New York: W.W. Norton, 2002.

McKenney, Tom C. *Jack Hinson's One-Man War*. Gretna: Pelican, 2009.

McLean, John. *One Hundred Years in Illinois, 1818–1918*. Chicago: Paterson, 1919.

Meloan, John McElrath. "Murray and Calloway County Closely Linked with Kentucky History, Tradition." In *History of Calloway County, Kentucky*. Murray: Murray Leger and Times, 1931.

Metcalf, F. "The Illinois Confederate Company." *Confederate Veteran*, May 1908.

Michael, W.H.C. "The Mississippi Flotilla." War Papers, Military Order of the Loyal Legion of the United States. http://suvcw.org/mollus/warpapers/NEv1p21.htm (accessed July 23, 2012).

"Miscellaneous Washington News." *New York Times*, August 30, 1861.

"The Mississippi Expedition." *New York Times*, December 14, 1861.

Montgomery, J.J. "Daring Deeds of a Confederate Soldier." *Confederate Veteran*, January 1899.

Moore, Frank, ed. *The Rebellion Record: A Diary of American Events, with Documents, Narratives, Illustrative Incidents, Poetry, Etc*. New York: G.P. Putnam, 1862–1868.

"More About General Forrest's Raid." *Paducah Sun*, March 28, 1902

Morrison, Marion. *A History of the Ninth Regiment, Illinois Volunteer Infantry*. Monmouth: J.S. Clark, 1864.

Mullen, Jay Carlton. "The Turning of Columbus." *Register of the Kentucky Historical Society*, July 1966.

Needham, Hawley V. *Journal of Private Hawley V. Needham, 134th Illinois Volunteer Infantry Regt., Company G*. www.jacksonpurchasehistory.org/jackson-purchase-during-the-civil-war (accessed April 4, 2012).

Neuman, Fred G. *The Story of Paducah*. N.P.: Young, 1927.

"Old Veteran, Confederate, An." *Confederate Veteran*, January 1897.

"Operations in Tennessee." *New York Times*, February 13, 1862.

"Operations in the West." *New York Times*, March 28, 1862.

"Operations on the Mississippi." *New York Times*, April 1, 1862.

"Operations up the Tennessee." *New York Times*, April 22, 1862.

Otey, Mercer. "Story of Our Great War." *Confederate Veteran*, June 1899.

"Outrages in Southern Kentucky." *New York Times*, August 27, 1861.

Palmer, John M. *Personal Recollections of John M. Palmer: The Story of an Earnest Life*. Cincinnati: Robert Clarke, 1901.

Parks, Joseph H. *General Leonidas Polk, C.S.A.: The Fighting Bishop*. Baton Rouge: Louisiana State University Press, 1962.

Perret, Geoffrey. *Lincoln's War: The Untold Story of America's Greatest President at Commander in Chief*. New York: Random House, 2004.

Pickett, William D. "The Bursting of the 'Lady Polk.'" *Confederate Veteran*, June 1904.

Piston, William Garrett, and Thomas P. Sweeney. "Missourians and the War on the Western Rivers." *North and South*, August 2009.

Polk, William M. "General Polk and the Battle of Belmont." In *Battles and Leaders of the Civil War: The Opening Battles*. Edited by Robert Underwood Johnson and Clarence Clough Buel. Edison, NJ: Castle, 1995.

Pope, John. *The Military Memoirs of General John Pope*. Edited by Peter Cozzens and Robert I. Girardi. Chapel Hill: University of North Carolina Press, 1998.

Quigley, Quintus Quincy. *The Life and Times of Quintus Quincy Quigley, 1828–1910: His Personal Journal, 1859–1908*. Edited by George Quigley Langstaff, Jr. No place: self-published, 1999.

Rabb, James W. *Confederate General Lloyd Tilghman: A Biography*. Jefferson, NC: McFarland, 2006.

Ramage, James A. "Grant's Occupation of Paducah." In *Kentucky's Civil War, 1861–1865*. Edited by Jerlene Rose. Clay City: Back Home in Kentucky, 2005.

"Reminiscences: Mother of the Confederacy." *Confederate Veteran*, April 1894.

Rennick, Robert M. *Kentucky Place Names*. Lexington: University Press of Kentucky, 1987.

Rennolds, Edwin H. *History of the Henry County Commands*. Jacksonville: Sun, 1904.

Rerick, John H. *The Forty-Fourth Indiana Volunteer Infantry*. Lagrange, IN: self-published, 1880.

"River Batteries at Fort Donelson." *Confederate Veteran*, November 1896.

Robertson, E.L. *Paducah, 1830–1980: A Sesquicentennial History*. Paducah: self-published, 1980.

Roe, L.P. Letter to mother. April 27, 1862. Collection of the author.

Ross, E.B. Untitled item. *Confederate Veteran*, August 1895.

Russell, William Howard. *My Diary North and South*. Boston: T.O.H.P. Burnham, 1863.

St. Clair, William R. "Feasting and Fighting." *Confederate Veteran*, January 1894.

Sanders, Charles W., Jr. *While in the Hands of the Enemy: Military Prisons of the Civil War*. Baton Rouge: Louisiana University Press, 2005.

Sarna, Jonathan D. *When General Grant Expelled the Jews*. New York: Schocken, 2012.

Schenker, Carl R., Jr. "Grant's Rise from Obscurity." *North and South*, June 2006.

"Secession Plot at Paducah, Ky." *New York Times*, May 11, 1862.

"Secession Spirit (1861) in Illinois." *Confederate Veteran*, January 1901.

Shelton, Phillip M. "Camp Beauregard, Graves County, Kentucky." *Register of the Kentucky Historical Society*, April 1963.

Sherman, William T. *Memoirs of General W.T. Sherman*. New York: Library of America, 1990.

_____. *Sherman's Civil War: Selected Correspondence of William T. Sherman, 1860–1865*. Edited by Brooks D. Simpson and Jean V. Berlin. Chapel Hill: University of North Carolina Press, 1999.

Singletary, Don. "The Battle of Belmont." *Confederate Veteran*, November 1915.

Smith, Henry I. *History of the Seventh Iowa Veteran Volunteer Infantry*. Mason City, IA: E. Hitchcock, 1903.

Smith, John T. *A History of the Thirty-First Regiment of Indiana Volunteer Infantry in the War of the Rebellion*. Cincinnati: Western Methodist, 1900.

Smith, Myron J., Jr. *The Carondelet: A Civil War Ironclad on Western Waters*. Jefferson, NC: McFarland, 2010.

_____. *The Timberclads in the Civil War: The Lexington, Conestoga, and Tyler on the Western Waters*. Jefferson, NC: McFarland, 2008.

Snead, Thomas L. "The First Year of the War in Missouri." In *Battles and Leaders of the Civil War: The Opening Battles*. Edited by Robert Underwood Johnson and Clarence Clough Buel. Edison, NJ: Castle, 1995.

"Some Stories Around Town." *Paducah Sun*, October 2, 1909.

"Southern News Through Louisville." *New York Times*, June 12, 1861.

Spence, Philip B. "Service for the Confederacy." *Confederate Veteran*, August 1900.

Stanley, Henry Morton. *The Autobiography of Sir Henry Morton Stanley.* Boston: Houghton Mifflin, 1909.

Stevenson, B.L. "Kentucky Neutrality in 1861." In *Sketches of War History, 1861–1865: Papers Read Before the Ohio Commandery of the Military Order of the Loyal Legion of the United States.* Vol. 2. Cincinnati: Robert Clarke, 1888.

Stickles, Arndt. *Simon Bolivar Buckner: Borderland Knight.* Chapel Hill: University of North Carolina Press, 2001.

Taylor, Jesse. "The Defense of Fort Henry." In *Battles and Leaders of the Civil War: The Opening Battles.* Edited by Robert Underwood Johnson and Clarence Clough Buel. Edison, NJ: Castle, 1995.

"Telegraph Under the Ohio." *New York Times,* August 18, 1853.

Thompson, Ed. Porter. *History of the Orphan Brigade, 1861–1865.* Dayton, Ohio: Morningside, 1991.

"Tobacco versus Treason." *New York Times,* May 4, 1862.

Tucker, Spencer C. *Andrew Foote: Civil War Admiral on Western Waters.* Annapolis: Naval Institute Press, 2000.

Twain, Mark. *Life on the Mississippi.* New York: Harper, 1917.

Ullrich, Dieter C. "Confederate Operations in the Jackson Purchase: A History of Camp Beauregard, Kentucky." *Filson Club History Quarterly,* October 2002.

"United Daughters of the Confederacy." *Confederate Veteran,* December 1900.

United States Naval War Records Office. *Official Records of the Union and Confederate Navies in the War of the Rebellion.* Series I. 27 Vols. Washington, D.C.: Government Printing Office, 1894–1917.

United States War Department. *The War of the Rebellion: A Compilation of the Official Records of the Union and Confederate Armies.* 129 Volumes. Washington, D.C.: Government Printing Office, 1880–1901.

Walke, Henry. "The Gun-Boats at Belmont and Fort Henry." In *Battles and Leaders of the Civil War: The Opening Battles.* Edited by Robert Underwood Johnson and Clarence Clough Buel. Edison, NJ: Castle, 1995.

_____. *Naval Scenes and Reminiscences of the Civil War.* New York: F.R. Reed, 1877.

_____. "The Western Flotilla at Fort Donelson, Island Number Ten, Fort Pillow, and Memphis." In *Battles and Leaders of the Civil War: The Opening Battles.* Edited by Robert Underwood Johnson and Clarence Clough Buel. Edison, NJ: Castle, 1995.

Wallace, Lew. *An Autobiography.* Vol. 1. New York: Harper, 1906.

_____. "The Capture of Fort Donelson." In *Battles and Leaders of the Civil War: The Opening Battles.* Edited by Robert Underwood Johnson and Clarence Clough Buel. Edison, NJ: Castle, 1995.

"The War in Kentucky." *New York Times,* November 1, 1864.

"The War in the Southwest." *New York Times,* November 21, 1862.

Ward, Ezra. *Generals in Blue.* Baton Rouge: Louisiana State University Press, 2006.

_____. *Generals in Gray.* Baton Rouge: Louisiana State University Press, 2006.

Wardner, Horace. "Reminiscences of a Surgeon." War Papers, Military Order of the Loyal Legion of the United States. http://suvcw.org/mollus/warpapers/ILv3p173.htm (accessed July 22, 2012).

Waters, John C. Papers. MS 88–01, Box 7. Forrest C. Pogue Special Collections Library, Murray State University, Murray, Kentucky.

Webb, W.S., and W.D. Funkhouser. *Ancient Life in Kentucky.* Berea: Kentucky Geological Survey, 1972.

Whitesell, Hunter B. "Military Operations in the Jackson Purchase Area of Kentucky, 1862–1865." *Register of the Kentucky Historical Society.* Part 1, April 1965; Part 2, July 1965; Part 3, October 1965.

Whitesell, Robert D. "Military and Naval Activity Between Cairo and Columbus." *Register of the Kentucky Historical Society,* April 1963.

Wiley, Bell Irvin. *Embattled Confederates.* New York: Bonanza, 1964.

_____. *The Life of Billy Yank: The Common Soldier of the Union.* Baton Rouge: Louisiana State University Press, 1990.

_____. *The Life of Johnny Reb: The Common Soldier of the Confederacy.* Baton Rouge: Louisiana State University Press, 1990.

Wills, Brian Steel. *A Battle from the Start: The Life of Nathan Bedford Forrest.* New York: HarperCollins, 1992.

Wills, Charles Wright. *Army Life of an Illinois Soldier.* Washington, D.C.: Globe, 1906.

Winter, William C., ed. *Captain Joseph Boyce and the 1st Missouri Infantry, C.S.A.* St. Louis: Missouri History Museum, 2011.

Wood, Richard G. "Construction of the Louisville and Paducah Marine Hospitals." *Register of the Kentucky Historical Society*, January 1958.

Woodworth, Steven E. *Nothing But Victory: The Army of the Tennessee, 1861–1865.* New York: Alfred A. Knopf, 2005.

Works Progress Administration. *Military History of Kentucky.* Frankfort: State Journal, 1939.

Wright, Steven L. "'Oh, God, What Is in Store for Us!': Kentucky's Illusion of Neutrality." Unpublished ms.

Wright, Steven L., ed. *Kentucky Soldiers and Their Regiments in the Civil War, 1861.* Vol. 1. Utica, KY: McDowell, 2009.

_____. *Kentucky Soldiers and Their Regiments in the Civil War, 1862.* Vol. 2. Utica, KY: McDowell, 2009.

Index

Adair, John M. 21
Adams, Michael 70
Adams, Richard 126
Adams, Theodore 37
African Americans 85, 159
agriculture 3, 4, 5, 13, 14, 196, 204, 210
Aiguer, Geoffrey 168
Akers, John 122
Akers, William R. 121
Alabama Troops (CSA): 1st Infantry 181; 27th Infantry 91, 112
Alexandria, Virginia 48
Allen, E.J. *see* Pinkerton, Allan
Alps 132
Alton, Illinois 123, 152
Ambrose, D. Leib 21, 100
American Tobacco Company 210
Anaconda Plan 35
Anderson, John 17
Anderson, Lucien 191
Anderson, Robert 33, 57–58
Anna 208
Arkansas Troops (CSA): 6th Infantry 52; 11th Infantry 161; 12th Infantry 161; 15th Infantry 91, 112
Army of the Mississippi 164
Army of the Ohio 94
Army of the Potomac 72, 215*ch*3*n*8, 222*ch*12*n*8
Army of the Tennessee 177, 222*ch*13*n*20
Arnaud, Charles de 44
Asboth, Alexander S. 207
Aurora, Kentucky 102, 103
Avery, Phineas Orlando 101

Bailey's Ferry, Tennessee 110, 113
Baldwin, William D. 133
Ballard County, Kentucky 13, 27
Baltimore & Ohio Railroad 8
Baptists 10, 192, 213*n*18
Barnes, George F. 200
Barry, A.J. 16, 17, 23
Bassett Family 199
Bates, Edward 34–35
Baxter, A.S. 97
Beadle, John H. 132

Beauregard, P.G.T. 105, 108, 155, 156, 179, 190
Bell, John 13
Bell, Tyree 198
Belmont, Missouri 43, 44, 54, 55, 62
Belmont, Battle of *see* Columbus-Belmont, Battle of
"The Belmont Quickstep" 86
Beltzhoover, Daniel 63, 64, 95
Ben-Hur 81
Benjamin, Judah P. 56, 59, 95, 156, 157, 158
Benson, Jo 86
Benton 37, 39, 169, 170, 171, 172, 173, 185
Benton, Kentucky 192
Bidwell, B.G. 136
Bird, John 20, 21
Bird's Point, Missouri 20, 21, 22, 23, 33, 47, 59, 61, 72, 77, 88, 97, 98, 109
Bissell, Joshua W. 164, 165, 166, 174, 175, 176, 185
Black Hawk War 98
Black Patch War 211
Blackburn, Luke P. 25
Blair, Francis "Frank," Jr. 57, 58
Blair, Montgomery 57
Blandville, Kentucky 74, 98, 100, 101
Bonham, D.W.C. 75, 93, 94
Boon, O.R. 28
Boston, Massachusetts 152
Boswell family 27
Bowen, John S. 55, 92, 94
Bowling Green, Kentucky 54, 56, 88, 90, 94–95, 97, 104, 107, 118, 130, 147, 156, 158, 160
Boyce, Joseph 55, 94
Boydsville, Kentucky 27
Bragg, Braxton 179, 200
Bramlette, Thomas E. 206
Bratcher Family 62, 66, 72
Breckinridge, John C. 13, 15, 147
Brilliant 207
Brinton, John H. 31, 34, 62, 66, 67, 69, 71, 72, 98, 108, 118, 126, 133, 217*ch*6*n*12, 217*ch*7*n*38, 218*ch*8*n*6
Brooks, Thorndike 27
Buchanan, James 15, 128
Buckner, Simon Bolivar 41, 97, 118, 127, **128**,

237

129, 130, 132, 133, 135, 139, 142, 143, 146, 147–149, 150–151, 152, 211
Buell, Don Carlos 94, 97, 104, 109, 123, 124
Buena Vista, Battle of (Mexican War) 81
Buford, Abraham 197, 198, 200–201, 202, 207, 208, 209
Buford, John 72, 201
Buford, Napoleon B. 64, 72, 81, 88, 160, 170, 177, 178–179, 182, 185, 201
Bulliss, Robert E. 190
Burnett, Henry C. 10, 13, 14–15, 17, 19, 150
Busbey Family 27

Cairo 39
Cairo, Illinois 17, 20–21, 22, 23, 24, 29, 30–31, 32, 33, 34, 36, 37, 40, 41, 43, 44, 46, 47, 59, 60, 61, 62, 72, 74, 77, 79, 82, 83, 84, 88, 96, 97, 98, 101, 104, 108, 109, 110, 121, 122, 123, 124, 125, 126, 138, 151, 152, 154, 155, 157, 159, 165, 166, 169, 173, 181, 193, 203, 204, 214*ch*3*n*1
Calloway County, Kentucky 3, 4, 27, 41, 102, 152, 196, 197, 209
Calloway Landing, Kentucky 103
Cameron, Simon 58
Camp Beauregard, Kentucky 55, 75, 92–95, 97, 100, 156, 212
Camp Boone, Tennessee 25, 28, 41
Camp Chase, Ohio 152
Camp Cheatham, Tennessee 25
Camp Clay, Ohio 22
Camp Defiance, Illinois 20
Camp Dick Robinson, Kentucky 22
Camp Douglas, Illinois 152
Camp Halleck, Tennessee 110
Camp Joe Holt, Indiana 22
Camp Johnston, Missouri 54, 62, 63, 66, 68, 69
Camp Nelson, Kentucky 22
Canton, China 113
Canton, Kentucky 129
Cape Girardeau, Missouri 33, 81
Cargill Hotel 28
Carondelet 39, 109, 113, 114, 121, 126, 131, 132, 136, 137, 138, 169, 181, 182, 183, 184, 185, 186
Carondelet, Missouri 37, 39, *42*, 83
Carson, Kit 33
Carter, Isaiah 5
Cartmell, J.M. 85
Casey, Peter 135
Caseyville, Kentucky 96–97
Catholics 10, 192
Cave-in-Rock, Illinois 79, 96
Cavin, Charles H. 126
Center Furnace 4
Centre College 14
Cerro Gordo Landing, Tennessee 120, 121
Chancellor 72
Chapman, J.F. 200
Charleston, South Carolina 15
Charm 65
Chattanooga, battles for 195

Cheatham, Benjamin F. 28–29, 53, 65, 67, 68, 71, 72, 88, 156
Chetlain, Augustus L. 60, 73, 75
Chicago, Illinois 20, 84, 152
Chicago & Cairo Railroad 7
The *Chicago Tribune* 80
Chickasaw Indians 3, 98
Chickasaw Oldtown, Alabama 3
Chinese 5
Cincinnati 39, 109, 113, 114, 115, 116, 117, 122, 124, 155, 169, 172
Cincinnati, Ohio 18, 35, 36, 37, 123, 194
The *Cincinnati Commercial* 14
The *Cincinnati Gazette* 116
City of Alton 40
Clark, George Rogers 8, 98
Clark, William 8
Clark's River 102
Clarksville, Tennessee 56, 90, 150, 154
Clay, Henry 10
Cleveland, Ohio 84
Cole, J. G. 9
Columbus, Kentucky 1, 2, 6, 16, 17, 18, 22, 23, 24, 26, 33, 40–41, 42, 43, 44, 48, 49, 51–52, 53, 54, 55, 56, 59, 60, 61, 62, 63, 64, 65, 67, 73, 74, 78, 80, 85, 88, 95, 97, 99, 100, 101, 104, 106, 107, 139, 153, 155, 156, 157, 158, 159, 160, 161, 162, 169, 170, 192, 201, 204, 205, 216*ch*5*n*20
Columbus, Ohio 152
Columbus-Belmont, Battle of 2, 57–72, 80, 81, 82, 85, 86, 88, 92, 94, 123, 217*ch*6*n*12, 217*ch*7*n*38, 218*ch*8*n*6
The *Columbus Crescent* 15
Columbus Rangers 40, 215*ch*4*n*1
Combs, Leslie 23
Commerce, Missouri 164
Conestoga 37, 44, 89–90, 97, *99*, 102, 103, 109, 113, 116, 119, 120, 121, 129, 130, 132, 169
Confederate Department No. 2 32
Constitutional Union Party 13
Cook, John 132
Cooper, Samuel 156
Corinth Campaign 222*ch*12*n*8
Corps of Topographical Engineers 9
Crisp Family 134
Croft, J.T. 190
Crossland, Ed 199
Crowell, Augustus 126
Cruft, Charles 141
Cullum, G.W. 104, 157, 158, 159, 168, 169
Cumberland Gap 25
Cumberland Presbyterians 10
Cumberland River 1, 3, 4, 6, 25, 26, 43, 54, 56, 60, 62, 79, 81, 89, 90, 97, 104, 107, 124, 125, 126, 127, 129, 134, 135, 150, 154
Cumberland Rolling Mills 90
Cypress Swamp, Missouri 175, 176

D.A. January 110
Dacotah 200

Davis, Charles H. 224*n*71
Davis, Garrett 23
Davis, Jefferson 16, 17, 19, 23, 26, 48, 49, 50, 56, 76, 86, 87, 158, 167, 206, 216*ch*5*n*11
Day, John B. 76, 78
Democratic Party 10
Department No. 2 (CSA) 32, 49, 54
Department of the Cumberland 33, 57, 203
Department of the Ohio 18, 97, 104
Department of the West 33
District of Cairo 81, 97
District of Northern Missouri 164
District of Southeast Missouri 43, 81
District of Western Kentucky 203
District of Western Tennessee 153
Dixon, Joseph 90, 91, 106, 127, 132
Dollins, James 71, 72
Donelson, Daniel S. 26
Doublin, E.J. 87
Doublin, John 87–88, 219*ch*8*n*33
Dougherty, Henry 61, 64, 67, 68, 71, 72, 80
Douglas, Stephen A. 13
Dove, Benjamin M. 151, 178
Dover, Tennessee 26, 108, 127, 149, 151, 152
Driggs, George W. 122, 123
Dublin, Kentucky 205
Duke, James Buchanan 210, 211
Dumas, Thomas J. 166
Dunbar 103, 119
Durbin, Arthur J. 93, 94

Eads, James B. 35, 36, 37, 39, 85, 173
Eastport 120, 121
Eddyville, Kentucky 42, 89, 90
Elliott's Mill, Kentucky 98, 101
Ellison, P.M. 197
Emerald Hill (plantation) 219*n*40
Empire Furnace 4
English 10
Episcopals 49
Essex 37, 109, 110, *111*, 113, 114, 117, 124
Ewing, Thomas 34

Fairplay 207
Falls of the Ohio *see* Louisville, Kentucky
Faulkner, W.W. 202
Faxson, Len G. 15
The *Federal Scout* 159
Feliciana, Kentucky 6, 55, 92, 93, 94
First Bull Run, Battle of 27, 152
First Congressional District, Kentucky 3, 10, 204
Fisher, George A. 198
Fitch, Le Roy 207
Fitzpatrick, Thomas "Broken Hand" 33
Florence, Alabama 120
Floyd, John B. 128, *129*, 130, 134, 139, 146, 147, 148, 149, 150, 153
Foote, Andrew H. 2, *38*, 39, 82–83, 84–85, 97, 101, 104, 105, 108, 109, 111, 113, 115, 117–118, 119, 121, 122, 124, 125, 132, 134, 135, 137,
138, 140, 143, 153, 154, 155, 157–158, 167–169, 170, 171, 172, 173, 176, 177, 179, 180, 181, 183, 184, 185, 186, 187, 223*ch*14*n*6, 224*n*70, 224*n*71
Force, Manning 164
Forrest, Jeffrey 148
Forrest, Nathan Bedford 2, 92, 129–130, 136, 142, 147, 148, 152, 197–198, 199, 200, 201, 202, 208
Fort Anderson 60, 191, *193*, 196, 197, 198, 199, 201, 202
Fort Bankhead, Missouri 161, 165
Fort De Russey, Kentucky 53, 101, 159
Fort Donelson, Tennessee 26, 54–55, 89, 90, 91–92, 97, 104, 107, 108, 111, 112, 115, 118, 119, 121, 124, 125, 126, 127, 128, 129, 130, 154, 155, 159, 168, 169, 221*ch*11*n*5, 221*ch*12*n*8, 222*ch*13*n*19
Fort Donelson, Battle of 2, 131–153, 156, 158
Fort Halleck, Kentucky 159
Fort Heiman, Kentucky 91, 107, 110, 111, 112, 116, 125, 132, 140, 188–89, 190, 207–208, 209
Fort Henry, Tennessee 25–26, 27, 55, 56, 89, 91–92, 97, 102, 103, 104, 105, 119, 121, 125–126, 127, 130, 132, 135, 137
Fort Henry, Battle of 2, 106–118, 123, 128, 136, 152, 154, 188, 221*ch*11*n*5
Fort Holt, Kentucky 47, 59, 72, 88, 97, 98, 100, 108, 109
Fort Jefferson, Kentucky 98, 101
Fort Massac, Illinois 8
Fort Pillow, Tennessee 161, 179, 201, 202, 203
Fort Sumter, South Carolina 15, 34
Fort Thompson, Missouri 161, 165, 167
Fort Warren, Massachusetts 152, 221*ch*11*n*11
Foster, John D. 178
Fox, Gustavus A. 35, 83, 84, 168
Frankfort, Kentucky 10, 16, 22, 154
The *Frankfort Daily Commonwealth* 25
Frémont, John C. *32*, 33–34, 35, 37–38, 42, 43, 44, 47, 57–59, 60, 61, 73, 74, 77, 83
Fugitive Slave Act 14
Fulton, Kentucky 28, 156, 211

Gamble, Hamilton R. 57
Gantt, E.W. 161
Garrard County, Kentucky 22, 51
General Anderson 150
General Polk 56
Germans 7, 10, 33
Gettysburg, Battle of 72
Gilmer, Jeremy F. 91, 106, 107, 111, 112, 115
Golconda, Illinois 79
Gorgas, Josiah 23, 56
Gracey, Frank P. 207
Grampus 171
Granger, Gordon 164
Grant, U.S. 2, 43, 44–*45*, 46, 47, 50, 56, 59–62, 63, 66, 67, 68, 70–71, 73, 74, 80–81, 82, 83, 84, 88, 96, 97–98, 100, 101, 103–104, 105, 108, 109–110, 113, 118, 121, 122–123,

124, 125, 126, 127, 129, 130, 133–134, 135, 153, 154, 173, 190, 192–193, 194, 195, 196, 203–204, 205, 206, 217*ch*6*n*8, 219*ch*9*n*3, 219*ch*9*n*17, 221*ch*11*n*5, 222*ch*13*n*19, 225*n*19
Graves, Rice 144
Graves County, Kentucky 3, 5, 6, 7, 55, 75, 94, 205
Great Lakes 7
Greensburg, Kentucky 22
Greif, J.V. 198
Grierson, Benjamin 59
Griffin, Patrick 92
Gurley, John Addison 194
Guthrie, J.V. 22
Gwin, William 119, 121

Halleck, Henry W. 77, 79, 81, 83, 89, 96, 97, 98, 101, 102, 103–105, 108, 109, 110, 113, 122, 123–124, 125, 152, 153, 157, 159–160, 168–169, 171, 174, 176–177, 187, 194, 195, 206, 219*ch*9*n*21, 223*ch*14*n*6
Hamilton, Schuyler 164, 165, 175
Hannibal 123
Hardee, William 78, 130
Harp Family 27
Harper's Weekly 21
Harris, Isham 24, 25, 26, 32, 49, 50, 55, 136, 216*ch*5*n*11
Harrodsburg, Kentucky 14
Hayden, Charles 91
Haynes, Milton Andrew 106, 112
Haynie, I.N. 133
Heiman, Adolphus 91, 92, 107, 112, 115, 119, 127, 128, 133, 139, 152
Henderson County, Kentucky 144
Henry, Gustavus A. 26, 90
Hickman, Kentucky 6, 23, 29, 37, 42, 44, 49, 157, 164, 170, 172, 177, 178, 179, 190, 192, 212
Hickman County, Kentucky 3, 27, 205
Hickman Creek 127
Hickory Creek 102
Hicks, S.G. 198, 199, 200–202
Hill 67
Hillman, Daniel 4–5
Hinson, Jack 196
Hirsh, Isaac E. 55
Hitchcock, Ethan Allen 124
Hoel, William R. 182
Hogg, Harvey 157, 177, 178
Hollis, George N. 88
Home Guard (Kentucky) 15, 19, 22, 197, 202
Hood, John Bell 216*n*5
Hopkinsville, Kentucky 22, 129, 130, 211
Hottenstein, John A. 182
Hubbard, John Milton 52, 92, 93, 176
Humboldt, Tennessee 158, 160
Hummel, Fred 45
Hungarians 33
Hunt, Spence 166
Hunter, David 59, 153
Hutchens, William D. 178

Illinois Central Railroad 7
Illinois Troops: Battery A, Chicago Light Artillery 44, 116; 2nd Cavalry 157, 177; 4th Cavalry 101, 110; 6th Cavalry 59; 7th Cavalry 21, 180; 7th Infantry 100; 8th Infantry 21, 40, 80, 141; 9th Infantry 44, 46, 75, 140, 141; 10th Infantry 20; 11th Infantry 142; 12th Infantry 44, 75, 141, 151; 17th Infantry 133; 18th Infantry 141; 20th Infantry 142; 21st Infantry 43; 22nd Infantry 68; 27th Infantry 64, 72, 88, 158, 160, 170, 177; 29th Infantry 102, 141; 30th Infantry 69, 141; 31st Infantry 66, 69, 141, 142; 40th Infantry 46, 75, 102, 154; 41st Infantry 75, 140, 141; 42nd Infantry 180, 182; 48th Infantry 133; 49th Infantry 133; 55th Infantry 21, 158; 122nd Infantry 200; 134th Infantry 203
Indian Creek 127
Indiana Troops: 11th Infantry 76, 144; 31st Infantry 132, 141; 44th Infantry 141; 52nd Infantry 189
Iowa Troops: 2nd Infantry 143, 150; 5th Cavalry 188, 189, 190; 7th Infantry 68, 121; 12th Infantry 122
Irish 7, 10, 14
Iron Banks *see* Columbus, Kentucky
Iron Banks Baptist Church 213*n*18
Iron Industry 4, 5, 6, 89
Island Number Ten, Tennessee 156, 160
Island Number Ten, Battle of 2, 161–187, 224*n*70, 224*n*71
Itra's Landing, Tennessee 110
Ivy 56

Jackson, Andrew 3, 10
Jackson, Mississippi 24
Jackson, Tennessee 25, 156
Jarrett, Emily Gant 45, 216*ch*4*n*13
Jefferson City, Missouri 59
Jews 10, 97, 192–195, 219*ch*9*n*3, 225*n*19
Johnson, Bushrod 128, 129, 133, 139, 144, 149, 151–152
Johnson, John M. 26, 50
Johnsonville, Tennessee 207, 208
Johnston, Albert Sidney 48, 54–55, 56, 88, 90, 95, 101, 106, 118, 128, 130, 139, 147, 156, 179, 216*n*5, 221*ch*12*n*8
Johnston, Joseph E. 216*n*5
Jonesborough, Illinois 96
J.W. Cheeseman 208

Kansas City, Missouri 58
Kaskaskia, Illinois 8
Kaskel, Cesar 192, 193–194
Kaskel, Julius 192, 193
Keiter, William 87
Kelley, David C. 129, 136
Kentucky House of Representatives 15, 19, 44, 50, 154
Kentucky Military Board 29
Kentucky Senate 14, 15, 19

Index

Kentucky Troops (CSA): 2nd Infantry 139, 142; 3rd (Mounted) Infantry 41, 199, 201; 7th Infantry 52; 7th (Mounted) Infantry 52, 199, 201, 202; 8th Infantry150, 201; 12th Cavalry 201, 202
Kentucky Troops (USA): 1st Artillery 199; 16th Cavalry 200; 17th Infantry 141; 20th Infantry 26; 25th Infantry 141
Kimbell, Charles B. 78
King, Henry Clay 26, 28, 190
King's Hell Hounds 190
Ku Klux Klan 210

Land Ordinance of 1785 3
Laning, James 109
Lauman, Jacob 132, 150
Lawrenceburg, Indiana 35
Lee, Robert E. 53, 212
Leighton (plantation) 48
Lenthall, John 36
Lexington 37, 41, 44, 61, 62, 70, 97, **99**, 102, 103, 109, 113, 119, 120, 121, 207
Lexington, Missouri 58
Lexington, Battle of 58
Lidlow, John 117
Lincoln, Abraham 13, 14, 15, 16, 18, 19, 21, 22, 23, 25, 33, 34, 35, 43, 55, 57, 58, 83, 98, 151, 155, 159, 169, 194, 209, 214*ch*1*n*8
Livingston 56
Livingstone, David 52
Logan, John A. 66, 69, 141, 142
Long, Stephen Harriman 8, 9
Louisiana Troops (CSA): 11th Infantry 65; 13th Infantry 52
Louisville 22, 39, 125, 132, 136, 137, 138, 144, 151, 169, 177, 178
Louisville, Kentucky 8, 9, 10, 35, 36, 41, 57, 85, 97, 194
Louisville & Nashville Railroad 94
The *Louisville Daily Democrat* 196
The *Louisville Daily Journal* 17, 24, 27, 28, 159
Lovelaceville, Kentucky 74, 100
Lowe, W.W. 188
Lynn Boyd 28

Mackall, William W. 179, 185, 186, 187
Madrid Bend, Kentucky 162
Magoffin, Anna Nelson Shelby 14
Magoffin, Beriah 14–15, 16, 19, 22, 25, 26, 29, 42, 44, 49, 50, 214*ch*1*n*8
Mallory, Stephen 56
Marion, Illinois 28
Mayfield, Kentucky 5, 7, 20, 26, 28–29, 55, 78, 87, 93, 156, 191, 192, 200, 202, 204–205, 210, 212
Mayfield Convention 17–19, 22
Mayfield Creek 100, 102
Maynadier, Henry B. 170
Mazeppa 207–208
McArthur, John 134, 140, 141

McClellan, George B. 18, 22, 23, 35, 77, 97, 105, 123, 159
McClernand, John A. 61, 64, 66, 67, 69, 72, 81, 97, 98–101, 103, 108–111, 113, 116–117, 119, 124–125, 126, 130, 132–133, 134, 135, 139, 140, 141, 142, 143, 144
McCown, John P. 53, 54, 156, 161, 162, 163, 164, 165, 172, 179
McCracken County, Kentucky 3, 7, 8, 155, 204
McCulloch, Ben 32
McLean, John 46, 60, 154
McPherson, James B. 109, 110
McRae 56
Meigs, Montgomery 36, 38, 57, 85
Melton, J.F. 27, 152, 198
Melvin, Kentucky 74
Memphis, Tennessee 1, 22, 23, 24, 26, 28, 29, 32, 49, 88, 104
Memphis & Charleston Railroad 88
Memphis & Ohio Railroad 119, 138
Meredith, Solomon 208
Methodists 10, 192
Mexican War 7, 9, 31, 32, 34, 63, 73, 88, 164, 179, 200
Michael, W.H.C. 117, 221*ch*11*n*5
Milburn, Kentucky 42, 74, 99, 100
Mill Springs, Battle of 104
Miller, J.H. 189
Miller, Thomas F. 102
Minnehaha 155
Mississippi River 1, 2, 5, 6, 17, 20, 23, 31, 32, 33, 35, 37, 39, 40, 43, 52, 53–54, 56, 59, 62, 63, 65, 71, 74, 77, 85, 87, 96, 155, 160, 161, 162, 165, 169, 174, 175, 186
Mississippi Troops (CSA): 1st Cavalry 156; 22nd Infantry 55, 93, 94
Missouri Compromise 14
The *Missouri Democrat* 70
Missouri River 58, 173–174
Missouri Troops (CSA): 1st Infantry 55, 75, 94
Missouri Troops (USA): 1st Light Artillery 132, 189; 8th Infantry144; 22nd Infantry 178
Mobile, Alabama 6
Mobile & Ohio Railroad 6, 7, 23, 53, 94, 100, 156, 213*n*8
Monroe, James 3
Montgomery, J.J. 150
Montgomery, Alabama 24
Montgomery County, Tennessee 26
Moore, Jennie Billings 209
Moose 207
Morgan, John Hunt 216*n*5
Morrison, Marion 75
Morrison, William E. 133
Morton, Oliver P. 60
Moss, George B. 16
Mound City 39, 169
Mound City, Illinois 21, 29, 37, 59, 60, 63, 83
Mt. Carmel Church, Kentucky 189
Mulligan, James 58
Munfordville, Kentucky 29

Murfreesboro, Tennessee 216*n*5
Murray, Kentucky 27, 102, 152, 192, 196–197, 198, 210, 211, 212
Muscle Shoals, Alabama 3, 8

Nashville, Tennessee 1, 10, 24, 86, 89, 97, 98, 118, 130, 139, 144, 146, 147, 148, 150, 153, 222*ch*12*n*8
Nashville & Northwest Railroad 6, 170
Needham, Hawley V. 203, 205
Negroes *see* African Americans
Nelson, William "Bull" 22, 25
New Era 37
New Haven, Connecticut 224*n*71
New Madrid, Missouri 32, 33, 37, 44, 99, 156, 161, 162, 164–166, 167, 168, 169, 170, 172, 173, 174, 175, 179, 180, 183, 184, 185, 187, 191
New Madrid Earthquake 57
New Orleans 56, 162, 183
New Orleans, Louisiana 5, 8, 23, 25, 170
New Orleans & Ohio Railroad 6, 7, 8, 200
New Uncle Sam 118
New York City 33, 194, 221*n*11
The *New York Herald* 4
The *New York Times* 7, 9–10, 27, 42, 77, 83, 86, 120, 191, 195, 205
Newport, Kentucky 22, 37
Noble, John 10, 11
Norfolk, Missouri 62
Norton, B.H. 204

Oehlschlaeger, George M. 45, 198, 200
Oglesby, Richard J. 21, 40, 41, 61, 62, 140, 141, 142
Ohio River 1, 6, 7, 8, 9, 17, 20, 21, 22, 24, 25, 28, 30, 35, 36, 42, 62, 78, 79, 97, 98, 198, 199
Ohio Troops: 20th Infantry 124, 164; 43rd Infantry 183; 54th Infantry 158; 56th Infantry 124; 71st Infantry 158; 72nd Infantry 201; 76th Infantry 124; 78th Infantry 124
Olive, Kentucky 42
Oregon Trail 33
Orphan Brigade (1st Kentucky Brigade, CSA) 127, 139, 144
Otey, Mercer 201
Owen, Harriet 5

Paducah, Kentucky 1, 2, 7, 8, 9, 10, 11, 13, 16, 17, 18, 20, 23, 24, 25, 28, 33, 41, 42, 45–47, 48, 51, 58, 59–60, 61, 73–74, 75, 76–77, 78, 79, 84, 96, 97, 102, 103, 108, 109, 110, 120, 122–123, 124, 126, 152, 153, 154, 155, 157, 158, 159, 160, 181, 188, 191–192, 193–194, 195, 196, 197–200, 201–202, 203, 204, 205, 206, 208, 209, 210, 211, 217*n*8, 221*n*11
The *Paducah Democrat* 9
The *Paducah Herald* (also *Tri-Weekly Herald*) 7, 10, 11, 13, 23
The *Paducah Journal* 9
Paine, Eleazer A. 21, 46, 74–75, 76, 77, 92, 98, 109, 123, 165, 186, 192, 203–206, 210, 219*n*21, 224*n*70, 225*n*46
Palmer, John M. 164, 165, 174–175, 184
Panther Island 103, 113
Paris, Tennessee 24, 108, 189–190
Pawpaw 198
Pekin, Kentucky 8
Peoria, Illinois 30
Peosta 30
Perryville, Battle of 216*n*5
Phelps, S. Ledyard 37, 89, 90, 97, 101–102, 108, 109, 116, 117, 119–121, 157, 158, 192, 219*n*3
Philadelphia, Pennsylvania 31, 73, 222*ch*12*n*8
Phillips, G.C. 93, 94
The *Picket Guard* 78
Pickett, Edward 178
Pickett, William D. 87
Pillow, Gideon 26, 29, 31–33, 44, 46, 48, 49, 54, 63–68, 85, 88–89, 129, 130, 131, 132, 136, 139, 142, 146, 147, 148, 150, 151, 153
Pine Bluff, Kentucky 41, 110
Pinkerton, Allen 23
Pinson, R.A. 156
Pittsburg 39, 125, 132, 136, 137, 138, 169, 185
Pittsburg Landing, Tennessee 177
Pittsburgh, Pennsylvania 7, 8, 37, 83, 84, 159
Planters' Protective Association 210–211
Plumley's Station, Kentucky 74
Plummer, Joseph B. 165–166
Pocahontas 41
Pocahontas, Arkansas 32
Point Pleasant, Missouri 165, 166, 173, 174, 184
Polk, Leonidas 2, 32, 44, 48–49, 50–*51*, 52, 53, 54, 55, 56, 61, 62, 63, 64, 65, 68, 74, 78, 85, 86–88, 89, 90, 91, 94, 95, 101, 106, 139, 155, 156, 157, 158–159, 161, 162, 216*n*5, 216*n*11, 223*n*6
Polk, William M. 64
Pook, Samuel 36
Pope, John 2, 164, 165, 166, *167*, 173, 174, 175, 176, 177, 179, 181, 183–184, 185, 186, 187, 224*n*42, 224*n*70
Pore, James 8
Pore, William 8
Porter, James D. 71
Portsmouth, Ohio 37
Powell, Lazarus 194
Prentiss, Benjamin 20, 21, 23, 24–25, 29
Price, Sterling 32, 58, 59, 61, 74, 80, 190
Prince 65
Prince, Henry 205
Princeton, Kentucky 210
Provisional Army of Tennessee 32
Pryor, Bill 202

Quigley, Quintus Quincy 10, 11, 13, 16, 24

Rawlins, John A. 108, 135
Reelfoot Lake 162, 178, 186

Index 243

Rennolds, Edwin H. 156–157, 162, 166
Republican Party 14, 33, 43
Revolutionary War 3, 8, 55
Rice, Dan 16, 198
Rich, Lucius 55
Riddle's Point, Missouri 174, 175
Riley, A.C. 75
Riley, F.A. 137
Roberts, George W. 180
Rocky Mountains 33
Rodgers, John 36, 37–39
Roe, Lorenzo P. 188, 189
Rosecrans, William S. 222*ch*12*n*8
Ross, Reuben 131, 135, 136, 138
Rousseau, Lovell Harrison 22, 203
Rucker, Edward W. 180
Russell, William Howard 20, 30, 31, 32
Russellville, Kentucky 42, 118

St. Charles Hotel 43
St. Clair, William R. 199
St. Francis Hotel 28
St. Johns Bayou, Missouri 175
St. Louis 39, 109, 113, 114, 124, 132, 135, 136, 137, 138, 144, 169, 172
St. Louis, Missouri 10, 23, 24, 32, 33, 34, 35, 36, 37, 38, 43, 44, 58, 59, 77, 81, 82, 83, 96, 103, 108, 123, 125, 152, 169, 171, 221*ch*12*n*8
Samuel Orr 41
Sanders, Kate 204
Sanderson, W.L. 74
Sauner, John S. 46
Savannah, Georgia 56
Savannah, Tennessee 121
Schwartz, Adolph 141
Scots-Irish 10
Scott, Thomas A. 168, 183
Scott, Winfield 31, 35, 73, 81, 161
Second Opium War 113
Sedgwick, John 31, 215*ch*3*n*8
Shanklin, Robert 204
Shawneetown, Illinois 79, 93
Shelby, Isaac 3, 14
Sheliha, Victor 179
Sherman, William Tecumseh 34, 73, 104, 124, 154, 155, 157, 158, 159, 192, 193
Shields, Augustine 28
Shiloh, Battle of 71, 155, 190, 191, 218*ch*8*n*6, 221*ch*11*n*5, 221*ch*12*n*8, 223*ch*13*n*19
Shirk, James W. 97, 103, 119, 200, 207
Sierra Nevada Mountains 33
Sikeston, Missouri 166
Singletary, Dan 63, 67
Sisters of the Holy Cross 60
slavery and slaves 5–6, 10, 13, 21, 41, 48, 57, 84, 89, 90, 91, 96, 106, 113, 150, 154, 196, 210
Smith, C.F. 47, 59, 60, 61, 63, 68, 73–74, 75–77, 78, 79, 80, 89, 97, 98, 100, 102–103, 105, 108–110, 111, 113, 116, 124, 125, 126, 130, 132, 133, 134, 135, 140, 143, 144, 146, 149, 150, 153, 219*n*21, 223*ch*13*n*19

Smith, Henry I. 121
Smith, Preston 65, 68
Smithland, Kentucky 1, 60, 90, 96, 109, 110, 129, 152, 154, 203, 207
Spanish-American War 210
Sparrestrom, Frederick 178
Spotsylvania, Battle of 215*ch*3*n*8
Springfield, Illinois 152
Springfield, Missouri 59
Stanley, David S. 186
Stanley, Henry Morton 52–53
State Guard (Kentucky) 15, 18, 23, 24, 28, 41
Stearns, H.P. 66
Steele, Oliver 144
Steiner, John H. 177
Stembel, R.N. 41, 61, 82, 84–85, 115, 117
Stevenson, William G. 54
Stewart, A.P. 156, 162, 167
Stewart, Davis 122
Stewart, Richard 63
Submarine 37
Swallow 37

Tappan, J.C. 63–64, 87
Tate, Sam 88
Taylor, Ezra 69
Taylor, George 40, 48
Taylor, Jesse 112–113, 114, 115, 117
Taylor, Zachary 73, 81, 164
Tennessee River 1, 3, 4, 6, 25, 43, 54, 56, 62, 78, 79, 89–90, 97, 124, 129, 138, 154
Tennessee Troops (CSA): 1st Heavy Artillery 112; 2nd Infantry 54; 3rd Infantry 142; 4th Infantry 52; 5th Infantry 87, 156, 162, 166; 6th Infantry 85; 7th Cavalry 52, 92; 10th Infantry 91, 92, 119; 12th Infantry 64; 15th Infantry 28, 65, 69, 72; 18th Infantry 142; 32nd Infantry 142; Maury County Artillery 131, 132, 138
Thayer, John A. 142
Thomas, George H. 104, 203, 222*ch*12*n*8
Thomas, Lorenzo 42, 58, 102, 219*n*21
Thompson, A.P. 198, 199
Thompson, M. Jeff 60, 61, 164
Tigress 124
Tilghman, Augusta 41, 221*n*11
Tilghman, Lloyd 7–8, 18, 23, 24–25, 28, 41, 54, 55, 76, 90, 92, 103, 106, **107**–108, 111–112, 115–116, 117–188, 122–123, 127, 152, 211, 221*n*11
Tipton, Missouri 58, 183
Tiptonville, Tennessee 162, 174, 175, 186, 224*n*70, 224*n*71
Transylvania University 14
Trask, W.L. 65
Trenton, Tennessee 200, 201
Troy, Tennessee 7
Trudeau, James 171, 172, 180
Turtle 170, 171
Tuscumbia 207
Tuttle, James 193
Twain, Mark 53, 67, 161

Tyler 37, 44, 61, 62, 70, 109, 113, 119, 120, 121, 132, 137, 138
Tyler, H.A. 201

Undine 208
Union City, Tennessee 27, 28, 29, 48, 95, 100, 156, 159, 179
Union League of America 192, 204
United Daughters of the Confederacy 211, 225n46
United States Colored Troops: 1st Infantry 197; 8th Artillery 199, 204
United States House of Representatives 14, 19, 194
United States Marine Hospital (Louisville) 8, 9
United States Marine Hospital (Paducah) 8, 9
United States Military Academy (West Point) 7, 48, 49, 72, 73, 88, 124, 161, 164, 179, 200
United States Senate 3, 33, 34, 194
University of North Carolina at Chapel Hill 48

Venable, C.D. 157
Venus 208
Vicksburg, Mississippi 1, 190
Vicksburg, Siege of 176, 195, 221*ch*11*n*5
Viola, Kentucky 74, 156
Virginia Theological Seminary 48

Wabash River 79
Wadesboro, Kentucky 3
Walke, Henry 61, 63, 64–65, 79, 81, 82, 83, 113, 114, 117, 118, 124, 126, 127, 131, 132, 135, 137–138, 151, 171, 181, 182–183, 184, 186
Walker, L.P. 23, 24, 49, 50, 214*ch*1*n*8

Wallace, Lew 73, 76–77, 78, 81, 102, 116, 124, 125, 134, 135, 141, 142, 143, 144, 146, 149, 150–151
Wallace, Matthew 110
Wallace, W.H.L. 61, 81, 110, 142
War of 1812 3
Wardlow, L.B. 93
Wardner, Horace 151
Washburne, Elihu B. 43, 173, 194
Washington, George 73
Washington, D.C. 14, 19, 34, 35, 153, 168, 194, 209, 222*ch*12*n*8, 224*n*71
W.B. Terry 41, 42
Wells, A.J.G. 211
Western (1st) Division, Department No. 2 (CSA) 52
Weston, Kentucky 98, 99, 100
Whig Party 10
Williams, R.K. 26, 28
Williamson County, Illinois 27
Wills, Charles W. 21, 30, 80, 173, 217*n*8
Wilson 102, 103
Wilson's Creek, Battle of 58
Winchester 172, 182
Wisconsin Troops: 8th Infantry 122
Wise, Henry A. 83, 168
Witter, Amos 62
Wood, George T. 29
Woodford County, Kentucky 72
Woodruff, W.E. 22
Woolfolk, Robert Owen 76, 78, 218*ch*7*n*13

Yandell, Lunsford P. 52, 85–86
Yates, Richard 20, 78

www.ingramcontent.com/pod-product-compliance
Lightning Source LLC
Chambersburg PA
CBHW051218300426

44116CB00006B/616